D1190263

RELIGION AND THE SOCIAL ORDER

Volume 2 • 1991

VATICAN II AND U.S. CATHOLICISM

RELIGION AND
THE SOCIAL ORDER

VATICAN II AND U.S. CATHOLICISM

Series Editor: DAVID G. BROMLEY
Department of Sociology
 and Anthropology
Virginia Commonwealth University

Volume Editor: HELEN ROSE EBAUGH
Department of Sociology
University of Houston

OFFICIAL PUBLICATION OF THE
ASSOCIATION FOR THE SOCIOLOGY OF RELIGION

VOLUME 2 • 1991

 JAI PRESS INC.

Greenwich, Connecticut   London, England

CONTENTS

List of Contributors   vii

Preface   ix

PART I.   SOCIAL AND HISTORICAL CONDITIONS OF VATICAN II

VATICAN II AND THE REVITALIZATION MOVEMENT
  Helen Rose Ebaugh   3

THE CHURCH AND MODERNIZATION
  Gregory Baum and Jean-Guy Vaillancourt   21

PART. II.   CHANGES IN THE INTERNAL DYNAMICS
OF THE U.S. CHURCH

THE DEMOGRAPHY OF AMERICAN CATHOLICS:
1965-1990
  Andrew M. Greeley   37

CATHOLIC YOUTH IN THE MODERN CHURCH
  Patrick H. McNamara   57

CHANGES IN THE PRIESTHOOD AND SEMINARIES
  Dean R. Hoge   67

FULL PEWS AND EMPTY ALTARS:
DEMOGRAPHICS OF U.S. DIOCESAN PRIESTS,
1966-2005
  Richard A. Schoenherr and Lawrence A. Young   85

AMERICAN SISTERS: ORGANIZATIONAL
AND VALUE CHANGES
  Marie Augusta Neal, S.N.D.   105

v

NEW ROLES FOR WOMEN IN THE
CATHOLIC CHURCH: 1965-1990
  Ruth A. Wallace   123

PART. III   THE CHURCH AND SOCIAL ISSUES: INSTITUTIONAL COMMITMENTS AND SHIFTING ATTITUDES OF CATHOLICS

CATHOLIC SEXUAL ETHICS SINCE VATICAN II
  James R. Kelly   139

THE CHURCH AND SOCIAL ISSUES:
INSTITUTIONAL COMMITMENTS
  Joseph P. Fitzpatrick, S.J.   155

THE CHURCH AND THE NEW IMMIGRANTS
  Kevin J. Christiano   169

THE SOCIAL MOVEMENT FOR CHANGE
WITHIN THE CATHOLIC CHURCH
  Katherine Meyer   187

PART IV.   CATHOLICISM IN WORLD PERSPECTIVE

WESTERN EUROPEAN CATHOLICISM
SINCE VATICAN II
  Karel Dobbelaere and Liliane Voyé   205

THE POST-VATICAN II CHURCH IN LATIN AMERICA
  Madeleine Adriance   233

PART V.   LOOKING TO THE FUTURE OF THE CHURCH IN THE UNITED STATES

U.S. CATHOLICISM: THE NOW AND FUTURE CHURCH
  Joseph H. Fichter, S. J.   249

VATICAN II AND THE RECONCEPTUALIZATION
OF THE CHURCH
  Helen Rose Ebaugh   267

LIST OF CONTRIBUTORS

Madeleine Adriance — Department of Sociology
Mount Ida College

Gregory Baum — Department of Religious Studies
McGill University

Kevin Christiano — Department of Sociology
University of Notre Dame

Karel Dobbelaere — Department of Sociology
Catholic University
Leuven, Belgium

Helen Rose Ebaugh — Department of Sociology
University of Houston

Joseph Fichter — Department of Sociology
Loyola University

Joseph Fitzpatrick — Department of Sociology
Fordham University

Andrew Greeley — Department of Sociology
University of Arizona

Dean Hoge — Department of Sociology
Catholic University

James Kelly — Department of Sociology
Fordham University

Patrick McNamara — Department of Sociology
University of New Mexico

Katherine Meyer

Department of Sociology
Ohio State University

Marie Augusta Neal

Department of Sociology
Emmanual College

Richard Schoenherr

Department of Sociology
University of Wisconsin-Madison

Jean-Guy Vaillancourt

Department of Sociology
University of Montreal

Liliane Voyé

Department of Sociology
Catholic University
Leuven, Belgium

Ruth Wallace

Department of Sociology
George Washington University

Lawrence Young

Department of Sociology
Brigham Young University

PREFACE

My presidency of the Association for the Sociology of Religion for the 1989-1990 term overlapped with the twenty-fifth anniversary of the closing of the Second Vatican Council in Roman Catholicism and the promulgation of the official decrees of the Council. Because much of my research has addressed issues of social change in the Catholic church, it was predictable that I would focus attention on this anniversary event.

While much has been written on the Council by theologians, historians, and journalists, as well as Sociologists, I know of no attempt to evaluate the overall impact of the Council on the church in the United States. There does exist a substantial literature that focuses upon specific institutions and aspects of post-Vatican II Catholic life, such as the priesthood, laity, religious men and women, liturgy, and changing parish and diocesan structures. The idea that motivated this edited volume was to ask "experts" (predominantly Sociologists, in this instance) who had done research in these specific areas to write chapters describing the major changes that had occurred and to evaluate the impact of these changes for the U.S. church both now and into the next century.

Part I focuses upon the social and historical factors that influenced Pope John XXIII to convene the twenty-first ecumenical council in 1962. While Vatican II is often depicted as a surprise event that Pope John sprang upon an unsuspecting Catholic world, in the first chapter I present the Council as part of a larger progressive movement that had been building in the church during the nearly 100 years since the last ecumenical council (The First Vatican Council) in 1870. In the second chapter, Baum and Vaillancourt place Vatican II in the larger struggle between the church and the forces of modernization that confronted Catholicism in the first half of this century.

Part II focuses upon changes that were effected by the Council in terms of the internal structures that make up the church. Greeley, in the third chapter, describes the demographic shifts that have taken place within the U.S. Catholic population since the Council and the implications of these shifts for the functioning of the church. In the fourth chapter, McNamara traces changes in the demographics, behavior, and attitudes of youth in the church over the past several decades. The fifth and sixth chapters address the issue of the decline in the number of priests that has occurred in the U.S. church in the past three decades. Hoge describes the decline in seminarians and analyzes factors that correlate with fewer new recruits. Schoenherr and Young present data on the diocesan priest decline and environmental factors that relate to priest demographics by diocese. The seventh and eighth chapters focus upon women in the modern church. Neal analyzes trends among religious women (Catholic sisters) in the United States while Wallace describes the new role of "associate pastor" that some women are assuming in priestless parishes.

In Part III, consideration is given to changes that have occurred in the church's stance toward social issues. Kelly, in the ninth chapter, discuses shifts in the attitudes of Catholics in regard to sexual ethics, especially premarital sex, birth control, and abortion issues. In the tenth chapter, Fitzpatrick traces shifts in the church's stance on social issues, especially rights of workers, liberation of the poor, care of refugees, peace, and disarmament. In the eleventh chapter, Christiano reviews the church's involvement with the recent immigrants, especially the Central American migrants, who seek asylum and opportunity in the United States. Meyer, in the twelfth chapter, emphasizes the conflicts experienced by the church in the struggle to implement the decrees of the Council, including the change movement that lead to and encompassed Vatican II.

The two chapters in Part IV contrast the response of the Catholic church in the United States with what is happening in Catholicism in other countries, in particular, Western Europe and Central America. Dobbelaere and Voyé describe the situation in Western European countries based on an array of survey data. They also argue the thesis that the changes that occurred after the Council were consequences of processes of modernization. Adriance, in the fifteenth chapter, describes post-Vatican II Catholicism in Latin and Central American countries. She contrasts the developments in these countries with the U.S. situation.

In the final section, Part V, consideration is given to summarizing the changes that have taken place in U.S. Catholicism since the Council and to making some predictions about the challenges facing the church as it enters the twenty-first century. In the sixteenth chapter, Fichter points out what he considers major shifts in the past twenty-five years and arenas that call for bold action on the part of the church in the future decades. In the final chapter, I present what I see as the major conceptual shifts that were legitimated by

Vatican II and the implications of these shifts for the structures of the church. I conclude by summarizing the major challenges of the church in the decade of the 1990s and into the next century, based upon the data and analyses presented in the chapters of this book.

I want to extend my appreciation to each of the authors who diligently prepared the materials that went into each chapter. I also owe thanks to David Bromley who is series editor of the Sociology of Religion series for JAI Press and who provided experience and sage advice at each step of the arduous process of putting together an edited book. Bill Howard, my graduate assistant during the project, provided help with the various editing and organizational tasks necessary for coordinating this volume.

Helen Rose Ebaugh
Volume Editor

PART I

SOCIAL AND HISTORICAL CONDITIONS
OF VATICAN II

VATICAN II AND THE
REVITALIZATION MOVEMENT

Helen Rose Ebaugh

Most of the literature dealing with the Second Vatican Council takes the Council itself as a starting point and focuses upon the far-reaching changes, both ideological and normative, introduced into the Catholic world by the Council. It is as if the Council burst upon the Catholic church as a meteor from outer space and created cataclysmic chaos in what was once a stable, secure, harmonious world. In fact, however, the Council (1962-1965) was simply one event in a much broader historical process that had its roots in centuries of church history, in particular, the nearly 100 years of strain and struggle that had gripped parts of the church since the First Vatican Council in 1870, a council called to condemn modernism and unify factions within the church.

By the time John XXIII ascended the papacy in 1958, the voices of protest and unrest gave a clear message that the church was failing to come to terms with the world in which the church was operating in the twentieth century. Pope John XXIII inherited a very troubled, divided, outdated church. He inherited a crisis situation which demanded bold action. Ecumenical or general councils have traditionally been a mechanism for pontiffs to deal with crises in the Church. In earlier ages, councils were used to settle doctrinal disputes; however, they were also convened, as with the Council of Trent (1545-1563), to revitalize church structures and correct internal abuses (Fesquet 1967; Hughes 1961). It was not surprising, therefore, that Pope John gave serious

Religion and the Social Order, Volume 2, pages 3-19.
ISBN: 1-55938-388-7

consideration to calling together church representatives from throughout the world as a way of relieving the crisis.

By the middle of the twentieth century, the seeds of discord and disagreement that arose and were never resolved during the First Vatican Council had reached a crescendo and become widespread, both among clerical and lay elements in the church. The opposition consisted, for the most part, of progressive, liberal thinkers who objected to the conservative stances taken at the First Vatican Council and advocated an updating of the church to accommodate modern society. After heated debates and numerous compromises throughout the four Council sessions, it is obvious from the Council documents, as well as the structural changes that eventuated from them, that the progressives won out. This raises two very interesting sets of questions: (1) How did the few lone voices of liberal theologians and bishops early in the century become mobilized and channelled into a collective voice of discontent? More specifically, what factors internal to the church contributed to the coalescence of the progressive faction and the legitimation of their stance by the Council? (2) What external factors in the broader society interacted with the opposition faction within the church to give greater legitimacy to their cause?

A SOCIAL MOVEMENTS APPROACH

It seems to me that the most fruitful way to address the questions is to view the council from a social movements perspective. Unlike formal systems theory or static organizational analysis, a social movements approach places historical events in the broader context of internal pressures that systematically work toward creating change in the system, and it provides a way of analyzing conflict between advocates of change and opposition groups.

In the 100 years between the Vatican councils, most of those dissenting from established church doctrine and practice remained "loyal opposition" in that protestors remained part of the official church structure and exercised "voice" rather than "exit" (Hirschman 1970). As a result, opposition groups and "mini-movements," as Seidler and Meyer (1989) call them, arose within the church around numerous issues. These voices of protest, which had been heard mainly on a national level, came together in unison at the Council and were strong enough to set an agenda of aggiornamento and change, even with the resistance of a strong, conservative opposition group.

While I will suggest five "stages" that characterize phases of a social movement, I do not intend to imply a rigid order or "natural history" (Smelser 1963) of a movement, nor do I argue for immutable boundaries between the stages. In reality, stages frequently interpenetrate each other and may even occur in reverse order than predicted. Like Seidler and Meyer (1989), I will use a stage model simply as a tool for understanding the myriad events, actors, and situations that were involved in the changes occurring in the church during the twentieth century.

Social movement theorists have suggested a number of models of the stages of social movement activity (Seidler and Meyers 1989; Smelser 1963; Turner and Killian 1987). The 5-stage model I will use is a synthesis of these various statements. Stage I, the development of structural strain (Smelser 1963),constitutes the preconditions or unrest that lead to tension buildup in the system because of the failure of the parts of the system or organization to work together in harmony. In the case of change in the Catholic church, this period extended between the two councils.

Stage II, coalescence of resources, is characterized by unrest becoming more open and focused and by the development of a "social myth" (Turner and Killian 1987) that supplies the justification for change. Movement leaders emerge, often as prophets, and the movement garners greater resources in the form of people, organization, power, and visibility. It was the progressive theologians like Yves Congar, Marie de Chenu, Karl and Hugo Rahner, Jean Danilou, de Lubac, Schillebeeckx, de Chardin, Hans Kung, and John Courtney Murray who developed the theological rationale for reform in the church. A primary function of the Council was to bring these theologians together with liberal bishops and cardinals who had organized in their respective countries to promote change in various structures of the church. For example, for decades, a vigorous liturgical movement had been going on within countries like Belgium, Holland, Germany, France, and the United States (McNaspy 1966).The astonishing growth of the United States Liturgical Conference was simply one example of like movements in these countries. Likewise, the issue of the renewal of religious life constituted the focus of the Sister Formation Movement in the United States as well as parallel efforts in European countries. The Council catapulted these national movements onto the international scene both by providing opportunity for communication and organization among spokesmen from various countries and through the media which helped define and focus issues, especially controversial and heated ones.

Legitimation, Stage III, occurs as a movement is able to effect significant changes in the formal structures of the system. The decrees and documents that were officially promulgated at the end of the council formally legitimated the prevailing liberal position that gained ascendancy and recognition during the Council debates.

Institutionalization, Stage IV, is the process of implementing change in terms of law, rules, official ideology, role changes, and the diffusion of a generalized belief system through education. The 25-year period since the Council has been one of implementation and is still not complete. Stage V is that of countermovements that develop as resistance to the structural and ideological changes. The number and strength of such countermovements in the Catholic church during the past ten years is evidence that the changes initiated by Vatican II have become institutionalized throughout the church.

STAGE I: STRUCTURAL STRAIN

The First Vatican Council was called in 1870 to unify the Catholic world as it confronted the issues of modernism that accompanied the social and political upheavals of the Industrial Revolution. The blueprint of a monolithic, authoritarian church in which the pope had infallible authority was challenged even before the final council documents were issued. The definition of papal infallibility, while it received a majority approbation, was opposed by a minority of bishops, even as the final votes were counted. Many of the dissenting votes came from American bishops who could not reconcile infallible papal authority with the tradition of nationalism and democracy that were part of their American experience. Of the 45 American bishops, 15 voted for the decree, 4 voted against, 5 approved with reservations, and 21 absented themselves (Ellis 1963). After the council, 55 bishops from around the world sent a formal protest to the pope explaining their absence from the voting in terms of their objection to the decree (Ellis 1963). Part of their objection was the fact that the Council had not discussed the bishops' role in church authority.

The objections of so many American bishops to the decree on papal infallibility was a major factor that coalesced into the "phantom heresy" (Cogley 1973; Greeley 1977) which Pope Leo XIII later called "Americanism" (Cogley 1973). Cogley summarizes this "heresy" as including the following ideas: the superiority of action over contemplation; individual conscience guided by the Holy Spirit sometimes transcends the need for sacraments and ecclesiastical authority; and the insistence that the church adjust its basic teachings to accommodate the findings of modern science.

In addition to the "American heresy," many American bishops joined voices with the modernist movement that had its origins in Europe. The modernists (condemned by Pius X in 1907) propounded such ideas as a Catholic interpretation of Darwinism, theology as evolving rather than as a static, unchanging system of truths, and the reconciliation of evolution and creation. In addition, they insisted on the need for the church to embrace democracy (Kurtz 1986). Throughout the 100 years between the two councils these two "heresies" polarized not only American bishops but the episcopacy and church theologians throughout the world.

Although Pope Leo XIII (1878-1903) had inaugurated a new stage in the church's relationship with the world by sensitizing clergy and laity to social responsibilities, his was merely an attempt to present a Christian alternative to the threat of socialism that was coming to dominate the Western world. His strategy was to demonstrate that the church already had a solution to the problems posed by the socialists and that the interests of the workers were better served by Catholicism than by the godless creeds of socialism or communism. His social doctrine was buttressed by his restoration of the philosophy and theology of Thomas Acquinas as the basis of Christian teaching. As McSweeney (1980, p. 68) argues, the rediscovery of Thomism was not a purely cognitive affair; it was the "centre of a political strategy intended to bring about the restoration of a Christian social order, an organic hierarchic society united by common values and common faith under the temporal kingship of secular rulers and under the authority of the Pope." Thomism provided the church with the most refined instrument of intellectual discipline and papal imperialism, resulting in further isolating Catholicism into a ghetto mentality. McSweeney (1980) sees Thomism as another form of ghetto, more subtle and less obtrusive but with essentially the same objective of recovering the church's dominance in society by regaining control of every aspect of Catholics' lives by shielding them from the enticements of secular thought.

Catholic Action was a movement inaugurated by Leo XIII to encourage Catholic laity to take a fuller part in social and political affairs. It was not intended to reduce hierarchic control over lay activity but rather to organize the laity into Catholic organizations supervised by the clergy. Trade unions, for example, were to be a form of Catholic Action, not a neutral sphere of activity independent of Catholics' beliefs and commitments (McSweeney 1980). As Von Aretin maintains, lay organizations, before Leo XIII, were fewer in number but enjoyed greater independence from clerical control (Von Aretin 1970).

Overall, Leo XIII stimulated Catholic scholarship by opening the Vatican archives to scholars, giving mild encouragement to biblical criticism, and making Newman a cardinal, despite his known liberal views and opposition to papal absolutism. However, all these efforts had the aim of redefining social, political, and economic involvements from the perspectives of Catholic theology and of restoring the power and influence of the church in its relationships with institutions of the modern world. Again, the consequence was to energize the laity by providing a Catholic approach to their worldly involvements, thereby regaining control over modern thought and institutions that posed a secular threat.

Had Leo XIII been followed by a more liberal or even moderate Pope committed to moving the church forward in its efforts to deal with the challenges of the late-nineteenth-century industrializing world, the structural strains that propelled the church into the pre-Vatican II crisis may never have eventuated in another Vatican council. However, Pope Pius X (1903-1914) took it as his agenda to stem the tides of modernism that he saw creeping into the church after Leo's reign. He first condemned modernism in a papal encyclical in 1907 and the following year demanded that all Catholic priests take an anti-modernist oath, a requirement that remained in effect as a condition for priestly ordination until the close of the Second Vatican Council. He accused the modernists of undermining papal authority by giving undue credence to the findings of modern science and permitting the intellectual freedom of the individual which the scientific ethic requires. While the anti-modernist stance of the Vatican waxed and waned somewhat during the ensuing 50-year period, dialog between Catholic intellectuals and secular scientists was curtailed by numerous restrictions placed on Catholic scholars by Rome.

In addition to the internal strains that were occurring within the ranks of theologians and Catholic intelligentia, the church was situated in a rapidly changing world. With advances in travel and communication after World War II, the nations of the world were becoming less and less isolated from one another and less and less European dominated. The Western world was learning about other, non-Christian religions, religions, in fact, that claimed more members than Christianity. Could the church continue, in its missionizing efforts, to condemn these religions as inferior? Was it possible to prove that the Bible was any more justifiable than the sacred writings of these other religions, some even older than Christianity? Also, archaeology was uncovering ancient data that challenged the church's traditional interpretation of the Bible.

In addition to a rapidly shrinking world, profound changes were taking place in the West itself which challenged some of the traditional positions of the church. From the nineteenth century on, democracy, equality, and personal freedom increasingly replaced the blind acceptance of hierarchic structures and systems of closed mobility. Greeley (1973) points to the personalist revolution as one of the most important developments of the twentieth century, reflected in progressive educational theories and the consciousness awakening of various minority groups.

Greeley (1973) also demonstrates how worldwide changes in population shifts presented challenges to the church, especially in terms of reproduction and the role of women in society. Overpopulation, low infant mortality rates, and long life expectancies, along with shifting attitudes and opportunities regarding women, made the church's traditional teachings regarding birth control, family life, and the place of women outdated and inappropriate in the modern world.

In several countries, like the United States and parts of Europe, Catholics were also moving beyond immigrant status and third and fourth generations were rising into the middle and upper classes, with greater emphasis upon education and professionalism. The ghetto mentality of traditional Catholicism gave way to attitudes that were more in line with upward mobility.

The reaction of the Vatican to the dissent that ebbed and flowed during these decades has been described by a number of authors as the deployment of a "seige mentality" (Brown 1969; Fesquet 1967; Kaiser 1963). The hierarchy feared for the purity of Catholic doctrine as it was bombarded by secular thought, strongly distrusted science and free scholarship (Ellis 1972; Kurtz 1986), and rejected growing pressures toward democracy. Dissent was countered by teachings of anti-modernism from 1908 until the death of Pope Pius XII in 1958 (McSweeney 1980).

The general unrest in the church was also evident in the numerous national movements that were gaining strength and visibility by the end of the first half of the twentieth century. While the Liturgical Movement had grown from a "timid trickle into a mighty tide" (McNaspy 1966) in a number of countries, it was only one of several reform movements that had gained the attention of both church and secular leaders. The Lay Movement, with Catholic Action as its center, had as its goals reaction against the pervasive clerical control that characterized the church, and support for greater participation and authority for the laity. As lay people in various countries, including Italy, France, Germany, and the United States, began organizing and holding lay congresses, they started to build a strong movement that threatened to gain some independence from clerical control. In Vaillancourt's (1980) analysis, the movement threat was serious enough to cause the Vatican to use measures of cooptation to assure that the laity would serve as a kind of "reserve clergy," faithful to the conservative policies of the Vatican, rather than to evolve into a protest movement within the church. In order to assure Vatican control of the movement, the First World Congress for the Lay Apostolate was held in Rome in 1951 and attended by Roman Catholic laity from 74 countries (Vaillancourt 1980).

The Social Gospel Movement also flourished in the four or five decades preceding the Council and set the stage for the council encyclical, "On the Church in the Modern World." Catholic social activists in the United States, Italy, and Germany raised the social consciousness of Catholics both in terms of direct aid to the victims of poverty, immigration, disease, and poor working conditions and also awareness of widespread social and economic changes that were needed to eradicate the social ills of society.

All of the above factors, both within the church itself and in changing societal conditions, served to highlight the fact that the monolithic, hierarchic church was becoming an anachronism in the latter half of the twentieth century.

STAGE II: MOBILIZATION

Crisis in itself is insufficient to propel discontent and strain forward into an organized social movement. Numerous times in church history, crisis has been resolved by retrenchment in the form of reactionary popes. By mechanisms of isolation and strong central autocracy, dissensus has been squelched by pontifical edicts. The question remains: why did this not happen in the mid twentieth century? What were the conditions that catapulted the church to reconceptualize its theology in relation to the world rather than retrench back to a "ghetto Catholicism?" What were the factors that mobilized widespread unrest into what became a full fledged social movement of liberalization and accommodation to the modern world?

There is no doubt that the personality and pastoralism of John XXIII was a crucial factor in the mobilization process. The question to be answered, however, is how Pope John XXIII, known as an open-minded reformist cardinal came to be elected as pope in a church that traditionally was dominated by more conservative leaders such as Pius XII. Part of the answer to his election must be understood in the context of the changes that had occurred in the church in the decade preceding his election, knowledge that the cardinals were well aware of as they gathered in Rome in 1958 to elect a new pontiff. A number of factors had coalesced to sharpen and focus the crisis in the church.

Pope Pius XII's encyclical, *Humani Generis,* issued in 1950, provided a rallying point for Catholic intellectuals who had felt that the church was becoming somewhat more open in its stance toward scientific inquiry. Theologians such as deLubac, Rahner, and Chardin had been arguing for some time that a distinction must be made between the content of the truths of faith and their modes of expression which not only could but must be adapted to the world in which they are articulated. While there was some speculation that Pius XII was softening in his position in regard to scientific discoveries, *Humani Generis* removed any doubt about his official position when he condemned "false opinions that threaten to undermine the bases of Catholic teaching" and maintained that "When the popes explicitly pronounce judgement on a hitherto controversial question, it is a clear indication to all of us that, according to the intention and will of the popes, it should no longer by subject to free discussion by theologians."

Despite the edicts of Rome, there were Catholic scholars like DeLubac, Congar, Rahner, Chenu, Teilhard de Chardin who were willing to forge ahead with theological ideas that tried to bring harmony between the newly developing scientific ideas and Catholic thought. It was their ideas that eventually, through much debate and anguish, became the prevailing orthodox theologies that prevailed at the Second Vatican Council.

Why were these dissenting theologians not formally censured, as had been the case numerous times before when dissident voices challenged the authority of Rome? The option of mounting a campaign similar to Pius X's squelching of the anti-modernists in the early part of the century was not as simple in the 1950s for a number of reasons. In the work of most of the modern theologians, the Pope was confronted with meticulous scholarship explicitly framed within the Catholic tradition and based solidly upon Scripture (McSweeney 1980). None of them could be accused of heresy because of their solid appeal to Catholic tradition.

In addition, the worldwide church of the 1950s was very different in composition from that of 50 years earlier. In the United States and Europe,

Catholics were educated and versed in scientific thinking. The writings of the liberal theologians like Chardin, Rahner, and Schillebeex were being read and championed by many clerics, nuns, and laity. The Pope realized the danger of widespread censoring of what had become well disseminated through the modern means of communication.

In spite of the conservative stance of *Humani Generis*, Pius XII was himself an educated scholar who read widely. He was well aware of recent social changes, as evidenced by his insistence that priests and nuns be professionally prepared to deal with the demands of their professional commitments. In fact, in 1952, he called to Rome all of the major superiors of religious orders of women and mandated that they prepare their nuns professionally on a par with their lay counterparts. In turn, this lead to the Sister Formation Movement in the United States and to the profound changes that resulted from an educated core of religious women (Ebaugh 1977; Neal 1990).

The professionalism of both nuns and priests was an important factor in the mobilization process that lead up to Vatican II. For the clergy, it meant a new orientation that included a sense of competence, maturity, ability to articulate with other related professionals, more volunteerism in selection of appointments, and specific training in roles such as counsellor, social worker, and business manager. For nuns, professionalization meant engaging in higher studies, often at institutions outside of their convents, and associating with lay people on a daily basis. The unanticipated result of such professionalization for both priests and nuns was the shifting of meaningful reference groups and exposure to knowledge and ways of thinking that were antithetical to the blind acceptance of faith and authority.

The Liturgical Movement of the 1950s was also a major factor that mobilized and educated both clerics and laity to new ways of thinking about rituals and practices of the church. What differentiated the modern liturgical movement from many liturgical revivals of the past was its stress on reforming of the liturgy itself rather than raising the level of devotion of the laity which characterized many earlier movements (McSweeney 1980).

The first major act of liturgical reform occurred in 1951 when Pius XII restored the Easter Vigil to its primitive form by greater involvement of the laity in the ritual and by institutionalizing the sacrament of Baptism into the liturgy. This action of the Pope was in keeping with the broader goals of the Liturgical Movement, namely, to revitalize lay participation and involvement in worship. Because the Mass was said in Latin, many Catholics struggled to follow along in their English missals or recited the rosary or read devotional literature while the priest performed his act at the altar. The new Easter Vigil Mass was the first concerted effort to draw laity more integrally into the ritual by introducing some preparatory rites in English, such as the renewal of Baptismal vows, a processional, and a lighting of candles ceremony. The new Vigil was a return to the customs of the primitive church. It placed the ritual in historical context, and suggested that the centuries old tradition of the Mass was amenable to change. This attitude not only prepared the laity for the liturgical changes that became the first agenda item of the Council, but also mobilized the liturgical reformists to push ahead for even greater changes.

As the cardinals gathered in Rome in the fall of 1958 to elect a new pope, the press was presenting the election as a straightforward political choice between left and right forces in the church. As Hebblethwaite (1968) describes, during the two weeks between the death of Pius XII and the start of the election conclave, the lobbying was discreet but intense among the conservative and liberal forces among the cardinals and their advisors. Don Roncalli (soon to be Pope John XXIII) was a favored candidate among the more reform-minded cardinals. He was seen as a progressive who was nevertheless moderate enough to gain the support of the conservative, traditional contingent who favored several more conservative cardinals who were committed to continuing the policies of the previous pontiff (Rynne 1968). After 11 votes, the progressives won out as Roncalli won the needed two-thirds plus one votes.

Two months after his election, Pope John XXIII announced an ecumenical council for the explicit purpose of aggiornamento, namely, updating the church to function in modern society. It was clear, in the way the announcement was made, that the pope was legitimating open discussion and entertaining the argument that the church was outdated and needed reform. In his opening remarks to the council delegates, he told the council fathers that their task was to make the church relevant to the world. It was not clear, at that point, just how this mandate would affect doctrine and structure; however, the basic intent of the Council was made very clear.

The announcement of the Council as well as the actual event was clearly a victory for the progressives and constituted a major resource for the advocates of change in the church. As the resource mobilization theorists demonstrate (Gamson 1975; Jenkins 1981, 1983; McCarthy and Zald 1977; Oberschaal 1973; Tilly 1978), the success of a movement depends primarily upon the types of resources (key people, organizations, finances, power) that the movement advocates are able to muster to their cause. The Council itself, with a myriad of discussions and debates that eventuated in the offical council decrees, became a major resource in the movement toward greater liberalization and modernization of the church.

Another resource in preparing for the Council was the group of liberal theologians whom Pope John XXIII called to Rome soon after he announced the Council. Even though many of the council committees were dominated by conservative theologians and clerics from the Roman Curia, the progressive theologians were very active in Rome providing lectures and seminars to the bishops (Rynne 1968). Not only did they provide rationales for council agenda items, but they, along with many other theologians, briefed the council delegates.

The Council was a critical factor both in the mobilization phase and in the actual legitimation of specific ideas and changes advocated by the progressives in the movement. In the course of the council debates, many bishops, as well as church members around the world who were keeping abreast of the Council's activities through the highly organized media present at the sessions, were mobilized as active participants in the process of aggiornamento.

STAGE III: LEGITIMATION OF MAZEWAY SHIFTS

Despite the heated debates that took place between the traditionalists and progressives during the council sessions, and the ambiguity in many of the final council documents, there is widespread agreement that the progressives who were advocating change won out in the official positions finally promulgated by the Council (Dulles 1988; McSweeney 1980; Rynne 1968; Seidler and Meyer 1989). The council legitimated many of the ideas and theologies that were developed by the liberal thinkers and writers in the several decades before the Council.

The election of Pope Paul VI in 1963 (after only one session of the Council was completed) was also a victory for the progressives because the new pope had made it clear that he supported aggiornamento and the direction the Council was taking. His election in 1963 was again very political and pitted the liberal, reform-minded cardinals against those who opposed change. The issue of whether aggiornamento would continue or be squelched in the church was at stake as the cardinals struggled with one another to select a new pope. The fact that it took eight ballots to elect Montini as successor to John XXIII shows that dissension still existed among the cardinals. Finally, however, the progressives won and Pope Paul VI was named Pontiff. In his acceptance speech the new pope committed himself to continuing the reform efforts of John XXIII when he convened the Second Vatican Council.

Basically, the Second Vatican Council legitimated the "revitalization movement" by developing the kind of shift in "mazeways" that Wallace argues is at the heart of revitalization (Wallace 1956, 1957). Pope John XXIII's call for aggiornamento was first and foremost a call for reconsideration of the church's systems of meaning as they applied to the modern world. He encouraged the council fathers to reconsider all aspects of the church's teachings in light of the rapid changes that were occurring in society and to revitalize the church's teachings and structures by making them relevant in a modern, industrializing world.

After three years of intense and conflict-ridden debate, the final documents of the Council indicate that a mazeway shift occurred in the church's position and attitude toward the world. While there is much debate about the implications of various of the documents, the vast majority of commentators agree that Vatican II legitimated a new theology. The most significant shift that occurred, and one that underlay all the documents, was the ratification of Pope John's distinction between the content of the church's doctrine and its form of expression, a distinction which introduced the possibility of relativity of both faith and morality. While nowhere explicitly stated, the basic implication in the documents is that the meaning of any statement of doctrine is open to interpretation; it is never finally captured in any form of expression that is valid for all times and cultures.

As McSweeney (1980) maintains in the document on Revelation, the Council came as near as the most optimistic new theologian could wish in defining the historical relativity of the church's teaching when it legitimated a relativist principle that destroyed the sense of doctrinal clarity and conceptual precision which was the basis of traditional Catholicism.

Likewise, the liturgical changes effected by the Council were based upon the principle of adaptation to the local culture. The rigidity introduced into the liturgy by Pope Pius V in 1570 and which remained basically unchanged in the subsequent 400 years was suddenly replaced by significant changes, not only in form, but in meaning. Active participation of the laity was emphasized; the vernacular was introduced as part of the process of adapting to the "genius and traditions of peoples"; the Mass as Eucharistic Meal (Agape), in which the laity took part as the altar and action faced them, was substituted for the traditional notion of Mass as sacrifice reenacted by the priest standing with his back to the people as audience.

Many of the other changes legitimated by the Council, such as the principle of collegiality, religious freedom, ecumenism, and the social mission of the church are also justified by the general notion that the church can no longer stand apart from the world as a hierarchic institution that possesses the sole truth that is immutable and immune from the pressures of the external world. In endorsing the principle of adaptation, the Council opened the way to reintepretation of doctrine and to a diversity of forms of expression.

The general outcome of the council debates was that the progressive theologians won a major victory and were able to achieve the legitimation of their liberal positions. The council documents institutionalized the principles of renewal and adaptation, themes that had served as the major motifs and goals of the progressive movement for several decades.

STAGE IV: IMPLEMENTATION

As movement theorists demonstrate in their numerous case studies, legitimation of ideas by a formal authority does not necessarily translate into smooth implementation strategies. The "contested accommodation" model described by Seidler and Meyer (1989) highlights the "spirals of conflict" that characterized implementation of Vatican II in the United States. The fact that change happened so rapidly in an institution that had been the epitome of stability and tradition, coupled with the fact that the legitimation took place in Rome by the hierarchy which was always isolated from the general populace of Catholics, meant that most elements in the church (clergy and laity alike) had very little time to assimilate the changes.

While it is true that the presence of the media during the Council meant that the Catholic world was kept abreast of the debates and positions that emerged, Rome was far away until the first of the changes began to be implemented on the diocesan and parish levels, primarily in terms of liturgical changes and greater participation by the laity in church affairs. The fact that the encyclical *Humanae Vitae*, condemning artificial birth control, appeared three years after the close of the Council also heightened lay involvement in issues of interpretation of church teaching and gave many of them an opportunity to implement the spirit of the Council's stance on morality by taking into account both personal and societal issues in deciding issues of morality (Greeley 1977).

Seidler and Meyer (1989), in their analysis of articles published in *The Catholic National Reporter,* show that the types of issues that became controversial and targets of conflict differed during the decades of the 1960s and 1970s. During the 1960s, the conflicts seem largely to reflect a progressive or radical challenge to traditional episcopal authority. Even though the Council had legitimated a progressive agenda, many bishops and pastors had difficulty accepting the implementation of new ideas and structures. In particular, issues of authority, freedom and changes in liturgy caused confrontations between the hierarchy and priests, nuns, and laity who were eager to move forward with renewal. Many priests and nuns expressed their dissatisfaction with the way renewal was progressing by exiting their professional roles (Ebaugh 1977, 1988; Hoge 1987; Schoenherr and Sorenson 1982, 1988; Schoenherr and Greeley 1974). While the 1970s carried forward some of these debates, the decrease in importance of authority conflicts reflected the hierarchy's growing acceptance of renewal efforts. By the 1970s, Catholics had not only accepted the general principle of change but were now using their greater voice in the church to confront specific issues, such as: attacking the National Conference of Catholic Bishops; fighting over the dismissal of parish councils, local nuns, and religious educators; demanding greater input into diocesan and parish decisions; and taking sides, often vociferously, on the new charismatic communities that were developing (Seidler and Meyer 1989).

STAGE V: COUNTERMOVEMENTS

One indication that a social movement has achieved legitimation and institutionalization is that countermovements arise to protest the new accommodation. Backlash movements are organized in an effort to stop, reverse, or slow down the gains made by a successful social movement. In the United States we have seen the frenzied attempt of the white supremists, the anti-feminists, and the right-to-lifers to reverse or retard the strides made by their counterpart movements. In the past decade we have seen a number of countermovements arise in the Catholic church to protest the directions that change has taken in the worldwide church.

The most notable of these backlash movements is Catholic Traditionalism, an international movement with the objective of reaffirming and restoring pre-Vatican II theology and cultic practices, symbolized in the Latin Tridentine Mass (Dinges 1989). The most visible central figure in the movement was the French Archbishop Marcel Lefebvre and his priestly fraternity, the Society of St. Pius X. After twenty years of vigorous protest against the legitimacy and authority of Vatican II, and after numerous attempts at negotiation and accommodation on the part of Rome, in June, 1988, the Archbishop incurred automatic excommunication when he consecrated four bishops without Vatican approval. As Dinges (1989) remarks, the primary reason that Vatican concern with traditionalist dissent focused on Lefebvre and his fraternity was that, unlike traditionalist enclaves organized around individual priests, Lebebvre had the power to both ordain and consecrate, thereby establishing a line of succession and possible schism, a fear that materialized with his excommunication.

In many ways, Pope John Paul II is part of the countermovement in his attempts to slow aggiornamento by taking a traditionalist stance on a number of issues. While he later reneged on his earlier action, for a number of years he allowed the archconservative French Archbishop Marcel Lefebvre to continue ordaining priests and deacons in Switzerland in defiance of a Vatican ban. He banned Hans Kung from teaching Catholic theology because of his liberal views, called the liberal Edward Schillebeeckx to Rome to reprimand him for some of his teachings, forbade Charles Curran to continue teaching at Catholic University because of his liberal positions on moral issues, and censored Archbishop Hunthausen. He condemned liberation theology, urged priests to get out of politics, reiterated his conservative stand on birth control, ordered religious women who signed a statement on abortion to retract it or risk expulsion from their orders, reiterated a traditional stance on homosexuality, and made it clear that he supported clerical celibacy and opposed the ordination of women. His stance on these various issues made it clear that he feared aggiornamento had gone too far.

SUMMARY

Much of the literature on the Second Vatican Council focuses upon the dramatic changes effected by the Council in worldwide Roman Catholicism.

There is no denying the reality and far reaching consequences of these changes. However, in this paper I argue that the Council was a result and final stage in the progressive social movement that was alive in the church in the 100 years since the First Vatican Council in 1870.

The various national mini-movements such as the Liturgical Movement, the Sister Formation Movement, the worker-priest movement in France, the Biblical Scholarship Movement, and the Social Action Movement pointed out the structural strains that existed in the church. In addition, the work of liberal theologians provided a Scriptural and theological rationale for many of the new ideas that presented a challenge to the traditional mentality that characterized much of the church's teaching and actions in the early part of the twentieth century.

As Pope John XXIII ascended the papal throne in 1958 he realized that a crisis existed in the church and that bold action was required to bring the church into the modern world. Against the advice of many of his advisors, he announced the Twenty-first Ecumenical Council in the Catholic church and began the mammoth task of establishing the preparatory commissions whose mandate was to prepare for the Second Vatican Council.

The major consequence of the Council was a radical shift in the church's self-conceptualization and stance toward modernity. The Council, in its official decrees, legitimated many of the ideas and theologies that were developed by the liberal theologians and advocated by the progressive movements that preceded the Council. Both the council delegates and laity throughout the church were prepared for the changes by participation in the precursor movements, the relatively open process that characterized the council sessions, and the vast media coverage of the council events in Rome.

The implementation of the council decrees in the 25 years since they were promulgated has been a history of both successses and conflicts on all levels of church structure. In the first decade of implementation, the conflicts were largely a challenge to traditional episcopal authority as many bishops and pastors resisted change. Confrontations between the hierarchy and those priests, nuns, and laity who were pressuring for renewal made headline news. By the decade of the 1970s increasing numbers of the hierarchy had accepted renewal efforts and the issues that gained public attention shifted to the confrontation on more specific issues such as attacks on the National Conference of Catholic Bishops, struggles of religious orders with Roman authorities, the dismissal of liberal religious educators, and efforts to gain greater collegiality and power on the part of Catholic laity.

Like most social movements, the post-Vatican Catholic church in the 1980s faced backlash, countermovements that protested the changes that were being made. The most notable of these countermovements was Catholic Traditionalism, an international movement that aimed to reaffirm and restore pre-Vatican II theology and practices. After intense struggle, the Catholic church officially denounced the most radical element in the movement by excommunicating its founder and spokesman, Archbishop Marcel Lefebvre. Despite this official action by the church, the Traditionalist Movement in its many forms remains very alive as a constant challenge to the spirit and changes introduced by the Second Vatican Council.

The implementation stage of Vatican II is far from complete as the church continues to live out the agenda set by the Council. To what extent Pope John's vision of a "renewed church" will materialize awaits the challenges that will arise both within the church itself and in the broader world throughout the decade of the 1990s and into the twenty-first century.

REFERENCES

Abell, A. 1960. *American Catholicism and Social Action.* Garden City, NY: Doubleday.

Brown, R. McA. 1969. *The Ecumenical Revolution.* Garden City, NY: Anchor-Image.

Burns, G. 1990. "The Politics of Ideology: The Papal Struggle with Liberalism." *The American Journal of Sociology* 95:1123-1152.

Cogley, J. 1973. *Catholic America.* NY: Dial Press.

Dinges, W.D. 1983. "Catholic Traditionalist Movement." Pp. 137-158 in *Alternatives to American Mainline Churches,* edited by J.H. Fichter. New York: Unification Theological Seminary.

_____. 1989. "The Quandry of Dissent on the Catholic Right," In *Sociological Studies in Roman Catholicism: Historical and Contemporary Perspectives.* Edited by Roger O'Toole. The Edwin Mellen Press.

Dulles, A. 1988. *The Reshaping of Catholicism.* New York: Harper and Row.

Ebaugh, H.R. Fuchs. 1977. *Out of the Cloister: A Study of Organizational Dilemmas.* Austin: The University of Texas Press.

_____. 1988. *Becoming an Ex: The Process of Role Exit.* Chicago: The University of Chicago Press.

Ellis, J.T. 1963. *Perspectives in American Catholicism.* Baltimore: Helicon Press.

_____. 1969. *American Catholicism.* Chicago: The University of Chicago Press.

_____. 1972. "The Formation of the American Priest: An Historical Perspective." Pp. 3-110 in *The Catholic Priest in the United States: Historical Investigations,* edited by J. T. Ellis. Collegeville, MN: St. John's University Press.

Fesquet, H. 1967. *The Drama of Vatican II: The Ecumenical Council, June 1962-December 1965.* New York: Random House.

Gamson, W. 1975. *The Strategy of Social Protest.* Homewood, IL:Dorsey.

Greeley, A.M. 1973. *The New Agenda.* Garden City, NY: Doubleday.

_____. 1977. *The American Catholic: A Social Portrait.* New York: Basic Books.

Hebblethwaite, P. 1968. *Inside the Synod: Rome, 1967.* New York: Paulist Press.

Hennesey, J. 1981. *American Catholics: A History of the Roman Catholic Community in the U.S.* New York: Oxford University Press.

Hirschman, A. O. 1970. *Exit, Voice and Loyalty: Responses to Decline in Firms, Organizations and States.* Cambridge, MA: Harvard University Press.

Hoge, D.R. 1987. *The Future of Catholic Leadership: Responses to the Priest Shortage.* Kansas City, MO: Sheed and Ward.

Hughes, P. 1961. *The Church in Crisis: A History of the General Concils, 325-1870.* Garden City, NY: Hanover House (Doubleday).

Jenkins, J.C. 1981. "Sociopolitical Movements." *Handbook of Political Behavior* 4: 81-183.

_____. 1983. "Resource Mobilization Theory and the Study of Social Movements," *Annual Review of Sociology* 9:527-553.

Kaiser, R. B. 1963. *Pope, Council and the World: The Story of Vatican II.* New York: Macmillan.

Kurtz, L. 1986. *The Politics of Heresy: The Modernist Crisis in Roman Catholicism.* Los Angeles: University of California Press.

Lyng, S., and L. R. Kurtz. 1985. "Bureaucratic Insurgency: The Vatican and the Crisis of Modernism." *Social Forces* 63: 901-921.

McCarthy, J., and M.N. Zald. 1977. "Resource Mobilization and Social Movements." *American Journal of Sociology* 82: 1212-1241.

McNaspy, C.J. 1966. "Liturgy." Pp. 133-136 in *The Documents of Vatican II,* edited by W. M. Abbott, S.J. New York: Guild Press.

McSweeney, W. 1980. *Roman Catholicism: The Search for Relevance.* New York: St. Martin's Press.

Neal, M. A. 1990. *From Nuns to Sisters: An Expanding Vocation.* Mystic, CT: Twenty-Third Publications.

Oberschall, A. 1973. *Social Conflict and Social Movements.* Englewood Cliffs, NJ: Prentice-Hall.

Rynne, X. 1968. *Vatican Council II.* New York: Farrar, Straus and Giroux.

Schoenherr, R., and A. Greeley. 1974. "Role Commitment Processes and the American Catholic Priesthood." *American Sociological Review* 39: 407-426.

Schoenherr, R. and A. Sorensen. 1982. "Social Change in Religious Organizations: Consequences of the Clergy Decline in the U.S. Catholic Church." *Sociological Analysis* 43:52-71.

Schoenherr, R., L.A. Young, and J.P. Vilarino. 1988. "Demographic Transitions in Religious Organizations: A Comparative Study of Priest Decline in Roman Catholic Dioceses. *Journal for the Scientific Study of Religion* 27: 499-523.

Seidler, J., and K. Meyer. 1989. *Conflict and Change in the Catholic Church.* New Brunswick: Rutgers University Press.

Smelser, N. 1963. *The Theory of Collective Behavior.* Glencoe, IL: Free Press.

Tilly, C. 1978. *From Mobilization to Revolution.* Reading, MA: Addison-Wesley.

Turner, R. and L.M. Killian. 1987. *Collective Behavior, 3rd ed.* Englewood Cliffs, NJ: Prentice-Hall.

Vaillancourt, J-G. 1980. *Papal Power: A Study of Vatican Control Over Lay Catholic Elites.* Berkeley, CA: University of California Press.

Von Aretin, K. O. 1970. *The Papacy and the Modern World.* London: Weidenfeld and Nicolson.

Wallace, A. F.C. 1956. "Revitalization Movements." *American Anthropologist* 58:264-281.

_____. 1957. "Mazeway Disintegration: The Individual's Perception of Socio-Cultural Disorganization." *Human Organization* 16:23-27.

THE CHURCH AND MODERNIZATION

Gregory Baum and Jean-Guy Vaillancourt

In this essay, we wish to interpret Vatican Council II as an effort of the Catholic church to respond to the challenges and expectations of modern society, without loosing its own identity in the process. We shall show that the openness to modernity in the conciliar teachings was not accompanied by an equivalent effort to insert these modern values into the church's own self-organization. The contradiction between what is taught ad extra and what is done ad intra has caused confusion and frustration in the Catholic church. This state of disarray can be overcome only when the ecclesiastical institutions come to embody the Church's own social teaching.

DEFINITION AND IMPLICATIONS OF MODERNITY

At the outset we must offer a definition of what we mean by "modernity." By that term sociologists usually refer to the new society created by the two great social transformations, the Industrial Revolution beginning in England in the second half of the eighteenth century and the democratic revolution, symbolized by the dramatic events of the French Revolution at the end of the same century. Industrialization and democratization are distinct historical processes that have not always gone hand in hand. A democratizing revolution created the United States of America in 1776 while large-scale industrialization only took place in the second half of the nineteenth century. Conversely, the industrialization of Quebec began at the turn of the twentieth century while

Religion and the Social Order, Volume 2, pages 21-33.
Copyright © 1991 by JAI Press Inc.
All rights of reproduction in any form reserved.
ISBN: 1-55938-388-7

the democratic modernization of Quebec matured only in the 1960s during the celebrated Quiet Revolution.

In Europe an affinity existed between industrialization and democracy. The development of industry produced new wealth for the members of the burgher class, thus giving them more power for the political struggle to transform an aristocratic into a democratic society. There is a close link between industrial capitalism and political democracy, if the latter is understood as a form of government that protects personal safety and property rights and interferes as little as possible in the societal process. Yet there is a tension between capitalism and democracy if the latter is understood as a form of government that serves the well-being of society as a whole and for this purpose encourages the participation of all the citizens. In such a situation, industrial capitalism stands out as nonparticipatory and hierarchically organized. This complex, shifting interrelation between capitalism and democracy makes the word "liberal" an ambiguous term. For some, liberal refers to a free market economy, unrestrained by government intervention, while for others liberal designates the political orientation toward greater equality and participation. *The concept of modernization used in the present essay refers exclusively to the political modernization that has produced modern, democratic Western society.*

The process of democratization includes values and institutions such as constitutional government, the division of powers, democratic participation, free elections, equality before the law, religious liberty, the secularization of the state, human rights, religious and ideological pluralism, respect for public opinion, and the right to organize political parties. Also included are the assumptions that government is responsible for promoting the well-being of society and the expectation that democracy is the ideal for the whole world.

These modern values and institutions have come to define the democratic ethos of Western society. All Western democracies pay at least lip service to this ethos, even if this high ideal is not fully supported by the values and institutions created by industrial capitalism. We note, moreover, that the democratic ethos is an embodiment of "the Enlightenment principle," the intellectual foundation of political modernization, which affirms that "human reason" empowers people to free themselves from the distorting and self-limiting myths of the past to become the rational subjects of their own social existence.

The process of political modernization is not free of ambiguity. It has problematic side effects, such as centralization, bureaucratization, and the enhancement of state power, developments analyzed and criticized by the early sociologists from Alexis de Tocqueville to Max Weber. Still, the democratic values and institutions have retained their appeal.

THE CATHOLIC CHURCH'S STANCE
TOWARD MODERNITY

In the nineteenth century the Catholic church vehemently rejected the emerging liberal, democratic society as well as the Enlightenment principle implicit in it. The most vehement repudiation, the Syllabus of Errors, promulgated by Pius IX in 1864, listed and condemned 80 erroneous opinions of modern society, including the rationalistic philosophical theories that legitimated the new social order. The eightieth condemned erroneous opinion was that "the Roman Pontiff could and should reconcile himself with and adjust to progress, liberalism, and the new society" (Denziger and Schoenmetzer 1963, p. 584, no. 2980).

Throughout the nineteenth century papal teaching lamented the revolutionary character of modern society, the rejection of traditional authority, the hostility to religion, the blind faith in human reason, the all-pervasive individualism, and the manner in which modernity undermined the common good of society, including the demand for human rights and religious liberty. Identified with the inherited feudal-communal society, the Catholic church, sensitive to the ambiguous side effects of liberal society, defended the position that the old institutions of solidarity, community, and tradition protected ordinary people more effectively from the arbitrariness of state power than did the new, liberal society. The church articulated a critique of modernity that was shared by many conservative or Tory social thinkers of Europe.

Leo XIII's *Rerum novarum* (1891) was the church's first official reaction to the growing industrialization of society and the far-reaching effect it had on the people of all classes. In that encyclical, the emphasis was on social justice. Leo XIII lamented that unrestrained capitalism undermined the common good and split society into two antagonistic classes, the self-serving owners of industry and the exploited and oppressed workers. He called upon national governments, made up of selfless, spiritual men, to stand above the competing interests of the classes, promote the common good, restrain the liberal economy, legislate social justice and protect the workers and the poor. While the pope condemned socialism, he defended the right of workers to organize their own associations, and he upheld the justice of their demand for a living wage. The Church here defended what is often called a "red Tory" position, adopted by progressive conservatives in many parts of Europe and Canada, which maintained that it is possible to promote social reforms while remaining faithful to time-tested traditions in the realm of politics.

It is significant that papal social teaching did not say a single word in favor of political modernization, including democracy, electoral participation, human rights, and pluralism. The idea that people were the sovereign subject of their society and hence the source of the power their government exercised over them seemed irreconcilable with Catholic tradition. In *Quadragesimo anno* (1931), Pius XII even suggested a "corporatist" organization of society as an alternative to political democracy (*Seven Great Encyclicals* 1963, p. 148, nn. 81-83). Envisaging the creation of corporations, made up of owners and workers belonging to the same industries, he recommended that representatives of these corporations form a national council, steered by government, that would promote the national economy in favour of the common good. Corporatism thus gave all men, be they owners of an industry or salaried workers, a certain voice in the making of economic policy.

The first positive statement upholding modern democracy is found in Pius XII's Christmas address in 1944 (Yzermans 1961, pp. 78-79). Toward the end of the war, the pope realized that, on the one hand, the Soviet atheistic communism was gaining ground, and, on the other hand, the conservative ideals, some of which were defended by Italian and Spanish fascism, were not destined to survive after the war. The pope now recognized the Western democracies as the societies in which the Church had the best chance of flowering. Still, the teaching of Pius XII showed only the slightest opening toward pluralism, human rights, and religious liberty.

For Catholics living in modern, democratic societies, this conservative aspect of the church's teaching was difficult to grasp. In the United States, in particular, with its liberal culture and the absence of a strong Tory tradition, Catholics were puzzled by the church's rejection of political modernization. Already in the nineteenth century, American Catholics wanted to participate on equal footing in building the liberal society, yet their adjustment to modernity and their turn to a spirituality more attuned to democratic values appeared to Rome as an Americanism worthy of condemnation.

In nineteenth-century Europe, the church remained on the whole identified with the conservative tradition. The efforts to make the Church respond more positively to democracy and pluralism were condemned. This embarrassed Catholics living as minorities in Protestant countries—in England, for instance (Chadwick 1970, pp. 416-422). It was only after World War II that Catholicism located in Western democracies, especially France and Germany, experienced a lively spiritual renewal and a new openness, sparked and defended by brilliant theologians, like Chenu, Congar, de Lubac, and Rahner, who gave expression to the aspirations of Catholics educated in an Enlightenment culture. These theologians were often censured by Rome. Also rebuked by Rome was the American theologian, John Courtney Murray, who defended religious liberty as a human right.

On January 25, 1959, John XXIII announced his intention to convoke an ecumenical council, to be called the Second Vatican Council, or Vatican II. One of the aims of the Council was to deal in an innovative way with the church's situation in the modern world. In his first encyclical letter of June 1959, *Ad Petri cathedram,* John XXIII specified: "The major aim of the council will consist in promoting the development of Christian faith, the spiritual renewal of the Catholic faith, and the adaptation of Church disciplines to the needs and methods of our times" (*Documentation Catholique* 1959, col. 907, our translation). What the Pope wanted was, in his own words, "a wise modernization" of the church, so that its internal structure could find a renewed vigor.

An ecumenical council is an extraordinary event in the life of the Catholic church. According to Catholic teaching, a general or ecumenical council exercises supreme magisterium and jurisdiction in the church. While these supreme ministerial powers are normally exercised by the pope, united with his bishops in spirit, at an ecumenical council this highest office is exercized by the legislative assembly, the gathered episcopate with the pope simply acting as president. An ecumenical council is one of the rare historical moments when the bishops from various parts of the globe are institutionally empowered to affect the teaching, the pastoral policy and the self-organization of the Catholic church.

Vatican II was such a rare occasion. Thanks to the influence of the bishops from the industrialized and democratic countries, especially from the lands along the Rhine (Belgium, France, Germany, and Holland), a leadership that was eventually endorsed by the great majority of the bishops, the Vatican Council significantly modified the church's relationship to the modern world.[1] An important event occurred at the beginning of the Council when the conciliar assembly rejected a draft document prepared by an ecclesiastical commission controlled by the Roman Curia and demanded the election of new conciliar commissions to be charged with the task of preparing the conciliar documents. Throughout the four sessions of the Council, it was the set of progressive Western European bishops, later joined by the American hierarchy, that exercised the greatest influence on the shaping of ecclesiastical policy. Behind the outspoken bishops and cardinals stood the important theologians from these countries, theologians who had laid, over the years, a theological foundation for an open approach of the church in regard to modern society.

Before turning to the conciliar texts, we must look at the historical moment at which the Vatican Council was held. The early 1960s was a time of great cultural optimism in Western Europe and North America. The interventionist Keynesian economic policies adopted after World War II in the North Atlantic countries were now producing enormous wealth under conditions that almost abolished unemployment and permitted working-class families to improve their standard of living. Welfare capitalism seemed to be the answer to the problem of poverty. There was hope that if this economic system could be exported to the poorer countries of Latin America, Asia, and Africa, these countries would also be able to develop, industrialize, produce wealth, and overcome the conditions of hunger and misery.[2] In America, John Kennedy gave expression to this optimistic perspective, and in Europe, Pope John XXIII became the symbol of this evolutionary hope.

It is not surprising that Latin American Catholics, examining the conciliar documents in the late 1960s, came to the conclusion that in its approach to modern society, Vatican II reflected the perspective of the middle class in the North Atlantic nations. The Latin American Bishops Conference of Medellin, in 1968, pronounced a judgement on modern, Western society, that clearly articulated the oppressive and exploitative structures, at which Vatican II had only hinted in vague fashion. The Latin American bishops accounted for the marginalization and the poverty of their people in terms of neocolonial exploitation and internal class oppression (Gremillion 1976, Medellin Documents, "Peace," pp. 455-458, nn. 2-13).

VATICAN II AND MODERNITY

The conciliar documents that clearly express the Church's positive response to modernity are the Decree on Ecumenism (*Unitatis reintegratio*), the Declarations on Religious Freedom and on the Church's Relationship to Non-Christian Religions (*Dignitatis humanae* and *Nostra aetate*), and more especially the Pastoral Constitution on the Church in the Modern World (*Gaudium et spes*). In these texts the Catholic church formally approves and recommends the values and institutions of political modernization, in particular, (1) religious pluralism, (2) human rights, (3) respect for personal conscience, even if in error, (4) democratic participation, and (5) universal applicability. These innovations, as we shall see, raise a number of theological questions.

In the conciliar texts, the church becomes reconciled with religious pluralism. In the Decree on Ecumenism, the Church acknowledges other (non-Catholic) Christians as Christians, as brothers and sisters in Christ through faith and baptism, and recognizes the other churches as ecclesial communities used by the Spirit to save and sanctify humanity. The Decree praises the ecumenical movement as a Spirit-inspired effort to reunite the divided Christian family and recommends dialogue, cooperation, and even in special circumstances, common worship.

In the Declaration on the Church's Relationship to Non-Christian Religions, the Church expresses a profound respect for the great world religions, especially biblically-grounded Judaism. It acknowledges that present in these religions are the rays of God's own light that mediate saving wisdom to their followers, even if the fullness of this light is available only in Jesus Christ. The church here recommends interreligious dialogue and cooperation.

In these two conciliar documents and in the important Declaration on Religious Liberty, the Catholic church recognizes religious pluralism as the historical reality of God's world. Vatican II clearly and unambiguously affirms religious liberty as a human right. Social justice demands that religious pluralism be respected and protected by government. What is necessary, therefore, is a certain separation of the state from any particular church, including the Catholic church. A special legal arrangement between the Catholic church and a national government is acceptable only if it guarantees the freedom of other religious organizations.

The conciliar documents are sensitive to the ambiguous underside of religious pluralism, namely the relativism of religious truth. While the Council recommends dialogue and cooperation among Christians and among members of the world religions, it still defends the Catholic Church's traditional self-understanding—albeit in a modified form—as the one, true community of Jesus Christ in the world. The ancient formula, "extra ecclesiam nulla salus," is here given a new meaning: it is understood not as invalidating the other churches nor even the great world religions, but rather as affirming that the divine grace variously present in these religious traditions, Christian and otherwise, has been mediated —in a hidden way—by the Catholic church. What this nonhistorical, metaphysical mediation means is not made clear. It is a notion that continues to raise great theological difficulties.

The Pastoral Constitution on the Church and the Modern World, *Gaudium et spes,* is the principal conciliar document, and the most startling one, recording the church's positive response to modern society. Here human rights, including the freedom of religion, are fully recognized. Because of the dignity of the human person and the essential equality of humans, "every type of discrimination, whether social or cultural, whether based on sex, race, color, social condition, language or religion, is to be overcome and eradicated as contrary to God's intent" (Gremillion 1976, p. 266, n. 29).

It is made clear that these personal rights include the equality of women and men. According to the Council, part of the broader desires of humankind for human equality is "the claim of women for equity with men before the law and in fact" (Gremillion 1976, p. 207, n. 9). And regretting that human rights are not yet universally honoured, the Council gives as an example "the case of a woman who is denied . . . access to education or cultural benefits equal to those recognized for men" (p. 266, n. 29).

The Council admits that the emphasis on personal human rights has had an ambiguous underside, the promotion of individualism and the undermining of social solidarity—such as is found in the liberal political tradition from John Locke to Margaret Thatcher. Against this atomistic, liberal tradition, the Council insists on the social nature of human persons and their rootedness in communities. People are destined to belong to one another and to be responsible for one another. Concern for the common good is not imposed upon men and women by an external authority: concern for the common good is generated in people as they discover themselves. We note that Vatican II recognizes not only the personal rights against discrimination mentioned above but also the solidarity rights, foreign to the liberal tradition, such as the right to work and the right to the necessities of life.

Gaudium et spes praises the excellence of liberty, the fruit of political modernization. "Only in freedom can human persons direct themselves toward goodness. Our contemporaries make much of this freedom and pursue it eagerly; and rightly so, to be sure. . . . Authentic freedom is an exceptional sign of the divine image in humans" (Gremillion 1976, pp. 255-256, n. 17).

The same document also recognizes the possible negative consequences of this freedom. "Often people promote freedom perversely as a license for doing whatever pleases them, even if it is evil" (Gremillion 1976, p. 256, n. 17). Yet if these people explore their own conscience, we are told, they will hear a summons to do good.

In this context, *Gaudium et spes* introduces an innovative theology of conscience, echoing the work of Karl Rahner, the theory that God is graciously present in the moral quest of individual people. The conciliar document tells us (1) that, in conscience, people are addressed by a law not of their own making, summoning them to do good and avoid evil (the natural law), and (2) that in conscience, "the most secret core and sanctuary of a person," people hear the echo of God's voice, summoning them to live up to "the law that is fulfilled by love of God and neighbour" (Gremillion 1976, p. 255, n. 16). What is affirmed here is that the natural law is not as natural as it appears: it is in fact "supernatural," that is, an echo of God's redemptive summons. God is graciously present in people's inner struggle to find the truth and do the right thing. That is why *Gaudium et spes* is able to propose that "in fidelity to conscience, Christians are joined with the rest of humans in the search for truth, and for the genuine solution to the numerous problems which arise in the life of individuals and from social relationships."

Here is the theological foundation for an open discussion among Christians and other citizens in regard to the great ethical issues of the day. What the church here admits is that it does not have all the answers. At the same time, open discussion does not imply an ethical relativism. On the contrary, God's guidance becomes available and the discovery of objective ethical norms is rendered possible precisely through respectful dialogue involving the whole of society. In this process, we are told, the erroneous conscience does not lose its dignity.

According to *Gaudium et spes* a just society is one in which the citizens are responsible agents and participate in the decisions that affect their lives. Political modernization is here judged to be in keeping with the Gospel. The following passages summarize the new social teaching.

> From a keener awareness of human dignity there arises in many parts of the world the desire to establish a political-jurisdical order in which personal rights can gain a better protection. These include the rights of free assembly, of common action, of expressing personal opinions, and of professing a religion both privately and publicly. For the protection of personal rights is a necessary condition for the active participation of citizens, whether as individuals or collectively, in the life and government of the state" (Gremillion 1976, p. 308, n. 73).

It is in full accord with human nature that juridical-political structures should, with ever better success and without any discrimination, afford all their citizens the chance to participate freely and actively in establishing the constitutional bases of a political community, governing the state, determining the scope and purpose of various institutions, and choosing leaders" (p. 310, n. 75).

Not discussed in *Gaudium et spes* is the ambiguity of the democratic revolution, that is the trend toward increasing centralization and bureaucratization, an aspect of modernity examined by Max Weber and other sociologists. Nor, as we shall see, does *Gaudium et spes* raise the difficult question of how the right to participate in decision making, demanded by justice, can be implemented in the Catholic church.

According to the Vatican Council, democratization is not simply a Western development that deserves praise; it is a development, summoned forth by reason, justice, and a growing sense of human dignity, that is destined to affect the whole of the human family. "Now, for the first time in human history, all people are convinced that the benefits of culture ought to be and actually can be extended to everyone. In every group or nation, there is an ever increasing number of men and women who are conscious that they themselves are the artisans and authors of the culture of their community. Throughout the world there is a similar growth in the combined sense of independence and responsibility" (Gremillion 1976, p. 250, n. 9). The summons to justice, freedom, and responsibility is here presented as a universal vocation.

The strongest statement that democratic participation is the ideal for the whole of humankind is made in the chapter of *Gaudium et spes* that deals with peace. For here peace is defined not as the absence of war, nor as the maintenance of the balance of power, but as an enterprise of social justice. Peace is not a static condition, a tranquil order, achieved once and for all, but an ongoing political endeavor creating the conditions of justice between nations and within nations. Only justice can overcome the outbreak of violence. To work for peace, therefore, includes the economic and political development of the nations that will deliver people from economic exploitation, political and military oppression, and the violation of human rights.

We have emphasized that the openness of Vatican II to political modernization was not a concession to secular Enlightenment philosophy but an original development of doctrine which recognized the presence of God, creator and redeemer, in the whole of human history. At first the reader is puzzled by the secular-sounding statement that "we are witnesses of the birth of a new humanism, one in which humans are defined first of all by their responsibility toward their brothers and sisters and toward history" (Gremillion 1976, p. 292, n. 55). But upon closer inspection, the reader discovers that the Council recognizes God's gracious presence as the ground, the vector, and the horizon of people's entry into their full humanity. Echoing the theology of Karl

Rahner and Henri de Lubac, the Council affirms that the mystery of redemption is active in the whole of history. The humanism of solidarity and responsibility is brought forth by God.

A CRITICAL REMARK

Before we move on to the Council's unfinished business, let us briefly reflect on the optimistic perspective adopted by the Council. *Gaudium et spes* vaguely recognizes, but does not analyse, the grave injustices existing in society and in particular the misery and hunger in the less developed regions of the world. The conciliar document suggests that a universal consensus is emerging in contemporary society that grave social and economic disparities among people are no longer tolerable. "Our contemporaries are coming to feel these inequalities with an ever sharper awareness. They are thoroughly convinced that the wider technical and economic potential which the modern world enjoys can and should correct this unhappy state of affairs. Hence numerous reforms are needed at the socio-economic level, along with universal changes in ideas and attitudes" (Gremillion 1976, p. 300, n. 63).

Gaudium et spes is hopeful that the contemporary form of capitalism, with its Keynesian, interventionist orientation, can be extended, with the generous help of the developed nations, to the regions of the world that still suffer from hunger, oppression, and lack of economic development. What is needed is economic reform and magnanimity. Catholic social teaching has always disapproved of "liberal capitalism" because it leaves the production and distribution of goods solely to market forces, but confronted with welfare or interventionist capitalism, the Vatican Council reacted more positively. For while there is room in welfare capitalism for the free enterprise of groups and individials (in accordance with the principle of subsidiarity), the government is responsible for promoting the economic well-being of all and for adopting economic policies that will benefit society as a whole (in accordance with the principle of socialization).

Vatican II did not analyze the economic forces that produced inequality and exploitation in the world, especially among the poorer nations of the Third World. Following a certain middle-class optimism, Vatican II looked with some hope to the extension of the Western economic system to the world as a whole. By contrast, the Medellin Conference (held in 1968) of the Latin American Bishops looked at the growing world system with fear because, in their judgement, it increased the dependency and powerlessness of their continent. We note that the World Synod of Bishops, held in Rome in 1971, decided to adopt the Latin American perspective rather than that of Vatican II: "We perceive the serious injustices constructing around the world a network of domination, oppression and abuses, that stifle freedom and keep the greater part of humanity from sharing in the building up and enjoyment of a more just and more fraternal society" (Gremillion 1976, p. 514, n. 3).

This more radical line of thought was developed by Pope John Paul II in the 1980s, first in *Laborem exercens* (1981) which analyzed the exploitative and alienating character of capitalism and communism (Baum 1982), and then in *Sollicitudo rei socialis* (1987) which denounced the devastating impact of the international financial institutions on Third World countries (Baum and R. Ellsberg 1989). This more radical approach represents the Church's response to the decline of Keynesian welfare capitalism in the 1980s and its replacement by Friedmanian monetarism with its trust in the logic of the market forces.

MODERNITY AND CHURCH STRUCTURES

Is the church's institutional apparatus capable of modernization? The Catholic church regards as of divine origin its basic ecclesiastical institutions responsible for teaching and ruling, *magisterium* and *regimen*. Still, the ecclesiastical organization has greatly developed over the centuries. The synodal structures that characterized the early church have been largely replaced by organizational patterns derived from feudalism and the subsequent aristocratic age. Power is here strictly exercised from above. No clear distinction is made between the legislative, executive, and juridical powers. Thus there exist no independent courts capable of judging whether bishops and popes have acted in accordance with the law. The concentration of power in the papacy, an ancient trend in the Catholic church, has been further intensified in recent centuries. As in all aristocratic societies, the people play only a passive role in matters of ecclesiastical teaching and polity.

Political modernization has generated a new ethic of governance. Modern men and women have ethical objections to an exercise of authority that is not open to dialogue and participation and not limited by checks and balances. How should the Catholic church respond to this ethical challenge?

This question was not clearly faced at the Second Vatican Council, even though the Council itself was one of the rare occasions in the Catholic church when dialogue and participation were able to influence public policy. At an important moment, the Council decided to divide its ecclesiological concerns into two separate sections, one dealing with the church ad extra and the other with the church ad intra. The fateful decision encouraged the illusion that these two aspects could be separated without causing serious confusion. If the church accepts on theological grounds the values and institutions of political modernization and at the same time refuses to democratize its own self-organization, then it inevitably generates frustration and dissatisfaction among its members. If openness and dialogue are recommended ad extra, Catholics expect, and demand on ethical grounds, a corresponding renewal of ecclesiastical life ad intra.

Vatican II introduced into the church the ideals of equality, co-responsibility, participation, and respect for personal conscience. It laid the dogmatic foundation for the democratization of the church. Defining the church as "People of God" in which all members, by virtue of their faith and baptism, participate in the threefold office of Jesus Christ, as prophet, priest and servant-king. Vatican II recognized that all Christians—not just the hierarchy—are teachers in the church, all are priests offering worship, and all exercise ministry in and for the church (Abbott 1966, "Lumen Gentium," chaps. 2 and 4, pp. 24-37, 56-65). The ministry of the hierarchy is not intended to replace the participation of the baptised, but on the contrary, to assure and foster their co-responsability. Moreover, by emphasizing the variety of gifts or charisms, the Council acknowledges that the Spirit uses the faithful, freely chosen, whatever their rank, to guide the church on its way through history. The term "collegiality," which the Council applied to the share of the bishops in the governance of the church universal, became the symbol of a participatory church open to the Spirit speaking in the people.

It is possible to introduce participatory institutions in the Catholic church without betraying the traditional papal-episcopal structure. Such a participatory church was in fact recommended by the Puebla Conference (held in 1979) of the Latin American bishops (Eagleson and Scharper 1979, "The Final Document," part 3, pp. 203-262). And at the end of their pastoral letter on economic justice, the U.S. Bishops were willing to "commit the Church to become a model of collaboration and participation" ("Economic Justice" 1986, p. 447, n. 358).

Yet Vatican II introduced almost no institutional changes providing for the participation of priests and lay people in the decisions affecting their lives in the church. Parish councils, priests' councils, and diocesan councils were recommended, but they were defined as purely consultative bodies, depending on the generosity of the pastors who convoked them and were willing to learn from them. Vatican II only hinted at a greater respect for personal conscience in the church. It did very little to protect the freedom of theological research and debate. No attempt was made to introduce independent courts in the Catholic church. Bishops, including the supreme bishop, the pope, continue to be simultaneously rulers and judges, a feature reminiscent of a previous age.

The contradiction between church ad intra and ad extra has become even stronger in the decades since the Council. The ecclesiastical authoritarianism introduced in the 1980s clashes with the bold social teaching of John Paul II which has defined humans, men and women, as "the subjects" of their society and the other institutions to which they belong (Baum and Ellsberg 1989, pp. 13, 24, 48, nn. 15, 25, 44). According to John Paul II, governments are unjust whenever they confine decision making to an elite, to a small group of men, thus depriving the people of what the pope calls "their subjectivity," that is to say, their right of participation and their call to co-responsibility.

Authoritarian governments, according to the pope, create frustrations among the people, prompting them to emigrate, to leave society, or to seek refuge in withdrawal and interior immigration.

The contradiction between the church's approval of political modernization and its refusal to institutionalize these values in its own life creates a dilemma. As Cardinal Konig suggested in November, 1989, the problems in the contemporary church are largely caused by the fact that the decentralization and participation recommended by Vatican II have as yet not been fully implemented. The issue involves far more than expediency. Because the Catholic church regards itself as the *magnum quoddam et perpetuum motivum credibilitatis* (Denzinger and Schoenmetzer 1963, p. 590, n. 3012), it must regulate its own institutional life in such a way that the ecclesiastical community appears to the public as a perfect image of social values derived from the Gospel, faithful to its own teaching, and in keeping with the ethical demands of the age.

NOTES

1. The story of the progressive bishops, told in all accounts of the Second Vatican Council, is recorded with a certain bitterness in Ralph Wiltgen's (1976) *The Rhone Flows into the Tiber.*
2. The best-known theoretical statement of this optimistic developmentalism is W.W. Rostow's (1960) *The Stages of Economic Growth: A Non-Communist Manifesto.*

REFERENCES

Abbott, W.M., S.J., ed. 1966. *The Documents of Vatican II.* New York: Herder & Herder.

Baum, G. 1982. *The Priority of Labor: A Commentary on Laborem exercens.* New York: Paulist Press.

Baum, G., and R. Ellsberg. 1989. *The Logic of Solidarity: Commentaries on Sollicitudo rei socialis.* Maryknoll, NY: Orbis Books.

Chadwick, O. 1970. *The Victorian Church, part 2.* London: Adam & Charles Black.

Denzinger, H., and A. Schoenmetzer. 1963. *Enchiridion symbolorum.* 32nd ed. Barcelona: Herder.

Documentation catholique 1959. Vol. 56.

Eagelson, J., and P. Scharper, eds. 1976. *Puebla Beyond.* Maryknoll, NY: Orbis Books.

"Economic Justice for All." 1986. *Origins* 16(November).

Gremillion, J., ed. 1976. *The Gospel of Peace and Justice.* Maryknoll, NY: Orbis Books.

Rostow, W.W. 1960. *The Stages of Economic Growth: A Non-Communist Manifesto.* Cambridge: Cambridge University Press.

Seven Great Encyclicals. 1963. New York: Paulist Press.

Wiltgen, R. 1967. *The Rhine Flows into the Tiber.* Choeleigh, Devon: Augustine.

Yzermans, V.A., ed. 1961. *The Major Addresses of Pope Pius XII,* vol. 2. St. Paul, MN: North Central Publishers.

PART II

CHANGES IN THE INTERNAL DYNAMICS
OF THE U.S. CHURCH

THE DEMOGRAPHY OF
AMERICAN CATHOLICS:

1965-1990

Andrew M. Greeley

This paper is divided into three sections, the first dealing with how many Catholics there are in America, the second with the changing demographic composition of American Catholics, and the third with the continuing of Catholic immigration.

HOW MANY CATHOLICS?

What proportion of Americans are Catholics?

Depending on your sources, the estimates range from 21 percent to 28 percent. The differences are not unimportant: each percentage point represents almost two and a half million people. There may be more than 16 million Catholics for which the low estimate does not account.

Table 1 presents six different estimates. The first is drawn from the largest single study of American religious affiliation ever attempted—the Current Population Survey of the Census Bureau (as it was then called) in 1957. If the proportion Catholic is the same today as it was then, then there are approximately 59 million Catholics in the United States, seven million more than reported in the *Official Catholic Directory* (1986).

Religion and the Social Order, Volume 2, pages 37-56.
Copyright © 1991 by JAI Press Inc.
All rights of reproduction in any form reserved.
ISBN: 1-55938-388-7

Table 1.   Various Estimates of Present U.S. Catholic Population

	Proportion	*Population in Millions*
U.S. Census (1957)	25	59
Gallup	28	65
NORC	25	59
Official Directory	22	52
Births*	25	59
Deaths**	21	49

Notes: *Ratio of baptisms to live births.
　　　　**Ratio of funerals to deaths.

Recent surveys of the Gallup organization estimate that 28 percent of Americans are Catholic which would mean a Catholic population of 65 million. The surveys done of religion at the National Opinion Research Center (NORC) since the early 1960s consistently report 25 percent of the population Catholic. The Gallup data, on the other hand, indicate an increase from 23 percent to 28 percent between the early 1960s and the present, a 20 percent increase in the proportion of Americans who are Catholic.

In Which Estimate Should the Most Confidence Be Placed?

The *Official Catholic Directory* figures are helpful but not conclusive because the quality of information available to a pastor when he fills out his annual form varies, as does the care with which the form is filled out. Note in Table 2 that while Gallup portrays an increase in the last quarter century and NORC no change, the *Directory* estimates indicate a decline (from 24% to 22%) in the proportion Catholic—which is compatible with an increase in numbers because the American population is growing at a faster rate than is the proportion affiliated with the church, if the Directory is to be believed.[1]

Baptism and burial records are likely to be more reliable than pastoral estimates of parish size, if only because of canonical regulations about keeping records and because the books are ready at hand when a pastor is required to tally the numbers (which does not necessarily mean that he looks at the books). Thus, at the present time, if the reports are accurate, a quarter of American births are Catholic and 21 percent of deaths are Catholic. These figures suggest that the Gallup numbers are too high—such a gross under-reporting by the country's pastors seems most improbable.

Moreover, the proportion of burials (Catholic burials as a fraction of death statistics) that are Catholic has been consistently at 21 percent since the early 1960s while the proportion of births (baptisms divided by birth statistics) has fallen from 31 percent in 1962 to 25 percent at the present (see Table 2)—a

Table 2.   Catholic Population Statistics from the
Official Catholic Directory by Year
(Percentage of Total U.S. Population)

Year	Total	Births*	Deaths**
1960	24	31	21
1965	24	31	21
1970	24	28	22
1975	23	27	22
1980	22	26	21
1985	22	25	21

Notes: *Ratio of baptisms to live births.
          **Ratio of funerals to deaths.

finding that is supported by the various fertility studies done at the University of Michigan and Princeton University which show that from the middle 1960s on the Catholic birth rate rapidly declined until it matched the national rate (despite the birth control encyclical).

Why the difference in birth rates and death rates? The higher birth rate causes the lower death rate because it produces a younger population. In NORC's *General Social Surveys* (Davis and Smith 1989) adult Catholics (over age 18) are three years younger on the average than adult Protestants (43 versus 46). The younger population is the result of higher birth rates in the past. It will take many years for the present lower birth rates to begin to age the Catholic population so that it becomes as old (on the average) as the Protestant population.

If Gallup's figures are too high and pastoral estimates too low, why then are the middle range figures (about a quarter of the country is Catholic) so stable in the last 25 years despite the demographic changes which are going on? The answer is that the figures mask a process by which Catholics leave the church and are replaced. In the General Social Survey 28 percent of the respondents said they were raised Catholic. The 25 percent currently Catholic is the result of an equation in which the number of converts and the natural increase from higher birth rates and immigration has been subtracted from the number of defectors. As a result of the decline in the Catholic birth rate and the decline in the number of converts there will be a slow erosion in years to come from the 25 percent figure, though not in actual numbers of Catholics as long as the American population continues to grow. (As we shall see subsequently, immigration may diminish or even cancel out this expected erosion in proportion Catholic.)

In 1960, some 15 percent of those who were raised Catholics are no longer Catholic. Taking into account the shifting age of the American population (and the propensity of some to return to their denominations as they grow older) that figure has not changed in the last quarter century (Hout and Greeley 1987). Thus, if the proportion Catholic erodes in decades to come it will be the result of changing birth and convert rates (and perhaps changing immigration rates) and not of changing defection rates. As I will note later in this paper, defection is particularly high among Hispanic Catholics and in this population the rate may actually be increasing.

About half of the defectors have left to join another religion, usually in conjunction with a marriage to someone of that religion (Greeley 1979). The other half leave to no religious affiliation. The Catholic defection rate is (and has been) more than half again as high as the Protestant defection rate.

Perhaps the most useful statistic for estimating how many Catholics there are in a given area is a fraction in which the numerator is the number of baptisms the previous year and the denominator is the number of live births in the same area. Thus, by way of example, (using the *Official Directory* for 1986 and the current *Statistical Abstract,* both of which present data for 1985) I calculate that in 1985 37 percent of the live births in the State of Illinois were baptized Catholic or that the population Catholic of the Prairie State is approximately 4.3 million. Diocesan statistics could be calculated using the same formula.

To save overworked Chicago chancery officials the trouble of calculating an estimate, I have done so for them: I estimate 2.57 million Catholics, a little less than 10 percent more than the report in the *Directory* (approximately the same as the national rate of underestimates). This technique must be used with special caution in any area in which there is reason to suppose that the age and ethnic group distribution of Catholics is radically different from the rest of the country as in the States of Florida, Texas, New Mexico, and California with their large Hispanic populations which are younger and more fertile than the national average. (The Hispanic birth rate is 20 per 1,000 as opposed to the 15.5 per 1,000 national rate.)

In many, if not most, cases, however, an estimate using this technique is likely to provide the best possible numbers until the church attempts a census as careful and as comprehensive as the government's. Table 3 presents the proportion Catholic estimated by this technique for each of the nine census regions of the country.

Table 4 presents the proportion Catholic and the estimated Catholic population for each of the states. In any state in which there have been many baptisms of the children of migratory workers from Mexico one should discount somewhat the estimates in this table, and especially as noted previously in such states as Florida, New Mexico, Texas, and California where there are large Mexican American populations.

The shape of the age pyramid of the Catholic population is rather different from that of the rest of the country—smaller at the top, larger in the middle,

Table 3. Proportion* Catholic by Census Region
(In Percent)

New England	58
Middle Atlantic	40
East North Central	37
West North Central	26
South Atlantic	11
East South Central	7
West South Central	23
Mountain	20
Pacific	17

Note: *Ratio of baptisms to live births.

Table 4. Catholic Population by State
(Estimated by the number of baptisms
as percent of live births in the state.)

	Percent Catholic	*Total Catholic Population* (*in thousands*)
New England		
Maine	27	314
New Hampshire	34	339
Vermont	31	166
Massachusetts	57	3,319
Rhode Island	53	523
Connecticut	55	1,746
Mid Atlantic		
New York	42	7,469
New Jersey	46	3,417
Pennsylvania	34	4,030
South Atlantic		
Delaware	27	167
Maryland and DC	19	953
Virginia	9	523
West Virginia	6	116
North Carolina	3	187
South Carolina	3	100
Georgia	4	239
Florida*	18	2,045

East North Central

Ohio	22	2,364
Indiana	16	879
Illinois	33	3,806
Michigan	24	2,818
Wisconsin	37	1,776

East South Central

Kentucky	13	484
Tennessee	4	190
Alabama	3	120
Mississippi	5	130

West North Central

Minnesota	34	1,426
Iowa	26	750
Missouri	19	956
North Dakota	31	212
South Dakota	31	219
Nebraska	26	449
Kansas	21	514

West South Central

Arkansas	4	94
Louisiana	33	1,478
Oklahoma	6	198
Texas*	24	3,929

Mountain

Montana	13	119
Idaho	23	121
Wyoming	15	76
Colorado	22	719
New Mexico*	42	690
Arizona	22	701
Utah	5	77
Nevada	17	150

Pacific

Washington	12	529
Oregon	11	296
California*	32	8,437
Alaska	10	52
Hawaii	22	231

Note: *Estimates in Florida, Texas, New Mexico, and California are problematic because of their large Hispanic population, with a younger than national average and a higher birth rate.

and then tapering down towards similarity at the bottom. It would be possible to estimate this pyramid from the age of a person at burial. One would calculate the number of deaths by gender in five-year age categories (one year for those under five) and multiply that number by the inverse of the age/sex-specific death rate. However national data for age-specific deaths of Catholics are not available.

An attempt was made to collect this information by the publisher of the *Official Catholic Directory*. It would have been a rather easy task for a pastor to go through his funeral record and tabulate such data. Unfortunately, only about a quarter of the pastors cooperated, making any such estimates virtually impossible.

It is reasonable to conclude that Catholics are about a quarter of the American people, a little less than 60 million in number. Until the American population reaches stability (births replacing deaths but not adding to the population) the Catholic numbers will continue to increase, although the proportion Catholic may decline slightly because of the decline in Catholic birth rate (if that decline is not cancelled by immigration).

There are four possible ways to prevent this slow erosion—more births, more converts, more immigrants, fewer defections. The last might seem the most promising, but it must be noted that, whatever the cause of defections, the present rate is not a result of the Vatican Council, post-conciliar changes in the church, nor changes in American society, because the rate has not changed since 1960. Whatever the nature of the defection problem, its causes are deeper than the current controversies in the church.

One might observe in passing that attempts at "evangelization," which do not ask questions about the high Catholic defection rate, seem to be misplaced—if not foolish. My research suggests that the most serious cause of defection—over and above the "average"—is the way authority is exercised, especially at the parish level (Greeley 1979).

The Mobility of Catholics

In 1961, half the Catholics in the country were immigrants or the children of immigrants. Yet a quarter of the college graduates in the country were Catholic (Greeley 1964). American Catholics had one foot in the immigrant era and one foot in the upper-middle-class professional suburb. Thirty years later, many observers both in and outside the Catholic church are not sure that the descendents of Catholic immigrants have succeeded in American society. In fact, there is no reasonable doubt about that success. In 1987 and 1988, the average white Protestant income was $24,899 (according to NORC's *General Social Surveys*). The average Catholic income was $28,367. Catholic income was fourteen percent higher than Protestant income.

In the middle 1980s,[2] 61 percent of the Catholics in the country were white-collar workers, as opposed to 55 percent of the white Protestants. Twenty-

ANDREW M. GREELEY

one percent of Catholics were professionals, as opposed to 19 percent of white Protestants. Thirty-nine percent of Catholics had attended college, as had 37 percent of white Protestants.[3]

In the beginning of the 1970s, 27 percent of the Catholic population had attended college and 29 percent of Protestants. Thus the Catholic increase in little more than a decade was 12 percentage points, a 44 percent increase in the number of college educated people within the Catholic population. Those clergy and hierarchy who think that somehow the Big change in the social status of their people is over could not be more wrong. If anything, the pace of change will increase because the proportion of Catholics attending college is still accelerating.

One way of mapping the social change of a population is to consider the educational and occupational decisions made by those who are young adults at different points in the population's history. The 20 thousand cases in NORC's *General Social Surveys* provide enough data for us to be able to "walk back" the Catholic population to the decisions of those who were born before 1900 and who made their career decisions during the First World War. Even at that time, when immigrants were still pouring into the country, 13 percent of young American Catholics were deciding to attend college. During the 1920s, the proportion remained steady at 13 percent. Despite the Great Depression, it rose to 18 percent in the 1930s. In the two decades after the war it increased again, first to 25 percent and then to 31 percent. The biggest increase in the century was during the 1960s when 47 percent of the Catholics coming of age elected to attend college (precisely at the time my own research was documenting the Catholic economic and educational revolution). In the 1970s the proportion increased to 52 percent and in the 1980s to 55 percent.

Catholic college attendance has doubled twice during the century. The proportion of young Catholics choosing professional careers has increased from 8 percent in the World War I era to 25 percent among young people reaching maturity today and the proportion of white-collar workers has risen from 44 percent to almost 70 percent.

These changes are impressive. They are also, given the history of American immigration, ordinary. The research of Barry Chiswick (1978) has shown that it takes the immigrant, on the average, 12 years to catch up in income with the native born of the same educational achievement. The sons of immigrants earn more income (by about 5%) than the sons of native born. America is indeed the land of opportunity, unless you happen to be Hispanic or native born black.

The mistake all along has been to assume that the children, grandchildren, and great grandchildren of Catholic (non-Hispanic) immigrants would somehow be excluded from this process of economic achievement because of handicaps imposed on them by their religion. It is safe to say that the assumption, however strongly some may still hold it (if only preconsciously), has been proven wrong. The Catholic story is merely the immigrant story, writ for a different religious group than the Protestant groups.

There are two different dynamics of upward mobility at work—that which affects the whole of society and that which affects those who at one time were disadvantaged in the society. The first is the enormous increase in higher education of the whole population in this century and the second is the even more rapid increase of certain groups which were catching up. We can picture both of these processes operating at the same time by imagining an ascending curved line (see Figure 1).[4] This represents the log of the odds of college attendance to non-attendance (the best way to measure proportions over time) from 1910 to the present for all white Americans. It is a slowly ascending curve.

Figure 2 smooths the curves in Figure 1 into trend lines. The top line is Irish Catholic, the middle two, (so close as to be almost the same line) are German Catholic and non-Catholic Americans. The bottom two lines, almost on top of one another, are the Polish and Italian Catholics. The ascent of that line to parity with the rest of the country is in a very simple sketch the story of the demography of American Catholics in this century.

One could draw similar upward swinging curves on other sheets of paper to represent proportion choosing white-collar and professional careers. The former is similar to the college attendance curve, the latter also climbs but the slope is more shallow.

Then we plot, on the same page, lines for four major Catholic European ethnic groups—Irish, German, Italian, and Polish. The German line is more or less the same as the national average. The Irish line begins in 1910 at a level already above the national average and continues to climb so that at the end of the series it is even more distant from the average. There is a sharp drop in the 1930s (during the Great Depression), but the Irish line is still above the national average even then. After the Depression, it soars again.

The Polish and Italian lines are below the national line and move up at about the same rate as the national line (the slopes are a little less steep) until the 1940s; then they suddenly turn sharply upward, cross the national line in the 1960s and at the present stand above the national average, though not yet as high as the Irish.

In a brief scheme, this is the story of Catholic ethnic groups in the twentieth century, one of them on the average, another above the average even at the beginning of the century, the final two "catching up" at the time of the G. I. Bill after the war and moving ahead in the last couple of decades. It is, I emphasize, not an unusual story in itself. What is unusual is that this path up the American ladder of dreams happened to groups who were not supposed to prosper and whose prosperity is still an affront to many, including some of their own (who perhaps like to think that they are ahead of their fellow ethnics).

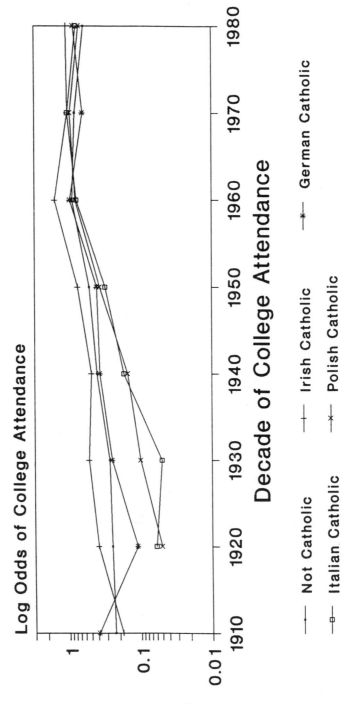

Figure 1. Odds of College Attendance by Religion and Ethnicity

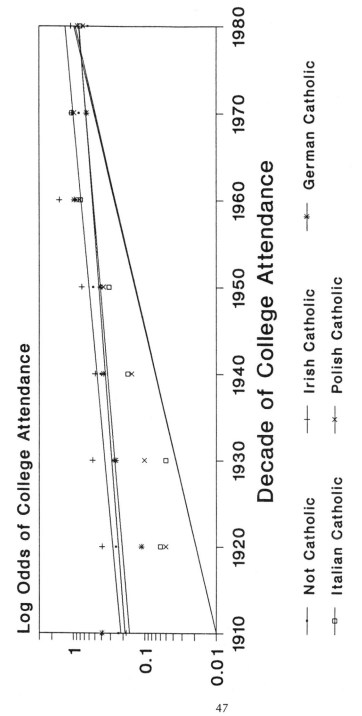

Figure 2. Trends in College Attendance by Religion and Ethnicity

47

Demographically the quarter century since the end of the Vatican Council was an era during which the more recent Catholic immigrant groups caught up with the rest of America in educational attainment. As a result, the proportion college educated in the Catholic population has accelerated dramatically and will continue to do so.

Oddly enough, the image of Catholics on the fringes of American society is shared by some Catholic leaders and theologians. Cardinal Joseph Bernardin writes, "The Church of the future in this country will not be able to rely on general social support, the structures of popular culture or the kind of civic leverage formerly wielded by priests in Bing Crosby movies." And theologian Avery Dulles writes, "We have as yet very few eminent Catholic intellectuals on the national scene. Catholics, whether clerical or lay, are not prominent in science, literature, the fine arts or even, I think, in the performing arts and communications. We have all too few Catholic political leaders and statesmen with a clear apostolic vision and commitment."

One can address the hypotheses in these two statements with data that show whether Catholics are adequately represented in the scholary and artistic elites. In the NORC's *General Social Surveys* (almost 23,000 cases) a little less than 2 percent of Americans fall in the category of scholars, writers, performers, and artists. Catholics are no less likely than anyone else (save for Jews) to be in that 2 percent. Moreover they are as likely to have Ph.D.s as anyone else. In addition, they seem to be successful in these areas because they earn five thousand dollars more than the national average for this category. Finally, they may not have what Father Dulles defines as "clear apostolic vision," but they go to church far more often than do their colleagues who are not Catholic, and more often than typical Catholics. About half of American Catholics go to Mass at least two or three times a month. Among those who fall in the artist-scholar-writer-performer category, 56 percent attend church regularly, a statistically significant difference (only 5% never attend Mass). Is this merely "nominal or perfunctory" membership?

Not only are the Catholic cultural elites still Catholic, they tend to be devout Catholics. If there are 40 million Catholic adults, there are almost a million Catholics who can make some claim to be part of the intellectual and cultural creative elites. More than half of them (approximately a half million) regularly show up at Sunday (or Saturday evening) Mass.

IMMIGRANT CATHOLICISM—STILL ALIVE?

Freedom of inquiry in the United States is limited by an extra-legal restriction on the right of the census to ask a religious affiliation question. Thus the issue of religion and immigration can be addressed statistically only by analyzing survey data. In this section, I propose to rely on data from NORC's *General*

Social Surveys (Davis and Smith 1989). I am at least as well aware as any critic of the limitations of this approach. For example, it is likely to underestimate Hispanics and hence Catholics among immigrants. It is impossible to specify the recency of the immigration event. The wording of NORC's question will include within the "immigrants" respondents who were born of American citizens residing out of the country. Moreover, 7 percent of the "immigrants" list their country of origin in another item as Puerto Rico, which is hardly a foreign country.[5]

As can be observed in Table 5, 42 percent of first generation Americans and 46 percent of second generation Americans are Catholic as opposed to 20 percent of the third generation. Eleven percent of Catholics are immigrants and 22 percent are the children of immigrants. Thus a third of American Catholics are immigrants or children of immigrants[6] Jews, "others," and those with no religion are also over-represented among immigrants. Protestants, in contrast, are drastically under-represented among immigrants—approximately only a third of immigrants. There does not seem to be a shift in these proportions in the last decade (see Table 6). The distribution is basically the same at both time periods.

Table 5.   Religion by Generation
(In Percent)

	First[1]	*Second*[2]	*Third*[3]
Protestant	34	37	71
Catholic	42	46	20
Jewish	5	7	1
None	10	7	7
Other	9	3	1
Total	100	100	100
(Total Respondents)	(N = 1003)	(N = 1855)	(N = 12,818)

Notes: [1]"Were you born in this country?" No.
      [2]"Were both your parents born in this country?" No.
      [3]"Were both your parents born in this country?" Yes.
Source: NORC's *General Social Surveys* for 1977-1988 (Davis and Smith 1989).

Table 6. Religion of Immigrants by Time of Survey
(In Percent)

	1977-1983	*1984-1988*
Protestant	35	32
Catholic	42	43
Jewish	5	5
None	9	10
Other	7	10
Total	100	100
(Total Respondents)	(*N* =514)	(*N* =489)

Source: NORC's *General Social Surveys* for 1977-1988 (Davis and Smith 1989).

The immigrants (though not their children) are a little less likely to attend church at least two or three times a month than third generation Americans and notably less likely to believe in life after death[7] although this is the result of a larger proportion saying that they are undecided on the subject (see Table 7). Immigrants and their children are as likely as third generation Americans to say that they are "strong" in their denominational affiliation. They are, however, much less likely to belong to "fundamentalist" denominations (Smith 1986).

The difference between the first and second generation and the third generation in belief in life after death cannot be accounted for by different proportions Hispanic, non-European, Catholic, or non-fundamentalist, nor by differences in age or education. Interestingly enough, the differences between generational groups (see Table 8) in belief in life after death is greater among older respondents than among younger respondents—there being no relationship between age and belief among the third generation and a negative relationship among the first and second generation. (Older immigrants and the older children of immigrants are less likely to believe in life after death than younger immigrants and their children.) Thus, the three items that measure religious attitudes and behavior in the *General Social Surveys* do not indicate that immigration will produce a less "religious" population or a more "religious" population. Forty-five percent of the Catholic immigration is "non-European" as opposed to 32 percent of the non-Catholic population; a third of the Catholic immigration is "Spanish Origin" (see Table 9).

The proportion of Protestants, and especially fundamentalist Protestants, in American society will diminish (if only marginally) as immigration accounts for a portion of the "natural" increase in the population. The country seems to be in the process of becoming more Catholic (and more Jewish, "other" and "none"). However, a closer look at the demography of American

Table 7. Religious Behavior and Attitudes by Generation
(In Percent)

	Generation		
	First	Second	Third
Church at least two or three times a month	42	46	45
Belief in life after death	67	67	81
"Strong" religious affiliation	44	45	44
"Fundamentalist" affiliation	14	12	38

Source: NORC's *General Social Surveys* for 1977-1988 (Davis and Smith 1989).

Table 8. Belief in Life after Death by Generation and Age

	Generation	
Age	First and Second	Third
20s	70%	78%
	(271)*	(2223)
30s	70%	81%
	(315)	(1954)
40s	68%	81%
	(229)	(1301)
50s	65%	83%
	(241)	(1020)
60s	67%	82%
	(334)	(915)
70s	64%	83%
	(336)	(782)

Note: *Number of respondents in parentheses.
Source: NORC's *General Social Surveys* for 1977-1988 (Davis and Smith 1989).

Table 9. Origins by Generation and Religion
(Percent Not European)

	Generation		
	First	*Second*	*Third*
Catholic	45%	14%	9%
	(414)*	(800)	(2209)
Not Catholic	32%	8%	15%
	(542)	(887)	(7363)

Note: *Number of respondents in parentheses.
Source: NORC's *General Social Surveys* for 1977-1988 (Davis and Smith 1989).

Catholicism suggests that the increase in Catholic affiliation may be less than meets the eye because of the defection rate of American Catholics and especially the defection rate of Catholics of "Spanish Origin" who constitute a third of the Catholic immigrants. As I reported in the first section of this paper, Catholics have constituted about a quarter of Americans for the last 30 years, but this constant proportion masks a shift in distribution within the Catholic population. The Catholic defection rate during the last third of a century has been routinely 15 percent—about one out of every six of those who are raised Catholic are no longer Catholic.[8] Indeed if one looks at the religion in which a respondent was raised, then half of the immigrants and their children were Catholic at one time.

That there are no traces of this decline in the proportion reporting themselves Catholic in national surveys is the result of the high proportion of Catholics among immigrants and their children. The tables in this section of the paper demonstrate that if it were not for the immigrants and their children Catholics would constitute only a fifth and not a fourth of the American population. Given the rate of decline of Catholics among "Spanish Origin" immigrants and their children, it may well be that the increase in Catholicism through immigration will do little more than replace those who have left the Catholic church.

Catholics of Spanish Origin are defecting to Protestant denominations at the rate of approximately 60 thousand people a year. Over the past 15 years this departure from Catholicism has amounted to almost a million men and women, almost one of ten (8%) of the Spanish Catholic population. This conclusion is based on an analysis of respondents of "Spanish Origin" in NORC's annual *General Social Surveys.* There are, according to the census, some 17 million Americans of Spanish Origin. It is routinely assumed that most, if not all, of these are Catholics. In fact, according to the *General Social*

Surveys only 70 percent of those of Spanish origins (Mexican, Puerto Rican, and "Other Spanish") are Catholic and 22 percent are Protestants. Thus, at the most, only 12 million of the population reported by the census are Catholic.

If one pools all the annual *General Social Surveys* since 1972, one has a Spanish Origin sample of 790, a sufficient number for analysis of the change in the last decade and the difference between Protestant and Catholic Hispanics. There are weaknesses in the *General Social Survey* sample: it has been assembled over 16 years, it is not based on a Hispanic sampling frame (which does not exist), it represents interviews only with those who speak English, it probably misses the poorest of Hispanic respondents (as do all surveys). However, it is, as far as I know, the only data set, based on a national probability sample, that provides detailed information on the religion in which a respondent was raised and the religion with which the respondent currently identifies.

In the first four years of the *General Social Surveys* (1972-1975), 16 percent of Spanish Origin respondents were Protestant (and 7% some other religion or no religion). In the four most recent years (1985-1988), 23 percent were Protestant (and 7% other or no religion). Thus, in the early 1970s, 77 percent of the Hispanics were Catholic. In the middle 1980s that had declined to 71 percent. The difference between the two time periods is statistically significant (at the .02 level). The Protestant segment of Americans of Hispanic origin is not only large, it is growing rapidly.

The defection rates are higher among Puerto Ricans (24%) and "others" (26%) than among Mexican Americans (15%). They are lower in the West (17%) than in the East (23%). Thirty-six percent of those who are currently Protestant were raised Protestant, making them at least second generation converts. A little more than three-fifths of both Catholic and Protestant Hispanics are native born. About a third of each group are the children of native born parents (so immigration does not seem to correlate with religious affiliation).

More than three-fourths of the Spanish Origin Protestants are either Baptists or Fundamentalists. Moreover, they are more likely to believe in life after death than their Catholic counterparts (80% as opposed to 64%), more likely to reject abortion on demand (79% as opposed to 69%), more likely to think that premarital sex is always wrong (37% versus 26%), and much more likely to attend church regularly: 23 percent of the Catholics go to church every week as opposed to 49 percent of the Protestants (29% more than once a week). Thus it would seem that the Protestant Hispanics have joined fervent Protestant groups in which their religion provides them with intense activity and community support. By some norms of religious behavior they are better Catholics than those who have stayed.

There are two explanations for the defection of Catholics to Protestant denominations, especially to the sects to which most of them seem to be going:

1.   Because the Catholic Church fails to reach the poorest of its Spanish members a vacuum has been created into which the sects can rush with their enthusiasm, their grass roots ministry, their concern about the religious problems of ordinary people, and their "native" (and married) clergy.

2.   The sects have a special appeal to the new middle class because they provide a means of breaking with the old traditions and becoming responsible and respectable members of the American middle class (much as Catholicism provides a middle-class niche for some upwardly mobile Blacks). The Catholic church's failure in this perspective is to provide community and respectability for the upwardly mobile Hispanic American. This explanation is supported by analysis done (most notably by the late Anne Parsons [1969] of Italian-American Pentecostals during the 1930s and 1940s, an analysis that saw the Protestant sects as a means of "Americanization" for some Italians.

This second model seems to fit the data in Table 10 better than the first. Protestant Hispanics are better educated, make more money, are more likely to be married, and are more likely to be managers and white-collar workers than Hispanic Catholics. Moreover, they come from backgrounds in which there was more paternal education.

Becoming Protestant has apparently an economic and social payoff for Hispanics. The second generation Protestants (those who say they were raised Protestant) have on the average 11.3 years of education and earned on the average $27,000 a year. Fifty-two percent of them are white-collar workers and 28 percent are managers. They remain fervent Protestants—26 percent of them attend church more than once a week.[9]

Table 10.   Differences Between Hispanic Catholics and Protestants

	Protestants (N = 197)	*Catholics* (N = 593)
Income	$25,000	$19,000
Education	10.8 years	10.4 years
Percent Managers	21%	13%
Percent White Collar	45%	38%
Married	70%	63%
Father's Education	7.1 years	6.3 years

Note: All differences are statistically significant at the .01 level.
Source: NORC's *General Social Surveys* for 1972-1988 (Davis and Smith 1989).

Protestant Hispanics do indeed look like an upwardly mobile middle class for whom the Protestant denomination provides both a way of becoming acceptably American and a support community in which they are comfortable as they break with their old religious heritage. It is not only their old religion which is left behind. Fifty-nine percent of Hispanic Catholics are Democrats, while only 44 percent of Spanish Protestants are Democrats.

The success of the sects, then, seems to be the result of the failure of the Catholic church to be responsive to the emotional, communal, and religious needs of some of the new Hispanic middle class. The loss of almost one out of ten members of its largest ethnic group is an ecclesiastical failure of unprecedented proportions, one that is matched only by the failure of the Catholic church in the first half of the nineteenth century to retain the affiliation of Irish rural proletarians (farm laborers) who migrated to the American South before the Great Famine (Greeley 1988; Shaughnessy 1925). Like many of the Hispanic migrants, the Irish speaking prefamine Irish laborers (the so-called bog Irish) were only loosely affiliated with organized Catholicism. However, unlike the present American Catholic church, that of the early nineteenth century lacked the resources of money and personnel to respond to the prefamine immigration.

CONCLUSION

The form of this paper is also a sketch of the demographic history of American Catholicism during the quarter century after the Second Vatican Council—rapid social and economic change between two massive immigrations. Since 1965, the children and the grandchildren of the pre-1920 immigration caught up with and indeed surpassed the rest of the country on the ordinary measures of achievement and at the same time remained Catholic. In the same time period, a new wave of immigration, almost half of which was Catholic in its origins, has arrived on America's shores. Some of that group seems to be leaving the church, threatening a possible long-term decline in the proportion Catholic.

The church which dealt successfully with the beginning of the century crisis seems incapable of responding to the end of the century crisis—even though it has far more resources available now than it did then.

It is hard to see how the Second Vatican Council can be blamed for this latter crisis. However, the independence of the American bishops at the Council may well have so frightened the Roman Curia that it decided to appoint only "safe" bishops—which meant bishops who could not respond to any serious problem, whether it be the disenchantmant of the old wave of immigrants with incompetence and insensitivity or the departure of the new wave.

A three-word summary of the last quarter century: success, then failure.

NOTES

1. Why would pastoral estimates decline? In part perhaps because of the impression that the number of their parishioners is declining and perhaps in part because they know they will be taxed on the numbers reported.

2. These statistics represent *General Social Surveys* data pooled in 4-year groupings.

3. Catholics include Hispanics; and Protestants do not include blacks.

4. The apparent down sweep of the line in the last two decades is caused by the fact that observations in the *General Social Surveys* began in 1972 and continue to the present. Many young men and women in the last two cohorts were still coming of age during the last two decades and were not yet embarking on their college education.

5. In this paper, those whose parents are born abroad are called "first" generation, those who are native born with at least one parent born abroad are called "second" generation, and those whose parents were born in the United States are called "third" generation—meaning third and subsequent generations.

6. In 1960, half of the Catholic population was either first or second generation American.

7. Question wording: "Do you believe in life after death?"

8. Some three-fifths of the "defectors" have joined another Christian denomination in conjunction with marriage, the other two-fifths have rejected all denominational affiliation. About half of this latter group eventually return to Catholicism during the life-cycle, a return taken into account in the over all 15 percent defection rate.

9. The *General Social Survey* is available at most university computer centers. The income variable, based on corrections for inflation developed by Michael Hout, may not be on all data sets yet.

REFERENCES

Chiswick, B.R. 1978. "The Effects of Americanization on the Earnings of Foreign-Born Men." *Journal of Political Economy* 86(5): 897-921.

Davis, J. A., and T.W. Smith. 1989. *General Social Surveys, 1972-1989. Cumulative Codebook.* Chicago: National Opinion Research Center.

Greeley, A. 1964. *Religion and Career.* New York: Sheed and Ward.

_____. 1979. *Crisis in the Church.* Chicago: Thomas More Press.

_____. 1988. "The Success and Assimilating of Irish Protestants and Irish Catholics in the United States." *Sociology and Social Research* 72:229-236.

Hout, M., and A. Greeley. 1987. "The Center Does Not Hold: Church Attendance in the United States, 1940-1984." *American Sociological Review* 52:325-345.

Official Catholic Directory. 1986. Wilmette, IL: P. J. Kennedy.

Parsons, A. 1969. *Belief, Magic, and Anomie.* New York: Free Press.

Shaughnessy, G. 1925. *Has the Immigrant Kept the Faith? A Study of Immigration and Catholic Growth in the United States.* New York: Longmans, Green.

Smith, T.W. 1986. *Classifying Protestant Denominations.* General Social Survey Technical Report No. 66. Chicago: National Opinion Research Center.

Statistical Abstract. 1985. Washington, DC: Bureau of the Census.

CATHOLIC YOUTH IN THE MODERN CHURCH

Patrick H. McNamara

The Vatican Council, as Dean Hoge reminds us in Chapter 5, "has been likened to an earthquake" whose "ripple effects" are still with us. If one thinks about young American Catholics, images of alienation, falling away, are-we-losing-a-whole-generation easily come to mind. As we shall see, such images are, for the most part, false. We come nearest a true picture by looking at the survey evidence from the 1970s and 1980s, then turning our attention to studies of young women and men attending Catholic schools. Do young American Catholics differ from their parents in how important religion is in their lives? How do they regard the Catholic church as an institution? Do Catholic schools affect their identity as Catholics and their responsiveness to Church leadership?

Three topics comprise this chapter:

1. a review of survey evidence bearing on young Catholics' beliefs and practices,
2. the effects of Catholic schools on the religiosity of young Catholics,
3. an assessment of the situation of young Catholics today.

Religion and the Social Order, Volume 2, pages 57-65.
ISBN: 1-55938-388-7

YOUTH CATHOLICS: BELIEFS AND
PRACTICES SINCE VATICAN II

The 1970s

The continuing survey research of Father Andrew Greeley and colleagues stands as the premier source of information about post-Vatican II Catholics. By 1974, Greeley, McCready, and McCourt (1976) found strong approval of many changes brought on by Vatican II. Catholics remained loyal to the church itself, though declines were evident in weekly Mass attendance and in acceptance of certain doctrinal and moral teachings: the authority of the pope, eternal punishment, birth control, divorce, and premarital sex.

Did age make a difference in how Catholics responded to these issues? The authors divided those sampled into four birth cohorts or "generations," labeling each by "events which marked their coming into maturity" (Greeley, McCready, and McCourt 1976): (1) a depression cohort born between 1901 and 1924; (2) a World War II cohort born between 1925 and 1934; (3) a Cold War cohort born between 1935 and 1943; and (4) a Vietnam cohort born between 1944 and 1954. The theory behind generational analysis is that persons born within a given time period are affected (though not necessarily in identical ways) by key events occurring during their lifetimes that lend a distinctive cast to their feelings, outlooks, and convictions. The teens and early twenties are ages particularly susceptible to value and attitude formation through these historical events. Being born in the United States between 1944 and 1954 meant, for example, "encountering" the Vietnam War (1965 to 1975) at its outset between the ages of 11 and 21. Few are unaffected whether they supported or opposed the war. By the same token, the Vietnam Generation also lived through the Second Vatican Council and the political and cultural changes associated with the late 1960s and early 1970s in America. Finally, this cohort comprises roughly the first half of the huge Baby Boom Generation born between 1946 and 1964; they made up 35 percent of the Catholic population under 70 years of age in 1974 (Greeley et al. 1976, p. 121).

Young Catholics 30 or under in the mid 1970s differed from their parents and grandparents. Compared to all adult Catholics a decade earlier, they were between 12 percent and 24 percent less likely to attend Mass weekly, to be very pleased with a son as priest, to be orthodox on matters of birth control, divorce, and premarital sex, and to go to Confession monthly. Members of the Vietnam Generation were also more likely to say they were no longer Catholics. By 1973-1974, "the Catholic Church had lost 30 percent of its college-educated people under 30." The comparable Protestant defection rate was 21 percent (Greeley et al. 1976, p. 146).

Greeley and his colleagues, however, were quick to point out that very little of the above differences was attributable per se to age. In an analysis that drew much attention, they concluded that by far the greater proportion of changes in belief and practice was due to a decline in acceptance of papal leadership, which, in turn, was linked to a declining approval of the church's sexual teachings (birth control, divorce, premarital sex). In a final statistical analysis, the authors linked the declines to the issuance in 1968 of the papal encyclical *Humanae Vitae* which reaffirmed the Catholic Church's traditional teaching rejecting artifical birth control. It was not the Vatican Council itself, they argued, which "caused" the declines; in fact, "the positive dynamics released by the Council prevented the loss from becoming worse" (Greeley et al. 1976, p. 152).

What is important about this analysis, recalling the generational perspective described earlier, is the light it shed upon subsequent survey results. In 1979, Greeley and colleagues focused explicitly upon Baby Boom Generation Catholics, contrasting those under 30 with those over 30. In *Crisis in the Church* (Greeley 1979) and in *Young Catholics* (Fee, Greeley, McCready, and Sullivan 1981), Greeley, Fee, McCready, and Sullivan reaffirmed the continuing "non-existent credibility" of the church for young people in the area of sexual ethics. For example, 73 percent of Catholics *under* 30 approved of premarital sex among engaged couples; by contrast, only 30 percent of those *over* 30 lent their approval (Greeley 1979, p. 60).

Most significant, perhaps, was a finding that has set the stage for a portrait characteristic of young Catholics from the mid 1970s to the present: Greeley (1979) cites a Chicago archdiocesan survey indicating that among those under 30 who reported receiving Holy Communion weekly and praying daily, approximately two-thirds approved of premarital sex among the engaged, divorce and birth control. Greeley labeled these respondents "communal Catholics"—younger and better educated women and men who continued to be distrustful and unaccepting of the church's teaching, particularly on these issues. But they still thought of themselves as good Catholics and attended Mass regularly. Beyond this, Baby Boom Catholics assume a stance of "self-consciously selecting" which teachings and practices they will accept. Whereas members of an earlier generation would probably have concluded that they could no longer be practicing Catholics (or even Catholics by identity), Baby Boom Catholics see nothing incompatible in continuing to attend Mass and receive the Sacraments while rejecting or simply disregarding certain teachings and norms. They resent any implication that they are "not really Catholics." These findings underline the much discussed "primacy of conscience" allegedly characteristic of a younger generation of Catholics: the inner "I" is the ultimate arbiter of what will be taken seriously in belief and behavior. Institutional authority per se is not seen as binding; it may, at most, provide one factor among many to be considered in forming one's beliefs and moral conscience.

The 1980s

In 1986, George Gallup and James Castelli (1987) surveyed Catholics nationally. A third of the nation's teenagers (but just 28 percent of the entire population) say they are Catholics. By this time, researchers could divide the Baby Boom Generation into two cohorts, the Vietnam Generation born from 1946 through 1957 and a post-Vietnam Generation born from 1958 to 1968. Catholics 18 to 29 years of age in 1986 (post-Vietnam) compared to those the same age in 1977 are more likely to read the Bible, pray the rosary, go to Confession, attend a meeting of a Catholic organization or a prayer meeting, make a retreat, and attend a spiritual conference, though the differences are, in many cases, very small. In a chapter devoted to teenage Catholics, the authors indicate that the latter are more permissive than their Protestant counterparts concerning sex, alcohol, and marijuana. Forty-two percent of Catholic teens as opposed to 37 percent of Protestant teens say religion is less important to them than it is to their parents; 49 percent of Catholic teens rate religious faith as a very important value compared to 57 percent of Protestant teens.

D'Antonio, Davidson, Hoge, and Wallace (1989) found in their Catholic laity study no late 1980s turn around from trends just cited. Those 18 to 29, as contrasted with those 30 and older, are *less* likely to attend Mass weekly (29 percent compared with 43 percent for those 30 to 54, and 53 percent for those 55 and over), to say the church is an important part of their lives, or to read the Bible on a regular basis. But on several moral issues—sexual relations outside of marriage, homosexual behavior, remarrying without an annulment, and practicing birth control—the 18 to 29 year olds were joined by Catholics 30 to 55 in believing that "final moral authority" should lie "with the individual or with a collaboration of church leaders and individuals." This research simply reflects the continuing "liberal" trend of the earlier Baby Boomers now entering middle age, whose attitudes and values are transmitted to their children. However, regardless of age group, frequent Mass attendance notably increases willingness to accept church authority (D'Antonio et al. 1989).

Mass attendance as an indicator of religiosity for Catholics has occasioned some recent controversy. Hout and Greeley's (1987) analysis suggests that the declining rate of Mass attendance among American Catholics leveled off in 1975 and has not gone down appreciably since then. A more recent analysis by Chavez (1989, p. 476) claims that "every successive cohort coming of age since about 1940 attended Church less often than the cohort before it." Protestants exhibit an early "revival" in the early 1980s, but for Catholics, the overall trend through 1986 shows "successive cohorts were less likely to be regular attenders at Church." One should keep in mind that the most notable decline refers to *regular weekly* attendance. Measured in terms of attendance two or three times a month, a substantial majority of Catholic teenagers and young people in their twenties continue to attend Mass regularly. Furthermore, there is some evidence that as young Catholics approach age 30, Mass attendance increases (Greeley 1985).

Criteria discussed above are far from being the only plausible indicators of identification with or loyalty to the church. The D'Antonio et al. study asked both whether respondents thought that the church was the most important part (or among the most important parts) of their lives; and whether one could be a good Catholic without (1) going to Mass every Sunday; (2) contributing annually to special collections for the pope; (3) obeying the teaching on birth control; (4) going to private Confession at least annually); (5) obeying the teaching on divorce and remarriage; (6) receiving Communion during the Easter season; (7) getting married in the church); (8) believing in the infallibility of the pope; (9) donating time or money to help the poor; and (10) obeying the church's teaching on abortion.

Thirty-seven percent of those 29 or younger gave the Church "high importance" compared to 45 percent for the 30 to 54 group and 66 percent for those 55 and over. The "good Catholic" questions were, with the exceptions of the last three items, answered yes (you can be) by majorities of the 29 or under group, with the 30 to 39 year-old group matching them closely. On the last three, "yes answers" lay between 45 to 49 percent. As the authors point out, Catholics in the late 1980s were "more likely to question the quality of a person's Catholicism if they don't help the poor than if they don't go to Mass on Sunday, or if they use contraceptives other than rhythm" (D'Antonio et al. 1989, p. 70).

In their conclusion, D'Antonio et al. (1989, p. 186) remark that "the 18-20 year olds, and those in their thirties and forties, have much lower levels of commitment than those over 55." But given the results set down above, "we are left to ponder the changes that are taking place regarding the meaning of commitment" (p. 186). American Catholics, like most Americans, cherish their autonomy. Church leaders in and of themselves are no longer acknowledged as arbiters of moral authority. The process of inviting lay consultation on the drafting of pastoral letters on nuclear war, on the American economy, and on the status of women, "provide a helpful model for a new approach to moral authority in the Church" (p. 188). Adopting this approach on future issues, according to the authors, would encourage Catholic lay persons to view church leaders' positions as reasonable, and thus more acceptable. To be taken seriously in decisions affecting their lives might well move young Catholics toward greater loyalty and commitment to the church (D'Antonio et al. 1989).

CATHOLIC SCHOOLS

The financial sacrifices of Catholic families account for the largest private school system in the United States. In pre-Vatican II decades, Catholic youngsters were to safeguard their faith by learning about it from the sisters, brothers, priests, and lay teachers who staffed the Catholic schools and brought religious values to classroom, schoolyard, and playing field. While no one claims attending Catholic schools guarantees an active Catholic graduate, Greeley and Rossi's 1963 research showed a significant relationship between attending Catholic schools all the way through college, and later involvement in Catholic organizations, adherence to ethical values, knowledge about the church, and "appropriate social and racial attitudes and values" (Greeley et al. 1976, pp. 13-14).

A decade later, despite closings and sharp declines in the numbers attending them, Catholic schools were still effective in transmitting Catholic values to young people (Greeley et al. 1976). However, Fichter's study of Jesuit high schools in the late 1960s showed that students (all boys) considered religion "a dull subject," less interesting than almost everything else in the curriculum. Whether it was taught well or badly made little difference in measures of Christian ethical behavior or moral attitudes. Coming from well advantaged families decidedly above the American average in social class, the boys were little affected in their outlooks by Catholic social teaching. They remained skeptical of programs aimed at alleviation of poverty and looked negatively upon social welfare payments. In fact, these attitudes became *more* unfavorable as students progressed from freshman through senior year. Family and cultural environments persisted as influences from freshman through senior year; attending a Jesuit high school promoted and reinforced class attitudes. Fichter predicted this situation would worsen as the proportion of lay to Jesuit faculty increased in the schools (Fichter 1973).

The 1980s saw several regional surveys of seniors in Catholic high schools, plus my own case study of a southwestern Catholic high school. The young women and men in these studies differed little from young Catholics surveyed nationally (see above) on issues of sexual morality, birth control, divorce, and abortion, with boys more likely than girls (save on the issue of birth control) to disagree with Catholic teaching. In terms of social morality, however, the majority of students was supportive on measures of racial integration, and believed the church *should* take stands on such issues as nuclear disarmament, racial discrimination, world hunger, and economic justice (McAuley and Mathieson 1986; McNamara 1991).

Seniors in the Catholic high school I studied from 1977 through 1989 were scarcely immune from the "selective Catholicism" and moral individualism revealed in national surveys. Catholic seniors are indeed willing to accept the church as a guide, but as one senior put it,

Unlike my parents, I have been raised in a generation in which every issue can be openly discussed, questioned, analyzed, and criticized with the possible result of altering what is believed or held as a truth. I seldom accept a teaching or "truth" unless I can justify this with my own truths, reason and values . . . I am seeking a level of spirituality quite different from my parents. They were content with a religious faith in which everything was determined for them and they simply believed and practiced as told (McNamara 1991, pp. 143-144).

Around a third of the school's seniors in the late 1980s expressed such sentiments, with no differences by gender. The high school I studied is typical, not of the many inner-city Catholic schools that have been forced to close in recent years, but of flourishing suburban college-preparatory institutions whose rising tuition costs are affordable mainly by the growing numbers of Catholic middle- and upper-middle-class families. The individualism of their daughters and sons is hardly surprising, resembling the views of the young upwardly mobile Americans interviewed by Bellah, Madsen, Sullivan, Swidler, and Tipton (1985). Moreover, the Hispanic seniors (about a third of the student body) were somewhat *more* likely (with no gender differences) than their Anglo counterparts to take a "selective" stance. As one Hispanic male put it,

Being a Catholic is very important. My parents pretty much stay with the traditional teachings of the Church. I, on the other hand, take and use only what I feel is right for me (p. 121).

No overall "generation gap" characterizes these seniors, however. Around 30 percent of them say little difference exists between themselves and their parents in what they believe and practice. In the vast majority of cases, regular Mass attendance and acceptance of orthodox beliefs and moral values did not differ between generations. Hispanic students are significantly more likely than Anglo students to fall into this category, and much less likely to express serious doubts or alienation from Catholicism (28 percent of Anglo seniors; 6 percent of Hispanics).

Young men and women graduating from high school are still searching for their identities, of course, a quest that may well extend into adulthood. If the church looks to its schools for future lay leadership, certainly no picture emerges of some "lost generation." A large majority of the 2000 seniors I surveyed sees the church as an important resource for forming their religious and moral positions—but not the only one. The church, then, is not an "enveloping institution," as it may have been for their parents, that projects a compelling moral authority. But caring and sensitive theology teachers, as this high school was fortunate to have, can make an enormous difference by creating an openness to church teaching that may come to a fuller flowering later in their students' lives. Certainly they were notably successful in helping the students see the church as an important voice deserving their respect when its leaders issue statements on the broad sociomoral issues of racism, world hunger, poverty, and unemployment. On matters of personal morality, these young women and men, particularly as we move further into the 1990s, may well be echoing not only the powerful currents of peer and media influence, but the more liberal stances of Baby Boom parents whose children are now coming into adolescence. This issue should loom large in any Catholic research agenda for the 1990s.

Let me return to the question of how young Catholics' views and practices might change over time. In 1987, I re-surveyed a small sample of 1978 and 1979 graduates from the school I studied. The following profile of these 54 well-educated men and women in their late twenties evinces no wholesale defection from the Catholic church. The majority opposes abortion except in cases of rape and incest; they appear expectedly liberal on other issues of personal and social morality. However, a little over half attend Mass at least monthly, while the remainder show up a few times a year or not at all. Less than half attend a parish regularly; nine out of ten belong to no parish organizations. None of this is particularly surprising, given what survey research tells us about the diminished participation of young American adults regardless of denomination. But if one looks beyond "institutional" religiosity, three-quarters pray at least weekly (half do so daily), 40 percent say religion is "of central importance and comes before all other aspects" of their lives; 62 percent have had a spiritual experience that "lifted them out of themselves"; almost nine out of ten agree they have a personal responsibility to share what they have with those who have less, and to oppose unjust practices in society; over half would support a city ordinance prohibiting discrimination against homosexuals. All in all, this is a group that seems spiritually alive and socially caring, though perhaps not conventionally religious (McNamara 1991).

CONCLUSIONS

Nothing in post-Vatican II research portrays a mass youthful exodus from the church, like refugees fleeing a shattered homeland. An older devotional Catholicism of ritual regularity, sense of sin, reliance on authority, and sense of the miraculous (Dolan 1987), may have yielded to "two or three times a month" Mass attendance and a primacy of "personal conscience" in beliefs and moral issues for both Baby Boom and post-Baby Boom Catholics. Nor do the voices of the young post-Vietnam Catholics that I and others have surveyed in our research echo bitter alienation or bored indifference. They can be reached by good preaching (all too rare, as Greeley and others have noted); they are more than willing to be consulted in and serve on diocesan synods and parish committees when asked; their values can be affected by caring and intellectually honest teachers in Catholic high schools and colleges. True, like most American teenagers, they accord few, if any, adult authorities credibility in the area of sexual mores which seem peer constructed and immune to adult "coaching." But this moral individualism does not render them deaf to the challenging messages of the American bishops' recent social initiatives. The church, they believe, has a legitimate role as a moral conscience in society. But given the current and impending priest shortage and the fact that fewer Catholic schools are serving a diminishing proportion of Catholic young people, how will they be socialized into the distinctive worldviews of their church? No easy answers lie on the horizon. What *is* safe to say, I think, is that continuation of moral stances and social patterns that seem antiquatedly authoritarian (birth control) and senselessly oppressive (refusal to ordain women) to young—and many not so young—Catholics makes this task of socialization that much harder no matter who undertakes it. Vigorous Catholic self-renewal that includes imaginative and participative liturgies and retreats, along with prophetic stances by leaders on sociomoral issues that engage the idealism of the young, would seem essential conditions for reclaiming any vital commitment of coming generations to the faith of their mothers and fathers.

REFERENCES

Bellah, R.N., R. Madsen, W.M. Sullivan, A. Swidler, and S. M. Tipton. 1985. *Habits of the Heart: Individualism and Commitment in American Life.* Berkeley: University of California Press.

Chaves, M. 1989. "Secularization and Religious Revival: Evidence from United States Church Attendance Rates." *Journal for the Scientific Study of Religion* 28(4):465-477.

D'Antonio, W., J. Davidson, D. Hoge, and R. Wallace. 1989. *American Catholic Laity in a Changing Church.* Kansas City, MO: Sheed and Ward.

Dolan, J. P. 1987. *The American Catholic Experience.* Garden City, NJ: Doubleday.

Fee, J., A. Greeley, W. McCready, and T. Sullivan. 1981. *Young Catholics.* New York: Sadlier.

Gallup, G. III, and J. Castelli. 1987. *The American Catholic People.* Garden City, NJ: Doubleday.

Greeley, A. M. 1979. *Crisis in the Church.* Chicago: Thomas More.

————. 1985. *American Catholics after the Council: An Unauthorized Report.* Chicago: Thomas More.

Greeley, A. M., W. McCready, and K. McCourt. 1976. *Catholic Schools in a Declining Church.* Kansas City, MO: Sheed and Ward.

Greeley, A.M., and P. Rossi. 1966. *The Education of Catholic Americans.* Chicago: Aldine.

Hout, M., and A. M. Greeley. 1987. "The Center Doesn't Hold: Church Attendance Rates in the United States: 1940-1984." *American Sociological Review* 52(June):325-345.

McAuley, E. N., and M. Mathieson. 1986. *Faith Without Form: Beliefs of Catholic Youth.* Kansas City, MO: Sheed and Ward.

McNamara, P. H. 1991. *Conscience First, Tradition Second: A Study of Young Catholics.* Albany, NY: SUNY Press.

CHANGES IN THE PRIESTHOOD AND SEMINARIES

Dean R. Hoge

The Second Vatican Council, the most consequential event in modern Catholic history, has been likened to an earthquake. Therefore one might expect that the decades after its close might be filled with after-tremors or shock waves. The effects of such a momentous event take a while to spread into all corners of the church, and they unleash further chains of reactions that nobody can predict. Indeed the 25 years since the Council can be interpreted in this way. The process is not yet finished; today in 1990 the ripple effects of the Council are still present.

This chapter will trace the most important effects of the Council on priesthood and seminary life. We will try to describe the principal events and to show their interrelations. It is impossible to explain the events with any precision, because historical explanation in such a case is only guesswork. No one can say exactly which events were "caused" by the Council or by any other event. Other social currents were also present in American Catholicism—including the American cultural revolution of the 1960s, the feminist movement, continued upward mobility and suburbanization, and the encyclical *Humanae Vitae* on birth control issued in 1968.

Religion and the Social Order, Volume 2, pages 67-83.
Copyright © 1991 by JAI Press Inc.
All rights of reproduction in any form reserved.
ISBN: 1-55938-388-7

THE EFFECTS OF THE COUNCIL

After the close of the Council in 1965 there was an initial time of several years when the effects of the Council were first felt, then a time of about a decade during which numerous tensions over the Council's directives were gradually resolved, and most recently a time when the worst was over but implications of earlier changes were still being worked out (Seidler and Meyer 1989). To understand the developments we should note that the Council did not take a great interest in the priesthood or seminaries as such; its energies were given to other issues including liturgy, religious freedom, and ecclesiology, and its effects on the priesthood in the United States were indirect by way of other concerns. We can identify three principal indirect effects from the new teachings on liturgy, ecclesiology, and authority.

The impact of the Council on liturgy had an immediate psychological impact. For many priests the changes were incomprehensible. How could anyone undermine the sacred liturgy that they had so long celebrated and defended as God-given? How could priests change from Latin to English, face the people, and even ask them to shake hands? Some priests adapted easily, especially younger ones trained in modern theology. But older priests felt embattled and tried to stand firm. Factions developed within each diocese pitting young priests against old.

Conciliar teachings on ecclesiology called for a new vision of the church as the "people of God," for a new view that the lay life was as good as the religious life, and for more participatory, consultative parish life. Some priests rejoiced, others were embittered. The Council encouraged the multiplication of ministries, to include deacons, extraordinary ministers, pastoral assistants, lectors, directors of religious education, and leaders of lay groups. All these persons were aware of the conciliar emphasis on the priesthood of the baptized, and they felt the right to have a role in ministry. No longer was the priest the sole minister in the parish. This was an unwelcome idea and a threat to many priests.

Church authority was now seen as residing with both the Pope and bishops, and lay people were to be included in decision making. The Council asked for quasi-democratic structures at all levels, including lay parish councils and diocesan pastoral councils. These teachings were unsettling to many priests— but they also contained a major victory for the priesthood in general, since the Council mandated councils of priests in each diocese.

In 1970, Pope Paul VI decreed that all dioceses should create priests' senates and advisory councils. Already some had them, and in others the priests had set up their own unapproved associations as a response to the new energies of the Council. These associations sometimes acted on their own, in defiance of the bishop. In some places there was even agitation for a labor union of priests (Stewart 1978, p. 24). In 1968, a national federation of these groups was founded—the National Federation of Priests' Councils. It began without sanction from the bishops, and it combined official priest senates and unofficial diocesan associations of priests (a total of 114 groups). Its initial agenda was priests' rights, and it had undoubted effect in many places. After a few years the bishops came to appreciate the NFPC and to work with it.

The new concept of priesthood included greater emphasis on professionalism, entailing greater individual autonomy free from close supervision, more collegial decision-making structures, and seminary education for social and pastoral leadership. The new ideal of the priesthood spread slowly and unevenly, depending on the local bishops and power structures. Priests gained more power in the appointment process, so that they began to be consulted about their own appointments, and factors other than seniority entered into appointments. Grievance committees and rules about due process were widely instituted. These were major gains in self-determination for priests, producing improved role satisfaction.

An important development was the burst of priestly resignations which began around about 1966 and peaked in 1969-1971. Also in 1966-1968 there was a fall-off in the number of seminarians, a trend which has continued until today. (We discuss both of these.) By the late 1980s, the main issues in the priesthood were the vocations shortage, the rise in lay ministries, and problems of morale. The immediate effects of the Council were receding, but the by-products were still creating stress in the system.

In the following sections we will describe important research findings, first regarding priests, then regarding seminarians, and finally on the priest shortage.

RESEARCH ON PRIESTS

After the Council, the problem of priestly resignations was alarming to all, and several research studies were launched. Why were so many young, capable priests leaving?

One major reason was the crisis of episcopal authority. In most dioceses, factions developed shortly after the Council (as noted earlier) in which the more progressive priests fought for quick implementation of Conciliar ideals, while the conservative priests—usually the older ones—opposed them. The bishops in most cases sided with the older conservatives and resisted change. This set the stage for standoffs between younger priests and unchanging bishops which infuriated the young priests and induced many to quit (Fichter 1968). Resignations increased fourfold from 1965 to 1969, and between 1966 and 1972, ten percent of all priests resigned (Schoenherr and Sorensen 1982). Those leaving were usually younger than 45, progressive in theology, enthusiastic about the Council, and restless with old-line episcopal authority (Schallert and Kelley 1970; National Opinion Research Center 1972). Figure 1 shows the rates

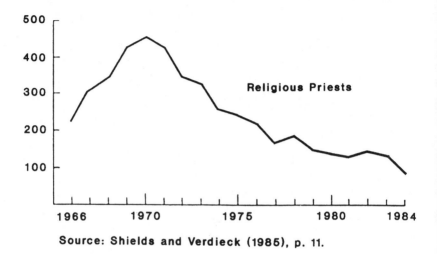

Source: Shields and Verdieck (1985), p. 11.

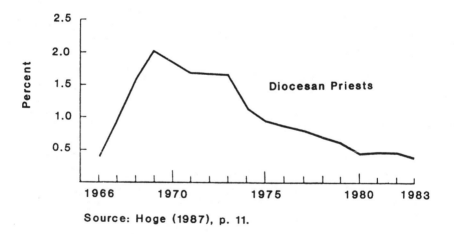

Source: Hoge (1987), p. 11.

Figure 1.   Resignations of Priests in the United States, 1966-1984

of resignation for both diocesan and religious priests. Between 1970 and 1980, about 15 to 17 percent of all diocesan priests and about 12 to 14 percent of all religious priests resigned (Hoge 1987, p. 10). The resignations receded after about 1971, partly because the ranks of young, progressive priests were so decimated by then that few remained.

The American bishops sponsored a major study in 1969 to see why so many priests were resigning. They commissioned a sociological study, a psychological study, and a volume of historical essays. They asked the National Opinion Research Center (NORC) in Chicago to do the sociological study, and the Center selected Richard Schoenherr and Andrew Greeley as codirectors. The NORC team surveyed a random sample of bishops, a random sample of active priests, and a random sample of resigned priests (see National Opinion Research Center 1972). The study produced a wealth of data on American priests. The major concern was on their role satisfaction and their intent to continue in their priesthood (versus resigning). The researchers tested two major factors. First, they accepted widespread accounts of difficulties young priests have with the total authority of bishops and religious superiors over them—situations which without doubt caused conflict and alienation among younger priests. Second, they wanted to test whether loneliness and the desire to marry was an important impetus leading to resignations. Using path models they found that both factors were present, and the second was the stronger of the two. Loneliness and the desire to marry was the single strongest factor behind the resignations.

The 1970 survey found unusually great age differences in theological beliefs; whereas the old priests strongly affirmed pre-Vatican teachings about faith, salvation, the priesthood, authority, and related topics, the young priests were different due to the influences of conciliar teachings. For example, on the statement, "God's Word comes to us through some of the great prophetic men of our times, such as Mahatma Gandhi and Martin Luther King," 86 percent of the priests under 35 years of age agreed, compared with 20 percent of the priests over 65. Also on the statement, "To doubt one article of faith that is *de fide* is to question the whole of revealed truth," 18 percent of the priests under 35 agreed, compared with 85 percent of those over 65. Such extreme age differences are very seldom found in social research.

In a separate survey of resigned priests, the NORC researchers found that 70 percent were married and another 8 percent were engaged; of those who had resigned four years earlier, 87 percent were married (National Opinion Research Center 1972, p. 285). The single event which most impelled them to leave was an emotional relationship with a woman. Most were now working in some sort of teaching or social service occupation. Thirty-six percent said they would like to return to priestly ministry as married priests, either full-time or part-time; but only 10 percent said they would like to be full-time again. In causing the resignations, it seems that weakness of faith was not a foremost factor; the main causes of the decision to resign were (a) loneliness and the desire to marry, and (b) problems dealing with the authority structure in the church.

Later Schoenherr and Greeley (1974) reanalyzed the data from active diocesan priests in search of structural factors influencing resignation rates. They expected that diocese size might be a factor—because relations between priests and chancery offices were more impersonal in large dioceses. Also, they hypothesized that decentralized dioceses might have lower resignations. But these hypotheses proved false. In addition, they found no impact of region of the United States, wealth of the diocese, average theological tendencies in the diocese, or average number of years in the diocese before a priest is appointed pastor. The only contextual factor they found to have an effect was the cumulative impact of many priests resigning in the same diocese; the more resignations in any diocese, the greater probability there was that more would resign.

An important study in the Archdiocese of Hartford resulted in a 1973 book by Douglas Hall and Benjamin Schneider. These researchers were asked to evaluate the priesthood in Hartford, especially with regard to priests' work satisfaction, overall morale, level of esteem received from other people, and feelings of whether their skills and competencies are being utilized. Hall and Schneider found rather low morale, especially among the young associates (curates). The associates complained of being given trivial jobs to do—or no jobs at all, of being treated as underlings by senior pastors, and of having no personal autonomy. Thus, the researchers recommended greater attention to the first assignments of priests after ordination, so that these assignments would provide psychological successes and build self-confidence. The young priests needed more mentoring, more feedback on their performance, and work assignments more central to their concepts of ministry. Hall and Schneider recommended that experiments should be started on various kinds of team ministries. The diocesan organization should also be reevaluated to make it more collegial and communicative.

Other important surveys of priests also were done during this time. In 1966, Joseph Fichter surveyed a random sample of diocesan priests who were curates, to get their views on the Council teachings and on conditions in their dioceses. He found them to be rather unhappy about clergy-bishop relations and curate-pastor relations. About half of these young priests were not on a first-name basis with their pastors (Fichter 1968, p. 121). The great majority wanted to change the process by which they get their job appointments. More than half (54%) reported that they were not working up to their capacity, an estimate which jumped to 79 percent for the curates who reported poor rectory relations. They were strongly in favor of dispensing with honorary titles for priests such as monsignor, domestic prelate, or papal chamberlain. Three out of five thought that priests should have freedom of choice to marry (for a similar survey see Fichter 1965).

Research on the priesthood in the 1980s was mainly related to questions of priestly morale, changes in the priestly task, and the shortage of vocations.[1] Schoenherr did detailed actuarial studies of the persons entering and exiting the priesthood, to predict the number available in years ahead. His predictions were shocking to many (see Schoenherr and Young's chapter in this volume, pp. 85-104). In 1985, Hoge, Shields, and Verdieck replicated portions of the 1970 priest study to get information on priestly morale and whether or not the priests of the 1980s were more active in encouraging vocations (Hoge, Shields, and Verdieck 1988; Verdieck, Shields, and Hoge 1988). They constructed a sample identical to that in 1970, though smaller in size, and they asked many of the same questions. The changes they found can be summarized under five headings.

First, the priests in 1985 were older. The median age in 1970 was 47.6 for all priests; in 1985 it was 53.4. The religious priests' median age had risen faster, since they had experienced more resignations in the last decade, and they had seen a greater dropoff in numbers of seminarians. More priests were retired; whereas in 1970, three percent of the priests said they were retired, in 1985, it was eight percent.

Second, there was an overall increased belief in God's ongoing revelation from 1970 to 1985, greater importance accorded to the role of an individual's personal conscience in moral decisions, a greater openness to Protestant theological thought, and reduced insistence on the uniqueness of priestly ministry over against the ministry of lay people. On many other topics, including beliefs about the nature of God, the sacraments, salvation, and the Church's social mission, there was no change.

The overall changes over 15 years were caused mainly by the simple mechanism that all priests had gotten 15 years older without any major change in their beliefs; hence as the old traditional priests died, they were replaced by younger liberal priests, with a resulting overall shift in the liberal direction. The extent of the shift was fairly small, because *the youngest priests in 1985 were decidedly more conservative than the youngest priests in 1970*. The 1985 survey thus confirmed what had been widely discussed among seminary educators for years—the young priests in the 1980s were more traditional in theology and less interested in the Church's social mission. The shifts are illustrated in Figure 2. The figure shows the 1970 and 1985 responses of priests in five age groups, on four questions. The solid lines connect the responses of the age groups in 1970, and the dots connect the age groups in 1985. The extreme slant of each line in 1970 depicts the sharp differences among the age groups. In 1985 the differences were smaller, and there was less polarization of age groups.

The asterisks in Figure 2 are placed 15 years after the points in the 1970 line, and they estimate where the 1985 line should be if all attitudes had remained constant. On the first two items (about revelation and the Christian

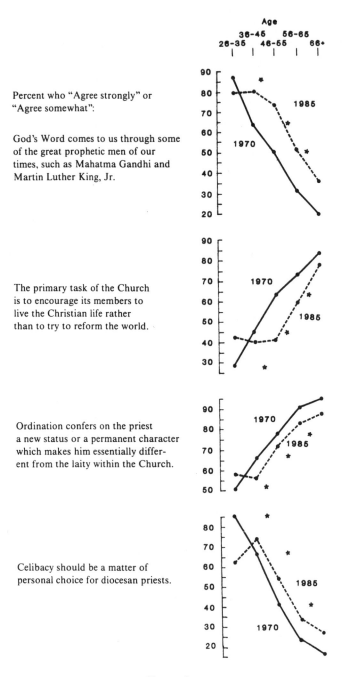

Figure 2.

life), the 1985 line is near the asterisks, indicating that individual priests' attitudes had indeed remained nearly constant. But on the last two items (regarding ordination and celibacy) the 1985 line is far from the asterisks, showing a conservative shift in individuals' attitudes since 1970.

Any conclusions about the nature of attitude shifts need to be tentative, for two reasons. The first is that 14 to 16 percent of the diocesan priests active in 1970 had resigned in the ensuing years, and it is known that the more progressive young priests were those most frequently resigning. Thus, the 1985 sample lacked those progressive persons, and was more conservative as a result. The second is that seminarians in recent years have tended to be of all ages, not just young men in their twenties. In a 1986 survey (discussed below), a third of the seminarians were over 30. Many older priests have been added to the priesthood population since 1970. The only safe conclusion is that, for whatever reason, there has been a modest shift in the direction of a critically understood faith, ecumenism, and openness to the Spirit, and it would have been greater if the youngest priests had not turned conservative.

Third, morale and work satisfaction rose between 1970 and 1985. This finding surprised everyone, coming as it did in a time of wide concern about sagging priestly morale. The explanation is either that the morale in 1970 was *really* low (so that in spite of low morale in 1985 it was still higher), or that the most dissatisfied priests had left during the intervening 15 years, thus raising the mean scores for the remainder. Probably both are true. In both 1970 and 1985, the priests with highest work satisfaction were those in educational apostolates, chaplaincies, or social service. Next highest were the priests in full-time diocesan administration or pastors of parishes with additional work outside the parish. Lowest were the full-time associate pastors. This pattern was found both in 1970 and 1985.

Fourth, the 1985 priests were more likely to encourage young men to enter the priesthood than those in 1970. The gain was sizable. Each questionnaire also asked about "4 to 5 years ago," and in the 1970 survey the priests reported a dropoff of encouragement from about 1965 to 1970. In the 1985 data the shift from about 1980 to 1985 was small.

Fifth, the percentage of priests in 1985 saying they might resign from the priesthood was lower than in 1970 (from 13 percent to 8 percent), and the percentage of priests 35 or younger who said they would probably or certainly like to get married, if priests were allowed to, dropped from 37 percent to 25 percent in 1985. Why the desire to marry dropped is unknown; possibly the growing legitimacy of single adult life in society in general influenced the priests, or possibly the level of homosexuality in the priesthood increased. There is no way to know.

The overall picture is one of return to stability after the troublesome post-Council years. The new theological views introduced by the Council were slowly permeating the priesthood, and morale was improving.

RESEARCH ON SEMINARIANS

At the close of the Council in 1965 there was much discussion in American Catholicism about seminaries (cf. Lee and Putz 1965; Poole 1965), and many criticisms were levelled against them. Some critics charged that the seminaries did not produce effective leaders; others that the seminaries over-emphasized spiritual formation at the cost of teaching practical skills; still others thought students were entering the seminaries at too young an age. CARA, the Catholic research center in Washington, D.C., sponsored a nationwide survey of Catholic seminarians, directed by Raymond Potvin and Antanas Suziedelis of Catholic University of America (Potvin and Suziedelis 1969). They surveyed students in 20 percent of all high school seminaries, college seminaries, and theologates in 1966, to learn about their backgrounds, their interests, their views of the priesthood, and their reactions to seminary experiences. A secondary aim was to get information on why so many seminary students drop out, so, one year later, the researchers requested follow-up information from the rectors on which seminarians had departed. The high school and college seminarians were fairly satisfied with their experiences, but the theological students were much less satisfied. Also religious theologians were less satisfied than diocesan theologians (Potvin and Suziedelis 1969, p. 71). The criticisms had mostly to do with quality of instruction; many students questioned if their training was relevant to their ministry. The majority of the respondents agreed that priests should have the option of marriage or celibacy (72% among the diocesan theology students), and students with this opinion were less satisfied than the others.

An important part of the analysis was the construction of two views of priestly roles, called "sacred" and "secular." The former stressed the traditional role of the priest as saying Mass, preaching the gospel, administering the sacraments, and living a holy life; the latter stressed leadership, counselling, relations with laity, and social witness (Potvin and Suziedelis 1969, p. 155). Seminarians stressing the sacred role tended to value celibacy more highly and to see the priesthood as higher in prestige. A year later, 22 percent of the seminarians had withdrawn, and the major predictors of withdrawal were the secular view of the priestly role, opposition to celibacy, dissatisfaction with seminary experiences, and high scores on the psychological dogmatism scale. Potvin and Suziedelis concluded that the problems in the seminaries were not so much a reflection of poor quality of the seminaries as they were a result of the unrest following the Council and a yearning for "relevance" among youth.

The late 1960s and 1970s was a period of unprecedented changes in Catholic seminaries. Robert Schreiter (1985, p. 6) observed:

> The period of the late 1960s saw the time of the greatest creative ferment in Roman Catholic seminary life . . . The changes which took place in the decade of 1965-1975 were certainly

the most important structural changes since the beginning of the seminary movement in this country.

The whole purpose of seminary education was being rethought. From their beginning in 1791, American seminaries had taken as their main purpose the preparation of priests who would be devoted and loyal to the church. The seminaries were placed in locations away from major cities and universities, and their major program emphasis was spiritual and moral rather than intellectual. But the documents of Vatican II ordered renewed study of the Scriptures, introduction of a greater practical element into the curriculum, and greater openness to ecumenical contacts and university training. The focus for most (not all) of the theologates became preparation for the professional ministry (Sanks 1984; White 1986). Multiple changes were made, of which we will mention six.

First, many small seminaries amalgamated into groupings and theological unions centered around major universities. Between 1967 and 1971, 56 of the schools merged, and another 30 did so in the following decade. The total number of theologates dropped from 133 in 1966 to 52 in 1988. These figures do not include high school and college seminaries, which closed at an even faster rate; the high school seminaries almost disappeared by the late 1980s, and the remaining college seminaries had severe enrollment problems. Enrollment of priesthood candidates in the theologates dropped from 8,916 in 1966 to 3,826 in 1989, a decline of 57 percent; the most precipitous declines were in the years 1966 to 1974, after which the declines became more gradual. But in spite of much hope and effort to recruit seminarians, the downward trend continued.

Second, all seminaries began field education and/or internship years, as a part of the shift toward professional education. Much more emphasis was put on preparing the new priests for the realistic demands of their future ministries.

Third, there were major shifts from strict rules, schedules, and discipline in student life to greater personal freedom. Dress codes were relaxed. Students were given freedom of movement on and off campus, and they were allowed to own cars.

Fourth, there was a dramatic shift away from the neoscholastic, pre-Vatican theological manuals to writings of current theologians. The language of instruction changed from Latin to English.

Fifth, most of the seminaries joined the Association of Theological Seminaries (ATS) (which includes Protestant seminaries), and in the process they subjected themselves to ATS standards. The vast majority received academic accreditation from the ATS.

Sixth, many seminaries began admitting non-priesthood candidates to their programs; the majority of these were women religious or lay women. In 1979, it was reported that 16 percent of all full-time students in the seminaries were laypersons, and by 1988 the figure was 39 percent. If all students, full-time and part-time are counted, the percentage who were non-ordination candidates in 1988 was 50.

Not all seminaries made the changes enumerated here, because many believed that priestly identity is more difficult to develop in seminaries affiliated with universities, in urban settings, and with women in the classrooms. In 1988, thirteen of the theologates were admitting no non-ordination students (Schuth 1989, p. 51).[2]

In 1984 and 1986, two new surveys of seminarians in theologates were made by Hemrick and Hoge (1985; 1987) and a third was done by Potvin (1985). The purpose was to take stock of the seminarians and find out their attitudes about priesthood and seminary life. Approximately 30 questions in the new surveys were repeats of those used in 1966.

It was found that the seminarians in the 1980s were older; mean age in 1986 was 30.0, compared with 25.2 for theologians in 1966. Fewer were preparing for the religious priesthood—24 percent in 1986, compared with 29 percent in 1966. Fewer had attended college seminaries—55 percent had been in college seminaries for all four years, compared with 94 percent in 1966. Seminarians in 1984 scored better, overall, on psychological measures than did those in 1966. They also seemed more ready to assume responsibility than in 1966, and reported better relations with superiors and with persons in authority.

Decisions about the priesthood had been made at a later age than was true in the 1960s—whereas 33 percent of the 1966 seminarians in theologates had decided definitely to become a priest while in elementary or high school, in 1984 only 12 percent had decided definitely by that time. There was a trend away from emphasizing witness to the world, and toward sacramental ministry; the 1984 seminarians expected to give greater emphasis to sacraments in their ministries, less to helping other people. Also, the 1984 seminarians tended to stress the essential and unchanging aspects of Catholic doctrine more than was done in 1966.

Compared with 1966, more of the 1984 seminarians emphasized the essential and unchanging aspects of Catholic doctrine, and more stressed that the primary task of the church is encouraging members to live the Christian life rather than to try to reform the world. The 1984 seminarians were less "activist" than in 1966. They also had a higher evaluation of celibacy, and fewer said they would like to marry if the church would permit it.

The seminarians were asked about several aspects of their seminary experiences, and comparisons were made with the responses in 1966. The 1986 seminarians were much more positive about seminary than were those in 1966. For example, one question asked, "Have you ever felt that many required activities in this seminary are a waste of time?" In 1966, 24 percent said "very often," and in 1986 it was only 10 percent. Another question asked, "Do you think the general training you received in this seminary is relevant for your vocation to the priesthood?"; 13 percent said "very relevant" in 1966. In 1986 it was 49 percent. Large shifts were found toward more positive evaluations of teachers, library facilities and guidance services, student-faculty relations, spiritual formation programs, internship opportunities, elective courses, and opportunities for intellectual autonomy.

The 1986 survey tried to discern the visions of future priesthood held by the seminarians, so 18 elements of priestly roles were given in the questionnaire to be rated in importance, and the same 18 were given to the seminary faculty for them to rate. In the 18 items, one major dimension was visible— "Institutional Orientation Versus Communal Orientation." Persons scoring at the institutional end think of the priesthood mostly in terms of its function in church structures; they see the priest as an official of the church, upholding its authority and maintaining its institutional identity. Persons at the communal end, by contrast, think of the priesthood in terms of the local Catholic community as the People of God and the role of the priest as spiritual leader in that setting. The faculty in these seminaries scored closer to the communal end than did the students, and the religious seminarians scored much closer to the communal end than did the diocesan seminarians.

RESPONSES TO THE PRIEST SHORTAGE

Of all the effects of the Council, the priest shortage—whether it was a direct effect or not—is the most consequential for the American Catholic church. As Richard Schoenherr has concluded on basis of his extensive research (see his chapter in this volume, pp. 85-104), the shortage in the United States will worsen, and the best estimate is that the number of active diocesan priests will decline about 43 percent from 1966 to the year 2005. The seminaries are now operating at a 59 percent replacement rate—for every 100 priests leaving the active ministry, 59 new ones are being ordained.

There are eleven discernible options for responding to the priest shortage (see Hoge 1987). They appear to cover all possibilities, so that even if nothing is done, one of the eleven will ensue. The first option is to reduce the *need* for priests, by redesigning the institutional church. Parishes could be restructured or combined, or Catholics could be reeducated to have lowered expectations of priestly services. For example, the Eucharist could be de-emphasized and offered less often. This option is objectionable for numerous theological reasons.

Second, existing priests could be reassigned or redistributed to get more involved in parish leadership. This could be done by taking priests away from other jobs which laypersons could do—such as teaching, administration, or counseling. It is a realistic option, one being carried out in many places today. But it has limits and will produce only a modest increase in priestly services in parishes.

Third and fourth, more parish priests could be obtained from religious orders or from foreign nations. These options are not realistic, except for getting limited numbers of priests from nations such as Poland or Philippines, who would be suitable to minister in certain types of ethnic parishes. Parish priests are not available in large numbers from religious orders.

Fifth, more seminarians could be recruited. This is the "of course" option which has been pursued energetically for decades. It is what has always been done. But fewer recruits can be found today, and it is improbable that enough can be obtained to overcome the severe priest shortage today.

Sixth, married as well as celibate men could be ordained to the diocesan priesthood. This is a hopeful option in that recent research among college students has indicated a large number of persons potentially interested in being married priests, if it were possible. We estimated, based on a 1985 survey of Catholic college students, that with optional celibacy the number of seminarians would increase fourfold. Also, in 1985, 63 percent of Catholic laity endorsed the idea. But many obstacles remain. Most important, the pope is opposed to the idea.

Seventh, women could be ordained. This is also hopeful in that a large number of women are interested, and all indications are that they are committed and able. Among Catholic adults, the idea was endorsed by 47 percent in a 1985 survey, so it would receive a little more initial opposition than optional celibacy for men. Again, the pope is in opposition.

Eighth, a term of service for the priesthood could be instituted, or an honorable discharge could be allowed after a set number of years. This idea would move the priesthood in the direction of a military career, with a definite duration and optional reenlistments. It would attract a large number of persons to the priesthood, according to the 1985 student survey. But the idea is in severe conflict with the church's theology of priesthood and thus is rejected by a great many priests and theologians.

Ninth, some resigned priests could be utilized as sacramental ministers. Due to the many resignations since the late 1960s, there are several thousand resigned priests eager to return to priestly duty. But the vast majority are married, and they want to return as married priests. So this option is really the same as the sixth option—that of optional celibacy. Until the celibacy rule changes, this option is impossible for most resigned priests.

The tenth and eleventh options call for use of other persons to fill in for priests. Option ten calls for expansion of the permanent diaconate, to provide many more deacons for parish leadership. This is a realistic option, in fact already happening. But there are limits to the usefulness of permanent deacons in parish leadership, because most work as deacons part-time (an average of 13 hours a week) and thus cannot undertake major program responsibilities. Also, there is an unsolved problem of tensions between deacons and priests in numerous parishes. In the future, permanent deacons will be major resources for parish leadership only when they work full-time.

Eleventh, lay ministries could be expanded. This is happening in many areas today. Full-time lay ministries are expanding everywhere. Lay leaders are taking over priestless parishes and replacing priests in non-sacramental ministries. This option has obvious limits, in that lay ministers cannot celebrate the sacraments, thus requiring services from visiting priests if priestless parishes are to have the Eucharist. Also lay ministers are of uneven quality today, causing mixed reactions from parish members.

The most realistic options for responding to the priest shortage in the decade ahead are the fifth (recruit more seminarians) and the eleventh (expand and develop lay ministries). In the long run, church teaching about celibacy needs to be reexamined and possibly changed in some situations to allow ordination of married men; this approach has the greatest potential for maintenance of Catholic church life in the future. Ordination of women may be a second step.

CONCLUSION

The 25 years since the close of the Council have been a time period packed with reform and innovation. There has been hope, despair, conflict, disillusionment, and bewilderment. Perhaps the effects of the Council were felt nowhere so intensely as in the priesthood and seminaries. But the priestly culture and seminary life have shown signs of settling down in recent years in a renewed form which will probably be in place for some years. The only major force likely to change it might be pressures from the priest shortage, causing relaxed institutional rules about who is eligible. If this occurs, another period of turbulence will begin. Meanwhile, sociological studies can be a genuine help to church leaders trying to discern the best future for the priesthood.

NOTES

1. For further studies on changes in the priesthod see Fichter (1974), Szafran (1976), and Bishops' Committee on Priestly Life and Ministry (1987). On priests' health see Fichter (1985).

2. For research on psychological characteristics of seminarians see Weisgerber (1977) and Godin (1983). On perseverance rates in seminaries see Lonsway (1972) and Weisgerber (1977). For a review of seminary research see Hoge, Potvin, and Ferry (1984).

REFERENCES

Bishops' Committee on Priestly Life and Ministry. 1987. *A Shepherd's Care: Reflections on the Changing Role of Pastor.* Booklet. Washington, DC: United States Catholic Conference.

Fichter, J. H. 1965. *Priest and People*. New York: Sheed and Ward.

―――――. 1968. *America's Forgotten Priests: What They Are Saying*. New York: Harper and Row.

―――――. 1974. *Organization Man in the Church*. Cambridge, MA: Schenkman.

―――――. 1985. *The Health of American Catholic Priests*. Booklet. Washington, DC: National Conference of Catholic Bishops.

Godin, A. 1983. *The Psychology of Religious Vocations: Problems of the Religious Life*. Translated by L. A. Wauck. Washington, DC: University Press of America.

Hall, D.T., and B. Schneider. 1973. *Organizational Climates and Careers: The Work Lives of Priests*. New York: Seminar Press.

Hemrick, E.F., and D. R. Hoge. 1985. *Seminarians in Theology: A National Profile*. Washington, DC: United States Catholic Conference.

―――――. 1987. *Seminary Life and Visions of the Priesthood: A National Survey of Seminarians*. Washington, DC: National Catholic Educational Association.

Hoge, D. R. 1987. *The Future of Catholic Leadership: Responses to the Priest Shortage*. Kansas City, MO: Sheed and Ward.

Hoge, D. R., R. H. Potvin, and K. M. Ferry. 1984. *Research on Men's Vocations to the Priesthood and the Religious Life*. Washington, DC: United States Catholic Conference.

Hoge, D. R., J. J. Shields, and M. J. Verdieck. 1988. "Changing Age Distribution and Theological Attitudes of Catholic Priests, 1970-1985." *Sociological Analysis* 49:264-280.

Lee, J. M., and L. J. Putz, eds. 1965. *Seminary Education in a Time of Change*. Notre Dame, IN: Fides.

Lonsway, F. A. 1972. *Ministers for Tomorrow: A Longitudinal Study*. Washington, DC: Center for Applied Research in the Apostolate.

National Opinion Research Center. 1972. *The Catholic Priest in the United States: Sociological Investigations*. (A. M. Greeley and R. A. Schoenherr, co-investigators.) Washington, DC: United States Catholic Conference.

Poole, S. 1965. *Seminary in Crisis*. New York: Herder and Herder.

Potvin, R. 1985. *Seminarians of the Eighties: A National Survey*. Washington, DC: National Catholic Educational Association.

Potvin, R., and A. Suziedelis. 1969. *Seminarians of the Sixties*. Washington, DC: Center for Applied Research in the Apostolate.

Sanks, T. H. 1984. "Education for Ministry Since Vatican II." *Theological Studies* 45: 481-500.

Schallert, E. J., and J. M. Kelley. 1970. "Some Factors Associated With Voluntary Withdrawal From the Catholic Priesthood." *Lumen Vitae* 25: 425-460.

Schoenherr, R. A., and A. M. Greeley. 1974. "Role Commitment Processes and the American Catholic Priesthood." *American Sociological Review* 39:407-426.

Schoenherr, R. A., and A. Sorensen. 1982. "Social Change in Religious Organizations: Consequences of the Clergy Decline in the U.S. Catholic Church." *Sociological Analysis* 43:52-71.

Schreiter, R.J. 1985. "Fragmentation and Unity in Theological Education." *Seminaries in Dialogue* (National Catholic Educational Association) 10:2-11.

Schuth, K. 1989. *Reasons for the Hope: The Future of Roman Catholic Theologates*. Wilmington, DE: Michael Glazier.

Seidler, J. and K. Meyer. 1989. *Conflict and Change in the Catholic Church*. New Brunswick, NJ: Rutgers University Press.

Shields, J. J., and M. J. Verdieck. 1985. *Religious Life in the United States: The Experience of Men's Communities*. Ringbound. Washington, DC: Center for Applied Research in the Apostolate.

Stewart, J. H. 1978. *American Catholic Leadership: A Decade of Turmoil 1966-1976*. The Hague: Mouton.

Szafran, R.F. 1976. "The Distribution of Influence in Religious Organizations." *Journal for the Scientific Study of Religion* 15:339-349.

Verdieck, M. J., J. J. Shields, and D. R. Hoge. 1988. "Role Commitment Processes Revisited: American Catholic Priests 1970 and 1985." *Journal for the Scientific Study of Religion* 27:524-535.

Weisgerber, C.A. 1977. *Testing the Seminarian: A Review of Research.* Washington, DC: Center for Applied Research in the Apostolate.

White, J. M. 1986. "American Diocesan Seminaries, 1791 to the 1980s." *Seminaries in Dialogue* (National Catholic Educational Association) 13:16-19.

FULL PEWS AND EMPTY ALTARS:

DEMOGRAPHICS OF U.S. DIOCESAN PRIESTS,

1966-2005

Richard A. Schoenherr and Lawrence A. Young

The two and a half decades since the Second Vatican Council have witnessed steady growth in Catholic church membership, mainly due to favorable demographic dynamics such as heavy immigration, high birth rates and a young age pyramid (Roof and McKinney 1987). The vitality of organized religion, though, depends not only on the growth of church membership, but also on the strength of its internal organization. Ironically, the Catholic church is facing a major organizational crisis since, despite the burgeoning laity, it is currently unable to recruit and retain sufficient priests.

In many ways this is a distinctively Catholic crisis. Recently, Hoge, Carroll, and Scheets (1988) studied parish leadership in Roman Catholicism and three comparable Protestant denominations. They found significant Catholic-Protestant differences in the ratio of clergy to church members. The contrasts they document epitomize one of the fundamental demographic contradictions within American religion today. Catholicism, on the one hand, is experiencing growth in membership but a shrinking priesthood population. Churches within

Religion and the Social Order, Volume 2, pages 85-104.
Copyright © 1991 by JAI Press Inc.
All rights of reproduction in any form reserved.
ISBN: 1-55938-388-7

mainline Protestantism, on the other hand, are characterized by declining church membership but a surplus of clergy.

In this chapter we wish to address the Catholic dilemma of full pews and vacant altars. The goal is to analyze past, current and future trends in the priest shortage. We document the decline in the number of Roman Catholic diocesan priests since the mid 1960s and report the results of demographic projections to 2005. We also alter the projection assumptions to assess future decline if entrances and exits were to improve by 25 percent. In addition, we test the accuracy of the projection models, using four years of recent data from a subsample of dioceses. The presentation begins with an overview of the findings.

HIGHLIGHTS

1.   The data indicate a probable decline of 40 percent in the number of diocesan priests over a 40-year period. The number of active diocesan priests, which stood at 35,000 in 1966, will fall to approximately 21,000 by the year 2005. Priests will be older, with almost half 55 or above and only one-eighth 34 or younger by 2005.

2.   The empirical data in the national study cover only the first 19 years (1966 through 1984) of this 40-year period. Projections were employed for the subsequent years. We devised three separate projections for clergy size: an optimistic, a pessimistic, and a moderate projection; the latter presumes that a certain leveling off of trends, as experienced in the years 1980-84, will continue into the next century. We believe the moderate projection is the most realistic. If the most optimistic assumptions prevail, the number of active diocesan priests in 2005 would be about 23,000, a 34 percent decline since 1966.

3.   The data reveal that the decrease in priestly ordinations is the most significant factor in the overall clergy decline—far more significant than resignations, retirements, or other factors. But analysis showed that if priestly ordinations were to be increased by 25 percent (other conditions remaining the same), the moderate decline in the number of U.S. diocesan priests between 1966 and 2005 would still stand at about 34 percent.

4.   To test these assumptions, trends in 12 dioceses were studied in detail for the years 1985-89, a four-year period beyond that covered by the full national study. The moderate projections are closest to the actual experience in those dioceses. When several other variables are considered as well, it seems likely that the trends currently are falling somewhere between the moderate and pessimistic projections.

DATA AND METHODS

Demographic data were gathered from official archives in a random sample of 86 Roman Catholic dioceses. The six-year project was sponsored by the U. S. Catholic Conference, which greatly facilitated access to sensitive data sources. For each diocese we constructed a population register of diocesan priests (see Shryock, Siegel et al. 1971). The registers contain full names and complete individual level data for all entrances into and exits out of the population of living priests from 1966 through 1984. For the 19-year national register, which is a concatenated file of data from the individual dioceses, $N = 36,370$. Using names in the registers allows us to control for under- and overreporting and to estimate census counts in a consistent fashion regardless of different local methods of recordkeeping.

Names and dates were taken directly from original archival material and were not dependent on the recall of diocesan officials, who, as it turned out, were as eager as we were to produce the most accurate data possible. In addition, we subjected the data files to an extensive series of computer programmed consistency checks. Insistence on historically accurate documents during the multiphase data collection campaign and methodically rigorous cleaning procedures during data processing has resulted in a highly accurate 19-year register of the population under study.

We used standard, and in some instances, modified demographic techniques to estimate the various entrance and attrition rates and to analyze change in size and composition of the clergy population. Projections beyond the last year of observation are based on average numbers of entrances and age-specific attrition rates experienced during the previous years. Techniques used in selecting assumptions for the projections were based on a variety of historical, organizational and statistical considerations described elsewhere (Schoenherr, Young, and Vilarino 1988).

Accordingly, the population projections utilize a mathematical model known as the cohort-component method described in Shryock, Siegel et al. (1971, p. 778). Formulas for the projection model and vital rates are given in a figure and table; major criteria used in determining assumptions for the projections are summarized in the next section. A full discussion of the projection assumptions and further details on methodology are provided in Schoenherr and Young (1990).

MAKING POPULATION PROJECTIONS

We attempt to describe the demographic transition of the clergy for a period of 40 years, only 19 of which are covered by empirical data. We rely on population projections to analyze the remaining 21 years. Admittedly, the plausibility of population projections decreases with each additional year, but forecasts over two decades are by no means useless. They shed light on the consequences of the "what-if" models contained in our projection assumptions. The population theory used in this analysis posits the simple question: What would happen to population size and composition over time if entrances and exits continued at assumed constant levels?

Population analysts increase the plausibility of their projections by hedging their bets. Instead of making one projection we usually make three, based on optimistic, pessimistic, and moderate assumptions. We prefer to describe each set of assumptions and let the reader make the final judgment.

One basic premise governs all the projections to be presented. We presume that the variation, selection, and retention mechanisms that determined the size and shape of the Catholic priesthood population for the past 20 years will continue unchanged for the next 20 years. With the assumption that only Catholic males who will be celibate will be recruited and retained, we constructed three different projection series.

In brief, our optimistic assumptions are based on the best possible interpretation of the historical data, the pessimistic on the worst possible past scenario and the moderate on the current trends in the sampled dioceses. The moderate assumptions are designed to produce a projection curve which falls approximately midway between the optimistic and pessimistic models.

The optimistic projection assumes that the relatively high ordinations and net migrations, on the one hand, and low resignations and retirements, on the other, experienced during specific years between 1966 and 1985, will dominate in the future. Furthermore, if any of these events showed consistent trends toward even more optimistic levels in the future than experienced in the past, estimates of their 1990-94 levels are used. The pessimistic projection assumes the opposite, namely, the relatively low ordinations and net migrations, and relatively high resignations and retirements that occurred during certain other past years are likely to continue in the years ahead. Similarly, if any of these events showed consistent movement toward more pessimistic levels, estimates of their 1990-94 levels are used.

The moderate projection or middle-of-the-road model results from assuming that the level of ordinations, net migrations, resignations and retirements occurring in 1980-84 will continue more or less unchanged from 1985 until the turn of the century. The assumptions about future death rates are based on life expectancy for white males in the United States produced from national census data; we use the same mortality assumptions for the optimistic, moderate and pessimistic models. Based on our reading of the data and understanding of the Catholic church in the United States, we make a few other reasonable adjustments to these assumptions. The modifications are described in Schoenherr and Young (1990).

An important caveat: Our population projections do not predict the future. They are merely forecasts of past trends based on reasonable assumptions. The forecasts in this chapter should be assessed carefully and used wisely.

CHANGE IN POPULATION SIZE, 1966-2005

Figure 1 shows the size of the active diocesan priest population for the United States from 1966 through 1984 and projections to the year 2005. In one sweep, the graph reports the changes in the number of priests during the first 19 years after the close of the Second Vatican Council and the most likely changes for the next two decades. Nationally, the long-term loss is apparent from the steep descending curve.

According to the top line on the right side of the figure, even under optimistic assumptions, the U.S. priesthood population would probably show a substantial loss in the four-decade period under study. The number of active diocesan priests in 2005 will be about 23,000, over 34 percent fewer than the 35,000 recorded for 1966. The bottom curve shows that if the pessimistic assumptions hold true, the average loss across the country would cut the population by more than half, reaching close to 53 percent between 1966 and 2005, with numbers of about 16,700.

The moderate assumptions are calculated to fall approximately midway between the optimistic and pessimistic extremes, which means, as Figure 1 shows, a drop of about 40 percent in the national population as a whole and thus the average diocese. If the trends of the early to mid 1980s continue—from which the moderate assumptions are taken—the number of active diocesan priests in 2005 will be slightly over 21,000.

CHANGE IN AGE DISTRIBUTION, 1966-2005

Figure 2 illustrates the changing age distribution of active diocesan priests at five-year intervals (the first is a four-year period because our historical data begin in 1966). The projected ages, which begin with 1985, are based on the moderate entrance and attrition assumptions. The moderate assumptions posit that declining ordinations would level off in 1985. As a consequence, the data for age composition presented in the figure may be somewhat optimistic if the drop in ordinations has not yet bottomed out.

As the first bar-graph in the figure and Column 1 in the accompanying chart show, U.S. dioceses, on the average, enjoyed a fairly well-balanced age distribution in 1966, with 21 percent of the active priests below age 35 and 29 percent age 55 or older. By 1985, the end of the census period, the average clergy population had aged notably with only about 10 percent in the youngest and 41 percent in the most senior age group. If the moderate assumptions hold

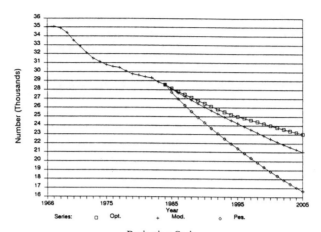

Series: □ Opt.   + Mod.   ◇ Pes.

Projection Series

Year	Optimistic	Current	Pessimistic
1966	—	35,070	—
1970	—	33,523	—
1975	—	30,785	—
1980	—	29,633	—
1985	28.141	28,077	27,721
1986	27,783	27,645	26,962
1987	27,444	27,236	26,247
1988	27,109	26,834	25,562
1989	26,779	26,442	24,909
1990	26,454	26,062	24,288
1995	25,017	24,230	21,421
2000	23,983	22,511	18,852
2005	23,040	21,030	16,653

Notes: [a]Census counts for 1966-84; projections based on optimistic, moderate, and pessimistic series for 1985-2005.

Projection model:

$$X_{ij} = [X_{i-1,\, j-1} + (A_{j-1}/2)](1-S_{j-1}) + (A_{j-1}/2)$$

Where:

X_{ij} is the age-specific population at the beginning of the year for age-group j in year i; A_{j-1} is the additions to age-group j-1; and S_{j-1} is the survival probability for age-group j-1.

And:

$$A_{j-1} = N_{j-1} + O_{j-1} + I_{j-1}$$

Where:

N_{j-1} is a number of returns from leaves of absence for age-group j-1; O_{j-1} is number of ordinations for age-group j-1; and I_{j-1} is number of incardinations for age-group j-1.

And:

$$S_{j-1} = (R_{j-1})\,(E_{j-1})(T_{j-1})(D_{j-1})(L_{j-1})$$

Where:

R_{j-1} is the resignation survival probability for age-group j-1; E_{j-1} is the excardination survival probability for age group j-1; T_{j-1} is the retirement survival probability for age-group j-1; D_{j-1} is the death survival probability for age group j-1; and L_{j-1} is the leave of absence survival probability for age-group j-1.

Figure 1.   Size of U.S. Diocesan Priest Population, 1966-2005[a]

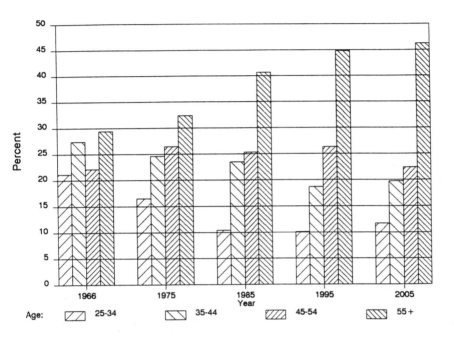

	Year				
Age	1966	1975	1985	1995	2005
25-34	21	16	10	10	12
35-44	27	25	23	19	20
45-54	22	26	25	26	22
55-64	18	21	26	26	28
65-74	8	10	13	17	16
75+	3	1	1	2	2

Note: [a]Census counts for 1966-75; projections based on moderate series for 1985-2005; see Figure 1 for projection model.

Figure 2. Age Distribution of U.S. Diocesan Priest Population, 1966-2005[a]

true to 2005, the imbalance in the national age distribution will increase considerably. Nearly half the active priests in the United States would be 55 or older while just a little over one-eighth would be under 35.

The dominant trend in the U.S. diocesan priesthood is one of movement from a young to an old population but with notable variations in the extent and speed of the change among individual dioceses. If trends persist, however, the percentage of younger priests eventually will begin to grow again, but during the process the numbers will continue to decline.

TOTAL PRIESTHOOD POPULATION

The data so far have been limited to active priests but the growing numbers of retired and semi-active clergy in the United States raise the question of how different the age composition of the total priest population is from that of the active clergy. Table 1 summarizes the same data presented in Figure 2 for active priests, includes comparable data for the total population, but uses mean and median age instead of the full age distribution.

Examining average age at the beginning, middle and end of the period reveals the amount of change that has occurred. First of all, differences between the mean age (arithmetic average) and median age (half the population is above and half below) reflect changes in the shape of the age pyramid as a population gets older. Thus, in 1966 the median is lower than the mean age, indicating a young population with a triangle-shaped pyramid. By 1985, the mean and median are practically identical, showing that the pyramid is beehive-shaped because the population is aging. In 2005, the median is higher than the mean, indicating an old population with an inverted triangle shape.

Table 1.   Mean and Median Age of Active and
All U.S. Diocesan Priests, 1966-2005[a]

	Year								
	1966	*1970*	*1975*	*1980*	*1985*	*1990*	*1995*	*2000*	*2005*
Mean									
Active	46.8	47.0	48.2	49.3	50.7	51.5	52.0	52.1	51.9
All	47.6	48.6	50.7	52.4	53.6	54.4	55.1	55.4	55.6
Median									
Active	45	46	47	49	51	52	53	53	53
All	46	47	50	52	54	55	56	56	57

Note: [a]Census counts for 1966-80; projections based on moderate series for 1985-2005; see Figure 1 for projection model.

Obviously, the active population is always younger than the total population. The gap, however, has been widening since the end of the Second Vatican Council. In 1966, the difference between the active and total population for both mean and median age was only one year and by 1985 it had grown to three years. In 2005, the mean and median age for the total population will be four years older than for the active priest population.

The age difference between active and total population is widening because the proportion of retired, sick and absent priests has been growing. In 1966, only 3.4 percent of U.S. priests were categorized as retired, sick or absent; by 1985 the proportion had increased almost fivefold, reaching 15.7 percent. In 2005, the retired, sick and absent category will account for 20.1 percent of the total priest population in the country.

Citing the median age is a more accurate indication of the age distribution when a population is very young or very old. In 1990, the median age of active U.S. priests was 52 and of all priests it was 55. By 2005, we project the median age of active priests will be 53 and that of the total population 57. Thus, between the beginning and end of the study period, the median age of active priests has gone up eight years and that of the total priesthood population 11 years.

MAJOR COMPONENTS OF GROWTH AND DECLINE

We have identified five entrance and six exit events that together determine the size and age composition of the priesthood population. A priest enters or re-enters the active clergy by ordination, incardination or return to active duty after a period of resignation, sick leave or awaiting assignment. He may exit from the active population by excardination, resignation, sick leave, awaiting assignment, retirement or, finally, death. The data displayed in Table 2 present the annual entrance, exit and net growth rates for the country over the census period. The rates give the average annual number of entrances or exits per 100 active priests and so can be read as percentages of the active population.

Entrance Rates

Examining Row 1 of the table, we see that annual ordination rates dropped sharply from 2.8 percent in the late 1960s to 1.8 percent in the early 1980s. The results shown in the last column indicate that, over the 19 years, the country experienced ordinations equalling 39 percent of the 1966 number of active priests.

The imbalance of incardinations over excardinations, or net migration, also played an important role in altering the U.S. clergy population. The surplus of incardinands over excardinands comes from either religious orders or foreign dioceses, because in the U.S. presbyterate each loss through

Table 2. Growth and Decline Rates of U.S. Diocesan Priest Population,
1966-84[a]; by Year and Transition Event
(Number of entrances or exits per 100 active priests)[b]

	Average Annual Rate			
Event	*1966-69*	*1970-74*	*1975-79*	*1980-84*	*Percent Gross Change 1966-84[c]*
Entrance					
Ordination	2.82	2.32	2.21	1.77	38.77
Incardination	0.22	0.41	0.60	0.67	8.18
Other entrance[d]	0.10	0.15	0.20	0.23	2.89
Exit					
Resignation	1.32	1.71	0.85	0.65	19.50
Excardination	0.08	0.18	0.30	0.37	3.97
Retirement	1.40	1.49	1.56	1.59	25.77
Death	1.19	0.94	0.77	0.77	15.58
Other exit[e]	0.27	0.28	0.30	0.29	4.86
Net decline	−1.13	−1.71	−0.77	−0.99	−19.84

Notes: [a]Crude rates based on census counts; formulas in order of appearance are as follows:

$$(O/P)k; \qquad (I/P)k; \qquad (N/P)k; \qquad (R/P)k;$$
$$(E/P)k; \qquad (T/P)k; \qquad (D/P)k; \qquad (L/P)k;$$
$$[(O + I + N - R - E - T - D - L)/P]k.$$

Where: O is the number of ordinations, I of incardinations, N of returns from leaves, R of resignations, E of excardinations, T of retirements, D of deaths, and L the number of leaves of absence during the calendar year; P is the total population of active incardinated priests at the beginning of the calendar year; and k is 100.
[b]Number of priests registered in the 19-year national census: 36,370.
[c]Using 1966 base figures and the cumulative numbers of entrance and exit events for numerators.
[d]Returns from sick leave, awaiting assignment and resignation.
[e]Sick leave and awaiting assignment.

excardination in one diocese is matched by a gain through incardination in another.

If we subtract excardination from incardination rates, as they appear in the table, we discover that the diocesan priest population experienced a gross increase through changes in affiliation because the cumulative difference is positive: 4.2 percent during roughly two decades. This accounted for over one-fifth of the population change that occurred.

If there had been no surplus incardinations, the overall decline in the national population between 1966 and 1984 would have been 24 percent rather than 20 percent. Thus, gains through incardinations are dampening the average clergy decline in the United States as a whole. In a further analysis we document that clergy migration is producing a notable gross increase in only certain regions and dioceses (Schoenherr and Young 1990).

In addition, leaves of absence and returns to active duty are important. Subtracting leave rates (labeled Other Exit in the table) from return rates (Other Entrance) produces a net decline, since the differences are negative.

The negative difference between the cumulative gain from returns and the cumulative loss from leaves, given in the last cell of Rows 8 and 3, respectively, is 2.0. Because the overall loss between 1966 and 1984 from all entrance and exit events was just under 20 percent, this 2 percent loss accounted for about one-tenth of the decline.

Thus, the effect on population change in the average U.S. diocese of both types of movement—immigration and leave—has been noteworthy.

Exit Rates

The period under study began with notably high attrition through resignations as the data in the fourth row of the table indicate. The exodus of American priests peaked at an annual rate of 1.7 percent during the early 1970s and then dropped in the early 1980s to a level only half as high as at the beginning of the census. The figure in Row 4, Column 5 reports that the resignation drain averaged a gross national loss of almost 20 percent in 19 years. Recruitment and retention both changed significantly during the period under observation. Ordinations dropped by about two-fifths while resignations were cut in half.

The overall picture is affected heavily not only by resignation from the active ministry but also by retirement and death. Table 2 reveals that retirement and death rates among the U.S. active clergy showed opposite tendencies since the mid 1960s. The number of retirements per 100 active priests rose steadily between 1966 and 1984 while deaths per 100 active priests declined notably.

Two explanations help account for these differences. First, retirement was a relatively new avenue of exit for U.S. priests after the Second Vatican Council, which closed in 1965. Although many dioceses had a large pool of priests who qualified for retirement at that time, formal programs had to be developed before those who were ready could retire. As a result, during the late 1960s most deaths occurred while the elderly priests were still categorized as active, thereby inflating preretirement mortality rates and deflating retirement rates.

Second, over the last two decades the life expectancy of U.S. white males has been increasing. So by the end of our census, fewer priests were dying before the age of retirement than at the beginning of the period. During the early years of the census, the combination of both situations artificially raised death rates among the active clergy and set retirement rates lower than expected.

Comparing the statistics in Rows 6 and 7 of the table shows that, throughout the entire census period, exits from the active clergy through retirement were higher than those through death. As the final column confirms, the decline for 1966-84 attributable to retirements was 25.8 percent while the loss through preretirement deaths was only 15.6 percent.

Overall Decline

The net gain or loss from all transition events is displayed in the bottom row of the table. Each five-year period showed net loss, with the average annual rate peaking at 1.7 percent in the early 1970s. The rate was notably less severe in the late 1970s but began to rise again in the first half of the 1980s.

High resignations accounted substantially for the early period of decline while low ordinations, sustained resignations and rising retirements can be blamed for the more recent period of loss. The decline may have been dampened, at least temporarily, by more favorable death rates experienced among white males in the United States.

ALTERING THE CHANGE PROCESS

Organizations have limited options in the face of declining recruitment and retention. Hoge (1987) lists them as threefold. Church leaders could reduce the need for priests, get more priests or expand lay ministry. Our empirical models permit us to explore only the second option, increasing the number of active priests.

Let us examine each element of the change process and ask which ones are the most powerful forces. Entrance and exit rates define the change process. Would increasing ordinations or net migrations slow down the decline more than reducing the number of resignations or retirements? To answer this question we designed a "what-if" experiment based on alternative scenarios of raising entrances and lowering exits by 25 percent. The base period for the experiment was 1980-84, because these years represent the "current" trends which have been incorporated in the moderate projections.

In a series of experimental models we compare what would happen if trends continue at the 1980-84 levels with what would happen if all but one of the transition events continue at those levels. In each scenario only one transition event is assumed to go up or down. Table 3 displays the size of the population when projected under the original and the altered assumptions, the percent change in size and the percent difference in the amount of change. The top rows of Sections 1 and 2 establish a base for the comparisons.

Thus, for example, the original model based on moderate assumptions projected that the size of the diocesan clergy population in 1995 would be 24,230. If, however, ordinations were to increase by 25 percent, clergy size would be considerably higher—25,497. Under all assumptions, population size

Table 3. Size of U.S. Diocesan Priest Population
Based on Original and Altered Projection Assumptions,
Percent Change from 1985 and Percent Difference
Between Change; by Year and Transition Event

		Year		
Assumption	*Event*	*1995*	*2005*	*2015*
		Size		
Original		24,230	21,030	19,050
Altered	Ordination (+ 25%)	25,497	23,195	21,917
	Net migration (+ 25)	24,446	21,395	19,500
	Resignation (− 25%)	24,614	21,607	19,713
	Retirement (− 25%)	24,822	21,660	19,592
		Percent Change		
		(From Jan. 1, 1985)[a]		
Original		14.2	25.5	32.5
Altered	Ordination (+ 25%)	9.7	17.9	22.4
	Net migration.(+ 25%)	13.4	24.2	30.9
	Resignation (− 25%)	12.8	23.5	30.2
	Retirement (− 25%)	12.1	23.3	30.6
		Percent Difference		
		(Between original and		
		altered percent change)[b]		
Altered	Ordination (+ 25%)	31.7	29.8	31.1
	Net migration (+ 25%)	5.6	5.1	4.9
	Resignation (− 25%)	9.9	7.8	7.1
	Retirement (− 25%)	14.8	8.6	5.8

Notes: [a]Size of active priest population on this date: 28,240; thus, percent change between 1985 and 1995 based on original assumptions is $(1 - (24,230 / 28,240)) *100 = 14.2$
[b]Scores are the difference between percent change based on original assumptions given in Row 1, Section 2, and percent change based on altered assumptions given in the other rows of Section 2.

grows smaller with each passing decade. So in Section 2, the top row of data shows that, according to our original moderate assumptions, the 1985 national priest population would decrease about 14 percent by 1995, 26 percent by 2005, and 33 percent by 2015.

Comparing statistics in the other rows of Section 2 demonstrates that ordinations are the most powerful force for change. Increasing the number of ordinations by 25 percent would curb the decline between 1985 and 1995 considerably. Instead of a 14 percent loss, the size of the average diocesan clergy would decrease by less than 10 percent, as the data in Row 2 for that year show. Altering assumptions for the other transition events would, nevertheless, still result in a 12 percent or 13 percent decline, according to the remaining figures in the column.

The bottom section of the table summarizes the contrasts. The scores are the percent difference between original and altered percent change. Thus the difference between the 1995 projected percent decline based on the original assumptions (14.2 percent) and that based on the altered assumption of increased ordinations (9.7 percent) is 31.7 percent.

That is to say, if all other trends occurred as projected but ordinations were one-fourth higher than the number used in our moderate projection model, the clergy decline between 1985 and 1995 would be about 32 percent less than originally projected. Not surprisingly, therefore, ordinations have the most powerful impact of any event tested in the experiment.

Retirements would have the next strongest impact. A similar decrease in retirements would lower the decline by almost 15 percent. Altering net migrations would have the least effect. Raising the net gain of incardinations over excardinations would retard the decline by less than 6 percent.

The bottom section of the table shows the effects of altering each of the entrance and exit trends over time. Raising the number of ordinations remains the most powerful force, but the impact is constant throughout the projection period, as Row 1 indicates. On the other hand, because age composition is also changing over time (as Figure 2 has demonstrated), the cumulative impact of lowering resignation and retirement rates would change apace. While the population is aging, reducing the rate of retirement would be more effective than reducing the rate of resignation because priests reaching retirement age are increasing while age brackets in which the risk of resignation is highest are decreasing.

Thus, comparing scores in Rows 3 and 4 shows that those for retirement are higher in 1995 and 2005 than those for resignation. By 2005, however, the proportion of younger priests would begin to grow, as our models predict. When the population is growing younger, the comparative impact of retirements and resignations is reversed.

So by 2015, reductions in resignations, which would lower the decline by 7 percent, would do more to dampen the decline than reductions in retirements, because the latter would slow it only about 6 percent. Although the differences are not large, reducing retirement has the greater short-term impact and reducing resignations the greater long-term impact on overall decline. The consequences of increasing the gain from incardinations remain the smallest, hovering around 5 percent for the entire period.

Without a doubt, increasing ordinations would have three to four times greater impact on checking the decline by 2005 than altering the next most powerful transition events, namely resignations and retirements.

Under the most likely scenario, based on our original moderate assumptions, the American diocesan priest population will decline 40 percent between 1966 and 2005. Under a 25 percent more optimistic ordination scenario, the moderate decline would still be almost 34 percent.

PLAUSIBILITY OF PROJECTIONS

The historical data used in this study are highly accurate because they were provided by reliable sources and subjected to meticulous verification and correction procedures. Projections, however, are based on assumptions that are more or less reasonable and must be evaluated carefully.

The single most important component of the model, in determining future trends, is the ordination assumption. Bear in mind that two decades of sustained seminarian decline have reduced the number of priest candidates enrolled in U.S. theologates by 58 percent. Between 1965 and 1989 the numbers dropped from 8,885 to 3,698 and it appears the decline is yet to bottom out (Catholic News Service 1990). So we see little probability that population size of the national clergy population will rise above the curve projected in Figure 1 by the moderate assumptions.

Test of Competing Assumptions

In our design, the historical period ends December 31, 1984, and projections begin January 1, 1985. Thus, as we neared the final stage of the U.S. Catholic Conference research project, dioceses already had experienced an additional four years of population change against which to check the plausibility of the competing assumptions. So we subsampled 12 dioceses, contacted our liaison persons and asked them to provide additional data covering January 1, 1985, to January 1, 1989. All 12 agreed to cooperate.

The subsample was drawn from a set of 48 dioceses in the original sample where data fluctuation during the census period was not excessive. The size of their combined active priest populations in 1966 was 3,737 which, when weighted according to sampling probabilities, represented 6,793 priests or 19 percent of the 35,070 active in the United States that year (see Figure 1).

As Table 4 demonstrates, however, the subsample overrepresents large dioceses in the Northeast, ignores small dioceses altogether and underrepresents dioceses in the West. During the analysis we discovered that the small and the newly established dioceses, which are also small, experienced irregular growth and/or decline during the historical period. As a result, their projections

Table 4.   Comparison of Full Sample and Subsample
of Dioceses; by Size and Region
(Percent)

	Full Sample[a]	Sub Sample[b]
Size (1968)		
Small (1-100)	30	0
Medium (101-200)	26	33
Large (201-500)	27	50
Extra Large (500+)	17	17
Total	100	100
Region		
New England	8	25
Middle Atlantic	16	25
East Northcentral	17	25
West Northcentral	16	0
Mountain	7	0
Pacific	12	8
East South[c]	7	8
West Southcentral	16	8
Total	99	100

Notes: [a] $N = 89$
[b] $N = 12$
[c] Combines South Atlantic and one diocese from the East Southcentral region.

were also wildly inconsistent. We therefore decided they would not provide an appropriate test and designed the subsample accordingly.

The regional imbalance in the subsample simply reflects that dioceses in the Northeastern part of the country experienced less extreme fluctuations in their data than those in other regions. We believe the subsample provides an appropriate test of our projections.

Results

Numbers.   The projection results for the 12 dioceses are summarized in Table 5. Column 1 gives census counts of active priests at five-year intervals until 1985 and at one-year intervals through 1989. The next three columns give the projected numbers under optimistic, moderate and pessimistic assumptions, beginning with one-year intervals through 1990 (to allow comparison with the new data) and then continuing with five-year intervals until 2005. Focusing

Table 5. Size of Diocesan Priest Population in
Subsample of Twelve Dioceses, 1966-2005

| | | Projection Series | | |
| | Census | | | |
Year	Counts	Optimistic	Moderate	Pessimistic
1966	6,793			
1970	6,505			
1975	5,869			
1980	5,736			
1985	5,373	5,489	5,366	5,289
1986	5,289	5,509	5,269	5,123
1987	5,233	5,534	5,185	4,967
1988	5,166	5,549	5,100	4,820
1989	5,133	5,561	5,019	4,679
1990	—	5,561	4,935	4,541
1995	—	5,310	4,547	3,913
2000	—	4,729	4,174	3,375
2005	—	4,496	3,865	2,939

on the data for 1989, we discover in Column 1 that the updated census recorded 5,133 priests in the 12-diocese subsample; our moderate projection for the same 12 dioceses, shown in Column 3 forecasted 5,019. Thus, the true curve falls very close to the moderate but between the moderate and optimistic projections. The population size recorded in the updated census numbers is only 2.2 percent higher than the moderate projection, so we conclude our projection models are reasonably accurate.

Rates. Comparing the annual ordination rate for 1980-84 shown in Row 1 of Table 6 with that for 1985-88 indicates that ordinations continued to decline, as expected. During 1980-84, there were 1.7 ordinations per 100 active priests per year and during 1985-88 there were only 1.5.

Likewise, annual immigration dropped considerably in the dioceses of the subsample during the 1980s, from 0.25 during the first half of the decade to only 0.14 immigrations per 100 active priests during the last half.

Because ordinations declined notably (about 10 percent from the early to the late 1980s) and immigrations dropped as well (about 44 percent during the same period), one would expect the actual decline curve to have fallen below the moderate projection curve instead of above it. Obviously, therefore, the lower entrance rates have been matched by lower exit rates, as the remaining transition statistics in the same two columns reveal.

Table 6. Growth and Decline Rates in Subsample
of Twelve Dioceses, 1966-89
(Number of entrances or exits per 100 active priests)

Event	*Average Annual Rates*					*Percent Gross Change*[a]	
	1966-69	*1970-74*	*1975-79*	*1980-84*	*1985-88*	*1966-84*	*1966-89*
Entrance							
Ordination[b]	2.85	2.39	2.31	1.69	1.51	39.10	–
Immigration[c]	0.15	0.27	0.26	0.25	0.14	3.99	–
Exit							
Resignation[b]	1.28	1.89	0.69	0.68	0.66	19.49	–
Retirement[b]	1.57	1.74	1.62	1.68	1.51	28.09	–
Death[b]	1.11	0.98	0.66	0.74	0.50	14.72	–
Net leave[d]	0.17	0.10	0.10	0.16	0.09	2.22	–
Net decline	−1.11	−2.05	−0.50	−1.32	−1.11	−21.43	−24.4

Notes: [a]Using 1966 figures for denominators and the cumulative numbers of entrance and exit events for
1966-84 and 1966-89 for numerators.
[b]See note [a] in Table 2, for formula.
[c]Incardination rate minus excardination rate; see note [a] in Table 2, for formulas of these rates.
[d]Leave rate minus return rate; see note [a] in Table 2, for formulas of these rates.

Although resignations in the subsample remained practically constant
throughout the decade, retirements dropped 10 percent during the 1980s,
deaths among active priests almost 33 percent, and leaves 44 percent, as a
comparison of figures in Columns 4 and 5 demonstrates. The impact of this
offsets the entrance figures, thus creating a population size slightly above that
forecasted by our moderate projection model. Note, however, the seeming
advantage is short-term because, as we learned from Table 1 and Figure 2,
the priest population throughout most of the United States continues to age
rapidly. Hence, rising retirement rates in future years are inevitable. Even if
retirement age is postponed, rising death rates in an aging population are
certain. Dioceses can put a damper on extended leaves, but that produces
relatively small gains in the active work force.

The final row and column of the table present the results of entrances and
exits during the roughly three decades studied. The annual net loss in the 12
dioceses peaked at two priests per 100 during the early 1970s, declined during
the late 1970s to an average of one-half per 100 and then rose again to well
over one priest per 100 throughout the 1980s.

Thus, the assumed decline, which we incorporated into our moderate
projection assumptions, continued to occur for the four years covered by our
additional data. In the average diocese of the subsample, the active priest

population at the beginning of 1989 was only about three-fourths its size in 1966, as the final statistic in the table demonstrates. The fact that decline continued as we assumed it would, lends credence to the projection models.

Caveat. A caution is in order when relating these findings in a complete way to the full national sample. Because, as we said, the subsample is not entirely representative (see Table 4), we can expect that the change process in the full sample will differ slightly from that of the subsample. The degree of difference cannot be measured, because data for 1985-88 are not available for the full sample. It is most probable, however, that the combined retirement and death rates in the full sample are going up in both the short and long run and not down, as they are in the short run for the subsample, simply because of the rapid-aging trend.

It is also probable that the declining trend in ordinations documented in the subsample is being experienced in the average diocese of the full sample— though, perhaps, not to the same degree—because the dioceses overrepresented by the subsample contain a much higher proportion of the clergy than the dioceses that are underrepresented. Thus, it is likely that the true curve for the 1989 national priest population would be very close to that for our moderate projections but might even fall between the moderate and the pessimistic projection curves.

The test has proven that the techniques used in the projection models for the 12 dioceses are accurate and reasonable. There is little doubt that the methods used in the projection models for the full national sample are equally accurate and reasonable—at least for the first four years of the projection period. Of course, new empirical data on ordinations, migrations and resignations become available each year. So observers will be able to reassess the accuracy of our assumptions periodically.

CONCLUSION

Since the close of the Second Vatican Council, structural innovation and change in the Catholic church has been the order of the day (Greeley 1977; Seidler and Meyer 1989). The ensuing years have also attested to steady growth in the Catholic lay population. In contrast, our data document unprecedented losses in size and rapid aging of the U. S. diocesan priesthood population during the same period.

Among the several dynamic forces of change noted in other chapters, our research calls attention, above all, to the decline in sheer numbers of ordained priests. We contend that the diminishing size of the priesthood population is the major driving force for social change in the waning years of the millennium. It is the growing priest shortage, primarily, but also in interaction with other preconditions for structural transformation, that is changing the face of the

U.S. Catholic church. Further conflict and change are inevitable as the contrasting demographic forces affecting priesthood and laity accelerate on their collision course.

REFERENCES

Catholic News Service. 1990. "U.S. Seminarian Number Down for Fifth Year in a Row." *The Catholic Herald: Diocese of Madison* (February 8), p. 10.

Greeley, A.M. 1977. *The American Catholic: A Social Portrait.* New York: Basic Books.

Hoge, D.R. 1987. *Future of Catholic Leadership: Response to the Priest Shortage.* Kansas City, MO: Sheed and Ward.

Hoge, D., J.W. Carroll, and F.K. Scheets, OSC. 1988. *Patterns of Parish Leadership: Cost and Effectivness in Four Denominations.* Kansas City, MO: Sheed and Ward.

Roof, W. C., and W. McKinney. 1987. *American Mainline Religion: Its Changing Shape and Future.* New Brunswick, NJ: Rutgers University Press.

Schoenherr, R.A., L.A. Young, and J.P. Vilarino. 1988. "Demographic Transitions in Religious Organizations: A Comparative Study of Priest Decline in Catholic Dioceses." *The Journal for the Scientific Study of Religion* 27:499-523.

Schoenherr, R.A., and L.A. Young. 1990. *The Catholic Priest in the United States: Demographic Investigations.* Madison, WI: Comparative Religious Organization Studies Publications, University of Wisconsin-Madison.

Seidler, J., and K. Meyer. 1989. *Conflict and Change in the Catholic Church.* New Brunswick, NJ: Rutgers University Press.

Shryock, H.S., J.S. Siegel et al. 1981. *The Methods and Materials of Demography.* 2 Vols. Washington, DC: U.S. Government Printing Office.

AMERICAN SISTERS:
ORGANIZATIONAL AND VALUE CHANGES

Marie Augusta Neal, S.N.D.

The *Decree on Renewal of Religious Life,* one of the sixteen documents of
the Second Vatican Council (Flannery 1975), mandated all institutes of women
and men living the vowed life in the Catholic church to engage in a pervasive
review of "the constitutions, directories, books of customs, of ceremonies" that
these be "properly revised" (Vatican Council II 1965, section 3, p. 3), to bring
them into line with the other documents of the Council. It would be a mistake
to assume that all the changes that have occurred in the past twenty-five years
in the organizational structure of women's religious institutes and in the
members' refocused perspective on ministry are a direct function of their
response to this decree on renewal. It would be equally erroneous, however,
to assume that this conciliar mandate to update structures had no significant
influence on the changes.

Between 1965 and 1990 I have surveyed the Catholic women in Institutes of
Religious Life three times: in 1967, 1980, and 1989. The first survey was a complete
population study to which 139,691 sisters responded, 88 percent of all those
contacted (Neal 1970/1971, 1971). The second survey, in 1980, was a stratified
random sample of 3,740 sisters drawn from 20 congregations on the basis of

Religion and the Social Order, Volume 2, pages 105-121.
Copyright © 1991 by JAI Press Inc.
All rights of reproduction in any form reserved.
ISBN: 1-55938-388-7

the congregation's pre- and post-Vatican Council belief scores as expressed by them in the 1967 survey. These scores were scaled and divided into five categories from very low to very high. The random sample was then drawn from each fifth. That survey, therefore, provides comparative data by religious belief.[1] The third survey (1989) was sent to a random sample of 3000 sisters selected from all congregations to which 74 percent (2140) responded.

This paper examines the organizational and value changes expressed in these three membership surveys which span the twenty-five years since the end of the Second Vatican Council. My objective is to analyze whether or not there is any significant causal link between religious belief and organizational structure.

CHANGES IN FOCUS OF RELIGIOUS LIFE

The vowed life has taken several characteristic forms throughout the history of Western society. The desert fathers gave advice to those who came out to see them; the monasteries, witness to the discipline of community life; the mendicants, the affirmation of serious philosophical and theological reflection; the apostolic orders, a call to alleviate the results of poverty; and the teaching communities, especially in the United States, to preparing the children of immigrants for responsible societal participation. The new ecclesial emphasis, however, is directly on human liberation for third world peoples (Cada 1979; Donovan 1989; Neal 1990; Nessan 1989).

For this mission, clearly articulated in *Populorum Progressio* (Paul VI 1967) and mandated by Vatican II in the *Pastoral Constitution on the Church in the Modern World* (Vatican Council II 1975a), the highly institutionalized life sisters were living in convents, schools, hospitals, and social service agencies was inadequate. Examined in the context of social structure and social change, it revealed itself as too conventionalized and restricted for effective participation in the transformation of the world that the Vatican Council's special option for the poor in global perspective called for. (See *Synodal Document on Justice in the World* [Synod of Bishops 1971, section 6].) The new social emphasis in religious belief suggested new forms of organization for life and action.

But fulfillment of the Church's mandate was not the only pressure to change which influenced religious congregations of Catholic women in the mid-1960s. There were pressures from a new professionalism stemming from formal educational upgrading in their preparation for ministry and from the consequential closer contact with life outside the convent structure. But here we will focus on the belief factor to determine the strength of its impact. From shortly after World War II, the Catholic church's search for God moved in a transition at once philosophical and theological from the transcendent to the immanent, that is, from seeking God outside of society and thus leaving its structure intact, to seeking God within the activity of daily life, in the lives and struggles of peoples (Ferree 1951; Nessan 1989; Suhard 1948).

The changed focus of the church from charity to social justice began to appear in theological writings after World War II, as sociological understanding of the co-optation of religion by entrenched interests in society spread (see Chenu 1957; Congar 1965; deLubac 1956). Specific concerns included: the use of the atomic bomb to end World War II, the continuation of racial segregation in American society, and the failure to effect the redistribution of world resources in the newly discovered poverty areas of the globe no longer remote, thanks to developing access through communication media and contact with third world missionaries. As expressed in his famous encyclical, *Pacem in Terris*, Pope John XXIII (1963) proclaimed that peace, poverty, and human rights are now the central concerns of the committed Christian.

As we review the process of change which culminated in Pope John's unequivocal statement, we see that the perhaps well-intentioned though ill-advised pre-conciliar emphasis has moved away from exhorting the advantaged elite to give of their largesse to the poor, to encouraging the poor as they organize themselves to claim their rights as human beings (Neal 1987). This startling ethic of common ownership was reintroduced in Vatican II: "When a person is in extreme necessity he has the right to supply himself with what he needs out of the riches of others" (Vatican Council II 1975a, section 69, p. 975), and footnoted with an even more explicit text from the writings of St. Thomas Aquinas in the thirteenth century: "In case of need all things are common property so that there would seem to be no sin in taking another's property; for need has made it common."[2]

People in third world countries in Christian Base Communities grappled with this new understanding of the gospel. They meditated, organized and acted to claim their rights (Berryman 1984; Cardenal 1976; Nessan 1989). At the same time, the first world religious congregations of women, inspired by the same mission expressed in the late 1960s as "an option for the poor," took the invitation of the *Decree on Renewal of Religious Life* as a directive to incorporate into their own organizational structure, rules and liturgy to respond to this mission.

RELIGIOUS BELIEFS

In each of the Sisters' Surveys the research design incorporated a measure of religious belief developed from a content analysis of significant contemporary church documents. In 1967, using the Vatican Council as the dividing line, the instrument developed was drawn from the writings of theologians defined at

Table 1.   Pre-Vatican and Post-Vatican Belief Items

		Percent Agreeing		
Item	*Theme*	*Y'67*	*Y'80*	*Y'89*
Pre-Vatican				
306	Chastity is the renunciation of all partial loves in order to embrace the perfection of love in a mystical union with Christ.	37	32	31
308	Vowed poverty means dependence on superiors, such that the use of all things falls under the authority and control of those who are set over the common life.	40	8	11
310	A truly obedient religious need seek no source other than her Rule and the will of her superiors to know what she should do.	31	9	11
312	Christians should look first to the salvation of their souls; then they should be concerned with helping others.	48	25	25
313	"Alone with the great Alone" expresses well to me the idea of God and the ideal of perfection.	20	9	13
315	A good way to explain the church is to explain the relationship of the pope to the bishops and of these to the priests, religious and laity.	25	14	16
317	I feel that the most important thing to realize about the sacraments is that they are channels for receiving grace.	54	42	50
319	The best contribution sisters can make to world problems is to pray about them.	30	17	19
322	I think of heaven as the state in which my soul will rest in blissful possession of the Beatific Vision	55	34	41
324	What my daily work consists of matters little, since I see it as a way to gain merit for heaven.	43	19	21
Averages		38.3%	21%	24%

Post-Vatican

307	The traditional way of presenting chastity in religious life has allowed for the development of isolation and false mysticism among sisters.	65	55	51
309	This generation of religious is being asked to rediscover evangelical poverty. This means a realistic search for ways to be meaningfully and lovingly poor and with the poor here and now.	80	80	80
311	Since Christ speaks to us through the events of our times, sisters cannot be apostolically effective in the modern world unless they understand and respond to social and political conditions.	66	58	59
314	The experience of dialogue among persons who are open and trusting provides the human analogy for understanding the Trinity as a life of communication and communion.	68	64	68
316	The charismatic gifts of the Spirit working in the laity are as necessary for the good of the church as the authoritative power of the hierarchy and the clergy.	86	78	76
318	Because baptism incorporates us into a community, the Christian life is necessarily social in all its dimensions.	65	69	71
320	The discipline of serious study, the effort of listening intently, of speaking honestly and openly appear to me as forms of asceticism more relevant today than imposed mortification and penances.	74	79	75
321	I think that sisters who feel called to do so ought to be witnessing to Christ through social and political action and speaking out on controversial issues as well as performing with professional competence among their lay peers in science labs, at conferences and on the speaker's platform.	44	74	67
323	When I experience moments of deep communication and union with other persons, these sometimes strike me as a taste of what heaven will be like.	59	67	69
325	I think of the work the people do as preparing the world for eternity and of human progress as advancement toward the accomplishment of God's plan.	75	68	60
Averages		68.2%	69%	67.6%

the time as "pre" or "post" Vatican in their orientations (Neal 1970/1971, 1971). As a further check on the validity of these formulations, the respondents were asked to indicate from a set of 12 items, which clustered the names of theologians categorized as pre- and post-Vatican, which sets included their preferred current thinking. (See items 269-280 in Sisters' Survey 1967.)[3] Decline in the preference for the theologians from whose writings the pre-Vatican items were derived went from 23 percent in 1967 to 13 percent in 1989 (Item 67). Twenty of these pre-post belief items were repeated in the 1980 and 1989 surveys. Two criteria were used for choosing them: degree of discrimination in 1967 and relevancy of language 13 years later. A comparison of the changes in response rate suggests several implications.

There is, as might well be expected, a considerable decline in choice of the "pre-Vatican" items from 1967 to 1989. These items can be summarized as perceiving God as remote and outside of daily experience but represented in the hierarchy of the church. For example, one item reads: "Alone with the great Alone expresses well for me the idea of God and the ideal of perfection" (Item 313 in Table 1). Another is: "A good way to explain the Church is to describe the relationship of the Pope to the bishops and of these to the priests, religious and laity" (Item 315). The first of these items declined from 20 percent assent to 13 percent from 1967 to 1989, the second from 25 percent to 16 percent. In 1967, using choices ranging from a straightforward "yes," indicating agreement, to a clear "no," 38 percent agreed with the pre-Vatican perspective. That percent had declined to 24 percent in 1989, even though with high exodus from religious life and declining recruitment, the percentage of sisters over 60 had increased from 20 percent in 1967 to 51 percent in 1989. There is not, however, a corresponding increase in the post-Vatican choice of "yes." In fact, the average post-Vatican response is almost identical with the 1967 level: 68.2 percent in 1967; 67.6 percent in 1989.

An item by item comparison, however, suggests the direction of change in belief. The affirmation that: "This generation of religious is being asked to rediscover evangelical poverty. This means a realistic search for ways to be meaningfully and lovingly poor and with the poor here and now" had an 80 percent agreement in 1967 and still had an 80 percent agreement in 1989. There is an increase of 6 percent to the affirmation that "Christian life is social in all its dimensions" (Item 318).

A strong affirmation of the holiness of good communication comes in an agreement that "the discipline of serious study, the effort of listening intently, of speaking honestly and openly appear as forms of asceticism more relevant today than imposed mortifications and penances," has 75 percent agreeing, the same as in 1967. The only item with a striking increase in affirmations rising from 44 percent in 1967 to 67 percent in 1989, declares that: "Sisters who feel called to do so ought to be witnessing to Christ through social and political action and speaking out on controversial issues, as well as performing with professional competence among their lay peers in science labs, at conferences and on the speaker's platform," up 23 percent in 1989 (Item 321).

Three items that received a substantially lower score in 1989 from that in 1967 are:

1.   The charismatic gifts of the Spirit working in the laity are as necessary for the good of the Church as the authoritative power of the hierarchy and clergy. (a decline from 86 percent in 1967, to 76 percent in 1989).
2.   I think of the work that people do as preparing the world for eternity and of human progress as advancement toward the accomplishment of God's plan (a decline from 75 percent in 1967, to 60 percent in 1989).
3.   Since Christ speaks to us through the events of our times, sisters cannot be apostolically effective in the modern world unless they understand and respond to social and political conditions (a decline from 66 percent in 1967, to 59 percent in 1989).

What these unexpected decreases mean requires examination of the entire survey, all of which cannot be contained in this one chapter, but my hypothesis at present is as follows. The trend in belief concerning God's action in society and the appropriate responses for women in the vowed life has not been a simple linear function marking a clear transition from seeking God on the mountain to transforming society into an environment of justice and peace. Rather two trends, at least, are evident. There is an increase in commitment to societal transformation. But this commitment tends to divide the community into activists and non-activists. Nevertheless, there is a simultaneous trend to a more gentle form of interpersonal relations, after a transitional period of conflictual confrontation. In the early period of renewal, just after the Council, the rule of silence was set aside but skill in dialogue had not yet developed in scriptural context to generate the needed acceptance of diversity.

Thus, two simultaneous efforts toward the refinement of religious life have characterized the intervening years: the one reflected in such developments as creation theology, centering prayer, eastern forms of mystical meditation and charismatic renewal developing a gentler people. This orientation was sometimes with, but sometimes separate from, the growth of a more politically active Christian base community type of social action. This latter dynamic was generated by the social teachings of the church which have accelerated the justice and peace commitment since the early 1960s, beginning with Pope John XXIII's *Mater et Magistra* (1961) and *Pacem in Terris* (1963). Such social activist emphasis has since had dramatic increase in Catholic social teaching. It is expressed well in the mission statements of the new Constitutions of some religious institutes (Neal 1990) but is not yet reflected well in interpersonal relations. In this, the religious orders have similar experiences to the commune experiments of other groups of men and women in the 1960s who tried participatory decision making in a communal way of life (see Kanter 1972).

FOCUS ON SOCIAL CONCERNS

While the 60s item belief measure of the Sisters' Survey of 1967 was directed to the Second Vatican Council teachings, the Survey of 1980 opened with a 55-item measure of religious belief and social action based on the decisions of the Call to Action Conference held in the United States in the bicenntenial year of American independence, 1976. This conference, named after Paul VI's encyclical *A Call to Action*, 1971, was modeled on the Medellin Conference of 1968 in Latin America, applying the decisions of Vatican II to that continent. Four years in preparation, the United States conference provided position papers further adapting the Second Vatican Council and subsequent documents to an active social ministry in justice and peace work outlined in the *Justice in the World* Synod of 1971.

The 55-item measure in the 1980 survey had the same intent as the pre-post measure in the 1967 survey, that is, to determine the strength of the belief in practice orientation of the religious congregations of women. The belief section of the 1989 survey, again with the same intent of measuring belief in practice, measured the response of the sisters to a specific church document, namely, *Sollicitudo Rei Socialis,* the encyclical of Pope John Paul II, issued on the twentieth anniversary of an earlier document, *Populorum Progressio.* This new document, promulgated on the very last day of 1987 to memorialize the earlier document, and called, in English, *On Social Concerns,* addresses the church's concern for world poverty. It expresses the policy developed over 100 years of Vatican teaching regarding the rights of the individual to share in the resources of society, in view of our common humanity. The 29 items for this measure were formulated to incorporate all the significant themes in the document. The responses ranged from "no" to "yes" on a 5-point Likert scale. Even the "probably yes's" are excluded in an attempt to highlight where full commitment is evident.

The responses ranged from a high agreement of 97 percent on one item to a low of 48 percent on another. Even though almost half of those surveyed fully agree with all the items, there is a steep decline as the statements call for more and more specific action and commitment to involvement in social transformation. While 97 percent agree that "The goods of creation are meant for all," (Item 1) and 90 percent that "Today the church is called to stand on the side of the poor, to discern the justice of their requests and to help to satisfy them without losing sight of the common good," only 49 percent agree that "private property is under a social mortgage" and that "those who possess it are bound to share it with those who need it," according to principles of justice and not solely of charity. The lowest affirmation, 48 percent, is given to the statement that 'Structures of sin' refer to an all-consuming desire for profit and thirst for power" (Item 3).

Between these two extremes of assent, items of intermediate intensity receive intermediate assent. For example, the statement: "Solidarity with 'the other' whether an individual, a people or a nation—not just as some kind of instrument, with a work capacity and physical strength to be exploited at low cost and then discarded when no longer useful, but as our 'neighbor,' a 'helper' to be made a sharer on a par with ourselves in the banquet of life to which all are equally invited by God," received an 87 percent response, while "What industry produces by processing raw materials with the contribution of work, must serve equally for the good of all," is assented to by only 67 percent. The statement that "All nations need democratic and participatory governments, rule of law and respect for basic human rights" was affirmed by 73 percent. This item is critical to the discussion of organizational change which will follow shortly.

To summarize this brief presentation of the belief segment of the 1989 survey, careful examination of these items suggests that the more general an item that calls for human caring and sharing, the higher the assent; the more specific the call to commitment to action in applying the justice agenda it calls for on the part of the individual, the more individuals resist that full, wholehearted assent to its meaning. The items that are derived from a social analysis are probably unfamiliar to some sisters because of the lack of a social analysis as part of the ministry in their local communities which have not yet accepted this new dimension of Christian social action for justice, despite its adoption in their constitutions and the involvement of the Pope and bishops in its creation (Schultheis, DeBerri, and Henriot 1987). This observation, of course, suggests the selectivity in traditional vowed obedience as it was applied in local areas where the local church had not yet adapted the option for the poor in its post-Vatican emphasis on liberation as distinct from development (see Nessan 1989; Williams 1989).

The reason for determining how many and who would agree with these statements was to find out who are the sisters ready and willing to carry out the church's mission to which these items give reference. Is it older sisters, better educated, or sisters who as students attended Catholic schools? Is it the influence of being brought up in different regions of the country, on a farm or in the city? In summary, are there any demographic variables that account for commitment to social action? Is it related to the transcendent/immanent religious belief scale measured by the pre-post items looked at earlier? Cross-tabulations indicate some significant relationship to the background variables, and 36 percent of those with high belief scores also have high social concerns scores. But when joined with other variables (items) such as commitment to the women's movement (Item 47), and membership in justice and peace groups working on community development with the poor (Item 45), the background variables drop out as insignificant while membership in social action groups accounts for most of the variance on commitment to social action measures. In a stepwise multiple regression, including age, education, social action, and the social concerns measure from the first 29 items taken from *On Social Concern*, the social measures account for almost all of the variance explained, 11 percent, but when the pre-post scale is entered, it increases the variance explained to 32 percent, the new value of R^2.

DEMOGRAPHIC CHANGES OF AMERICAN SISTERS

Before pursuing this analysis further, we should look briefly at a profile of American sisters today, as compared with their 1967 profile, especially because membership has declined radically in this 23-year span. Today's population of sisters in the United States is 60 percent of what it was in 1967 and the rate of entrance to religious communities as of 1984 was 15 percent of what it was in 1966 (Neal 1984). Whereas 22 percent of sisters were under thirty in 1967, only 1 percent are now. Fifty-one percent are over sixty now while only 20 percent were that old in 1967. The ethnic distribution is still similar to what it was 20 years ago: about 31 percent are of Irish ancestry, 25 percent, German; 8 percent French or French-Canadian; 4 percent Italian; 8 percent Polish; 3 percent African; 2 percent Hispanic; less than 1 percent Asian. Seventy-one percent are at least second generation and 25 percent are beyond fourth generation in America.

By several measures, sisters today, as in 1967, are distinctively of working-class background. Only 7 percent have professional parents and only 10 percent are daughters of managers or owners of businesses. This is similar to 1967. Almost a fourth come from farm families and 22 percent, from households whose heads are semi-skilled workers of various kinds. Only 33 percent define themselves as middle class and 1 percent as upper class. Over half of their parents received only an eighth grade education or less. The strikingly different quality of their backgrounds in 1989 compared with 1967, is their own education, most of which they received as members of their institutes. Today, 86 percent have a baccalaureate degree or higher. This number was only 62 percent in 1967, yet that in itself was high in comparison with other Americans in the 1960s. Educational advancement actually began in the mid 1930s, with the prior encouragement of Pope Pius XI, whose 1929 encyclical on Catholic education encouraged the professional development of those doing service work in the local church. The location of sisters predominantly in the East, 44 percent, and in the Midwest, 34 percent, has scarcely changed since 1967. One difference is that ten percent more are graduates of Catholic elementary, high schools and colleges than in 1967. The percent now is 70 percent.

ORGANIZATIONAL CHANGES IN RELIGIOUS ORDERS

In the language of renewal among women in religious congregations, the concept "collaborative decision making" expresses a highly valued mode of interaction. Revision of Constitutions during the past two decades has dealt seriously with devising models of participative decision making. This is a radical transition in forms of governance from 1967 when a "Mother General" was assisted by an elected Council of two to four women whom she was expected to consult when making all decisions and whose vote she was required to have for certain canonically indicated decisions, including purchase and selling of properties and the reception of new members. Proposed new forms of governance are much more inclusive in division of labor. Many institutes now not only require accountability of members to administration, but of administration to members, gathered in formal assembly to review their reports and develop new policies.

There is much less tendency today to define the governance role itself as sacred and coming directly from God. This shift in emphasis may be related to the women's movement which rejects the historical negative effects of a long tradition of patriarchy extending back to the early Middle Ages wherein Roman law gave the father of the family life and death control over his dependents, including women, children, and slaves (Lerner 1986). It also may be associated with the early American experience of town governance in which the citizens experienced themselves as a community of peers. Not only did they elect their representatives from among their colleagues but they also received from those elected as their "public servants" to administer policy established by the assembly of the whole, an account of how and why they made the choices they did with the limited authority extended to them by the assembly. Whatever the tradition or model from which the new structures of government derive, the shift in belief in the holiness of obedience introduces a new theology of God's will. The item reflecting this shift reads: "Inherent in our developing understanding of mission is the belief that God, who continues to speak to us in diverse ways today calls to us wih special insistence through the voices of the dispossessed and the materially poor as they attempt to organize themselves to claim their rights as human beings" (Item 344 in 1989 survey). Seventy-eight percent accept this item in 1989; 81 percent in l980. What it does in practice is to shift emphasis in governance from the sacralization of obedience to the voice of the superior to the sacralization of participation in decision making by all members. This is linked to the new mission emphasis of affirming the efforts of the dispossessed seeking their human rights by learning to make just demands for their fair share of the resources of the society in which they live (Neal 1987; Nessan 1989).

Sisters who have worked in third world settings, especially in Latin America, and who have used the method of *Conscientization,* made known to a wider community through the writings and work of Paulo Freire (1970), have greatly influenced their religious institutes to recognize the biblical grounding of this process among peoples historically dispossessed (Adriance 1986; Gallo 1988). Now, through literacy programs, and in contact with the wider world through media technology, these third world peoples are coming to take command over their own development and associating it with their religious beliefs about God and God's action in the world (Berryman 1984; Williams 1989). The adoption of this action in the world towards its transformation in justice has become a component of Liberation Theology as seen in the writings of Gustavo Gutierrez (1973) and other theologians whose reflection/action mode of theologizing characterizes places where the poor gather to raise to consciousness the political, social and economic oppressions of their lives and to take action together to change those conditions (Cleary 1990; Ellis and Maduro 1989).

Whatever the source of the model of participatory decision making used in their religious congregations, the Sisters' Survey of 1989 reveals that sisters in general have adopted it as a value associated with their religious life. They have done so to such a degree that the faith dimension of "blind obedience" to the expressed will of "the superior" has almost been eliminated as a faith position in the keeping of the vows. For many women in religious institutes, the vow of obedience has come to mean a search for God's expressed will in carrying out the justice and peace commitment in the "special option for the poor." For these religious women, preparing for mission by coming to understand the social context in which poverty occurs toward working to change those conditions becomes the essence of their vow of obedience, as they strive to carry out that mission of the church in the context of the charism of their specific congregation and the intent of their founding members. This commitment, expressed as "government for mission," has come, through the past quarter century since the Council, to inform Sisters' methods of governing themselves. In so doing they have been moved by the principle that "people have a right to participate in the decisions that affect their lives" reiterated in church documents that focus on the plight of the world's poor nations seeking human liberation.

This orientation to mission is relatively new, and follows the critiques of authoritarianism following World War II and especially the devastating effects of the holocaust and Eichmann's argument that "he only did what he was told." As educated women, Catholic sisters had to let go of a naive obedience in which informed decision making was lacking. The renewal process revealed that such ingenuousness had, in fact, become a part of the superior/subject relationship of some in religious life. The caricature of the naive sister in the communication media from the early 1950s onward made this reality evident to an observant public.

The findings of social psychology, evident in works like *The Authoritarian Personality* (Adorno, 1950), Erving Goffman's *Asylums* (1961), as well as in

Kanter's *Commitment and Community* (1972), were major contributions in the social science literature. They demonstrate the kind of research and analysis that raised the consciousness of women in religious congregations to the organizational changes needed to provide themselves a formation to mission adequate for the task of societal transformation that the Second Vatican Council called the church to effect (Neal 1965).

Sisters' concern for organizational restructuring did not begin with the Council. But the Council's mandate to update the Constitutions became the occasion to create more effective structures, sufficiently supportive of their newly developed advanced education and responsibility for mission to make the life credible to themselves, now competent for the mission, and attractive to new members ready and willing to undertake the mission for which the congregation existed.

One of the main realities of the renewal period is that not all the members of institutes of women were equally committed to the new direction of the Council to give priority to the needs of the poor. All sisters did not think that the Council was right in placing human liberation so central to the mission of the church. Some found that mandate too secular for their understanding of their religous commitment and others realized that they joined religious congregations to be nuns, not sisters (Neal 1990). Working through this dilemma is still in process in religious congregations of women, as the following data indicates.

To an item in the belief scale that reads: "A truly obedient religious need seek no source other than her Rule and the will of her superior to know what she should do" (Item 310), already in 1967 only 31 percent agreed with this item, but in 1989 that percent was reduced to 11 percent. Furthermore, of those agreeing, 58 percent were over 70 years of age. Clearly, this statement, commonly expressed prior to Vatican II, is no longer normative for women in vows.

The test of its application is seen in the following set of responses. Asked in 1989 for their preferred form of decision making, 43 percent chose the assembly of the whole and administrators accountable to it; 44 percent chose lawfully chosen delegates who then choose the administrators; and only 11 percent chose "A government that places decision making ultimately in the hands of lawfully chosen superiors who in turn accept responsiblity for the outcomes and to whom the members are accountable" (Item 357). This item was not included in the 1967 survey but was included in 1980 and in 1989. The results in 1980 were 45 percent, 45 percent, 10 percent, respectively. This consistency between 1980 and 1989 is unusual. The consistent low affirmation of centralized or hierarchical government remains, even when the question is phrased in a negative form. Asked for agreement to the statement: "The decisions that we need to make about our life and work are highly specialized and require a degree of knowledge that takes too much time to accumulate for all to participate; therefore, I think full participation in decision making is unwise," the "no's" and "probably no's" equal 61 percent while the straight "yes's" are again 11 percent (Item 162) Finally, the statement: "A small representative group should be elected and delegated to become informed and make the decisions for us" has a 69 percent rejection and a 10 percent full acceptance in 1989 (Item 163).

At this point it seems clear that for sisters in general, participation in decision making is intended and expected. Asked if it was related to their mission to the poor, 70 percent agreed that it is or probably is (Item 165). This last item is the measure of "government for mission." In 1980, this affirmation was higher. It was then 83 percent.

Asked what method of administration was characteristic of their group, 9 percent of sisters in 1980 said that "the major superior makes the decisions with the advice of her council where required by canon law." In 1989 that percent had risen to 26 percent, and the percent of those groups wherein the General Council only administers decisions made by the assembly had declined from 38 percent to 24 percent (Item 168). This trend back to an earlier structure would not be expected from the leverage of new theologies but can probably be accounted for by the insistence on that traditional form of government by the New Code of Canon Law and the Congregation for Institutes of Consecrated Life (CICL), the Vatican organization which accepts Constitutions for the Church.[4]

In 1983, the New Code of Canon Law was promulgated. Much to the concern of many involved in the process of revision of Constitutions, it reinforced rather than revised church insistence on what has come to be known in theological language as "personal authority" or "religious authority," namely, the requirement that vowed obedience be made to a person believed to be holding the place of God for the one making the vows. If the new value of "government for mission" had been formalized in the new Canons, the value proclaimed in church documents for government and economic participation of the poor in the decisions that affect their lives would have been formalized for church structures as well, in recognition of their normative power as models for life in other institutional settings. Because this did not occur, women in religious institutes are left with a dilemma. Shall they witness to their faith as expressed in *The Social Concerns* scale and violate the Canons by structuring their government according to their beliefs about responsible participation? Or should they conform to the Canons and contradict their belief already in practice that persons should participate in the decisions that affect their lives not out of willfulness but out of a basic belief in government for mission? That dilemma still characterizes the lived experience of Catholic sisters today.

In conclusion, the evidence is substantial that a new belief trend in the Catholic church stemming from its recognition of the struggles of third world peoples for participation in the decisions that affect their lives has, in fact, influenced the congregations of Catholic women to restructure their decision making systems to forms of participatory decision making within their own structures for community living. However, the practice of decision making in these same congregations, as well as the practice of belief in the "special option for the poor" stemming from the decrees of the Second Vatican Council, is influenced not only by the new faith mandate to stand with the poor as they reach out to take what is rightfully theirs, in the biblical sense that the land belongs to the people (Leviticus 25), but also by several other factors. These factors include: retention of old beliefs in the practice of "blind obedience" on the part of some members; conflict between the new emphasis on justice as a basis for the sharing of resources and the continuing operation of the old elite model of charity of the rich giving of their largesse to the truly powerless poor; and the trained professional trying to maintain her integrity and at the same time exercise good will in the practice of new forms of governance when many elements of the experiments are in flux. Finally, the fact that the church has yet to recognize these experiments as normative is itself a source of pain even as the development of peoples is a sign of hope.

NOTES

1. A short article in *Probe* (Neal 1981) is the only published report that contains the actual data from the Sisters' Survey of 1980. There are references to the data in Neal (1984, 1990).
2. This reference is from St.Thomas Aquinas's *Summa Theologica,* Second Part of the Second Part, Question 6, Answer 7.
3. Item numbers are being provided here even though the survey instrument is not included. It is available on request from the author.
4. The Code of Canon Law and the Congregation for Institutes of Consecrated Life (CICL) have a powerful influence on the structure of government in religious institutes. That influence is a major variable in the shift to conformity to the traditional obedience relationship in some institutes, but for this analysis it is only one factor among many faith factors in the church today.

REFERENCES

Adorno, T. W. et al. 1950. *The Authoritarian Personality.* New York: Harper and Row.
Adriance, M.C. 1986. *Opting For the Poor: Brazilian Catholicism in Transition.* Kansas City, MO: Sheed and Ward.
Aquinas, T. 1947. *Summa Theologica.* 3 Vols. Translated by the Fathers of the English Dominican Province. New York: Benziger Bros.
Berryman, P. 1984. *The Religious Roots of Rebellion.* Maryknoll, NY: Orbis Books.
Cada, L., R. Fitz, G. Foley, T. Giardino, C. Lichtenberg. 1979. *Shaping the Coming Age of Religious Life.* New York: Seabury.
Cardenal, E. 1976. *The Gospel of Solentiname.* Maryknoll: NY: Orbis Books.
Chenu, M. D., OP. 1957. "Toward a Theology of Work." *Cross Currents* 7:175-187.

Cleary, E. L. 1990. *Born of the Poor: The Latin American Church Since Medellin.* South Bend, IN: Notre Dame University Press.

Code of Canon Law. 1983. Prepared by the Canon Law Society of Great Britain and Ireland. London: Collins. (English translation of Codex Iuris Canonici, promulgated by Pope John Paul II).

Congar, Y. 1965. *Lay People in the Church.* Westminster, MD: Newman Press.

Donovan, M. A. SC. 1989. *Sisterhood as Power: The Past and Passion of Ecclesial Women.* New York: Crossroads.

Dorr, D. 1983. *Option For the Poor: A Hundred Years of Vatican Social Teaching.* Maryknoll, NY: Orbis Books.

Durkheim, E. 1965. *Elementary Forms of Religious Life.* New York: Free Press.

Ellis, M.H., and O. Maduro. 1989. *The Future of Liberation Theology.* New York: Orbis Books.

Ferree, W. 1951. *The Act of Social Justice.* Dayton, OH: Marianist Publications.

Flannery, A., OP, ed. 1975. *Vatican Council II: The Conciliar and Post-Conciliar Documents.* New York: Costello.

Freire, P. 1970. *Pedagogy of the Oppressed.* New York: Seabury.

Freud, S. 1961. *Civilization and Its Discontents.* New York: W.W. Norton.

Gallo, J., SND. 1988. *Basic Ecclesial Communities: A New Form of Christian Response to the World Today.* Ph.D. dissertation, Boston University.

Goffman, E. 1961. *Asylums.* New York: Doubleday.

Gutierrez, G. 1973. *A Theology of Liberation.* Maryknoll, NY: Orbis Books.

John XXIII. 1961. *Mater et Magistra* [Mother and Teacher]. Boston: St. Paul Editions.

_____. 1963. *Peace on Earth (Pacem In Terris).* Boston: St. Paul Editions.

John Paul II. 1988. *On Social Concerns (Sollicitudo Rei Socialis).* Boston: St. Paul Editions.

Kanter, R. 1972. *Commitment and Community.* Cambridge, MA: Harvard University Press.

Lerner, G. 1986. *The Creation of Patriarchy.* New York: Oxford University Press.

de Lubac, H. 1956. *The Splendor of the Church.* Translated by M. Mason. New York: Sheed & Ward.

Marx, K., and F. Engels. 1959. *Basic Writings on Politics and Philosophy.* Edited by L. S. Fever. New York: Doubleday.

Neal, M. A., SND. 1965. *Values and Interests in Social Change.* Englewood Cliffs, NJ: Prentice Hall.

_____. 1970/1971. "The Relation Between Religious Belief and Structural Change in Religious Orders: Developing an Effective Measuring Instrument." *Review of Religious Research* Part I, 12(1):2-16; Part II, 12(3):153-164.

_____. 1971. "A Theoretical Analysis of Renewal in Religious Orders in the United States." *Social Compass* 18(1):7-25.

_____. 1981. "The Sisters' Survey 1980: A Report." *Probe* 10(5):1-7.

_____. 1984. *Catholic Sisters in Transition From the 1960s to the 1980s.* Wilmington, DE: Michael Glazier.

_____. 1987. *The Just Demands of the Poor.* New York: Paulist Press.

_____. 1990. *From Nuns to Sisters: An Expanding Vocation.* Wilmington, DE: Twenty Third Publications.

Nessan, C.L. 1989. *Orthopraxis or Heresy: The North American Theological Response to Latin American Theology.* Academic Series: AAR, No. 63. Atlanta, GA: Scholars Press.

Paul VI. 1967. *Populorum Progressio. (On the Development of Peoples).* Boston: St.Paul Editions.

Pius XI. 1929. *The Christian Education of Youth.* Boston: St. Paul Editions.

Rahner, K. 1960. "Reflections on Obedience." *Cross Currents* 10:362-374.

Schultheis, M.J., E.P. De Berri, P.H. Henriot. 1987. *Our Best Kept Secret: The Rich Heritage of Catholic Social Teachings.* Washington, DC: Center of Concern.

Suhard, E.C. 1948. *Growth or Decline: The Church Today.* South Bend, IN: Fides Publishers.

Synod of Bishops. 1971. *Synodal Document on Justice in the World.* Second General Assembly, Rome, November 30, 1971. Boston: St. Paul Editions.

Vatican Council II. 1965. *Decree on the Renewal of Religious Life (Perfectae Caritatis).* Boston: St. Paul Editions.

_____. 1975a. *Gaudium et Spes (Pastoral Constitution on the Church in the Modern World).* Pp. 903-1001 in Flannery (ed.), *Vatican Council II: The Conciliar and Post-Conciliar Document.* New York: Costello.

_____. 1975b. *Lumen Gentium (Dogmatic Constitution on the Church).* Pp. 350-440 in Flannery (ed.), *Vatican Council II: The Conciliar and Post-Conciliar Documents.* New York: Costello.

Vatican Congregation for Religious and Secular Institutes. 1983. "Essential Elements in Church Teaching on Religious Life." *Origins* 13(8):133-142.

_____. 1975. *Ecclesiae Sanctae (Norms for Implementing the Decree on the Renewal of Religious Life, 1966.).* Pp. 626-633 in A. Flannery (ed.), *Vatican Council II: The Conciliar and Post-Conciliar Documents.* New York: Costlelo.

Weber, M. 1905/1980. *The Protestant Ethic and the Spirit of Capitalism.* New York: Charles Scribner.

_____. 1922/1963. *Sociology of Religion. 1963.* Boston: Beacon Press.

Williams, P.J. 1989. *The Catholic Church and Politics in Nicaragua and Costa Rica.* Pittsburgh, PA: University of Pittsburgh Press.

NEW ROLES FOR WOMEN IN THE CATHOLIC CHURCH:

1965-1990

Ruth A. Wallace

INTRODUCTION

This chapter discusses the changing role of women in the Catholic church since the Second Vatican Council, with a principal focus on those positions previously reserved solely for the clergy, to which women have been newly appointed. Before looking at the factors that facilitated the movement of women into these new roles, and the constraints and opportunities experienced by them, I begin with a microsociological perspective on women's invisibility in Rome during the Vatican II deliberations. The question I begin with is, "Where were the women during Vatican II?"

THE COUNCIL AND THE PRESENCE OF WOMEN

The central participants in the Council were the 2,540 bishops and a few male heads of religious orders who had voting rights at the Council. In addition,

Religion and the Social Order, Volume 2, pages 123-136.
Copyright © 1991 by JAI Press Inc.
All rights of reproduction in any form reserved.
ISBN: 1-55938-388-7

there were approximately 450 priests invited as experts ("periti"), and some Protestant observers and representatives from non-Christian religions, all of whom were men.[1] These experts were allowed to be present at the Council deliberations but had no voting rights.

Beginning with the second session of the Council in 1963, a few lay auditors were also invited. Abbott (1966, p.500) states that by the end of the Council in 1965 there were 12 laywomen and 10 religious women from different parts of the world present in Rome who participated as "auditrices." Their 27 male counterparts were called "auditores." These 49 lay auditors were present during the Council deliberations, but they had no vote and could not speak. At the various commission meetings held all over Rome, however, the auditors had the right to speak as well as listen. The list of auditors included three from the United States: Sister Mary Luke Tobin, the Mother General of the Sisters of Loretto; James Norris; and Martin H. Work.

There were a few women present at peripheral activities, such as the noon Council summary and the daily press briefings on the Council debates. Well-known American Catholic lay women, like Dorothy Day, Patricia Crowley, Abigail McCarthy, and Mary Daly could be seen at these briefings. Some women were also present at public talks given occasionally by eminent theologians. I was one of the four American nuns invited by Cardinal Leon Joseph Suenens to assist in organizing a series of afternoon discussions on current topics on the Council's agenda during the fourth session of the Council in 1965. The people we invited to participate in these discussions included lay men and women, Protestant observers and their wives, members of the press, priests, and bishops. A few women could also be seen at occasional weekend conferences and at informal gatherings at Roman restaurants.

Some of my personal observations in Rome from September to November, 1965, may be helpful in understanding women's "place" during the Council. There were many dramatic displays of patriarchal symbolism. An unforgettable sight, for instance, was the daily convergence of hundreds of bishops from all over the world dressed in their colorful regalia at the doors of St. Peter's. No woman or layman could be seen among them because the front entrance was reserved solely for the voting members of the Council.

How did the women who were not auditors participate in the Council? If they could procure tickets from a bishop, women were permitted to be among those participating in the Mass celebrated before the day's Council deliberations. However, they were instructed to leave immediately after the liturgy, because only bishops, periti, auditors and staff could be present for the Council deliberations. Because of the limitations placed on the role of auditor, a woman's voice was never heard during the Council deliberations.

On the other hand, within the Vatican itself women were highly visible in the lower-status roles of secretary, cook, and housekeeper. But as members of the laity, women were virtually invisible and entirely silent when decisions were being made regarding important structural changes affecting all members of the church.

FACTORS AFFECTING WOMEN'S
GREATER PARTICIPATION

In this section I explore those Vatican II changes which facilitated the movement of women into new roles in the church.[2] Initially I take a brief look at the Council documents and their implementation, and then examine changes in the new Code of Canon Law, before turning to factors outside the church which facilitated women's entrance into new roles.

Vatican II Documents and Their Implementation

A perusal of the Vatican II documents reveals that there were only a few instances where any attention was given to the contribution of women to the church. Given the invisibility and silence of women during the Council, it is not surprising that women's issues are seldom addressed in the documents themselves, even in the document on the laity that was supposedly addressed to laywomen and laymen alike. However, one statement in the document on the laity that was inserted only during the final drafting, reads: "Since in our times women have an ever active share in the whole life of society, it is very important that they participate more widely also in the various fields of the Church's apostolate" (Abbott 1966, p. 500).

How was this Council statement regarding women's increasing participation implemented? We should keep in mind that during the pre-Vatican II era, there were some women in important positions, like administrators of Catholic hospitals, presidents of Catholic women's colleges, and principals of high schools and grammar schools. However, these were not viewed as strictly "clerical" roles, and the vast majority of women occupying these positions were members of religious communities.[3]

In those sections of the world where bishops and priests encouraged women and laymen to participate more actively after the council, some women gradually assumed more prominent roles. At the parish level they accepted new ministerial roles such as lectors, Eucharistic ministers, acolytes, and directors of religious education. A study of Catholic parishes in the United States 20 years after the Council found that 52 percent of members of parish councils, 60 percent of eucharistic ministers, and half of the lectors were women. When asked who were the "most influential parishioners," exclusive of the pastors, the respondents produced a list that was 58 percent women (Leege and Trozzolo 1985, pp.56-57).

In our national study of the laity (D'Antonio, Davidson, Hoge, and Wallace 1989) we found that a majority of Catholics think the laity should have the right to participate in the following areas: deciding how parish income should be spent (80% agreed), giving occasional sermons at Mass (69% agreed), teaching in diocesan seminaries (68% agreed), deciding whether or not to have altar girls (66% agreed), being in charge of a parish when the priest is absent (65% agreed), and selecting the priests for their parish (57% said they should have the right).

Prior to Vatican II, women were invisible in such roles as student or faculty member in seminaries; it was only after the Vatican Council ended in 1965 that women were admitted to schools of theology for ministerial preparation. I would argue that the increase in women's presence as students and professors in seminaries is a micro-interactional change which will have important repercussions at the macro-structural level. Keep in mind that before 1965 only those priests who went to college before entering the seminary could have had the experience of a college education which included women as students and/or teachers. Before the Council ended, most future priests studied for their college degrees in seminaries or schools of theology, where the only women visible were the "good Sisters" who did the cooking, laundering, and other housekeeping tasks. Thus many of the priests today, as well as most of the bishops, have had little experience beyond high school in working with women as intellectual equals.

At the present time, however, approximately a fourth of the students enrolled in Catholic theological schools in the United States are women (Baumgaertner 1988, pp.90-92). In part, because of this breakthrough, some women are now serving in positions that were formerly reserved to the clergy, such as superintendents of schools, professors in seminaries, directors of Catholic Charities, and editors of diocesan newspapers. Because the percentage of women entering seminaries as students is on an upward trend, we can expect that the daily interaction between these women, their fellow students, and co-workers, will have an impact on the future behavior of the seminarians and priests as pastors of parishes and as administrators in chancery offices.

The New Code of Canon Law

Another Vatican II-related change which was an important facilitator for women's increased participation was the revision of the church's legal order. Realizing the importance of changes in church law for the implementation of Vatican Council decisions, Pope John XXIII called for the revision of Canon Law. The new Code of Canon Law, which was promulgated in 1983, made some provisions for the expansion of women's roles in the church. While still excluding women from the ordained ministry, the new Code opened the following positions to women on the diocesan level: diocesan chancellors, auditors, assessors, defenders of the marriage bond, promoters of justice, judges on diocesan courts, and members of diocesan synods and financial administrative councils.

Another new role to which women have been appointed, and one that I have been researching recently, is that of pastoral administrators of priestless parishes. The legal change which opened the door for the recruitment of women to this position can be found in the revised Code, Canon 517.2, which provides for persons other than priests to exercise pastoral care in a parish.

How did this change come about? The earliest version of the proposed law, drafted in 1977, was sent to the Catholic hierarchy and other consultative bodies of the church throughout the world in 1978. After observations of these groups were forwarded to the Vatican office, discussions of this proposed canon took place on April 19, 1980. As we might expect, some of the discussants in Rome "did not welcome the notion that a parish be entrusted, even in part," to a non-ordained person.[4] How were they convinced otherwise?

It was the intervention of Archbishop Rosalio Jose Castillo Lara, from Venezuela, that was the turning point in this deliberation (Renken 1987). He told the committee about the experience in his own diocese, where the priest shortage was so acute that he had entrusted the pastoral care of some communities to women religious. Archbishop Lara expressed much satisfaction with this arrangement, and he also argued that it was spiritually fruitful. This intervention by a Third World bishop was what convinced the committee, and the proposed canon was approved. The final version of the canon, now promulgated as Canon 517.2, reads:

> If the diocesan bishop should decide that due to a dearth of priests a participation in the exercise of the pastoral care of a parish is to be entrusted to a deacon or to some other person who is not a priest, or to a community of persons, he is to appoint some priest endowed with the powers and faculties of a pastor, to supervise the pastoral care.

For women, of course, the inclusionary clause in the wording of Canon 517.2 is "some other person who is not a priest." If the earlier arguments of some of the committee members had prevailed, this clause would have been deleted. Canon 517.2, therefore, created a new role for women in the Catholic church. I will expand on the consequences of this new role in the second half of this chapter.

DEMOGRAPHIC CHANGES AND THE CONTEMPORARY WOMEN'S MOVEMENT

Important demographic changes in the United States and the contemporary women's movement are the external factors that have expedited women's entrance into new roles in the church. Chief among the demographic changes are women's greater participation in the labor force, their increased rate of college attendance and their completion of postgraduate degrees (Kroe 1989, pp.11-13).

The increasing shortage of priests, however, is also a key factor, especially with respect to new roles which had previously been reserved solely to priests. Like Rosie the Riveter, women are being recruited to help out in a manpower shortage crisis. Appointing women as chancellors of dioceses, as canon lawyers in the diocesan tribunal, and as administrators of parishes frees priests for other diocesan needs, just as women in factories freed male factory workers to fight in the Second World War. As Schoenherr's analysis in Chapter Six reveals, the priest shortage is already at a crisis stage in some dioceses, and it shows no signs of abating. In contrast to the World War II manpower shortage, there is no anticipation of a future influx of male workers. The recruitment of women to positions in the church which were formerly reserved to the clergy is not expected to be a short-term situation.

The contemporary women's movement, which entered a phase of intense mobilization soon after the adjournment of the Vatican Council, had important repercussions for Catholic women. It raised public consciousness regarding the second-class rank of women in the church. In the gender caste system of the Catholic church only men can attain the higher status of clergy. All women, even those who join religious communities, are relegated to the ranks of the laity.

Have Catholics become more critical of the church's official position regarding women's ordination? Greeley (1985, p.182) analyzed data from general social surveys at the National Opinion Research Center. Asked whether they thought "it would be a good thing if women were to be ordained as priests," American Catholics showed a 15 percent increase in positive responses over an 8-year period. In 1974, 29 percent agreed with the statement, but by 1982, 44 percent agreed. At present, slightly over half of Catholic adults no longer view the priesthood as a male prerogative, a 23 percent increase from 1974 to 1985 (Hoge 1987; Woodward, Stranger, Sullivan, Margolis, and Vokey 1985).

Some support for women's ordination has come from professional groups within the church, such as the Catholic Biblical Association of America which issued a report in 1979 concluding that the evidence in the New Testament, "while not decisive by itself, points toward the admission of women to priestly ministry" ("Report of Catholic Biblical Association" 1979).

In the early 1980s, a few bishops wrote pastoral letters addressing the question of sexism in the church, and encouraged a re-thinking of the position of women. The following are some examples: Matthew Clark (1982), Victor Balke and Raymond Lucker (1981), and Peter Gerety (1980). Near the end of the decade, the American bishops as a group published the first draft of a pastoral response to women's concerns. Although the document condemns sexism as a sin, it falls far short of the expectations of many Catholics, because the document sidesteps the issue of women priests, and only recommends that the question of women being ordained *as deacons* "be investigated" (U.S. Bishops 1988). The second draft was no stronger than the first (U. S. Bishops 1990).

The women's movement was instrumental in other ways as well. Many American Catholic women experienced a heightening of their critical consciousness as they worked for the passage of the equal rights amendment and for their own feminist organizations, such as the Women's Ordination Conference and Catholics for a Free Choice. These experiences helped Catholic women to reflect on their countless hours of unpaid parish service as well as their exclusion from the most important functions in the ministry. The use of gender-neutral language, an important agenda item of the contemporary women's movement, has gradually penetrated the Catholic church in the United States. For example, a consensus statement resulting from a symposium on Women and Church Law sponsored by the Canon Law Society of America in 1976 reads, in part:

> We ask that the National Conference of Catholic Bishops, in conjunction with other Episcopal Conferences, work to replace sexist language in liturgical texts. We ask that such language be replaced in conference statements, in existing church legislation, and carefully avoided in any future statements and legislation (Coriden 1977, p. 159).

Some language revision in scripture readings, in hymns and prayers, and even in the revised Code of Canon Law has been accomplished, though much still remains to be done. The elimination of sexist language is an important phase in the process of women's empowerment.

The Vatican II documents, some provisions in the new Code of Canon Law, demographic changes, and the contemporary women's movement have expedited the movement of women into new church roles. However, the transition of women into these new roles has not been an entirely smooth one. There is no doubt that these facilitating factors helped to create new opportunities for women in the church. Nonetheless, there are a number of constraints encountered by these women in their role transition process. In the next section I present some data illustrating these constraints and opportunities from my recent study of women administrators of priestless parishes.

CONSTRAINTS AND OPPORTUNITIES OF WOMEN "PASTORS": A PRELIMINARY REPORT

Because the law that allowed for lay administrators of priestless parishes (Canon 517.2) was promulgated in 1983, it is only recently that women have been appointed to this position. Although this is an intermediate role between lay parishioner and parish priest, it can be viewed as on the "cutting edge" of role expansion for women in the church.

Previous research on this phenomenon is understandably sparse, since it is so new. Gilmour's (1986) study of priestless parishes was limited to nine midwestern parishes in the United States. Gilfeather's (1977, p. 53) study describes the activities of 80 religious women appointed as administrators of parishes in dioceses throughout Chile, who are, in her words," taking the lion's share of responsibility for the spiritual welfare of the inhabitants." Sociological studies of Protestant clergywomen are also beginning to emerge (Carroll, Hargrove, and Lummis 1983; Lehman 1985), but the role performance of these subjects is not complicated by the quantity of institutional constraints found in the Catholic church.

Between June and December of 1989, I traveled to 20 priestless parishes throughout the United States where women had been appointed by the bishop as pastoral administrators. All had served in this capacity for at least a year, two had been pastoring for as many as eight years, and most had three or more years of experience. Names and addresses of the women included in this study were obtained from the 1988 *Official Catholic Directory,* from women pastors whom I had interviewed in an exploratory study (Wallace 1988), and from other people knowledgeable about this phenomenon.[5] All 20 women whom I contacted by letter and phone agreed to participate in the study.

In order to compare the experiences of lay women with that of nuns, I selected nine parishes headed by lay women and eleven headed by nuns. (To my knowledge these nine lay women were the only ones in the United States who had administered a parish for at least a year.) Where possible I selected parishes headed by nuns that were adjacent to the lay-led parishes. I also aimed for rural-urban differences, but this proved to be impossible because most of the parishes headed by women are located in small rural towns and villages. Geographically the 20 parishes are dispersed in 12 states located in the middle atlantic, east and west north central, south atlantic, and pacific regions of the United States.

When I visited these parishes, I stayed for the weekend, usually three days and two nights. I conducted four in-depth interviews in each parish, one with the woman pastor[6] one with the priest who was the sacramental minister, and two with parishioners who were members of the parish council, one female and one male. The interviews ranged from one hour to two and a half hours in duration. I also conducted interviews with three women who had been recently terminated as pastoral administrators, bringing the total number of interviews to 83.

I also kept field notes of my observations at the various parish functions that I attended over the weekend, including the worship services where she and/or the priest were the presiders, and other parish activities, like baptisms, weddings, visits to the sick, coffee gatherings after liturgies, church dinners, and meetings of the parish council. Because in most cases I was a guest in their homes, I was able to observe the women pastors in their daily lives and to discuss a variety of topics with them. Each woman also provided me with printed materials where available, such as the history of the parish, their contract and job descriptions, parish bulletins, installation ceremony, and articles written about and by the pastoral administrator.

Analysis of these data did, indeed, shed some light on the constraints and opportunities of the women heading these parishes. The remainder of this chapter is a preliminary report of my findings.

The chief constraint experienced by these women results from a law of the church which restricts priestly ordination to males. This restriction means that even though women are doing the work of a priest in these parishes, they cannot be considered as members of the clergy. Because they are officially designated as lay persons, some of the central pastoral duties that are the essence of the priesthood, such as celebrating Mass and conferring the sacraments, are reserved for a priest, often called the "sacramental minister."

The priest is typically located in a nearby parish and travels from a distance for weekly visits to the parish. In some cases he is serving as many as three parishes and the distances between them are formidable; consequently, many of the women pastors preside at "priestless" communion services every other weekend, or oftener. With regard to the sacraments, some women report having heard confessions informally, although they cannot "validly" give absolution. In remote parishes the women pastors often preside at marriages and funerals outside of Mass, and almost all of them regularly preside at the graveside ceremony after the funeral service.

Although non-ordained persons are not permitted to perform the sacrament of the anointing of the sick, it is often difficult to find a priest to officiate at the critical moment. In one parish the woman pastor told how she solved a dilemma for a dying woman who was in dreadful pain, but who was, as her husband described it, "holding on" for the last sacrament. After trying unsuccessfully to locate a priest, the pastoral administrator arrived at the hospital room, leaned down to speak into the ear of the dying woman, and, as she reported it:

> I made sure she knew who I was and what I was doing and I said we would go through the whole rite just as if she had a priest. Her husband said that was what she wanted, and I wasn't gone ten minutes when she let go. And she was in terrible pain.

The pastoral duties that women pastors routinely perform include the following: scheduling Masses in coordination with the sacramental minister, presiding at prayer and communion services in the absence of a priest, preaching, planning and evaluating liturgies, preparing parishioners for baptism and marriage, counseling, processing marriage annulment cases, supervising religious education programs, visiting sick and elderly parishioners, supervising outreach programs (e.g., clothing or food distribution centers), supervising the upkeep of parish buildings, managing parish finances with the assistance of the parish finance council, attending parish council meetings, and representing the parish at clergy conferences and local ecumenical gatherings.

Most of the women manage to transform their limited empowerment from a constraint to an opportunity. Because they are not placed above their parishioners in the separate and privileged position befitting the clerical state, the women tend to identify very strongly with the parishioners. Pastoral administrators make a point of learning the names of each parishioner. For example, one woman heading a parish of 500 members was praised by her parishioners for her practice of addressing each person by name as she distributed communion to them on Sunday. Women pastors also tend to visit the families in their homes, another activity that was well received by parishioners. Many of the parishioners reported that they had no recollection of such visits by previous pastors. One pastoral administrator explained it to me this way: "Most priests want the people to come to them; we go out to the people."

Women pastors are typically very successful in their ability to involve the parishioners in shared responsibility for the parish. In some parishes, 80 to 90 percent of the parishioners are actively serving on parish committees and performing tasks on a volunteer basis such as cleaning the church, maintaining the church grounds, keeping financial records, typing the weekly bulletin, distributing food and clothing to the needy, teaching in the religious education program, planning the liturgies, leading youth groups, singing in the choir and taking on other liturgical roles such as lector and eucharistic minister. One woman compared her leadership style with that of the previous pastor in this way:

> Our styles are different. He had a different vision of his role than I have of my role as a pastor. I suppose I am more people oriented, and by that I mean that each person has something valuable to share with everyone else and I try to recognize that, help them identify it, and draw it out because I think that the whole parish is enriched when everyone is sharing their ability in ways of ministering to the parish, so that we do it together.

The collaborative leadership style of women pastors moves them a step further in their vision of the future. Many of them view the parishioners as "owning" the parish, and themselves as "enablers." In their words, "the parish belongs to the parishioners." In their attempt to bestow ownership of the parish on the parishioners, many of the women pastors have trained some of them to "take over" when they are no longer there. For example, in one instance when the priest failed to show up for Mass on Sunday, and in the absence of the woman administrator, one of the trained parishioners presided at the communion service. In some parishes the parishioners and the pastoral administrator take turns presiding and preaching at the communion services held during the week. This provides important "inservice training" for the parishioners.

Another institutional constraint concerns the tenure of pastoral administrators. These women are generally viewed as temporary substitutes; in fact the appellation "priestless parishes" connotes a deprivation, and consequently a lower status for the parish. One of the women voiced her refusal to accept such a negative identity in this way:

> I don't know who coined that phrase. We have never referred to ourselves as a priestless parish. We never refer to the Sunday Assembly as a Sunday Assembly in the absence of a priest. Those are all negative things and the focus is then put on the important person as the priest rather than the importance of the community.

An additional constraint for the pastoral administrator concerns title and dress. Even though the women are responsible for pastoring a parish community, the title of pastor is denied them, because by church law it is restricted to ordained priests. One could argue that there are few examples of a role which has been so thoroughly monopolized by men as that of a Catholic pastor, who is typically called "Father," a title which explicitly excludes women. Because there are, as yet, no church-wide norms regarding the exact title to be used, it is the local bishop's prerogative to decide what to call them. About half of the women I visited have the title pastoral administrator; some are called pastoral coordinator; a few are parochial ministers; and one each has the title of pastoral director, parish lay administrator, and parish life coordinator.

In everyday life, however, parishioners often refer to these women as "pastor," as do some of the priests. Several of the women reported receiving mail from the diocesan office addressed to "pastor" or "reverend," and three of them reported that their bishops publicly introduced them as "pastor." It is commonplace for the parishioners to refer to them and to introduce them as the pastor. In the words of one of the women, "I have had people tell me, 'Well, you are the pastor, really.'"

Symbolic clothing is another constraint. While the clerical collar can be worn by women clergy in Protestant denominations, it cannot be worn by their Roman Catholic counterparts because the collar symbolizes the clerical state. A few of the women I visited regularly wear an alb (a long white robe) while on the altar during liturgical ceremonies. In three of the dioceses the guidelines for pastoral administrators state that the alb is the ceremonial dress for the laity, consequently these dioceses *require* that pastoral administrators wear the alb at all ceremonial functions.

About half of the women I visited argued vehemently against accepting any of the clerical trappings. Married women and nuns alike identified very strongly with the laity, as the following statement illustrates:

> I dress in liturgical colors. In other words, if I am preaching during Advent, I wear a purple dress. My whole message to everyone in this parish is that I am a lay person and they are lay people. We had a group of people here who wanted me to wear an alb, and I said that just separates me from the people. I am just not into clerical dress.

Another institutional constraint involves the relationship between the women pastors and the priests. Even though they are in charge of the parish, there are restrictions on the authority of these women, for they must depend on a priest to perform all of the central ritual roles. Typically the priest travels from another parish on Saturday or Sunday to perform the service, and leaves almost immediately afterwards. Although he may scarcely know the parishioners, the priest must also be called in to perform their baptisms, hear their confessions, witness their marriages, and preside at the anointing of the sick. The women administrators responsible for preparing their parishioners for these sacraments report that the greatest point of tension occurs here, at the moment when they must place themselves in the "back of the church" and let the "real pastor" take over during the ceremony itself. This is how one of them described her feelings about this tension:

> It just doesn't seem right. It's very frustrating. There is nothing I can do about it. We have very good priests, for which I am grateful. But I don't like it. I feel it is a real insult to women.

This institutional constraint, which most strongly exemplifies their limited empowerment, is one that cannot be surmounted. It also appears to be a constraint which cannot be converted into an opportunity. On the other hand, as several of the women pointed out to me, their parishioners who witness these points of tension tend to identify strongly with their pain, anger, and frustration. Young couples preparing for marriage, young parents preparing for their child's baptism, and dying parishioners alike ask, "Why don't you do it? We want *you*." It appears that the witnessing of the most difficult point of tension in the lives of women pastoral administrators is changing parishioners' attitudes about the priesthood.

The fact that guidelines, titles, and job descriptions vary from diocese to diocese is a clear indication that the pastoring role of women in the Catholic church is still in an early stage in its evolution. External factors like demographic changes and the women's movement played an important part in moving women into this new position. In addition, the changes of Vatican II and legal changes in the church's code, were necessary conditions for their present appointment. Data on recruitment to the priesthood indicate that the tenure of women heading parishes will not be short-term, and that the numbers of such women will continue to increase. Although it would be premature to assess the overall impact of this phenomenon, I am convinced that the creativity exhibited by women pastors in the way they deal with the constraints of their new position has the potential to lead to the transformation of an institution.

ACKNOWLEDGMENTS

Support for this research was provided by grants from the Lilly Endowment and the National Science Foundation. I would like to thank Helen R. Ebaugh for her comments on this chapter.

NOTES

1. See *Concilio Ecumenico Vaticano II: Commissioni Conciliari* for a list of the council participants. I want to thank Rev. Francis X. Murphy, CSSR for bringing my attention to this document.

2. Some of this discussion is adapted from my earlier work on women in the church, in particular "Catholic Women and the Creation of a New Social Reality" (1988), and "Women in the Church: Limited Empowerment," in D'Antonio, Davidson, Hoge, and Wallace (1989).

3. It is important to remember that religious women, because of their gender, cannot be ordained, and thus have never been members of the clergy. However, because of their vows, they are usually set apart from the laity, and accorded a "higher level" in the eyes of most Catholics. In a certain sense this leaves religious women in a state of limbo. The Council Fathers underlined the special status of religious orders of men and women by addressing a document on the renewal of religious life, entitled "Perfectae Caritatis."

4. See John A. Renken (1987), "Canonical Issues in the Pastoral Care of Parishes without Priests."

5. I am especially indebted to Kay Sheskaitis, IHM, an expert on this topic, who was at that time Director of Ministry for the Archdiocese of Portland, Oregon.

6. Although the title pastor is reserved for priests, these women are, in effect, pastoring these parishes. See later discussion of the constraint regarding titles.

REFERENCES

Abbott, W. M., S. J., ed. 1966. *The Documents of Vatican II*. New York: America Press.
Balke, V. and R. Lucker. 1981. "Male and Female God Created Them." *Origins* 11:333-338.
Baumgaertner, W.L., ed. 1988. *Fact Book on Theological Education: 1987-88*. Vandalia, OH: Association of Theological Schools in the United States and Canada.

Carroll, J.W., B. Hargrove, and A. T. Lummis. 1983. *Women of the Cloth: A New Opportunity for the Churches.* San Francisco, CA: Harper and Row.

Catholics for a Free Choice. 1988. "All Work and No Say." *Conscience* 9:3-25.

Clark, M. 1982. "American Catholic Women: Persistent Questions, Faithful Witness." *Origins* 12:273-286.

Concilio Ecumenico Vaticano II: Commissioni Conciliari. 1965. (4th edition) Vatican City: Polyglot Press.

Coriden, J., ed. 1977. *Sexism and Church Law: Equal Rights and Affirmative Action.* New York: Paulist Press.

D'Antonio, W.V., J.D. Davidson, D.R. Hoge, and R.A. Wallace. 1989. *American Catholic Laity in a Changing Church.* Kansas City, MO: Sheed and Ward.

Gerety, P. 1980. "Women in the Church." *Origins* 10:582-588.

Gilfeather, K. 1977. "The Changing Role of Women in the Catholic Church in Chile." *Journal for the Scientific Study of Religion* 16:39-54.

Gilmour, P. 1986. *The Emerging Pastor: Non-Ordained Catholic Pastors.* Kansas City, MO: Sheed and Ward.

Greeley, A.M. 1985. *American Catholics Since the Council: An Unauthorized Report.* Chicago: Thomas More Press.

Hoge, D.R. 1987. *The Future of Catholic Leadership: Responses to the Priest Shortage.* Kansas City, MO: Sheed and Ward.

Kroe, E. 1989. *National Higher Education Statistics: Fall 1989.* Washington, DC: U.S. Department of Education.

Leege, D.C. and T.A. Trozzolo. 1985. "Who Participates in Local Church Communities?" *Origins* 15:49-57.

Lehman, E. C. 1985. *Women Clergy: Breaking through Gender Barriers.* New Brunswick, NJ: Transaction Books.

John Paul II. 1983. *Code of Canon Law.* Latin-English edition. Washington, DC: Canon Law Society of America.

Renken, J.A. 1987. "Canonical Issues in the Pastoral Care of Parishes without Priests." *The Jurist* 47:506-519.

"Report of Catholic Biblical Association." 1979. *Origins* (December 17).

The Official Catholic Directory. 1988. New York: Kenedy.

U.S. Bishops. 1988. "Partners in the Mystery of Redemption: A Pastoral Response to Women's Concerns for Church and Society." *Origins* 17:757-788.

_____. 1990. "One in Christ Jesus: A Pastoral Response to the Concerns of Women for Church and Society." *Origins* 19:717-740.

Wallace, R.A. 1988. "Catholic Women and the Creation of a New Social Reality." *Gender and Society* 2:24-38.

Woodward, K.L., T. Stranger, S. Sullivan, M. Margolis, and R. Vokey. 1985. "Church in Crisis." *Newsweek* (December 9), pp. 66-75.

PART III

THE CHURCH AND SOCIAL ISSUES: INSTITUTIONAL COMMITMENTS AND SHIFTING ATTITUDES OF CATHOLICS

CATHOLIC SEXUAL ETHICS SINCE VATICAN II

James R. Kelly

At first glance the Second Vatican Council seemed merely to restate what most knowledgeable persons had always thought *was* the Roman Catholic teaching about family and sexuality. In the Council documents there was, to be sure, no diminution in the pivotal importance Roman Catholicism has always attributed to the family. The "Decree on the Apostolate of the Laity" (Abbott 1966) and the "Decree on the Pastoral Constitution In The Modern World" repeat long-standing Catholic teaching that society and civilization depend on the family, that "the family is the foundation of society," "the first and vital cell of society." The centrality and indispensability of the family has distinguished Catholic social thought from much of modern political theory, ranging from early Marxism, which thought marriage a bourgoise impediment to revolutionary justice, to liberal capitalism, whose individualistic market focus ignored the family.

In traditional Catholic social thought the long-range moral progress of a people depends more on the health of the family than on the expansion of the economy. Indeed, in Catholic social thought the development of the

Religion and the Social Order, Volume 2, pages 139-154.
Copyright © 1991 by JAI Press Inc.
All rights of reproduction in any form reserved.
ISBN: 1-55938-388-7

economy and the policies of the state are most importantly judged in terms of their impact on the family. In our era, this gives Catholic social thought both nostalgic and critical airs. Because in Catholic social thought the family remains permanently the pivotal social institution, the state (or political collectivity) is *a priori* denied the possibility of becoming a focus of intense ideological feeling. But in Catholic social thought the state is perpetually required to find ways of adapting economic imperatives to the health of the family.

Besides placing enormous social and cultural importance on the family, Roman Catholicism has raised the family to an extraordinarily high ideological significance. Vatican II documents repeat the traditional teaching that marriage is a "sacrament" that images and symbolizes the love that Christ has for the church. This teaching dramatically links the indissolubility of marriage with the indissolubility of the bond between Christ and the church. In other words, the Catholic laity are invited to analogically understand the unalterable love of Christ for the church by reflecting on the Christian marriage they have experienced, a rather risky invitation, it would seem, in the modern era. Nevertheless, it is clear that the traditional ideal of marriage carries enormous symbolic importance in the Catholic way of thinking about the church, divine providence, and even about politics and social policy. Because the teaching about marriage is so densely interwoven with so many other dimensions of Catholic social and moral thought it is almost self-evident that traditional formulations of marriage and sexuality will prove strongly resistant to change. Despite extraordinary ideological pressure from modernity, and the difficulties many laity experience in living Catholic sexual ethics in secular and pluralistic cultures, history suggests that normative Catholic teaching about marriage and sexuality can be expected to change mostly in pastoral accommodation. But these changes in praxis might have lasting significance for Catholic theology, especially if its moral theologians continue to return to an earlier mode of pastorally sensitive moral casuistry (Jonsen and Toulmin 1988; Mahoney 1989).

Despite the appearance of sameness, the Council decree on "The Church In The Modern World" contained themes that have profoundly altered the Catholic way of understanding marriage. The council changed not the core elements of Catholic teaching, but the interrelationships among the elements, especially the theological emphases on the elements of the intention of commitment, the procreation of children and the achievement of marital affection which, together, comprise in Catholic thought the constitutive elements of the anthropological reality of marriage. These changes in theory have, but not without continued conflict, affected pastoral practice. These changes will continue to affect Catholic moral reflection about such questions as contraception, divorce, and homosexuality.

The teaching of the Second Vatican Council emphasized the centrality of love in the definition of marriage. The Council replaced the traditional but juridical term of "contract" with the biblical notion of "covenant." The Council brought to fruition a long history of Catholic philosophical reflection and described marriage in predominantly "personalistic" rather than in legal terms. Marriage was no longer described negatively as a "remedy for concupiscence" in a life inferior to consecrated virginity, as it was in the Augustinian tradition that heavily molded Catholic-Christian thought about sexuality. The Council described marriage as a life-long commitment to a community of love and mutual growth.

THE ONGOING CONTROVERSY
OVER HUMANAE VITAE

Through the middle ages and up to the Second Vatican Council the "primary" end of marriage was defined as procreation and the "secondary end" was the love of the spouses (see Mackin [1982] for the complicated history of this teaching.) In the decree "The Church in the Modern World," the Council no longer subordinated the "end" of love to the "end" of procreation. Indeed, the Council did not employ the traditional terms of "primary" and "secondary" ends, even though close observers (Mackin 1982, p. 264) contend that Pope Paul VI attempted at the last moment to restore this distinction to the decree.

On July 29, 1968, Pope Paul VI released his encyclical Humanae Vitae which both continued the personalist emphasis of the Second Vatican Council that marriage is above all a committed union of permanent sharing between husband and wife *and* the magisterium's traditional teaching that artificial contraception was not simply opposed to ecclesiastical law but also in conflict with the requirements of human dignity, the core element of the natural law tradition that has characterized Roman Catholic moral reflection. The Pope taught that every conjugal act (save those during naturally infecund periods) had to be open to the possibility of conception, for the "unitive" and the "procreative" ends of marriage could not be deliberately severed. The Pope's teaching went counter to the majority opinion of the "Pontifical Commission on Population, Family and Birth" which the Pope himself had commissioned to study birth control after the Council Fathers had honored his request that they not consider the topic of birth control (for a detailed account, see Kaiser [1985]). The majority of the commission had come to agree with Noonan's (1965, p. 532) conclusion that "the recorded statements of Christian doctrine did not have to be read in a way requiring an absolute prohibition" of artificial contraception. More specifically, the majority of the commission were persuaded that as an end of marriage the procreation of children should be seen in the overall commitment of the spouses but not necessarily in each single act of marital intercourse. Even the authors of the Pontifical Commission's minority report reaffirming the teaching against contraception conceded that moral reasoning alone could not sustain the ban.

Humanae Vitae was and is widely criticized by Catholics, as well as others. Just two days after its promulgation, 87 Catholics signed a statement of dissent published in The New York Times. Soon afterward, six hundred Catholic theologians signed a statement of dissent. Twenty years later, many of the same arguments against any absolute prohibition of artificial contraception were still being made by prominent theologians. On January 15, 1989, Bernard Haring, a well-known moral theologian, published an article in *Il Regno,* an Italian Catholic magazine, in which he called for the Pope to establish a commission to reexamine the issue of contraception. About a week later, Haring was joined by 162 European theologians in a statement that mostly criticized Pope John Paul II's appointment of bishops not recommended by the local churches but which also contained a criticism of the Pope's apparent description of the ban on birth control as a "fundamental truth of faith" ("The Cologne Declaration," March 1989, pp. 633-634). Haring wrote of the dangers of "psychological schism." But in the United States, and probably throughout most of the world, the teaching of Humanae Vitae and its strong defense by the present Pope (Familiares Consortio 1981) causes far less disagreement among the laity, not because it is accepted but because either it is not preached or is interpreted as a difficult ideal not always or everywhere achievable. Here some empirical studies can help us.

Greeley, McCourt, and McCready (1976) found that only 32 percent of Catholics in a national sample said that they believed that the church had a right to teach them what they should think about birth control. They argued that Humanae Vitae was the major cause in the decline in Mass attendance documented among American Catholics since the Second Vatican Council. But other studies have not been able to explicitly confirm this (D'Antonio, Davidson, Hoge, and Wallace 1989, pp. 44, 97; Hoge 1981) and the fact that Church attendance during the same period declined in liberal Protestant denominations, in which there were no controversies about contraception, suggested that something even more complex was happening. Because the size of the Catholic population had grown since 1968 while the decline in mass attendance has been stable for a decade, Greeley (1989a, p. 52) more recently has himself argued that it is not likely that people are turning away from the Church today because of the birth control issue; more likely, they reject the Church's teaching, practice birth control as a matter of conscience, and go to Church or not for other reasons. Only 10 percent of those who rejected the ban on artificial contraception and said they had little confidence in Catholic officials completely abandon church attendance (Greeley 1989a, p. 50).

D'Antonio et al. (1989, p. 135) found that, in a random national sample, Catholics were more likely (43%) to say that the ban on contraception had no effect on their religious commitment than they were to say (35%) that it weakened their commitment. An early study (Moore 1973, p. 28, Table 2-1) showed that the papal ban on contraception probably had little effect because of the broad sympathies of parish priests with their laity's concern for effective family planning. Few made an issue of contraception when hearing confessions and the great majority said that they either accept the penitent's judgement about the morality of contraceptive practice or they discourage contraception but do not withhold absolution because of it. Greeley (1989b, pp. 194-195) reports that, in general, defections from Catholicism are small (no more than one of every seven "born" Catholics) and that those on the margin of the church are "not significantly more likely than others to question teachings on birth control, divorce, abortion, artificial insemination and premarital sex."

AMERICAN CATHOLICS AND ABORTION

Abortion greatly divides the nation but, ironically, it seems not to have polarized Catholics at the local level (D'Antonio et al. 1989, p. 187), though this statement requires some qualification. Gallup and Castelli (1987, p. 52) report that "permissive Catholic attitudes toward birth control and premarital sex do not extend to abortion." The Notre Dame Study of Catholic Parish Life (Gremillion and Castelli 1987, pp. 42-43) observes that "Core Catholics reject abortion on demand or as a form of birth control." Both studies add that while American Catholics overwhelmingly reject unrestricted abortion, only a small percentage (other studies find between 10-15 percent) say they oppose legal abortion in all cases. Actually, in their attitudes toward abortion Catholics are much like other Americans, accepting legal abortion (at least in the first and early second trimesters) for the so-called hard cases of rape, incest, severe fetal deformity and severe maternal health problems. Systematic study has not been able to find that Catholics are less likely than Protestants to have abortions (Henshaw and Silverman 1989, p. 168). While magisterial Catholic moral thought opposes all *direct* abortions, the teaching of the American Bishops has followed the classical principle of prudence (Degnan in Jung and Shannon 1988, pp. 250-255) and taught that Catholics are morally obliged to seek to stop as many legal abortions as "possible." The bishops' support for the unsuccessful 1983 "Hatch Amendment," which would have returned to the states (as the July 3, 1989, Supreme Court ruling *Webster* vs. *Reproductive Health Services, et al.* has done to some extent) the right to restrict legal abortion, clearly shows that official Catholic teaching does not expect that western societies will enact laws prohibiting all abortions because probably few states, if any, would prohibit all direct abortions. McBrien (1987, p. 168) summarizes centuries of Catholic social thought with his observation that "disagreement over the political application of a moral principle does not necessarily imply disagreement over the moral principle itself." The hundreds and hundreds of polls about abortion yield collective support to his contention that "Many, indeed the majority, of those who oppose abortion on moral grounds also oppose an absolute legal prohibition. They want to leave *legal* room for abortion in the cases of rape, incest, danger of the mother's life, or radical deformity of the fetus" (1987, p. 168). Catholic and Protestant opinion about abortion is fairly similar; and regarding public policy, officials from most of the Christian denominations are actually fairly similar, although the failure of the churches to pursue an ecumenical approach regarding legal abortion has obscured those similarities (Kelly 1989).

ATTITUDES TOWARD PREMARITAL SEX

There has been a great shift among Americans in general with regard to attitudes toward matters sexual, and this shift arguably has been greatest among Roman Catholics. Although it is only a case study, perhaps by its specific focus Moberg's (Moberg and Hoge 1986, pp. 104-117) longitudinal study of Catholic students at Marquette University captures most dramatically the largeness of this shift in attitudes. In his 1961 survey, Moberg had not even thought to include a question about premarital sexual intercourse; indeed, in that survey a majority answered that "heavy necking" was morally wrong. But by 1987 only a third of the seniors (and a fifth of freshman) said they thought premarital sexual intercourse was always wrong. It might be that Marquette students when answering the question were thinking about sexual relations within at least some form of committed relationship, as 64 percent agreed it is wrong to have more than one sexual partner. Moreover, Marquette students clearly had not renounced marriage nor lost the hopes of earlier generations that marriage would be both fulfilling and permanent. In a question that included such powerful competitors as "careers" and "wealth," 59 percent of the senior men, and 72 percent of the women, said that they expected their "greatest future satisfaction" from "family and marriage," which is an even higher response than that given by the class of 1961.

The shift toward more permissive views of premarital sex found by Moberg at one Catholic college have been replicated by more comprehensive studies. Greeley, McCready, Sullivan, and Fee (1980) found that while in 1963, 83 percent of weekly communicants in their 20s thought premarital sex was wrong, by 1979 only 34 percent continued to say this. This finding about Catholics certainly mirrors larger trends found more generally among Americans. A 1985 report of the National Center for Health Statistics reported that the proportion of woman who delayed sexual intercourse until marriage declined from 48 percent among women who married in 1961 to 1964, to 21 percent marrying during the years from 1975 to 1979. The largest decline in postponing intercourse until marriage occurred during the years that followed the conclusion of the Second Vatican Council, from 1965 to 1969 (*New York Times,* April 17, 1985, p. C14). In other words, immediately after the Second

Vatican Council, American Catholics were at the intersection of any number of revolutions about such fundamental matters as religion, conscience and authority, sex, patriotism, family, and nation. It would have been easier for Catholics to organically assimilate the Council if the larger world had agreed to stay somewhat more in place during these years.

Greeley (1989a, p. 91, Table 8.3) reports that between 1972 and 1985 the "sexual revolution" affected Catholics more than Jews and Protestants, and that among all groups something more complicated than a complete erosion of past normative sentiments has occurred. Some features of traditional western sexual norms seem stable. While only about a third of sampled Catholics were willing to agree that premarital sex was always wrong, the vast majority of Catholics (as well as white Protestants and Jews, 71%) continue to describe extramarital sex as always wrong.

ARE CATHOLICS ANY DIFFERENT?
CATHOLIC DIVORCE RATES

While the magisterial statements of Roman Catholicism continue the high valorization of marriage (indeed, in his 1981 exhortation Familiaris Consortio, Pope John Paul II described the family as the "domestic church") and decry divorce, American Catholics increasingly seem more American than Catholic in terms of beliefs about marriage and in their marital related behavior. The Notre Dame study of affiliated Catholics found that 64 percent thought "the church should liberalize its position on divorce" (Gremillion and Castelli 1987, p. 38). (Unfortunately, they did not ask if by "divorce" respondents meant "annulment.") But less than a third of a national sample of Catholics said that individuals on their own, without church consultation, should decide if a divorced Catholic should remarry without getting an annulment (D'Antonio et al. 1989, p. 85). Past studies found that Roman Catholicism does have some inhibiting force on the divorce rates of Catholics, especially if they are practicing Catholicism. While the religiously committed are generally less likely than the unaffiliated to divorce, past studies reported that Catholics were far less likely than Protestants to legally end their marriages. But these differences have gradually declined, and more recent studies such as McCarthy (1979, p. 179) and Bumpass and Sweet (1972) have found a Catholic-Protestant differential of only about 3 percent. This difference is statistically significant but intuitively it seems far less than one might expect from Catholic normative teaching about the indissolubility of marriage. The key factor in divorce rates seems not so much to be official teaching about marriage (because all American religious traditions speak to some degree about the "sanctity" of marriage), but the degree of active involvement in the tradition. Still, normative beliefs seem to count for something. McCarthy (1979, p. 191) reports that active Catholics are still much less likely to separate than their Protestant counterparts. Greeley et al. (1980, p. 155) report that the Catholic "ever divorced" rate has increased from 15 percent in 1972 to 18 percent in 1980. They describe this change as "inching up" but "hardly revolutionary." They remark that despite the changing attitudes among Catholics toward divorce and the "ready availability of ecclesiastical annulments" the Catholic divorce rate should be described as stable. Time will tell. Certainly the practices of Roman Catholic "marriage tribunals" have altered (Deedy 1986, p. 321; Kelleher 1973, pp. 127-142) . A recent book for divorced Catholics (Twomey 1982) lists more than 30 factors that diocesan marriage courts have used to determine when "in the eyes of the church law a valid sacramental marriage never existed." As psychological factors are increasingly admitted as tribunal evidence, the church can claim to be continuing its tradition of regarding sacramental marriage as indissoluble *even* as the numbers of annulments steadily increase.

FAMILY SIZE

The broad findings about Catholics and divorce—that Catholic attitudes about divorce are converging with those of most Americans and that Catholic-Protestant divorce differentials are no longer very large—can also describe Catholic attitudes about family size and contraception. While many investigators now speak of a convergence (Westoff 1979) of Protestant and Catholic attitudes toward family size and family planning, there remain, for the moment at least, some differences. For example, as of the mid 1970s Hendershot and Mosher found a statistical "half-child" variation (3.04 vs. 2.47) differentiating (white) Catholics and (white) Protestants. They also found Catholics who received communion at least once a month tended to have larger families than less observant Catholics. So while it is true that all categories of American women had fewer children during the period studied—hence a general convergence within all identifiable groupings towards smaller families—fertility differences between religiously observant Catholic woman and all others actually increased during the period 1971-1975.

More recently, Blake (1984) also found a broad convergence toward smaller family expectations among all categories of students but she also found small but consistent differences differentiating Catholics, especially those who attended Catholic schools and who were religiously observant, from others. Johnson (1982) found that women graduates of Catholic colleges anticipated having more children than women graduates of Protestant affiliated colleges and, though they married later than their Protestant peers, actually averaged .29 more children.

What sense should we make of such findings? Obviously Catholics, like other Americans, anticipate and have fewer children than in the past. But it cannot be said that their patterns of contraceptive use are much different from others. But neither can it be said that being a knowledgeable and observant Catholic makes no difference at all in terms of expectation of number of children, actual family size, and even of contraceptive usage and likelihood to divorce. When interpreting these statistics, depending on our interests or, more likely, our guesses about the future, we can emphasize either the convergences with mainstream Americans, especially with affiliated Protestants, or the remaining differences distinguishing Catholic attitudes and marital behavior from other Americans. Overall, the data probably reflect more the common sense observation that being Catholic in American culture still makes some serious difference in terms of attitudes toward sexuality and family among those who take their Roman Catholicism seriously. But the differences are not as sharp or as clear as in the past, and they seem stable at present. American Catholics seem loyal to Catholicism (D'Antonio et al. 1989, 114-185; Gallup and Castelli 1987, chap. 15; Greeley 1989a, pp. 46-47; Seidler and Meyer 1989, p. 168), but by conventional indices of religious commitment they are more selectively attached to their religion than was generally the case before the Second Vatican Council.

ATTITUDES TOWARD HOMOSEXUALITY

During the annual "Gay Rights Parade" in New York City, a mandatory protest stop is made in front of St. Patrick's Cathedral, the residence of the Roman Catholic Archbishop of New York City. As is usually the case, at first glance the normative Catholic position seems simple and its political implications obvious. Especially since *Humanae Vitae* the teaching that each sexual act must be open to the possibility of the transmission of human life means that homosexual acts must be judged as intrinsically disordered. But despite this ideological hostility to any principled moral acceptance of homosexuality, magisterial Catholicism has sought its own nuanced approach to the psychological and moral complexity of homosexuality. Catholic documents have been careful to distinguish between a homosexual orientation and homosexual acts, usually describing the orientation as morally neutral (Sacred Congregation 1975, p. 8; see 1986, p. 9 for a less nuanced statement) and homosexual genital sex as morally impermissible. The moral counsel given to homosexuals is the same as that given to all the unmarried, the practice of celibacy. Thus, the American bishops have been instructed by Vatican authorities not to give official status to groups of Catholic homosexuals who publicly contend for church endorsement of loving homosexual acts as moral.

The record of the Catholic bishops with regard to civil rights of homosexuals has been generally in advance of public opinion, though gay activist groups will have much to criticize. Support for AIDS research and for AIDS victims has been frequently expressed. The general principle underlying official Catholic reactions to homosexual concerns has been supportive when they can be interpreted as a matter of general respect for the human person—such as the right to employment, nondiscrimination, health care, protection against the intolerant (Canadian Bishops 1989, pp. 25-27; Bishops of the California Catholic Conference 1988, p. 156)—and hostile to any policy or politics that would explicitly require a public definition of homosexuality as a sexual style morally equal to marriage between heterosexuals.

From their analysis of the available public opinion data, Gallup and Castelli (1987, pp. 63-65) conclude that "one area where Catholics are considerably more tolerant than Protestants involves homosexuality." For example, they were more likely than Protestants to support equal job opportunities for homosexuals. Although the questions did not include the distinction between orientation and behavior found in official Catholic discussions of homosexuality, Gallup and Castelli report that Catholics were more likely than Protestants (unfortunately they do not distinguish among denominations) and the general population to accept homosexuals as elementary school teachers and as clergy.

MORAL TRADITIONALISM
AND SOCIAL CRITIQUE

The common practice of researchers of attitudes of American Catholics on questions of marriage and sexuality is to say that Catholics practice a "selective" Catholicism. That is, like most Americans, American Catholics value autonomy and the rights of the individual conscience. They believe their society is egalitarian and democratic and they increasingly apply these criteria to religion as well. While reports of a "selective Catholicism" (Greeley 1989a, p. 47; Gremillion and Castelli 1987, p. 37) certainly have strong empirical warrant, the data also raise puzzling questions concerning the low rate of defection from Catholicism (Greeley 1989b, p. 195) and why disagreement about the church's teaching about sexual morality seems ultimately not to cause a withdrawal of loyalty. The answers to these questions lie on the three levels of church structure, moral culture, and the tendency of individuals to wish exemption from church teaching for themselves while affirming it in principle. It might be that Catholics, in effect, practice "situation ethics" even while they affirm the value of general norms. Perhaps this bothers intellectuals more than ordinary men and women.

The organizational reactions of Catholicism to the laity's increasingly "pick and choose" approach to Catholic moral thought is a key variable in the development of American Roman Catholicism. Official Catholic reaction has been to defend its moral traditionalism by deepening its political and cultural radicalism. This explicit linking makes both its moral and its social thought more coherent and more plausible; this strategy also seeks to make the contemporary world more hospitable to Catholic social and moral teaching. Magisterial Catholicism has increasingly recognized that only when coupled with a politically progressive social teaching can Catholicism make plausible its moral traditionalism. In brief, however unlikely the coupling may seem, in the postmodern era the retention of moral traditionalism requires a more radical social teaching.

The basic argument made here is that in the modern era what we might call the basic premise of sociology has been widely diffused in academic and ecclesial reflection. All moral activity has a social context or, to speak more plainly, any injunction that individuals be loyal to a moral code, such as preserving marriages or avoiding abortion, requires that the surrounding society make such behavior possible by providing the economic and community help that moral activity requires. This has been most evident in the Catholic debate about legal abortion.

Although the notion of a "consistent" ethic or a "seamless garment" approach, which links opposition to abortion to efforts to lessen poverty, to reduce military spending and to oppose capital punishment, has become associated with Cardinal Joseph Bernardin's December 6, 1983, address "A Consistent Ethic of Life" given at Fordham University, this approach, and not a single issue approach to abortion, had always characterized the American Catholic Bishops' position (Kelly 1989). From the start, church officials have acknowledged that women with unwanted pregnancies were more likely to forego abortions if they received help before and after the birth of their child. In 1967 the only national center of opposition to legal abortion was the United States Catholic Conference's Family Life Bureau, then directed by Father James McHugh. In a memo to McHugh the late Bishop W. Curtis, the Bureau's episcopal advisor, advised that pro-life activists ought to work to obtain help for women with problem and unwanted pregnancies and advised "cooperation with our welfare institutions that provide shelter, education, counseling, and future opportunity for the unwed mother" (Kelly forthcoming). Recent pastoral letters and encyclicals have pushed consistency far beyond the point of welfare assistance. The church's evolving teachings on questions of sexual equality and social justice show that only in the context of an increasingly radical critique of western economic systems does the church's teaching about sexual ethics and gender justice make internal sense (Kelly 1986). The thesis advanced here is that within Roman Catholicism the requirement of making internal sense of its arguments for moral traditionalism is itself a strong organizational propellent toward a radical critique of modern economic structures.

MORAL CONSERVATISM AND
ORGANIZATIONAL VITALITY

There is an unnoted aspect of the Catholic church's retention of moral traditionalism that can help us understand the existence of both severe dissent and continued vitality in the contemporary church. Efforts by the official magisterium to defend the plausibility of its sexual ethic and by the laity to follow them under the conditions of modern life have spawned not, as we have seen (Greeley 1989b, p. 195), widespread defection but a proliferation of church groups and organizations. There is a surface irony here. Because many of the traditional teachings of Roman Catholicism are so difficult to adapt to contemporary conditions they have required organizational innovations that engage many thousands of the laity as either voluntary or paid staff. All dioceses have extensive programs in "natural family planning," which respects the natural cycle of infecundity. In natural family planning programs both wives and husbands are taught to carefully observe the mucus content of the cervix to prevent unwanted conceptions by avoiding intercourse when its "lubricative" quality signals the presence of ovulation. Feminist critics (Greer 1984) of conventional Western means of birth control have praised natural family planning methods and these methods permit magisterial authorities to present the ban on artificial contraception as not precluding other ways of limiting births which are congruent with its interpretation of natural law.

All dioceses have "Pre-Cana" marriage preparation programs for those thinking of marriage and "Cana" for engaged Catholics. In 1978, the United States Catholic Conference Commission on Marriage and Family Life recommended that each parish should have a family ministry committee chaired by a volunteer couple or a full- or part-time coordinator, and by the early 1980s almost half of all American parishes did (Gremillion and Leege 1989, p. 5). Only about a fifth of all parishes have explicit ministries for the divorced and separated, but Catholic Family Ministry officials note that most divorcing Catholics prefer help and support groups from a parish where they are not personally known and that the centralization of such programs in several dispersed parishes means that programs are close for most of those who need them. Programs such as "Marriage Encounter" designed to enhance marriages by, among other things, increasing communication skills have attracted over 1.5 million American couples since 1968. "Dignity," a group of Catholic homosexuals who seek an explicit change in magisterial teaching about the morality of some forms of homosexuality, has more than 100 chapters throughout the United States. "Courage," which accepts church teaching that homosexuals should abstain from genital sex, has ten chapters. While there has been enormous debate about the moral acceptability of homosexuality, masturbation, and divorce, there has been widespread acceptance of the need for sex education in the Catholic schools (United States Catholic Conference 1983; Sacred Congregation 1986). The teacher's manual about AIDS developed by the National Catholic Educational Association (1988, p. 3) includes in its orientation for teachers and parents the reminder that they teach young persons "a compassionate response for all suffering members, including those who suffer from the effects of AIDS."

While they report a large amount of laity dissent from traditional Catholic teaching about sexuality, a surprising number of the same commentators also describe what they call the vitality of American Roman Catholicism (Castelli and Gallup 1987, p. xv; D'Antonio 1989, pp. 184-185; Greeley 1989a, pp. 46-47; Seidler and Meyer 1989, p. 168). But there are both theoretical (Kelly and Campion 1970) and common sense reasons why we should not be surprised to find that dissent, even from core moral teachings, might not in itself lead to weakening of a religious tradition and, indeed, might even engender institutional vitality by being the catalyst for organizational innovations involving lay participation. Needless to say, not all traditional teachings can be rationally justified and thus plausibly maintained. Catholic teachings, first of all, cannot be judged irrational or be experienced by most as patent impediments to human flourishing. They must even seem to be, however difficult, truer than the available alternatives. In my interviews of Directors of Catholic Family Life Directors one shrewdly observed that while parents might have trouble with the ban on artificial contraception themselves, they do not mind the church's teaching that there is an "inseparable connection" between the "unitive and the procreative meaning" of genital intercourse (Paul VI 1968, #12) as ideological support for their discouragement of premarital sex. Most parents would prefer that their children not be sexually active before marriage and many Catholics seem in effect to regard the teaching of *Humanae Vitae* as a dramatic reminder that sex is most human within bonds of commitment that do not exclude the loving care of children. While individuals might not always want the criteria of consistency to be applied to their own behavior, they might still want a coherent moral teaching available for the moral formation of their children.

Something similar seems to be evolving in questions of marriage and divorce. The magisterium continues to teach the indissolubility of marriage while in practice marriage tribunals are able to declare an increasing number of unhappy unions as lacking an element essential for their validity. Directors of diocesan family ministry offices have sometimes informed me that "annulments are possible for most Catholics seeking one." One observed that in the case of most divorcing couples there is evidence of an "immaturity that precludes a valid reception of the sacrament of marriage." He defined the requisite maturity for the sacrament as the "considered understanding that I will be the instrument by which God will love my spouse." This is a high requirement for maturity but, conversely, a low requirement for annulment.

In short, it is only a surface paradox that the American Catholic church can be characterized both by dissent and vitality. The moral traditionalism that sparks dissent also leads to organizational innovations that engage many hundreds of staff and many thousands of laity. While the normative moral theory of Catholicism emphasizes principles, the actual practice within Catholicism permits moral accommodation through the sacrament of reconciliation. Departures from moral teachings concerning contraception and divorce are either ignored, reinterpreted, or considered as leaving intact core and valued attitudes towards love and sexuality. The very systematic qualities of Catholic moral thought, and its efforts toward internal coherence, make it somewhat immune even from its internal critics who continue to privilege its core insights while seeking greater accommodation to marginal and tragic cases, especially where the application of even valued principles seemingly leads to psychological harm, as in some cases of abortion, homosexuality, and divorce. But for the reasons described in this essay, for the immediate future, observers of Roman Catholicism should expect more pastoral accommodation but little change in magisterial teaching about love, sexuality, and the family. Of some significance are the findings (D'Antonio et al. 1989, pp. 172-173) that Catholics who adhere to traditional moral norms are more likely than less traditional Catholics to agree with the pastoral letter "Economic Justice for All." The more immediate questions are how in an ecumenical framework American Catholics will be encouraged to work with those who do not share in any absolutist way the church's teaching on sex and marriage but value the church's teaching on social justice and peace so that the reshaping of modern economies and politics, which the Church increasingly acknowledges is necessary for the living of its sexual ethic, is made more likely (Kelly 1986).

REFERENCES

Abbott, W. M., S.J., ed. 1966. *The Documents of the Vatican II.* New York: Guild Press.

Blake, J. 1984. "Catholicism and Fertility: On Attitudes of Young Americans." *Population and Development Review* 10(2)329-340.

Bumpass, L.L., and J.A. Sweet. 1972 "Differentials In Marital Instability: 1970." *American Sociological Review* 37:754-766.

Committee (Ad Hoc) on Marriage and Family Life. 1987. *A Family Perspective on Church and Society: A Manual for All Pastoral Leaders.* Washington, DC: United States Catholic Conference.

Curran, C. 1976. "Dialogue with the Homophile Movement." *Catholic Moral Theology in Dialogue.* South Bend, IN: University of Notre Dame Press.

———. 1986. *Faithful Dissent.* Kansas City, MO: Sheed & Ward.

D'Antonio, W.V. 1988. "The American Catholic Family: Signs of Cohesion and Polarization." In *The Religion & Family Connection: Social Sciences Perspectives,* edited by D.L. Thomas. Provo, UT: Religious Studies Center, Brigham Young University.

D'Antonio, W.V., and J. Davidson, D.Hoge, and R. Wallace. 1989. *American Catholic Laity.* Kansas City, MO: Sheed & Ward.

Deedy, J. 1986. *The Catholic Fact Book*. Chicago, IL: Thomas More Press.

Ford, J.C., G. Grisez, J. Boyle, J. Finnis, and W.E. May. 1988. *The Teaching of Humanae Vitae: A Defense*. San Francisco, CA: Ignatius Press.

Gallup, G. Jr., and J. Castelli. 1987. *The American Catholic People: Their Beliefs, Practices, and Values*. Garden City, NY: Doubleday.

Greeley, A.M. 1989a. *Religious Change in America*. Cambridge, MA: Harvard University Press.

————. 1989b. "On the Margins of the Church: A Sociological Note." *America* (March 4), pp. 194-198.

Greeley, A., K. McCourt, and W. McCready. 1976. *Catholic Schools in a Declining Church*. Kansas City, MO: Sheed & Ward.

Greeley, A.M., W. McCready, T. Sullivan, and J. Fee. 1980. "A Profile of the American Catholic Family." *America* (September 27), pp. 155-160.

Greer, G. 1984. *Sex and Destiny*. New York: Harper & Row.

Gremillion, J., and J. Castelli. 1987. *The Emerging Parish: The Notre Dame Study of Catholic Life Since Vatican II*. San Francisco: Harper & Row.

Gremillion, J., and D. C. Leege. 1989. "Post-Vatican II Parish Life in The U.S.: Review and Preview." *Notre Dame Study of Catholic Parish Life,* Report no. 15, June. Sound Bend, IN: University of Notre Dame Press.

Henshaw, S.K., and J. Silverman. 1989. "The Characteristics and Prior Contraceptive Use of U.S. Abortion Patients." *Family Planning Perspectives*. 20(4):158-168.

Hoge, D. R. 1981. *Converts, Dropouts, Returnees*. New York: Pilgrim Press.

Johnson, N. E. 1982. "Religious Differentials in Reproduction." *Demography* 19(4).

Jonsen, A.A., and S.R. Toulmin. 1988. *The Abuse of Casuistry: A History of Moral Reasoning*. Berkeley: University of California Press.

Jung, P. B., and T.A. Shannon, eds. 1988. *Abortion and Catholicism: The American Debate*. New York: Crossroad.

Kaiser, R.B. 1985. *The Politics of Sex and Religion*. Kansas City, MO: Leaven Press.

Kelleher, S. J. 1973. *Divorce and Remarriage for Catholics?* New York: Doubleday.

Kelly, J.R. 1984. "Catholicism and Modern Memory: Some Sociological Reflection on the Symbolic Foundations of the Rhetorical Force of the Pastoral Letter 'The Challenge of Peace.'" *Sociological Analysis* 45(2): 131-144.

————. 1986. "Residual or Prophetic? The Cultural Fate of Roman Catholic Sexual Ethics of Abortion and Contraception." *Social Thought* 12(2):3-18.

————. 1989. "Ecumenism and Abortion: A Case Study of Pluralism, Privatization and Public Conscience." *Review of Religious Research* 30(3):225-235.

————. Forthcoming. "Learning and Teaching Consistency: Catholics and the Right-to-Life Movement." In M. Segers and T. Byrnes, *The Catholic Church and Abortion Politics*. Boulder, CO: Westview Press.

Kelly, J.R., and D.Campion. 1970. "Loyalty and Dissent: Reflections of Two Sociologists. *America* (June 27), pp. 679-680.

L'Osservatore Romano. 1989. "The Moral Norms of 'Humanae Vitae.'" *Origins* 18(2): 629-632.

Mackin, T., S. J. 1982. *What is Marriage?* New York: Paulist.

Mahoney, J. 1989. *The Making of Moral Theology: A Study of the Roman Catholic Tradition*. Oxford: Clarendon Press.

McBrien, R.P. 1987. *Caesar's Coin: Religion and Politics in America*. New York: Macmillan.

McCarthy, J. 1979. "Religious Commitment, Affiliation, and Marriage Dissolution." In *The Religious Dimension: New Directions in Quantitative Research*, edited by R. Wuthnow. New York: Academic Press.

Moberg, D.O., and D. R. Hoge. 1986. "Catholic College Students' Religious and Moral Attitudes, 1961 to 1982: Effects of the Sixties and the Seventies." *Review of Religious Research* 28(2): 104-117.

Moberg, D.O., and J.McEnery. 1976. "Changes in Church-Related Behavior and Attitudes of Catholic Students, 1961-1971." *Sociological Analysis* 37(1):53-62.

Moore, M.J. 1973. *Death of a Dogma? The American Catholic Clergy's Views of Contraception.* Chicago: University of Chicago Press.

Mosher, W.D., and G.F. Hendershot. 1984. "Religion and Fertility: A Replication." *Demography* 21(2):185-191.

National Catholic Educational Association. 1988. *AIDS: A Catholic Educational Approach.* Washington, DC: NCEA.

National Conference of Catholic Bishops. 1986. Economic Justice For All: Catholic Social Teaching and the U.S. Economy. *Origins* 16(24):409-455.

_____. 1988. *Partners in the Mystery of Redemption: A Pastoral Response to Women's Concerns for Church and Society* 17(45)757-788.

Nelson, R.J. 1989. "The Ecumenical Challenge of Ethical Issues." *Origins* 18(45):761-770.

Newman, J.H. 1961. *On Consulting the Faithful in Matters of Doctrine.* Kansas City, MO: Sheed and Ward.

Noonan, J. T. 1965. *Contraception: A History of Its Treatment by the Catholic Theologians and Canonists.* Cambridge, MA: Harvard University Press.

_____. 1972. *Power to Dissolve: Lawyers and Marriages in the Courts of the Roman Curia.* Cambridge, MA: Harvard University Press.

Paul VI. 1968. *Humane Vitae.* Boston, MA: Daughters of St. Paul.

Paul, John II. 1981. *Familiares Consortio* [On The Family.] Washington, DC: United States Catholic Conference.

Provost, J. 1989. "Canon Law and the Role of Consultation." *Origins* 18(47):794-799.

Sacred Congregation for the Doctrine of the Faith. 1975. *Declaration of Certain Questions Concerning Sexual Ethics.* Washington, DC:United States Catholic Conference.

_____. 1986. *Letter to the Bishops of the Catholic Church on the Pastoral Care of Homosexual Persons.* Washington, DC: United States Catholic Conference.

Saxton, S.L., P. Voydanoff, and A. A. Zukowski, eds. 1984. *The Changing Family: Reflections on Familiaris Consortio.* Chicago: Loyola University Press.

Seidler, J., and K. Meyer. 1989. *Conflict and Change in the Catholic Church.* New Brunswick, NJ: Rutgers University Press.

Shils, E. 1981. *Tradition.* Chicago: University of Chicago Press.

Shrum, W. 1980. "Religion and Marital Instability: Change In The 1970s? *Review of Religious Research* 21(2):135-147.

Twomey, G.S. 1982. *When Catholics Marry Again: A Guide for the Divorced, Their Families and Those Who Minister To Them.* Minneapolis, MN: Winston.

United States Catholic Conference. 1983. *Educational Guidance in Human Love: Outlines for Sex Education.* Washington, DC:United States Catholic Conference.

Wallerstein, J.S., and S. Blakeslee. 1988. *Second Chances: Men, Women, and Children a Decade After Divorce.* New York: Ticknor & Fields.

Westoff, C. F. 1979. "The Blending of Catholic Reproductive Behavior." In *The Religious Dimension,* edited by R. Wuthnow. New York: Academic Press.

Witzman, L.J. 1987. *The Divorce Revolution: The Unexpected Social and Economic Consequences for Women and Children in America.* New York: Free Press.

THE CHURCH AND SOCIAL ISSUES:
INSTITUTIONAL COMMITMENTS

Joseph P. Fitzpatrick, S.J.

INTRODUCTION

Vatican II's concern for the involvement of the church in important social and cultural issues was not new; however, it did give a new orientation toward the church's social teaching and social action. The emphasis on the church as "a pilgrim people" rather than a triumphal domination over the world by God's representatives; the acknowledgement of the positive values of modern culture and technology; the need of the church to relate itself effectively to the "modern world," and the statement of social issues in a new context of care of refugees and the liberation of the poor, and a plea for peace and disarmament were to have a new impact on the involvement of Catholics as well as the institutional Church in current social movements. Also, the participation of Catholics in contemporary social movements is a more militant challenging of the authority of governments where issues of justice are involved. This chapter briefly reviews significant antecedents to Vatican II, significant texts of the Council, and important consequences in regard to the church's teaching on social issues.

Religion and the Social Order, Volume 2, pages 155-168.
Copyright © 1991 by JAI Press Inc.
All rights of reproduction in any form reserved.
ISBN: 1-55938-388-7

ANTECEDENTS TO THE COUNCIL

Many forms of social teaching and social action prevailed in the life of Catholics in the last century and the early part of this century. However, the first document that achieved international attention and proclaimed the concern of the church for social justice and the rights of labor was the great encyclical of Pope Leo XIII, "Rerum Novarum" [On the Condition of the Working Classes] ([1891]1981). The encyclical was a strong statement about the rights of workingmen to organize and bargain collectively. It became known as the great charter for the workingmen of the world. The encyclical acknowledged the causes of radical movements in the injustices of the capitalist system. It asserted the natural right to private property but also the limitations of that right; it insisted on the obligation of the State to intervene in economic enterprises to promote justice and the common good. It called for a solidarity of employers and employees to direct economic activity to the common welfare, thus avoiding the laissez faire exploitation by employers or the class war of the Communists. It was the beginning of a series of papal documents that represent the core of Catholic social thinking during the early part of this century.

"Rerum Novarum" was followed in 1931 by the encyclical, "Quadragesimo Anno" [Reconstructing the Social Order] (Pius XI [1931]1981). This encyclical restated the basic teachings of "Rerum Novarum" but emphasized the new developments in capitalism, the monopolies of giant corporations and their international impact, and the way societies become structured to ensure maximum profits for the corporations. Thus the focus of "Quadragesimo Anno" was the need to reorganize the economic and political structures so that productive and commercial enterprises would serve the common good and not perpetuate a form of economic oppression.

This was the period of the growth of Soviet Communism under Stalin. It was also the period of the development of the American labor unions. Father John A. Ryan of Catholic University became the great scholar promoting a social policy based on principles of natural law, emphatically proclaimed by the church. There was also the development of the Catholic Rural Life Conference under Father Luigi Ligutti; the development of Catholic labor schools to train workingmen and women in the techniques of trade unionism; the formation of large-scale Catholic Charities by many dioceses; movements like The Catholic Worker under Dorothy Day and Peter Maurin; and the impact of Father Charles Coughlin, the well known, but very controversial radio priest. Catholic Action and the Lay Apostolate became commonly used terms to refer to the involvement of the laity in giving Catholic ideals a presence in the secular world. The National Catholic Welfare Conference was established in 1922 to coordinate the social action of the dioceses. Their Social Action Department, originally directed by

Father Raymond McGowan and more recently by Msgr. George Higgins, has been very influential.

Most of these movements developed out of a perspective of the need to reform the social order, to correct the abuses of capitalism, to support the growing labor movement and to promote a just political and economic system that would serve the common welfare. They were marked by great enthusiasm and impressive dedication. They were also marked by a sense of identification with the Church and were defined as an extension of the church's apostolate in the world.

VATICAN II: INSTITUTIONAL CHANGE

A new direction came out of Vatican II in "Gaudium et Spes" (The Constitution of the Church in the Modern World) (Abbott 1966). This decree had been preceded by two remarkable documents of Pope John XXIII, "Mater et Magistra" (Christianity and Social Progress) ([1961]1976), and "Pacem in Terris" (Peace on Earth) ([1963)1976).

By the time John XXIII became Pope, the world had gone through enormous change: the Second World War; the development of nuclear weapons; the decline of agriculture; the impact of the problem of population; massive movements of people as refugees, displaced persons, and immigrants; the end of Colonialism; the creation of the United Nations; the rise of television; the communication revolution; and unbelieveable technological advances. The encyclical "Mater et Magistra" took note of many of these changes, reaffirmed the teaching of "Rerum Novarum" and "Quadragesimo Anno," asserted the right of all peoples to share in the benefits of these developments; and their right to the opportunity to the full development of themselves as human persons and children of God. The letter was written as the First Development Decade was underway, the ten-year plan sponsored by the United Nations to bring the benefits of modern economic development to economically underdeveloped nations. The plan was inspired by the vision of a development of national and international economies on the model of a reformed capitalism in which the condition of poor persons and poor nations would be corrected. The First Development Decade was an acknowledged failure, evidence that development of poor nations could not be achieved by seeking to make the benefits of capitalist economies available to them.

The letter "Pacem in Terris" proved to be a much more significant statement. It was the first encyclical addressed not only to Catholics but to all men and women of good will. It has probably received more universal attention than any other encyclical. Four new developments were cited as "signs of the times": the increasing influence and participation of the working classes in social and political affairs, the importance of women, the end of Colonialism, and the struggle for the rights of racial and ethnic minorities. The letter also has a section on the problem of racism, and the need to eliminate it, and on the rights of refugees and immigrants to move from one area to another. The section on the arms race and the need for disarmament revealed the alertness of Pope John XXIII to the dangers of nuclear warfare. His insistence on the curtailment of the arms race was unusually strong. This was, indeed, a statement of the church to the modern world. The church acknowledged a new range of problems and Pope John's response was well informed, sophisticated, and up-to-date. All of this set the stage for the developments of Vatican II.

The Council followed the lead of John XXIII and, in "Gaudium et Spes," formulated a statement of social teachings that gave a new orientation to the involvement of the church in social, economic, and political issues. The new spirit of the Council was reflected in Pope John's opening speech to the Council. He said of the church: "She will look to the future without fear" (John XXIII[1962]1966, p. 712). He spoke with regret of those who, "In these modern times can see nothing but prevarication and ruin . . . They behave as though at the time of former Councils everything was a full triumph . . . " (p. 712). And he continues:

> We feel we must disagree with those prophets of doom who are always forecasting disaster, as though the end of the world were at hand . . . Divine Providence is leading us to a new order of human relations which by men's own efforts and even beyond their very expectations, are directed toward the fulfillment of God's superior and inscrutable designs (p. 712).

In the same address, Pope John spoke critically of previous interference of kings and government leaders which was often damaging, and he rejoiced in the freedom in which the Second Vatican Council was conducted. He emphasized the benefits of many modern developments: "She [the church] must ever look to the present, to the new conditions and new forms of life introduced into the modern world which have opened new avenues to the Catholic apostolate" (p. 712). He affirmed the need to be true to the teachings of the Church but added that this: " . . . should be studied and expounded through the methods of research and through the literary forms of modern thought" (p. 715). Thus Pope John XXIII struck the keynote, affirmed the spirit in which the Council was to proceed, adhering faithfully to the true doctrine of the church, but embracing every aspect of modern technology and culture that can enable modern men and women to appreciate the meaning for our times of the life and word of Jesus.

It was in "Gaudium et Spes" that the spirit of this opening speech is clearly reflected.

Thanks to the experience of past ages, the progress of the sciences, and the treasures hidden in the various forms of human culture, the nature of man himself is more clearly revealed and new roads to truth are opened. These benefits profit the Church, too (Abbott 1966, p. 246, para. 44).

For the first time in a Church document, the concept of culture was carefully examined. After commenting on the variety of cultures, the document continued: "All of these values can provide some preparation for the acceptance of the message of the gospel—a preparation which can be animated with divine love by Him who came to save the world" (Abbott 1966, p. 264, para. 57).

The Constitution addressed the many forms of oppression and asserted the need to defend the basic rights of men and women, extending beyond liberation from oppression to the right to full development as a human person. "Therefore, by virtue of the Gospel committed to her, the Church proclaims the rights of man. She acknowledges and greatly esteems the dynamic movements of today by which these rights are everywhere fostered" (Abbott 1966, p. 241, para. 41). There is a long section on the importance of marriage and the family, the basis of human societies and is an emphasis on education as an essential element of the cultural development to which men and women have a right. "It is appropriate that they should be able to assume their full proper role in accordance with their own nature" (p. 267, para. 60). A strong plea followed that Catholics should seek the benefits of modern science: "In pastoral care, appropriate use must be made not only of theological principles, but also of the findings of the secular sciences, especially of psychology and sociology" (p. 269, para. 62).

In the discussion of population issues, the right of people to emigrate was strongly defended: "The personal right of migration, however, is not to be impugned." (Abbott 1966, p. 274, para. 65) After a strong plea to Catholics to participate in public life by voting and using their influence with governments to demand justice for all, the document finally addressed the issues of modern warfare. "Peace is not merely the absence of war . . . Instead it is rightly and appropriately called 'an enterprise of justice'" (p. 290, para. 78). There is praise for those who take a pacifist stand, provided they do not endanger the rights of others, and genocide is particularly condemned as is the use of money to build weapons which should rightfully be spent to feed the poor. "The arms race" was called "an utterly treacherous trap for humanity and one which injures the poor to an intolerable degree" (p. 295, para. 81). And, "Any act of war aimed indiscriminately at the destruction of entire cities or of extensive areas along with their populations is a crime against God and man himself. It merits unequivocal and inhesitating condemnation" (p. 294, para. 80) The document encouraged involvement in efforts to create international institutions that can prevent war and promote justice and peace.

Thus a new charter for social action was presented that went far beyond labor/management issues, the functioning of the economy, or the development of peoples. The central importance of human rights was emphasized; the protection of refugees; involvement in the political process for the promotion of justice; and the unrelenting effort to eliminate war and the stockpiling of weapons, especially nuclear weapons. This was urged in a spirit of reverence for the benefits of modern science and technology, modern scholarship and organization. Thus social theory and social action gave a new direction to the social movements which will be described briefly below.

SOCIAL ACTION ISSUES

Civil Rights

One of the striking developments of the past 30 years has been the development of the Civil Rights Movement in society as well as among Catholics. "Gaudium et Spes" expressed its thanks to the many institutions that were directed toward the securing of human rights. Long before Vatican II, President Franklin D. Roosevelt had defined the four basic freedoms: from fear, from want, freedom of speech, freedom of worship. There followed some years later, in 1948, the Universal Declaration of Human Rights by the United Nations and, in 1966, the International Bill of Rights. In 1954, the Supreme Court of the United States declared that segregated schooling was a violation of the civil rights of Black children.

The Civil Rights Movement in the United States developed strongly in the late 1950s and early 1960s; and the civil rights legislation of this period placed the full power of law behind civil rights and the elimination of discrimination on the basis of race. The Voting Rights Act of 1965 secured the voting rights of Black people. The movement, which began as a struggle of Black citizens, later spread to all minority groups, particularly the Hispanics, who were coming to the United States in large numbers and the Native Americans. Many Catholics joined the famous March On Washington led by Reverend Martin Luther King, Jr. in 1963, as well as the march in Selma, Alabama, in June, 1965. They marched, as well, in support of the civil rights legislation of 1965. In many instances this was ecumenical activity in collaboration with other religious and civic groups.

But the promotion of civil rights became a major concern of Catholics both before, but particularly after, Vatican II. The Catholic Interracial Councils had come into being before Vatican II. Actually, the National Council on Race and Religion in which Catholics played an important part had been established in 1963, but its influence continued to be strong after Vatican II. The National Catholic Conference on Interracial Justice, an outgrowth of the Interracial

Councils, was another influential Catholic voice. The strong statements in "Pacem in Terris" and in "Gaudium et Spes" reflected this involvement of Catholics, and encouraged its continuance as a major religious commitment in the light of the Gospel.

Immigration and Refugee Issues

Refugee and immigration issues became important social issues nationally and internationally after World War II. Because of the political division of territories after World War II, there were two million refugees in Europe who had to be resettled; millions of others were displaced (Holborn 1975, p. 26). Between 1948 and 1951, about 410,000 displaced persons were resettled in the United States alone; between 1953, when the Refugee Relief Act was passed, and 1957, when it terminated, about 261,000 refugees from Europe were resettled in the United States (pp. 569-571). This new and major challenge evoked a large scale response throughout the Catholic world. In the United States, the U.S. Catholic Conference established Catholic Relief Services to assist in the resettlement. This was only the beginning of problems. No one could foresee at the time that refugee problems were to become critical throughout the world in the 1970s and 1980s (*World Refugee Survey* 1987). It is understandable that this issue should have been addressed in papal pronouncements, and in "Pacem in Terris" and "Gaudium et Spes."

Following the Cuban Revolution in 1959, one million Cubans fled to the United States. The Archdiocese of Miami played a major role in their resettlement. But it was not until the 1970s and 1980s that the refugee problem reached levels of disaster. In 1987, there were more than 13 million refugees throughout the world in need of protection and assistance. Between 1975 and 1985, the United States alone resettled over one million refugees (*World Refugee Survey* 1987, Table 8). The U.S. Catholic Conference established the Catholic Committee on Refugees and has been the major private organization involved in the resettlement effort in the United States. The U.S. Catholic Conference could do this because it could call upon the broad network of parishes where families volunteered to sponsor refugees. In terms of social action, this makes pre-World War II Catholic social action look miniscule. The greatest burden of care for refugees, however, is not the United States; it is Africa, one of the poor nations that has the least resources to care for its people. Numerous international agencies, including Catholic Relief Services, are involved in the effort to provide care.

Many of the religious communities of priests, nuns and brothers have accepted responsibility for the care of refugees at home or abroad (Centrum Ignatium Spiritualitatis 1983). In 1980, Father General Pedro Arrupe identified the service of refugees as a high priority of the Society of Jesus. Since then, Jesuits have labored in Africa, Central America, and South East Asia. As of

1983, twenty-five Jesuits were fulfilling appointments to assist the refugees. The Jesuit Refugee Service has played a major role in Central America.

Sanctuary

In the United States, apart from the resettlement of refugees from abroad, another particular aspect has developed among refugees who are officially identified as "illegally" in the United States. These are refugees who fled to the United States from Central America, largely from El Salvador, Nicaragua, and Guatemala, as well as from Haiti. No one knows how many there are, but the number is substantial, well over one million (Crittenlen 1988). These people are asking for asylum, namely, a political status that enables a refugee to remain in the United States and be gainfully employed until they may safely return to their homeland. They claim to have fled from the danger of persecution or death, but the Immigration and Naturalization Service of the United States (INS) officially defines most of them as "economic" rather than "political" refugees, and has made a consistent effort to send them back to their country of origin. The activities of INS have been very discriminatory. They are favorable to refugees from governments that the United States opposes, and unfavorable to refugees from governments that the United States supports. For example, in 1987, 87 percent of the refugees from Nicaragua who applied were granted asylum in contrast to 4 percent for refugees from El Salvador and Guatemala. Even the Supreme Court criticised the INS for "seemingly purposeful blindness" when interpreting the law in a way "strikingly contrary to plain language and legislative history" (*World Refugee Survey* 1987, p. 75). As a result, a widespread movement among religiously affiliated people has developed to provide sanctuary to these people to prevent their being returned to their own countries.

The sanctuary movement is inspired by a long Judeo/Christian tradition that, once a fugitive from justice entered the precincts of the temple, the synagogue, or the church or religious institution, the fugitive would be given protection until some just solution of the case could be arrived at. This tradition was applied to the refugees fleeing from Central America. It began as a simple process of granting sanctuary to particular families. But, as threats of arrest and trial increased, a well-organized system of legal services was developed, with provision for medical care of the refugees, and a network of concerned citizens throughout the country who agreed to cooperate with the movement. It has been challenged by the U.S. government for engaging in illegal activities (harboring illegal immigrants). Some involved individuals have been tried, convicted, and sentenced. But the movement goes forward with substantial success. Hundreds of refugee families have received protection and care while militant efforts are made to change the behavior of the Immigration and Naturalization Service. In June, 1984, there were 130 Sanctuary Centers conducted by a wide variety of religious groups (*Sanctuary Movement Fact Sheet* 1984).

Legalization of Illegals

One other aspect of the immigration problem has been that of the millions of persons who have been in the United States illegally. Many of these have been here for a number of years, but they lived in the shadows, always fearful that the INS would identify them, apprehend them, and deport them to their home country. The U.S. Congress has long been concerned about them and sought to develop legislation that would grant them legal status in the United States. Finally, the Immigration Reform and Control Act of 1986 (U.S. Congress 1986) was passed. This provided for all immigrants who had been in the United States illegally before January 1, 1982, the possibility of legalizing their status. They may obtain permanent residence status in a two-stage process; they then qualify to apply for U.S. citizenship after five more years of residence.

In terms of Catholic social action, this effort to assist the illegal immigrants in the process of legalization required a great deal of counseling, assistance in assembling documents, and preparation of the application for legalization. After the "temporary resident" period, the process required the training of immigrants in English and American history and government. The U.S. Catholic Conference together with local dioceses and parish groups assembled thousands of volunteers who assisted the immigrants in the process. It still goes on and represents an extensive social action effort in support of illegal immigrants.

The majority of the illegal immigrants are Hispanic, therefore, much of the effort toward legalization and for refugees is in their support. But attention to Hispanics goes far beyond refugee and immigration services. Hispanics now number more than 20 million persons in the United States, and they constitute the largest percentage of immigrants entering the United States with permanent visas. If this trend continues, the Catholic church will be predominantly Hispanic by the year 2050 (Fitzpatrick 1984). Thus major efforts toward evangelization are in progress, together with efforts to enable the Hispanics to participate fully in American life while preserving their native language and culture to the extent that this may be possible.

The bishops of the United States issued a pastoral letter in 1985, *The Hispanic Presence: Challenge and Commitment* asserting the values of Hispanic culture and its contribution to Catholic life in the United States, (National Conference of Catholic Bishops 1983). The bishops also made a strong plea for a policy of cultural pluralism which would enable the Hispanics to retain their cultural values while they move into the mainstream of American life. The bishops have established a Secretariat for Hispanic Affairs at the U.S. Catholic Conference, with regional Catholic Centers for Hispanics in areas where large numbers of Hispanics reside. However, most favorable of all have been the initiatives of the Hispanic people themselves. They have already had two important national assemblies, called Encuentros (Encounters), grass roots religious movements to enable them to sustain a strong Catholic life in the United States. Many dioceses have Offices of the Hispanic Apostolate. Thus the presence of Hispanics has become the focus of extensive Catholic social action in collaboration with Hispanics, in fulfillment of the teaching of "Pacem in Terris" and "Gaudium et Spes" that every effort must be made to enable the immigrants and refugees to establish themselves in our midst as the latest Catholic newcomers to this nation, which always has been a nation of immigrants.

Peace and Disarmament

Long before Vatican II, the call for peace was frequently pronounced by the Vatican and by Catholic associations around the world. Pax Christi International and its regional chapters have long proclaimed a Christian pacifism. One of their active participants has been Bishop Thomas Gumbleton, Auxiliary Bishop of Detroit. However, two developments in recent years have encouraged the church to speak more boldly, namely, the War in Vietnam, and U.S. Government intervention in Central America. When the U.S. Government activated the draft during the Vietnam War, large numbers of Catholics declared themselves to be conscientious objectors. Not only were they supported by Pax Christi, but many dioceses set up a process to certify the validity of the claims in conscience of many who declared themselves conscientious objectors.

The peace movement, however, went far beyond the issue of conscientious objection. Protests against the Vietnam War were frequent and sometimes violent. Civil disobedience became a common practice of peace activists. Student movements appeared throughout the nation and associations such as the Fellowship of Reconcilition, an ecumenical group, became active in many cities. The Catonsville Nine, led by Father Daniel Berrigan, S.J., and his brother Philip, were one of the most militant groups. They removed the files from a Draft Board Office in Catonsville, Maryland, and burned them in protest against the draft and the Vietnam War. A similar group, The Plowshares, led by Father Daniel Berrigan, invaded a General Electric plant in King of Prussia, Pennsylvania, and damaged the nose-cone of a nuclear weapon.

Many of the dioceses of the United States established Offices of Justice and Peace. Catholic groups and ecumenical groups demonstrated regularly at the research sites where scientists were developing plans for nuclear weapons. Bishop Hunthausen of Seattle, Washington, where nuclear submarines are berthed, led numerous demonstrations of protest against the nuclear submarines and weapons. One very dramatic moment in the church's effort for peace occurred on October 4, 1965, when Pope Paul VI spoke before the General Assembly of the United Nations:

> We feel we are making our own the voice of the dead and the living; of the dead who fell in the terrible wars of the past; of the living who have survived those wars, bearing in their hearts the condemnation of those who would try to revive wars; and also of those living who are rising fresh and confident, the youth of the present generation, dreaming as they are fully entitled to do, of a better human race. And we also make our own the voice of the poor, the disinherited, the suffering and those who hunger and thirst for justice, for the dignity of life, for freedom, for well-being and progress (Paul VI [1965]1976, p. 381).

The pope brought the audience to its feet with resounding applause with his impassioned plea: "No more war, war never again! Peace, it is peace which must guide the destinies of peoples and of all mankind" (p. 383).

In May, 1983, the National Conference of Catholic Bishops issued their pastoral letter on war and peace, *The Challenge of Peace: God's Promise and Our Response* (National Conference of Catholic Bishops 1983). This letter had been many years in preparation and had gone through three drafts before the final version. The Bishops reviewed the teaching of the church about war and presented arguments used for a just war. They affirmed the legitimacy of conscientious objection and the value of nonviolence. Most of the letter deals with nuclear weapons. They condemned the use of vast resources for the stockpiling of nuclear weapons while millions of the human family are starving; they condemned nuclear "first-strike" as morally indefensible and asserted that the principle of deterrence could be justified only as a step toward disarmament. The response to the letter was enormous. It was discussed and commented upon for months and was given serious study by governments and private citizens. It was challenged, not only by non-Catholics but by some Catholic groups as well who questioned the competence of the bishops to speak about such technical matters, or who felt that peace could be preserved only by a balance of nuclear weapons. The letter became a major resource to Catholics and non-Catholics in their protests against nuclear weapons and nuclear war.

Finally, the policy of the United States during the 1980s of supporting the government and the army of El Salvador against the insurgence, which arose in the late 1970s and the policy of seeking to destroy the Sandinista government, which had defeated the dictatorial Somoza regime in a revolution in 1979, aroused widespread and vigorous protest in the United States. The protests mounted, especially after the assassination of the great Archbishop Oscar Romero on March 24, 1980, and the brutal violation and killing of three Catholic nuns and their lay co-worker in December, 1980. The National Conference of Catholic Bishops issued a condemnation of the involvement of the United States with military aid, military advisers and billions of dollars of support for the army of El Salvador. It also condemned the attempt of the United States to overthrow the Sandinista government by supporting with money, equipment, and training the armed invasion of Nicaragua by a military group called the Contras. These peace movements had all the enthusiasm and drive of the movements against Communism in the 1930s. Thousands of organizations, largely secular but with many Catholic participants, constitute a powerful popular movement. It is difficult to evaluate the success of these groups. It may be that their protests have curtailed U.S. intervention rather than stopped it. Nor can it be said that Catholic participation was a consequence of Vatican II; it existed long before. The legitimacy, however, of these protests against war and the demonstrations for peace were strongly supported and involvement was encouraged by official Catholic statements.

The Preferential Option of the Poor

The preferential option for the poor is discussed in Chapter Fifteen. This was definitely a consequence of Vatican II. It represented a dramatic shift of the Latin American Bishops and the church away from an identification with the wealthy and powerful to a position of advocacy for the poor and their continuing struggle for liberation, peace, and justice. The main inspiration for this statement came from the Second Conference of the Latin American Episcopal Conference at Medellin, Colombia, August 24-September 6, 1968. The Conference sought to define the transformation of the Latin American Church in the light of the Council. The declaration of the conference was supported by the decisions of the Second Synod of Bishops after Vatican II which took place in 1971 (Gremillion 1976). This meeting touched on the central issues of the 1970s: the refugee problem, the increasing gap between rich and poor nations, the danger of a new economic colonialism replacing the political colonialism recently ended, human rights throughout the world, the arms race which it defined as " . . . a threat to man's highest good; it threatens to destroy all life from the face of the earth," and the need for peace. It stated a remarkable commitment to justice in surprisingly strong words:

> Action on behalf of justice and participation in the transformation of the world fully appear to us as a *constitutive dimension* of the preaching of the Gospel, or, in other words, of the Church's mission for the redemption of the human race and its liberation from every oppressive situation (Gremillion 1975, p. 514, emphasis added).

A third meeting of the Latin American Episcopal Conference took place in Puebla, Mexico, in February, 1979. Its conclusions basically supported the conclusions of the second meeting in Medellin. The development of Liberation Theology and the Basic Christian Communities constitute some of the most dramatic social involvements of the church after Vatican II.

Thus the official position of the church was clear. Liberation Theology, although widely controversial, became the most significant theological innovation of the post Vatican II era, not only in Latin America but throughout the world. Although the basic ecclesiastical communities (comunidades de base) have flourished in Latin America, their influence has had an impact in the United States as well. Community organization in the context of the parish has resulted in the promotion of justice and the enrichment of the faith. For example, Mission Dolores in Los Angeles reflects the American adaptation of the basic Christian communities. Sanctuary for refugees, predominantly Hispanic, advocacy for refugees and immigrants, solidarity with the poor, and a vital Catholic parish life represent what the Puebla documents called "integral liberation."

The famous Community Organization Program called COPS in San Antonio is another example of the close relationship between community organization and parish life. The Jesuit experimental parish, Holy Name, in Camden, New Jersey, with its parish staff, its traditional parochial school, its community development activities of legal services provided by a Jesuit priest-lawyer, and medical services by a Jesuit priest-medical doctor is another example of the effort of the church in the United States to serve the poor.

Diocesan offices of justice and peace seek to direct resources and personnel to programs for the poor, and the Bishops' Campaign for Human Development raises funds through the parishes for the support of worthy community development efforts. Drug prevention programs and youth service programs, such as the well-known Centro Sor Isolina Ferre in Ponce Playa, Puerto Rico, are increasing. Covenant House, the national and international network of homes for runaway youths, despite its current difficulties, is a significant effort developed by Catholics for the service of youths in trouble.

Neighborhood and housing efforts for the poor are other examples of church involvement with social issues. The New York Archdiocese has invested millions in the rehabilitation of abandoned buildings or the construction of new homes for poor and lower income persons. The Northwest Bronx Community and Clergy Coalition has saved that section of the Bronx from devastation. The South Bronx People for Change is an effort of Hispanics in the South Bronx parishes to bring their area to life again. As Senator Daniel Patrick Moynihan stated in his preface to a book about the re-awakening of the Bronx: "After much travail and much failure, and much avoidance of the obvious, the people of the South Bronx and the Catholic Church have got together and have set to work. And the Lord's work it is. And more, it is news, *Good News"* (Jonnes 1986, p. xxiv).

As the church moves further into the decade of the 1990s, the problems featured in the Council are still with us. However, the vision of the Council is now shared by millions of Catholics who, by their own efforts or in collaboration with other religious groups or secular organizations, are hard at work in the pursuit of human rights, advocacy for peace and disarmament, care of refugees and immigrants, the service of the faith by the promotion of justice, and the effort to bring about integral liberation by a preferential option for the poor. Despite difficulties and discouragement, there is evidence that the church has clearly read "the signs of the times," and Catholics are seeking to build a better world in the spirit of Vatican II.

REFERENCES

Abbott, W.M., S. J., ed. 1966. *The Documents of Vatican II.* New York: Herder and Herder.

Abell, A.J. 1960. *American Catholicism and Social Action: A Search for Social Justice, 1865-1950.* New York: Hanover House.

Centrum Ignatium Spiritualitatis [Center of Ignatian Spirituality]. 1983. *Refugee Service and Mission Today.* Vol. XIV:1. Rome, Italy.

Crittenlen, A. 1988. *Sanctuary.* New York: Weidenfeld & Nicholson.

Fitzpatrick, J.P., SJ. 1984. "The Latin American Church in the United States." *Thought* 59:244-254.

Gremillion, J., ed. 1976. *The Gospel of Peace and Justice.* Maryknoll, NY: Orbis.

Holborn, L.W. 1975. *Refugees: A Problem of Our Time.* Metuchen, NJ: Scarecrow Press.

John XXIII. (1961)1976. "Mater et Magistra" (Christianity and Social Progress). Pp. 143-200 in *The Gospel of Peace and Justice,* edited by J. Gremillion. Maryknoll, NY: Orbis.

————. (1962)1966. "Opening Speech to the Council" in Abbott. Pp. 71-719 in *The Documents of Vatican II.* New York: Herder and Herder.

————. (1963)1976. "Pacem in Terris" [Peace on Earth]. Pp. 201-242 in *The Gospel of Peace and Justice,* edited by J. Gremillion. Maryknoll, NY: Orbis.

Jonnes, J. 1986. *We're Still Here: The Rise, Fall and Resurrection of the South Bronx.* New York: Atlantic Monthly Press.

Latin American Episcopal Conference. 1970. *The Church in the Present Day Transformation of Latin America in the Light of the Council.* 2 Vols. Bogota, Colombia: General Secretariat of CELAM [Latin American Episcopal Conference].

————. 1979. *Puebla and Beyond.* Edited by J. Eagleson and P. Sharper. Maryknoll, NY: Orbis.

Leo XIII. (1891)1981. "Rerum Novarum" (On the Condition of the Working Classes). In *The Papal Encyclicals, 1878-1903,* vol. 1, edited by C. Carlen, IHM. Wilmington, NC: McGrath.

National Conference of Catholic Bishops. 1983. *The Challenge of Peace: God's Promise and Our Response.* Washington, DC: U.S. Catholic Conference.

————. 1985. *The Hispanic Presence: Challenge and Commitment.* Washington, DC: U.S. Catholic Conference.

Paul VI. (1965)1976. "Address to the General Assembly of the United Nations." Pp. 379-386 in *The Gospel of Peace and Justice,* edited by J. Gremillion. Maryknoll, NY: Orbis.

Pius XI. (1931)1981. "Quadragesimo Anno" (Reconstructing the Social Order). In *The Papal Encyclicals. 1878-1903,* vol. 22, edited by C. Carlen, IHM. McGrath.

Sanctuary Movement Fact Sheet. 1984. Chicago: Chicago Religious Task Force.

U.S. Congress. 1986. *Immigration Control and Reform Act of 1986.* 99th Congress, 1st session. Public Law 99-603.

World Refugee Survey. 1987. Washington, DC: U.S. Committtee for Refugees.

THE CHURCH AND THE NEW IMMIGRANTS

Kevin J. Christiano

INTRODUCTION: A CHURCH AND ITS PEOPLE

Theological currents emanating from the achievements of the Second Vatican Council place a heavy emphasis on a conception of the church as "the people of God." If this vision of ecclesial life is valid, it would seem to follow that in order to learn about the problems of the Catholic church in America, one would intend first to examine its people. Who are they, and what in their experience, past and present, has contributed to their sense of identity? Where are they, and how did they come to make of these locations their homes? Most important, what do they wish, at this moment and in these places, for their life together as members of a body of believers? These are, as scholars would say, empirical questions.

One area for improved empirical inquiry is the relationship between the American church and the most recent newcomers to our shores. These people include, among others, migrants from the island of Puerto Rico to the American mainland (Fitzpatrick 1987a); workers streaming north from Mexico (Massey, Alarcón, Durand, and González 1987); refugees from Central

Religion and the Social Order, Volume 2, pages 169-186.
Copyright © 1991 by JAI Press Inc.
All rights of reproduction in any form reserved.
ISBN: 1-55938-388-7

America (Bau 1985) and southeast Asia (Kelly 1986); and "boat people" from Cuba (Pérez 1986) and Haiti (Stafford 1987b).[1] In the same manner that immigrants from Europe in the latter half of the nineteenth and the first quarter of the twentieth centuries built much of what American Catholicism is today, so "new" immigrants from predominantly Catholic nations in Latin America, in the Caribbean region, and along the Pacific rim, undoubtedly will influence the future of the church in the United States. Hence, a modest amount of effort expended in studying these groups is virtually certain to yield useful results.

Because new immigrants, as a group, are disproportionately Catholic in allegiance, they often look to the church to nurture them in the new land while connecting them to memories of their old one. Further, the Catholic church has compiled long experience in meeting the material and spiritual needs of immigrants. Very few transnational voluntary organizations can match the systems of aid that the Catholic church provides to migrants. Concern for new immigrants resonates richly with the American Catholic heritage (Zendzian 1988). Some observers have ventured so far as to assert that the story of the immigrant in American society is to a large degree also the story of how Catholicism grew and flourished in this country. More pointedly, if the United States is "a nation of immigrants" (Kennedy 1964), then surely Catholics in America, native-born or not, are uniformly members of an "immigrant church" (Dolan 1975; Linkh 1975; Liptak 1989). In this case, what is past promises to be prologue as well. Immigration, in short, is the once-and-future reality of the Catholic church in the United States.

As central as the immigrant is to the study of American Catholicism, it is surprising to detect two patterns in the ample literature that is available on the "new immigration." First, little of the research deals, except indirectly, with religious beliefs and behaviors. Second, little of the remainder, which is still critical as contextual matter, is ever cited in discussions of the church in the United States and its future. In part, this mutual blindness may be attributed to a customary lack of overt connections between the disciplines that study religion and those devoted to immigration.

Economists, geographers, and demographers (the primary students of immigration in the academic realm) focus their attention on issues such as labor force participation. They are not particularly interested in the subject of religion—nor are they able to be. To illustrate, an extensive (though dated) analysis of demographic data on Hispanics in the United States (Jaffe, Cullen, and Boswell 1980) allocates merely one paragraph to the religious backgrounds of respondents to the 1970 Census, and that only to remind the reader that no data exist in the census to perform analyses by religion. "We assume that religion has, or had in the past, some undetermined influence," they speculate (Jaffe et al. 1980, p. 4). "Furthermore," they add, "we have the impression that the specific type of Catholicism varies from one Spanish-American group to another. Such variations in religion presumably have differential influences on the subjects of our interests (p. 4)." All of this would be axiomatic to a sociologist of religion, and the authors, too, believe the recognition of religious differences to be significant: "Because we think that this topic is important, we raise it," they explain (p. 4). "We can, however, say no more on it," they finally admit, "because we have no data and the subject is far too broad for inclusion in our study" (p. 4). Of course, neither the Census Bureau nor the other major source of federal statistics used by researchers on movements of people, the Immigration and Naturalization Service (INS) of the Department of Justice, gathers information on the religious affiliations of migrants (cf. McCready 1985, p. 54).

The neglect of migration studies by religious researchers is no better. To be sure, much is said, in the Catholic press and elsewhere, about the challenges that new immigrants pose to older images of church life and the structures that are employed for its organization. However, these remarks too frequently are undisturbed by any contact with sociological data. What Allan Figueroa Deck notes about Protestant evangelization of Hispanic populations in the United States could be uttered equally as readily with respect to the Catholic church's relations with any number of ethnic groups:

> ... there continues to be a lack of serious social-science studies of the phenomenon. What that means is that our grasp of the issues is still anecdotal, our judgments are not as well informed as they ought to be or could be. This is profoundly harmful to the church ... We keep expressing our concerns, repeating previous anecdotes ... but we fail to do anything different or new (Deck 1988, p. 486).

The purpose of this chapter is to start to rectify, however tentatively, some of the imbalance between anecdote and fact that marks writing on the relationship between the Catholic church and new immigrants to the United States. A simple review of relevant sociological research should establish a rudimentary factual base for the continuing debate over this relationship. In addition, it might isolate topics and suggest avenues for further exploration.

The analysis in this chapter begins with a synopsis of statistics charting trends in the latest migrations to America. It then turns to an examination of how some of the people who form those trends approach their own religion. Next, the direction of the gaze is reversed, and the discussion takes up the stance of religious leaders toward the new populations of immigrants. The range of ways in which the Catholic Church and its members persist in a tradition of service to the newest arrivals in our midst is described in the part that follows. Finally, a concluding section evaluates the prospects that new immigrants have for cultural survival and religious continuity.

A NATION OF IMMIGRANTS:
THE SCOPE OF THE NEW INFLUX

In 1965 (the same year, coincidentally, that saw the closing of the Second Vatican Council), the United States extensively revised its immigration statutes (Reimers 1985, pp. 63-90). Above all, these reforms ended a discriminatory system of national-origin quotas that had been in place in one form or another for more than 40 years. Henceforth, immigration to the United States was to be regulated by an explicit ranking of preferences that made no allusion to race or ethnicity. In addition, the 1965 amendments nearly doubled the total number of persons allowed legally to immigrate each year (at first, from 158,000 to 290,000—not counting parents, spouses, and children who are unmarried minors), and expanded the categories of immigration on which no limits were imposed (Massey 1981, p. 58; Reimers 1981, pp. 4-5).

With the removal of restrictions based on national origin, the sources of immigration to the United States shifted noticeably (Bean, Frisbie, Lowell, and Telles 1989, pp. 95-96; Bean, Schmandt, and Weintraub 1989, p. 1; Bean and Sullivan 1985, pp. 68-70; Cafferty 1985, pp. 36-38; Cafferty, Chiswick, Greeley, and Sullivan 1983, p. 95; Reimers 1981, p. 2). Whereas three-quarters of immigrants to this country between 1900 and 1968 (when the reforms of 1965 took effect) were from Europe, almost two thirds of those arriving since 1968 have come from Asia or Latin America (Massey 1981, p. 58; Reimers 1985, pp. ix-xv). Refugees, who are often admitted through special exemptions from the law, likewise derive mostly from Asia and the Latin regions of the Western Hemisphere (Massey 1981, pp. 59-60).

The annual volume of legal immigration has increased since the period immediately following liberalization of the relevant statutes (Massey and Schnabel 1983, pp. 212, 214-217), although the composition of the flow has remained substantially the same. In 1978, a full decade after the historic reforms, 600,000 legal immigrants entered the United States; in 1980, the total rose to 800,000 (Simon 1986, p. 17). The largest group of immigrants hailed from spots in the Western Hemisphere (Massey 1981, p. 58; Simon 1986, p. 36).

Especially well represented in this new stream of immigrants are persons from Mexico.[3] Other prominent nations "sending" immigrants and refugees include the Philippines, Cuba, the Dominican Republic, Haiti, and Vietnam (Allen and Turner 1988, pp. 25-26; Hoge 1987, pp. 38-39; Massey 1981, p. 58). In all of these nations except the last, Roman Catholicism has historically been the dominant faith. And although Catholics are a minority among Vietnamese, they were twice as likely as their proportion in the population would imply to be among those who fled the country soon after the fall of the Saigon government in 1975. Whole parishes, it is reported, migrated together after the Communist invasion (Kelly 1986, p. 141).

It should be no shock, then, to be told that "many" of the new immigrants, according to one educated—if overly safe—guess, "are probably Catholic" (Zendzian 1988, p. 44). Add to these numbers the "largely Catholic" migrant worker population of the United States (Zendzian 1988, p. 44), a portion of which reflects earlier undocumented migration from Mexico (Cafferty et al. 1983, pp. 103-105; Massey 1981, pp. 60-62; Passel 1986); Catholic migrants from Puerto Rico (who are already United States citizens); and Catholic residents whose status was recently legalized under the alien amnesty program; and one quickly sees the demographic profile of the American church changing.

These changes, moreover, are not about to cease (cf. Exter 1987). Persons with new immigrant backgrounds should become more and more of a presence in the Catholic church as time goes on. Census statistics indicate that many of the ethnic groups that are heavily represented in the new immigration are characterized by median ages well below the national figure. For example, Mexicans and Puerto Ricans are relatively young (Fernandez and Cresce 1986, p. 8; Fitzpatrick 1982, p. 125; 1983, p. 222; González and LaVelle 1985, pp. 9-10; Massey and Schnabel 1983, pp. 221, 224-227; NCPCH 1982, p. 13; Pérez 1986, p. 133; Schwartz 1988, p. 45). Some new immigrant groups are similarly distinguished by a level of fertility that is higher than average. Mexicans, Puerto Ricans, and Filipinos, for example, have larger families than are evident in the native-born population (Bean and Swicegood 1985; Bean and Tienda 1987, pp. 206-209; Cafferty et al. 1983, pp. 108-109; Fernandez and Cresce 1986, p. 9; Fitzpatrick 1983, p. 222; Massey 1981, pp. 65-67; Schwartz 1988, p. 45). These comparisons suggest that, barring rapid accommodation to American norms, the effects of the new immigration, on the church as well as on society, will be felt for some time to come (Gann and Duignan 1986, p. 267).

AN IMMIGRANT CHURCH: STYLES OF FAITH IN A NEW WORLD

The implications of statistics such as the ones introduced above are not lost on all contemporary analysts of the Catholic church in the quarter-century following the Second Vatican Council. "If present trends continue," Joseph P. Fitzpatrick (1983, p. 222) has warned, "the church of the next century will be predominantly a church of the young, rapidly increasing, poor Hispanic families." It makes sense, then, to believe, as Fitzpatrick predicts elsewhere, that "the Hispanic population may well give a particular character to the Catholic Church in the United States during the 21st century, as the Catholic immigrants from Europe gave their particular character to the Church during the present century" (Fitzpatrick 1987b, p. 125). Perhaps not coincidentally, the largest body of empirical research on the religious patterns of any new immigrant group takes Hispanic Catholics as its subject. For these reasons, it would be wise to review here the record of that research.

The population that, for statistical purposes, is designated "Hispanic" is in many respects quite heterogeneous. The category embraces middle-class Cubans in Miami, Puerto Ricans working at the minimum wage in New York, and Mexican farm laborers in the Southwest. In addition, data often do not distinguish within this category between immigrants and the native-born. Nevertheless, because the constituent elements of this population share some common orientations toward religious beliefs and behaviors, it is possible to make some generalizations about them.

To start with, most Hispanics in the United States are Roman Catholics. Estimates of the exact proportion, however, vary from a high figure of roughly 80 percent (Gann and Duignan 1986, p. 267; Gremillion and Leege 1989, p. 4) to a low of about 70 percent (Castelli and Gremillion 1987, p. 96; Gallup and Castelli 1987, p. 140; Gann and Duignan 1986, p. 272; Greeley 1988, p. 61; 1990, pp. 8, 120), with several others putting the true fraction somewhere in between (e.g., Greeley 1979, pp. 118-119; Lucas 1981, pp. 4, 15). Of course, a modest amount of variation in such estimates is to be expected as researchers move from sample to sample, but other factors may be at work as well.

Nationality differences within the Hispanic subgroup may account for some of the discrepancies. One analysis of pooled data from national surveys found that 82 percent of Mexicans in the United States identified themselves to interviewers as Catholics (Greeley 1979, p. 115). A more narrow study of 995 Hispanics residing in the Archdiocese of New York (two-thirds of whom were Puerto Ricans) discovered that 84 percent claimed to be Catholic (OPR 1982, vol. 1, pp. 21, 26; cf. Castelli and Gremillion 1987, p. 79). Both of these percentages are above the averages for Hispanics as a whole.

A more likely explanation, however, is that the fluctuating statistics on denominational identification indicate real changes in affiliations, probably in response to proselytizing of Hispanics by other churches. The evidence for this view includes the fact that the lower measurements of Hispanic allegiance to Catholicism are also the most recent. This topic is too important to dispense with here, so it is examined in more detail in a later section.

There is less dispute among sociologists over the style of Hispanic religiosity—as opposed to the sheer numbers of Catholic Hispanics. William C. McCready (1985, p. 51) captures the essence of the relationship between the Catholic Church and its Hispanic faithful in an understated phrase: "organized Catholicism" and Hispanics, he says, are "somewhat at arm's length." Hispanic religiosity is essentially personalistic (NCPCH 1982, pp. 36-37); Hispanics, according to Fitzpatrick (1983, p. 238; 1987a, p. 119) "are 'Catholic' because they belong to a Catholic people." Religious commitment, therefore, is not merely or even mainly a consequence of individual preference, and fidelity to a religious tradition is not necessarily manifested in a high level of involvement in the church as an institution. Instead, where and when religious practice does occur, Fitzpatrick notes, it is "marked by the quality of *personalismo*, the pattern of close, intimate personal relationships that is characteristic of Spanish cultures everywhere" (Fitzpatrick 1983, p. 238; 1987a, p. 119; cf. Bogen 1987, pp. 148-149; Lucas 1981, p. 55). A typical person raised in one of these cultures, by and large, is not what another study (Grebler, Moore, and Guzmán 1970, p. 450) has labeled "a strongly practicing 'Mass-and-Sacraments' Catholic."

Empirical research across a range of venues bears out these impressions. A pioneering survey of over 1,000 Hispanic Catholics in the metropolitan areas of the United States with the greatest densities of Spanish population (González and LaVelle 1985, p. 23; cf. Castelli and Gremillion 1987, pp. 86-93)[4] found that fully 83 percent of those responding said their religion was "very important" to them. The survey also revealed that Hispanic Catholics are decidedly orthodox in their adherence to traditional teachings of the Church (González and LaVelle 1985, pp. 28-40). This fact notwithstanding, they appeared, at the same time, to exhibit comparatively low thresholds of religious practice and to participate less regularly in the activities of local parishes (González and LaVelle 1985, pp. 72-94, 126-131).

Clearly, a gulf stretches between many Hispanics and the church to which they are nominally tied. Many Hispanics, including some who are most active in formal Catholicism, also reported an attachment to items of folk religious devotion. For example, a third of the respondents in the survey had erected home altars, and over 13 percent had at some time followed spiritualist or syncretistic religious formulae (González and LaVelle 1985, pp. 95-98, 145).

Other, more limited research on Hispanics has verified the basic pattern of loyalty to Catholic doctrine (OPR 1982, vol. 1, pp. 29-35), coupled with relaxed norms concerning the frequency of participation in church rituals (Castelli and Gremillion 1987, p. 82; Gallup and Castelli 1987, p. 143; Gann and Duignan 1986, p. 271; Grebler et al. 1970, pp. 473-477; Greeley 1979, p. 119; McCready 1985, p. 59; Markides and Cole 1984; OPR 1982, vol. 1, pp. 55-65); a vibrant spirituality; and a varied parachurch sacramentality that is carried on within the household (Gallup and Castelli 1987, p. 145; NCPCH 1982, p. 37; OPR 1982, vol. 1, pp. 49-51, 54-55, 67-68).

The Hispanic style of religious conduct may be traced partially to the migrant origins of many Spanish-speakers in the modern United States. In Mexico (which supplies the largest group of Hispanic immigrants), the legacy of a revolution has firmly entrenched an anti-institutional stance in governmental dealings with the Catholic church, and anticlerical thinking in popular attitudes toward the church's functionaries. For these and other reasons, Spanish cultures in the Americas produced few priests, and those who did receive a vocation to the priesthood rarely followed their people into migration (Deck 1989, pp. 58-63; McCready 1985, p. 51). The effects of this history can be read in the contemporary statistics on the availability of Hispanic priests in the United States. In 1980, there were maybe 1,500 Hispanics out of an American presbyterate with in excess of 58,000 members (González and LaVelle 1985, p. 173). Of the Hispanic clergy, no more than a third were born in the United States; the balance were brought from Spain and from parts of Latin America (Lucas 1981, p. 40), often specifically to minister to the Spanish-speaking population.

Hence, Hispanic Catholics in this country learned by necessity to function as religious people without much steady reliance on the clergy. In the relative absence of the clerical direction to austerity and order that greeted earlier waves of Catholic immigrants, Hispanics retained an earthy notion of the divine rooted in the immediacy of everyday experience, and a corresponding disinclination to regard the disciplines that were imposed by the official church as the last word on what is holy.

THE IMMIGRANT PRESENCE: "GIFT" AND CHALLENGE

In ideological terms, at any rate, the Catholic Church in the United States has been quick to praise the presumably special virtues of new immigrant groups and to welcome their members into the fold. For example, the American bishops, in their pastoral letter on *The Hispanic Presence* (NCCB 1984; cf. Castelli and Gremillion 1987, pp. 93-96), refer to this Catholic minority as "a blessing from God" to the entire church (NCCB 1984, p. 3; cf. Castillo 1986, p. 22). In a passage ideally suited to evangelism for "possibility thinking," the bishops instruct Catholics to view the growing Hispanic population not "simply as a large pastoral problem," but also as "a unique pastoral opportunity" (NCCB 1984, p. 4). Individual writers have likewise adopted a positive approach to immigration. Fitzpatrick (1987b, p. 5), for one, encourages American Catholics to perceive new contacts with "the cultures of the world . . . as a gift from the Lord at the present time." Silvano M. Tomasi (1989, p. 31) echoes this opinion: "Immigrants are a blessing," he contends; "they bring new vitality."

But if new immigrants are a gift to the Catholic church, they mostly resemble a present conferred at a surprise celebration—that is, their reception has not been preceded by much conscious preparation or advance planning. And as with a surprise gift, there is some obvious confusion over where to place the new acquisition. Consequently, many immigrants complain that the church barely exerts itself to reach them, tries little to understand them, and fails to accept them on any but its own terms. This failure is nothing new in church history. At times, a drive to "Americanize" Catholic newcomers constituted the deliberate policy of the hierarchy (Grebler et al. 1970, pp. 445, 459-461; Linkh 1975); at other moments, a kind of simple neglect was more salient.

In this religiously competitive society, other churches have attempted historically to meet the unmet needs of Catholic immigrants, and thereby to recruit at least some of them into their ranks. This, too, is not a novel problem for American Catholicism (see Abel 1933), though fear in response to Protestant "proselytism" waxes and wanes periodically. Thus, in the immediate aftermath of the massive twentieth-century immigration from Europe, Gerald Shaughnessy (1925) could title a book-length inquiry, *Has the Immigrant Kept the Faith?* Yet, by 1967, Catholic clergymen informed a field investigator in California that proselytism, once thought to be a mortal threat to the Church, was "not important" and of "negligible impact" (Grebler et al. 1970, p. 470). Today, renewed concern about losses of Catholic membership in the face of Protestant evangelization, particularly among minorities, has provoked the bishops of the United States to empanel an ad hoc committee on "A Pastoral Response to the Challenge of Proselytism."

Concern about competition from sects has developed especially with respect to Hispanics (Bogen 1987, p. 149; Castelli and Gremillion 1987, pp. 91-93; Gallup and Castelli 1987, pp. 139-141; Gann and Duignan 1986, p. 272; NCCB 1984, pp. 19-20; Saldigloria 1980, p. 167), and this competitive pressure is definitely not an illusion. Findings from Gallup polling indicate that almost three-quarters of Hispanic Catholics have been the recipients of membership appeals from Protestant groups (Gallup and Castelli 1987, p. 139; Lucas 1981, p. 89). Subsequent surveys have yielded comparable results (see González and LaVelle 1985, p. 147).

The first (and so far only) researcher to gauge quantitatively the recent "leakage" away from the church by the largest Catholic minority is Andrew M. Greeley (1990, pp. 10, 120-124). Extrapolating from data in the General Social Surveys, Greeley concluded that across a 15-year period in the 1970s and 1980s, nearly one million Hispanic Catholics left the church for Protestant bodies, a rate of about 60,000 defections per year. "The survey . . . suggests that the rate is much higher than previously estimated," he writes (p. 61). Indeed, it represents "an ecclesiastical failure of unprecedented proportions" (p. 62). Greeley's calculation has been diffused rapidly, both with and without credit to him, through Catholic publications nationwide (see, e.g., Duin 1990).

The evangelical and pentecostal bodies that have challenged the church for the allegiance of traditionally Catholic ethnic groups offer some undeniable attractions. Next to the "staidly institutional" Catholic church (NCPCH 1982, p. 37), they allow an informal and individual mode of religious expression. Their style, in keeping with the Hispanic emphasis, is highly personal. In addition, there is a minimum of stratification in the congregation: leaders are drawn directly from among the people (Deck 1988, pp. 486-490; Lucas 1981, pp. 91-93; Tomasi 1989, pp. 33-34). "They see in each convert a possible minister," asserts Patricio Flores (1980, p. 192), the Archbishop of San Antonio and the first Mexican-American in the Catholic hierarchy.

Blame for Catholic losses to sects, in the usual sociological explanation (e.g., Poblete and O'Dea 1960), rests on the "anomie" that is felt by newly arrived immigrants who, because they are now distanced from bonds of community that were forged in their old culture, are aimless and adrift. To compensate, this argument holds, the newcomers seek comfort and security in an institution that will buffer them, if only temporarily, from the shock of assimilation. The small scale and personal interaction that practically define sectarian churches impart social status, emotional fulfillment, and a sense of belonging to a class of people who, in this interpretation, would otherwise fall outside the margins of society. The problem with this explanation, however, is that defection is no more common, according to Greeley (1988, p. 61), in the second generation than in later cohorts. More accurate, defection appears to be related to upward economic mobility.

Religion, in fact, does not always serve to bind new immigrants to their community. As Susan Buchanan Stafford learned in her participant observation in a Haitian Catholic parish in Brooklyn (Stafford 1987a), the church, because it is taken so seriously by members of the community, can be transformed readily into an arena of conflict. This was the case when the Brooklyn parishioners divided sharply over the appropriate language to use in the liturgy: French (the option favored by immigrants in the congregation who were downwardly mobile or upwardly aspirant) or Haitian Creole (a vernacular more closely associated with popular expression).

THE ROLE OF THE CHURCH:
FROM "PASTORAL CARE" TO SANCTUARY

The Catholic Church in the United States has long pursued vigorously what its bishops, in a significant 1976 resolution, termed "The Pastoral Concern of the Church for People on the Move" (Liptak 1989, p. 196; Tomasi 1989). As Pope John Paul II has reminded Catholics, "the fact that the Church carries out extensive relief efforts on behalf of migrants and refugees should not be a source of surprise to anyone," for "the Church is ever mindful that Jesus Christ himself was a refugee, that as a child he had to flee with his parents from his native land" (quoted in OPCMR 1986a, p. 5; cf. NCCB 1987, p. 4).[5] Thus, one recent study of New York (Bogen 1987, p. 140) observes that the Roman Catholic church, in conformity with this commitment, "stands out as the largest private provider of services to immigrants in the city, and in the country as well."

Much of the church's concern for migrants takes the form of religious ministry to people who, because of their travels, are separated from the services of a normal parish.[6] But the projects of the Catholic church additionally entail efforts in resettling refugees, locating employment and housing opportunities for immigrants, teaching English as a second language, advising newcomers about the complexities of immigration law, and assisting the undocumented in regularizing their status (see Bogen 1987, pp. 140, 143-148; Castelli and Gremillion 1987, p. 83). The bulk of this activity is conducted under the auspices of diocesan Catholic charities and local chapters of aid organizations like the St. Vincent de Paul Society. However, the American bishops have a standing committee on migration and tourism, and in 1983 they established their own agency, the Office of Pastoral Care of Migrants and Refugees (OPCMR), to stimulate research, disseminate information, plan catechetical outreach, and advocate better treatment for immigrants (Deck 1989, p. 85; Liptak 1989, p. 196).[7]

This office has produced regular reports on the church's involvement with an impressive array of new immigrant groups, from traditionally Catholic nationalities such as Haitians (OPCMR 1986a) and Filipinos (Castillo 1986), to the Hmong (Liptak 1989, pp. 198-199; OPCMR 1986b), a largely illiterate Lao minority whose prevailing religion is a brand of animism (Kelly 1986, pp. 141, 147). The office even monitors developments in new Catholic immigration from "old" sources, such as Poland (OPCMR 1985; cf. Mostwin 1989). For some, however, such centralized activity by the official church is not enough.

The United States is the destination of choice for thousands of Central Americans who risk an arduous and even dangerous trek northward in search of a respite from war and political repression in their native lands. The clandestine migration of such refugees, as well as the precarious conditions of their lives upon arrival, naturally thwart attempts to count them. Yet one figure, reported in a respected news journal (*The Economist* 1987, p. 31), may serve to indicate the scale of the problem. The estimate holds that possibly a tenth of the normal population of a single Central American nation, El Salvador, is now resident illegally in the United States (cf. Crittenden 1988, p. xvi).

In recent years, one of the most controversial methods by which individual Catholics and some of their congregations have placed themselves at the service of new immigrants to the United States is through participation in a religious movement to establish church-based "sanctuaries" around the country for these refugees. In fact, religious resources—both symbolic and concrete ones—in large measure powered the movement for sanctuary at its inception. Among its symbolic resources were the appeal to an ethic of hospitality set above the purely instrumental, and the insistence on a sphere of life set apart from— and impenetrable by—the profane powers of the state. The movement's concrete resources, too, were not inconsiderable: the devoted labors of scores of clergy, religious, and lay persons from a variety of denominations, and the ready use of the facilities that they controlled.[8]

The tradition of churches granting safe haven to people in flight is both honored and ancient; it dates at least to the time of the Old Testament (see, e.g., Numbers 35: 6-34). Though religious in its inspiration, the practice of sanctuary much later took on the form of a legal privilege when some of its elements were incorporated into English law, which in turn functions as the foundation for judicial reasoning in the United States (Bau 1985; Crittenden 1988, pp. 62-63). However, the concept of sanctuary was never fully revived from its dormant state during most of American history. Thus, those who invoke its protection for their conduct today encounter a popular presumption of lawlessness. Rather than hearkening to a venerable humanitarian principle, the deeds of sanctuary workers appear, to federal prosecutors and to commissioners of the INS, to represent little more than open defiance of the law—a plain challenge whose true purpose, they suspect, is to score dubious political points against the foreign policy of the United States government.

In the best publicized prosecution of sanctuary activists, a federal grand jury in Phoenix indicted Jim Corbett and John Fife (to many, the founders of the movement), and fourteen others in early 1985 on a total of 71 counts of conspiracy and violations of immigration law. Among the co-defendants were two Catholic clergymen and three nuns (MacEoin 1985a, pp. 24-25; Tomsho 1987, p. 167). In spite of the fact that several prominent members of the sanctuary leadership are priests or sisters, however, the official church has kept a safe distance from the movement. The American hierarchy as a body has lent no direct support to sanctuary activities (Crittenden 1988, pp. 201-202; Davidson 1988, pp. 84-85, 98). Indeed, one bishop with experience in migrant affairs, Anthony Bevilacqua (now of Philadelphia), explicitly opposed the movement. Many others in roles of authority in the Church have withheld their endorsements from sanctuary or have maintained a discreet silence on the issue (Bau 1985, p. 188n). Nevertheless, several prelates with liberal sympathies, such as Rembert Weakland of Milwaukee and Raymond Hunthausen of Seattle, were early and vocal supporters of sanctuary (Crittenden 1988, pp. 105, 201; Davidson 1988, p. 76; MacEoin 1985a, pp. 26-27).

Sixteen months after their indictment, after a trial lasting 19 weeks, and after nine days of jury deliberations, eight of the sanctuary leaders charged in Phoenix were convicted on 18 of the 30 counts of which they were accused. Three persons were acquitted entirely. Of the original defendants, three others had entered guilty pleas before the start of the trial, and two more had had the cases against them dismissed (Crittenden 1988, p. 323; Davidson 1988, pp. 94, 148-150; Tomsho 1987, pp. 205-206). The convicted parties were sentenced to between three and five years on probation (Crittenden 1988, p. 335; Davidson 1988, p. 155). None went to jail.

The sanctuary movement remains active in communities across America, although its leaders and their work receive less police scrutiny and considerably less publicity than before. Indeed, the outcome of the Arizona trial appears effectively to have swept sanctuary from the front pages of the nation's newspapers and indirectly to have assured the government that the situation along the border is under some control.

Although assistance to refugees continues, workers for sanctuary are themselves divided on the question of their basic mission. One faction of members regards sanctuary aid as a response to an imperative emerging from profoundly religious commitments, albeit one with unavoidable political implications. Another views sanctuary (and its attendant critique of United States involvement in Central America) as an essentially political project carried out by people who, incidentally, are connected by religious affiliations (Bau 1985, pp. 29-38; Crittenden 1988, pp. 92-93, 202-205; Davidson 1988, pp. 80-84, 131-134). In this, as in so many other contemporary crusades, the necessity of balancing the things that are Caesar's against those that are God's has created conflicts that endure both within the group of activists and between their campaign and the authorities in the wider society.

THE FUTURE: A "POSTIMMIGRANT" CHURCH?

The American ideology values diversity as a prime resource from which a restless people over the years constructs and reconstructs a feeling of national unity (*E Pluribus Unum*). But in American society, the practical indices of success are desired as well. Provisions for new immigrants in the Catholic church have therefore had to tread a fine line between helping to open access to opportunity for these newcomers (a goal that most Americans endorse) and pressuring them to assimilate (a danger that many would now condemn). What is more, the proven tools for accepting immigrants into the flow of church life in this country have for the most part fallen out of favor. Gone, it seems, is the de jure "national parish," which cultivated the solidarity of ethnic groups by guaranteeing the persistence of their languages and customs within a homogeneous community of worshippers (Bogen 1987, pp. 141, 143, 150-151; Deck 1989, pp. 58-59; Fitzpatrick 1982, pp. 129, 137-138; 1983, pp. 236-237; 1987a, pp. 128-130; Tomasi 1989, pp. 32-33). And fading fast, it appears, is enthusiasm among pastors for maintaining neighborhood-centered Catholic schools, which entire generations of immigrants relied upon in the past to propel their ascent into the middle class (cf. Keely 1989).

Nevertheless, contemporary church leaders are sharply attuned to the popular rise in racial and ethnic consciousness since the Council. Accordingly, local ordinaries have attempted, largely on their own, "to work out measures to assist in preserving necessary aspects of immigrant culture while also addressing the issue of ethnic incorporation" (Liptak 1989, p. 194). What, precisely, qualifies as a "necessary" element of one's ethnicity, and why the

Church should be disposing on it, is not clear. But ecclesiastical innovation proceeds without pause.

Through a process called "inculturation," a concerted effort is currently being made to reconcile age-old liturgical rites with the distinctive symbols of different ethnic subcultures. On the organizational level, too, change is occurring. "Modified personal parishes," which simulate the functional virtues of the "national" congregations found in a previous time, have been granted a canonical foothold in some dioceses (cf. Deck 1988, p. 487), as have "pastoral centers" for specific linguistic minorities (Liptak 1989, p. 199). For others, the introduction of "base communities" to the United States has encouraged the application of a religious faith learned in the security of the old world to daily trials endured in the new. Everywhere, official flexibility and pastoral sensitivity are the nominal watchwords of the hour.

Whether the institutional arrangements of the 1990s will remain relatively static features of the Catholic experience in the United States, or whether they will be replaced like their predecessors with something newer still, no one knows. Already, though, a call has arisen from some for "third-stage policies for the postimmigrant era of the American church" (Liptak 1989, p. 201). What is in doubt is whether an institution as closely associated with the frustrations and fortunes of immigrants in American society as the Catholic Church could ever really expect such an era to commence, and whether the church's own historical identity in this land of immigrants could be sustained for long if one did.

For American Catholics, to be truthful, there may never be a "postimmigrant" church. But there always will be "postimmigrant" church members—that is, onetime immigrants who are full-time Catholics. Their numbers, in fact, will increase with time. The matter of how they are integrated into the people of God in America is worthy of a great deal more thought than has been given it to date.

ACKNOWLEDGMENTS

The author wishes to thank Jay P. Dolan, Helen Rose Ebaugh, Philip Gleason, and Douglas S. Massey for their assistance with the research for this essay. He confesses that, at times, he did not follow all of their sensible advice.

NOTES

1. A comprehensive listing of references to research on the "new" immigration appears in Cordasco (1987). Some basic demographic data on these populations are reported by Allen and Turner (1988) and Simon (1986). Massey (1981) develops a more sociological approach in his overview.

2. As a statistical summary, this work has since been superceded by Bean and Tienda (1987).

3. One claim insists that 42 percent of all legal immigrants to the United States during the 1970s were from Mexico alone (Cafferty 1985, p. 34). But note the much lower proportions that are attributed to Mexicans in Massey and Schnabel (1983, pp. 216-217). It may be more accurate to say that Mexicans account for approximately this fraction of all legal *Hispanic* immigration to the United States (Massey and Schnabel 1983, pp. 219, 221). See also Schwartz (1988, pp. 43-44).

4. The senior author of this first report was made an auxiliary bishop for the Archdiocese of Boston in 1988.

5. Woznicki (1982) furnishes a short but thorough analysis of the philosophical and theological underpinnings of the Catholic church's concern for migrants and refugees. See also NCCB (1987).

6. To demonstrate the lengths to which this ministry reaches, the Catholic bishops even sponsor a "Circus and Travelling Show Apostolate," which brings religious services to itinerant performers.

7. Reverend Silvano M. Tomasi, C.S., a respected immigration researcher who headed this office, was appointed by the Pope in 1989 to a position in the Vatican as Prelate Secretary of the Pontifical Council for Migrants and Travelers.

8. Because of the public nature of the movement's cause and the protracted trials of its leaders, journalistic writing on sanctuary is quite extensive. Yet a number of book-length treatments provide a perspective that is at the same time broader and deeper. Historical background and legal precedents for the concept of sanctuary are explained carefully in Bau (1985). The origins and development of the movement itself are documented by Crittenden (1988), Davidson (1988), and Tomsho (1987), while Loder (1986) conveys the firsthand view of one committed participant. The speakers at two symposia on sanctuary present largely opposing positions on the merits of the movement. Statements of support for seekers and sponsors of sanctuary are collected in MacEoin (1985b), but more critical remarks predominate in Thomas (1986).

REFERENCES

Abel, T. 1933. *Protestant Home Missions to Catholic Immigrants*. New York: Institute of Social and Religious Research.

Allen, J. P., and E.J. Turner. 1988. "Where to Find the New Immigrants: Look for Koreans in Baltimore, Mexicans in Chicago, Laotians in Minneapolis and Fresno, and Cambodians in Providence and Seattle." *American Demographics* 10 (September):22-27, 59-60.

Bau, I. 1985. *This Ground is Holy: Church Sanctuary and Central American Refugees*. New York: Paulist Press.

Bean, F.D., W. P. Frisbie, B. L. Lowell, and E.E. Telles. 1989. "The Spanish-Origin Population in the American Southwest." Pp. 65-112 in *Mexican and Central American Population and U. S. Immigration Policy*, edited by F.D. Bean, J. Schmandt, and S. Weintraub. Austin, TX: The Center for Mexican American Studies, The University of Texas at Austin.

Bean, F.D., J. Schmandt, and S. Weintraub. 1989. "Introduction." Pp. 1-4 in *Mexican and Central American Population and U. S. Immigration Policy*, edited by F.D. Bean, J. Schmandt, and S. Weintraub. Austin, TX: The Center for Mexican American Studies, The University of Texas at Austin.

Bean, F.D., and T.A. Sullivan. 1985. "Immigration and Its Consequences: Confronting the Problem." *Society* 22(May/June):67-73.

Bean, F.D., and G.Swicegood. 1985. *Mexican American Fertility Patterns*. Austin, TX: University of Texas Press.

Bean, F.D., and M. Tienda. 1987. *The Hispanic Population of the United States*. New York: Russell Sage Foundation.

Bogen, E. 1987. *Immigration in New York*. New York: Praeger.

Cafferty, P.S.J. 1985. "The 'New' Immigration." Pp. 33-48 in *Hispanics in the United States: A New Social Agenda,* edited by P.S.J. Cafferty and W.C. McCready. New Brunswick, NJ: Transaction Books.

Cafferty, P.S.J., B.R. Chiswick, A.M. Greeley, and T. A. Sullivan. 1983. *The Dilemma of American Immigration: Beyond the Golden Door.* New Brunswick, NJ: Transaction Books.

Castelli, J., and J. Gremillion. 1987. *The Emerging Parish: The Notre Dame Study of Catholic Life Since Vatican II.* San Francisco, CA: Harper and Row.

Castillo, N.M. 1986. *Introduction to Filipino Ministry.* San Francisco, CA and Washington, DC: Archdiocese of San Francisco, in cooperation with the Office of Pastoral Care of Migrants and Refugees, United States Catholic Conference.

Cordasco, F. 1987. *The New American Immigration: Evolving Patterns of Legal and Illegal Emigration; A Bibliography of Selected References.* New York: Garland.

Crittenden, A. 1988. *Sanctuary: A Story of American Conscience and Law in Collision.* New York: Weidenfeld and Nicolson.

Davidson, M. 1988. *Convictions of the Heart: Jim Corbett and the Sanctuary Movement.* Tucson, AZ: The University of Arizona Press.

Deck, A.F., S.J. 1988. "Proselytism and Hispanic Catholics: How Long Can We Cry Wolf?" *America* 159(December 10):485-490.

_____. 1989. *The Second Wave: Hispanic Ministry and the Evangelization of Cultures.* Mahwah, NJ: Paulist Press.

Dolan, J.P. 1975. *The Immigrant Church: New York's Irish and German Catholics, 1815-1865.* Baltimore, MD: The Johns Hopkins University Press.

Duin, J. 1990. "Hispanic Catholics: They're Changing American Catholicism. They're Also Leaving the Church at the Rate of 60,000 a Year." *New Covenant* 19(January):9-13.

The Economist. 1987. "Immigration: Sanctuary for Salvadorans?" *The Economist* 303(May 2):31-32.

Exter, T. 1987. "How Many Hispanics? Hispanics Will Account for One-Fifth to One-Half of the Nation's Population Growth Over the Next 25 Years. What is the Best Guess?" *American Demographics* 9(May):36-39, 67.

Fernandez, E.W., and A.R. Cresce. 1986. "The Hispanic Foreign-Born and the Assimilation Experience." *Migration World Magazine* 14(5):7-11.

Fitzpatrick, J.P., S.J. 1982. "The Puerto Ricans." Pp. 118-145 in *Contemporary American Immigration: Interpretive Essays,* edited by D.L. Cuddy. Boston: Twayne.

_____. 1983. "Faith and Stability Among Hispanic Families: The Role of Religion in Cultural Transition." Pp. 221-242 in *Families and Religions: Conflict and Change in Modern Society,* edited by W.V. D'Antonio and J. Aldous. Beverly Hills, CA: Sage.

_____. 1987a. *Puerto Rican Americans: The Meaning of Migration to the Mainland.* 2nd Edition. Englewood Cliffs, NJ: Prentice-Hall.

_____. 1987b. *One Church, Many Cultures: The Challenge of Diversity.* Kansas City, MO: Sheed and Ward.

Flores, P. 1980. "The Church: Diocesan and National." Pp. 187-195 in *Prophets Denied Honor: An Anthology on the Hispano Church of the United States,* edited by A.M. Stevens Arroyo, C.P. Maryknoll, NY: Orbis Books.

Gallup, G., Jr., and J. Castelli. 1987. *The American Catholic People: Their Beliefs, Practices, and Values.* Garden City, NY: Doubleday.

Gann, L.H., and P.J. Duignan. 1986. *The Hispanics in the United States: A History.* Stanford, CA and Boulder, CO: Hoover Institution on War, Revolution, and Peace, and the Westview Press.

González, R.O., O.F.M., and M. LaVelle. 1985. *The Hispanic Catholic in the United States: A Socio-Cultural and Religious Profile.* New York: Northeast Catholic Pastoral Center for Hispanics.

Grebler, L., J.W. Moore, and R.C. Guzmán, with J.L. Berlant, T.P. Carter, W. Fogel, C.W. Gordon, P.H. McNamara, F.G. Mittelbach, and S.J. Surace. 1970. *The Mexican-American People: The Nation's Second Largest Minority.* New York: The Free Press.

Greeley, A.M. 1979. "Ethnic Variations in Religious Commitment." Pp. 113-134 in *The Religious Dimension: New Directions in Quantitative Research,* edited by R. Wuthnow. New York: Academic Press.

_____. 1988. "Defection Among Hispanics." *America* 159(July 23-30):61-62.

_____. 1990. *The Catholic Myth: The Behavior and Beliefs of American Catholics.* New York: Scribner.

Gremillion, J., and D.C. Leege. 1989. "Post-Vatican II Parish Life in the United States: Review and Preview." *Notre Dame Study of Catholic Parish Life* 15(June):1-14.

Hoge, D.R. 1987. *The Future of Catholic Leadership: Responses to the Priest Shortage.* Kansas City, MO: Sheed and Ward.

Jaffe, A. J., R.M. Cullen, and T.D. Boswell. 1980. *The Changing Demography of Spanish Americans.* New York: Academic Press.

Keely, C.B. 1989. "The Catholic Church and the Integration of Immigrants." *Migration World Magazine* 17(5):30-33.

Kelly, G.P. 1986. "Coping with America: Refugees from Vietnam, Cambodia, and Laos in the 1970s and 1980s." *Annals of the American Academy of Political and Social Science* 487(September):138-149.

Kennedy, J.F. 1964. *A Nation of Immigrants.* Revised and enlarged Edition. New York: Harper and Row.

Linkh, R.M. 1975. *American Catholicism and European Immigrants (1900-1924).* Staten Island, NY: Center for Migration Studies.

Liptak, D., R.S.M. 1989. *Immigrants and Their Church.* New York: Macmillan.

Loder, T. 1986. *No One But Us: Personal Reflections on Public Sanctuary by an Offspring of Jacob.* San Diego, CA: LuraMedia.

Lucas, I. 1981. *The Browning of America: The Hispanic Revolution in the American Church.* Chicago: Fides/Claretian Books.

MacEoin, G. 1985a. "A Brief History of the Sanctuary Movement." Pp. 14-29 in *Sanctuary: A Resource Guide for Understanding and Participating in the Central American Refugees' Struggle,* edited by G. MacEoin. San Francisco, CA: Harper and Row.

_____. ed. 1985b. *Sanctuary: A Resource Guide for Understanding and Participating in the Central American Refugees' Struggle.* San Francisco, CA: Harper and Row.

Markides, K.S., and T. Cole. 1984. "Change and Continuity in Mexican American Religious Behavior: A Three-Generation Study." *Social Science Quarterly* 65(June):618-625.

Massey, D.S. 1981. "Dimensions of the New Immigration to the United States and the Prospects for Assimilation." *Annual Review of Sociology* 7:57-85.

Massey, D.S., R. Alarcón, J. Durand, and H. González. 1987. *Return to Aztlan: The Social Process of International Migration from Western Mexico.* Berkeley, CA: University of California Press.

Massey, D.S., and K.M. Schnabel. 1983. "Recent Trends in Hispanic Immigration to the United States." *International Migration Review* 17(Summer):212-244.

McCready, W.C. 1985. "Culture and Religion." Pp. 49-61 in *Hispanics in the United States: A New Social Agenda,* edited by P.S.J. Cafferty and W.C. McCready. New Brunswick, NJ: Transaction Books.

Mostwin, D. 1989. "The Unknown Polish Immigrant." *Migration World Magazine* 17(2):24-30.

National Conference of Catholic Bishops (NCCB). 1984. *The Hispanic Presence: Challenge and Commitment.* A Pastoral Letter on Hispanic Ministry, December 12, 1983. Washington, DC: Office of Publishing and Promotion Services, United States Catholic Conference.

———. 1987. *Together a New People: Pastoral Statement on Migrants and Refugees.* Washington, DC: Office of Publishing and Promotion Services, United States Catholic Conference.

Northeast Catholic Pastoral Center for Hispanics (NCPCH). 1982. *The Hispanic Community, the Church, and the Northeast Center for Hispanics: A Report* [Bilingual Edition]. New York: Northeast Catholic Pastoral Center for Hispanics, Inc.

Office of Pastoral Care of Migrants and Refugees (OPCMR), Bishops' Committee on Migration and Tourism, National Conference of Catholic Bishops. 1985. *The Pastoral Care of Polish Immigrants: Notes from Recent Research.* Washington, DC: National Conference of Catholic Bishops.

———. 1986a. *A New Moment in the Haitian Diaspora: Fourth Annual Convention of the Haitian Apostolate U. S. A.* Washington, DC: National Conference of Catholic Bishops.

———. 1986b. *Welcome into the Community of Faith: A Report on the Cambodian, Hmong, and Laotian Apostolate.* Washington, DC: National Conference of Catholic Bishops.

Office of Pastoral Research (OPR), Archdiocese of New York. 1982. *Hispanics in New York: Religious, Cultural, and Social Experiences* [2 Vols.]. New York: Office of Pastoral Research, Archdiocese of New York.

Passel, J.S. 1986. "Undocumented Immigration." *Annals of the American Academy of Political and Social Science* 487(September):181-200.

Pérez, L. 1986. "Cubans in the United States." *Annals of the American Academy of Political and Social Science* 487(September):126-137.

Poblete, R., S.J., and T. F' O'Dea. 1960. "Anomie and the 'Quest for Community': The Formation of Sects Among the Puerto Ricans of New York." *American Catholic Sociological Review* 21(Spring):18-36.

Reimers, D.M. 1981. "Post-World War II Immigration to the United States: America's Latest Newcomers." *Annals of the American Academy of Political and Social Science* 454(March):1-12.

———. 1985. *Still the Golden Door: The Third World Comes to America.* New York: Columbia University Press.

Saldigloria, R.F., S.J. 1980. "Religious Problems of the Hispanos in the City of New York." Pp. 166-169 in *Prophets Denied Honor: An Anthology on the Hispano Church of the United States,* edited by A.M.Stevens Arroyo, C.P. Maryknoll, NY: Orbis Books.

Schwartz, J. 1988. "Hispanics in the Eighties." *American Demographics* 10(January):42-45.

Shaughnessy, G., S.M. 1925. *Has the Immigrant Kept the Faith?: A Study of Immigration and Catholic Growth in the United States, 1790-1920.* New York: Macmillan.

Simon, J.L. 1986. "Basic Data Concerning Immigration into the United States." *Annals of the American Academy of Political and Social Science* 487(September):12-56.

Stafford, S.B. 1987a. "Language and Identity: Haitians in New York City." Pp. 202-217 in *Caribbean Life in New York City: Sociocultural Dimensions,* edited by C.R. Sutton and E.M. Chaney. Staten Island, NY: Center for Migration Studies of New York, Inc.

———. 1987b. "The Haitians: The Cultural Meaning of Race and Ethnicity." Pp. 131-158 in *New Immigrants in New York,* edited by N. Foner. New York: Columbia University Press.

Thomas, M.H., ed. 1986. *Sanctuary: Challenge to the Churches.* Washington, DC: The Institute on Religion and Democracy.

Tomasi, S.M., C.S. 1989. "The Pastoral Challenges of the New Immigration." *Migration World Magazine* 17(3/4):27-34.

Tomsho, R. 1987. *The American Sanctuary Movement.* Austin, TX: Texas Monthly Press, Inc.

Woznicki, A.N. 1982. *Journey to the Unknown: Catholic Doctrine on Ethnicity and Migration.* San Francisco, CA: Golden Phoenix Press.

Zendzian, P. 1988. "The American Church Celebrates Its Immigrant Heritage." *Migration World Magazine* 16(4/5): 44.

THE SOCIAL MOVEMENT
FOR CHANGE WITHIN
THE CATHOLIC CHURCH

Katherine Meyer

Changes in Catholicism initiated by Vatican II have rightfully been called revolutionary (Brown 1969; Ellis 1969; Pelikan 1983). Church structures and norms were altered dramatically. In the 25 years following the Council, conflict surrounded the implementation of change. The purpose of this paper is to put the event which was Vatican II and its aftermath in a larger framework of organizational modernization with a particular focus on the United States. The modernizing process has been a struggle that combined movements, conflicts, and countermovements and a struggle that had earlier roots.

THE BACKGROUND FOR CHANGE

The Catholic church entered the twentieth century with a traditionalist and defensive mentality and a bureaucratic and centralized structure. It had resisted modernity for five centuries while Protestantism and other movements adapted to contemporary forces. With Vatican I in 1870, Catholicism solidified its anti-

Religion and the Social Order, Volume 2, pages 187-201.
Copyright © 1991 by JAI Press Inc.
All rights of reproduction in any form reserved.
ISBN: 1-55938-388-7

modernist stance. Yet, forces for change were at work. Technological developments of the industrial age affected all churches profoundly, including the Catholic church. Improved transportation and communication increased contact with Asian and African cultures and religions. European ethnocentrism and Western absolutism were undermined. Investigations in archaeology modified interpretations of scripture, the development of the human race and earlier civilizations. Improvements in reproducing manuscripts increased scholarly access to ancient literature and history. Medical advances that produced more leisure time and greater longevity altered religious conceptions. Personal fulfillment became a goal for the burgeoning middle class. Development of contraceptives paved the way for new attitudes about sexuality.

Many technological advances produced changes indirectly through the new social structures they spawned. Monarchical styles of leadership were challenged by the growing dominance of democratic civil governments, the extension of suffrage to women, blacks, and other less privileged groups, and the increased literacy and education of the common people. Bureaucracy's need for input from accountants and financial advisers made it impossible for elites to rule without consultation. The growth of urban areas called for new approaches to evangelization and social action. The position of women in society changed drastically and challenged the assumption of traditional church teaching about family life and related issues. The emergence of new nations and the era of development in the Third World undercut old missionary patterns. In the United States, Catholics moved more solidly into the middle classes. The success of Catholicism in a pluralist religious structure furthered principles of religious tolerance and freedom of conscience (Murray 1960). European religious denominations worked together after World War II and the Holocaust; in the United States, religious groups bonded around civil rights issues.

Ideas that had been around for awhile, such as liberty and equality, gained new strength. More recent ones, like personal growth and development, blossomed. Norms like professional autonomy and occupational satisfaction became established among Catholic clergy and women and men religious, who historically had been a professional elite but lost ground compared with doctors, lawyers, and other groups over the centuries.

INTERNAL PRESSURES

Combined with these general societal forces surrounding and pervading the Catholic church, there were internal pressures advancing change as well. Scholars set forth new conceptualizations of the church. They struggled to preserve a viable Catholicism (Dulles 1974, 1977; McBrien 1973) as traditional understandings were eroding. Sometimes these new conceptualizations were a religious version of secular values and systems, such as consultation or a search for community. Sometimes ideas from social science were incorporated to expand religious understandings. And sometimes the values and structures of early Christianity were brought to bear on contemporary challenges.

The debate and clarification which predated Vatican II and continues today provided momentum. Theologians and other groups within the church poured out energy to redirect the church toward theology consistent with contemporary understandings. The product was not a common Catholic theology (Küng 1976; Tracy 1981). Rather several brands of ideological reconstruction vied for ascendancy. The most prominent was an image of a church consistent with the contemporary world in its teachings and practical in its solutions to the felt restrictions of the traditional church. This image was basically ratified by Vatican II. Traditionalist Catholicism set forth as its ideal the vision of the church espoused at the Council of Trent in 1870, a protectionist one. Charismatic Catholicism encouraged liturgical reform via Pentecostalism and communal living, but discouraged social activism, emphasizing primarily a concern for personal morality (McSweeney 1980).

Tensions among various visions of the church produced refinements and developments. For many years, theologians concentrated on different aspects of the religious realm—worship, doctrine, social action. Eventually their isolated activities coalesced into a more generalized intellectual movement for updating the church. Even within the reconstructing mainstream there were competing formulations and emphases. One emphasis of activist Catholics might be called political Catholicism (McSweeney 1980). An anti-institutional Catholicism sought rapid and basic change in authority structure (Davis 1967; Ruether 1975, 1977). With all these intellectual and intergroup tensions, the main movement advanced toward a reformulation of church teachings which retained the essence of Catholicism while accommodating contemporary structures and information.

Prior to Vatican II, church officials attempted to limit or exclude the penetration of the contemporary environment. A series of proclamations and activities followed in the wake of Vatican I (1869-1870) which itself had ratified the church's image as an organization protecting itself. Leo XIII in 1879 and Pius X in 1907 issued encyclicals against modernism. Pius X required clergy to take an oath against it. The Holy Office and the *Index of Forbidden Books* served as tools against secularism. In the 1940s and 1950s, frequent warnings were issued about the dangers of attending secular universities. Catholic integrists organized by Monsignor Umberto Benigni and apparently with the knowledge of Pius X zealously campaigned against theologians, biblical and Christian journals (Aubert 1978; Poulat 1969a, 1969b, 1977). Their excesses generated strong opposition in the last days of Pius X. While official reactionary policies of the late nineteenth and early twentieth centuries rarely reached the extremes of integrism, fundamentalist policies endured until Vatican II (Brown 1969; Hennesey 1981). Council deliberations articulated reaction to that fundamentalism within the church.

Environmental penetration, various groups engaged in reconstruction of ideology, and resistance from church officials characterized almost a century prior to Vatican II. There was a general state of tension; sporadic jousts with the official church occurred. If we think of social movements as originating amidst structural readiness, the situation was conducive for development of an organized force for modernization. In the four decades prior to the Second Vatican Council (1920-1959), the church moved beyond general strain and conduciveness. With the groundwork laid, the thrust toward modernizing progressed into stages of a recognizable social movement.

LEGITIMATION AND MOBILIZATION

Several mini-movements developed which were often partly endorsed by the official church. They spawned breaks with tradition. Noticeable among them were the liturgical movement, a closely related movement encouraging use of the vernacular in liturgy, a movement aiming to implement the social gospel, and a movement focused on a renaissance of Scripture scholarship. These movements were more than conceptually distinct tendencies. Each had its own articulators, its own goals, and distinct, developed movement organizations and member networks. They were notable agents of ferment in the church, particularly in the United States, but elsewhere as well. They were superceded only in the 1960s by an overarching movement for modernization.

Vatican II legitimized these mini-movements and the broader modernization one. The Council (1962-1965) along with its preparatory meetings (1959-1962) deliberated over updating the church (Rynne 1968; Fesquet 1967). Official council constitutions and other documents endorsed the goals of mini-movements. Pope John XXIII justified calling the council by stating that the church's structures and theological expression needed to be turned upside-down or inside-out (Murphy 1981). The Council Fathers debated an array of issues (Brown 1969; Fesquet 1967; Kaiser 1963; Rynne 1968). Reforming the church along biblical lines, tolerance for other religions, addressing Third World social and liturgical concerns, incorporating contemporary psychological understandings of marriage and family life, allowing for multiple sources of revelation, and encouraging freedom of conscience were just some revolutionary ones. After dramatic debates, interventions and exchanges, the Council Fathers resolved these and other basic questions in the direction of a pastorally oriented, reformed, and modern church.

When social movements are analyzed, a period of mobilization often precedes one of legitimation. The change process in the church worked differently. The governing body of Catholicism (pope and bishops) placed the issues of mini-movements, trends, and change on the agenda for the council. Bishops, theologians, and official non-Catholic Observors educated various groups of Council Fathers in both formal and informal sessions (Cullman 1968; Kaiser 1963; Rynne 1968; Fesquet 1967). These legitimating activities were the main focus of precouncil and early conciliar days. So, the legitimation stage came early. Simultaneously, people and resources were mobilized in support of or against the movement for change. Council deliberations were reported regularly in the press by attending journalists and Official Observors (Brown 1969; Cullman 1968). Frank reporting stimulated Catholic discussion around the world. Movement leaders emerged. There were theologians (K. Rahner, Congar, Danielou, Kung, Murray, Schillebeeckx) and Council Fathers (Alfrink, Bea, Dopfner, Frings, Koenig, Leger, Lercaro, Lienart, Suenens, Montini, who later became Pope Paul VI). American cardinals and bishops (Meyer, Ritter, Holliman, and Cushing to some extent) rallied support for change. Archbishop Helder Camara and other prelates from the Third World were outspoken proponents. And Popes John XXIII and Paul VI advanced aggiornamento or updating.

A coherent ideology and overarching theme developed toward the end of the council. Though there were variations and nuances of conceptualization, ideas about the church centered on openness, restructuring, modernizing, and a pilgrim and pastoral stance (Fesquet 1967; Fichter 1977; Kaiser 1963; Küng 1968; Murphy 1981; Novak 1964; Rynne 1968; Suenens 1968). These visions of the church became rallying cries of the progressives. Slogans, chants, and symbols appeared, especially in liturgies where a communitarian emphasis replaced individual pietism. Problems in the traditional church and its structures were articulated and a theology emerged that served as a rationale for change.

Resources were identifiable. Key leaders, media exposure, and legitimation were mentioned earlier. Affected groups (clergy, religious, laity) were both socializers and socialized through media, formal, and informal study. Additional organizations, networks and media emerged in large numbers. For example, in the United States, the first nondiocesan Catholic paper (the *National Catholic Reporter*) was founded in 1964. And the visibility of Popes John XXIII and Paul VI and the council were strong resources for change. John XXIII was particularly esteemed as an international leader not only by Catholics. Leadership, ideological development, and resources all gave evidence of a mobilization phase accompanying the legitimation stage of the movement for change.

Another evidence of mobilization was the emerging strength of countermovements. Confrontations and resistance were evident in the halls of the Council itself (Brown 1969; Fesquet 1967; Rynne 1968). Integralists who wished to retain all traditional doctrines of the Church resisted religious liberty, episcopal authority, and the election of Cardinal Montini as pope (Paul VI) in 1963. Outside the Vatican, controversy arose over Vatican decrees being implemented during the council era. There were strong reactions to liturgical reform by the laity (*National Catholic Reporter* 1964-1965). The introduction of interactive liturgies and the diminution of Marian devotions, Latin hymns, and recitiation of the rosary were resisted. In the United States, bishops such as Cardinals Spellman of New York and McIntyre of Los Angeles opposed the changes because they reduced mystery and distracted the people (Hennesey 1981). The French Archbishop Marcel LeFebvre began a traditionalist movement specifically directed against Vatican II in the years immediately following the council (McSweeney 1980).

Early legitimation of the aggiornamento movement had consequences. Changes in ritual and understanding seemed abrupt and dramatic because of the little time allowed for large segments of the Catholic world to digest the new ideas. Preceding or at least occurring simultaneously with mobilization, early legitimation produced a bifurcated process of mobilization which at the time appeared as one process. There was mobilization to provide support for reform and mobilization to promote implementation. Local clergy needed to both introduce change and explain the rationales. Consequently, for many clergy and Catholics, mobilization was half-hearted. Also, the church employed a traditional mode in calling for the changes to be implemented. Although in many respects Catholics may have seemed traditional, they apparently absorbed enough of the democratic ethos of their time to expect change to be voluntary or at least developed through a process of consultation. Further, to some, the new rules appeared to violate deeply held Catholic truths.

The movement for church reform never had a distinct mobilization period. Mobilization not only accompanied legitimation but also spilled over into the implementation phase. Bestriding legitimation and implementation, mobilization dramatized and heightened the visibility of those phases, at the least. At most, it may have confounded the actual dynamics of the processes.

Mobilization is a key element in any movement. The very definition of a movement centers on collective effort (Freeman 1983; Killian 1973; Turner and Killian 1972). Analysts focus on it as a time when resources are marshalled to either promote a movement's success or failure (Gamson 1975; McCarthy and Zald 1977; Oberschall 1973; Tilly 1978). Certain features of mobilization, such as emergence of leadership, a coherent ideology, slogans, countermovements, and conflict often merit theoretical and empirical discussion in themselves (Lang and Lang 1978; Mottl 1980; Smelser 1963; Wilson 1973). Specialists in collective behavior attend to conflicts and crowd activities of this period (Meyer and Seidler 1978; Perry and Pugh 1978; Seidler et al. 1977). The general public recognizes a movement as such because conflict is greatest, voices are most strident and publicity is most memorable. In fact, there can be recognizable movements which are only mobilized, never either legitimated or implemented. The stretching of mobilization across the legitimizing and part of the implementing stages and the emergence of bifurcated mobilization due to early legitimation are central to the drama of reform which was Vatican II.

MOBILIZATION AND IMPLEMENTATION

When the Council ended, the arena for confrontations and mobilizations moved from Rome to local dioceses, parishes, and other local settings (Hennesey 1981), the very places where implementation was to occur. From approximately 1965 to 1971, mobilization and implementation went hand in hand. In the United States, battles over interpretation of Vatican II decrees raged. If analysts think that church reform was a top-down organizational change rather than a movement, those battles dispel that possibility with their strong evidence of heavy involvement of members lower in the church's hierarchy. There were loosely affiliated movement segments among the grass roots, much as there had been loosely affiliated mini-movements (along with some uncoordinated avant garde efforts) prior to and through Vatican II. The underground church (Boyd 1968; Steeman 1969) experimented with changes not currently approved. Nonterritorial parishes, floating churches, and territorial parishes containing a progressive priest and change-oriented parishioners quickly incorporated new structures and rituals. Lower level clergy became another movement segment, pushing for change and explaining new ideas to the laity (Greeley 1977; National Opinion Research Center [NORC] 1972; Seidler 1979). A majority of women religious was another leading force for change along with men religious—both clerical and nonclerical. These groups opposed middle-of-the-road and traditional leadership by bishops. Their effort was not unified but rather segmented and polycephalous.

Paul VI continued to promote change after the Council from the top of the church hierarchy. A synod of bishops was assembled in 1967; decrees established parish and diocesan pastoral councils and priests' senates (Hennesey 1981); scholarly and ecumenical Biblical work was advanced; and ecumenism in general was advocated. During Paul's administration, mechanisms were set in motion for complete liturgical, homiletic, biblical and pastoral renewal at the local level (Murphy 1981). These hierarchical actions contributed to the struggle against the long-entrenched Catholic system as did the grass roots efforts. Although this system had been defeated at Vatican II, it persisted in the curia and in the habits of hierarchy and lay Catholics. Efforts to change it required more than a simple adjustment of institutional mechanisms.

Conflict characterized the mobilization-implementation stage in the United States. Bishops and parish priests could promote or block change in their respective spheres because of their key organizational positions (Haughey 1971; Schoenherr 1987; Spencer 1966; Vallier 1969). They could promote it by initiating new modes of worship, by establishing structures of shared governance, by encouraging discussion of council documents, by becoming involved in ecumenism, and by appointing others to make changes in religious education, church music, etcetera. Blockage could be by default, by countermanding progressive initiatives under their supervision or by minimizing the importance of council-derived directives from Rome. Bishops and priests displayed varied responses in both promoting and blocking change.

Priests especially were besieged by anguishing differences separating them from their bishop, other priests or members of their congregations—women and men, religious and lay persons (Fichter 1968, 1974; Hadden 1969; Hoge and Carroll 1975; NORC 1972; Steeman 1969; Wood 1981). The strain was heightened by numerous factors. Different theologies were used to support different administrative/professional perspectives in a diocese. Prior to Vatican II, there were certainly different ideas about administration but not different theologies to support them (Greeley 1973, 1977, 1981; Fichter 1968; Hall and Schneider 1973; NORC 1972). A sense of righteousness prevailed on each side (Greeley 1981). Where conflict occurred among persons at separate authority levels (e.g., bishop and priest, pastor and parishioners), sanctions were often employed (Dulles 1974; Fichter 1974). There was controversy over what constituted an appropriate sanction (Etzioni 1961; Murphy 1981), and there was controversy over whether authority was hierarchical or collaborative (Dulles 1974; Küng 1976; McKenzie 1966). Different perspectives toward authority, different theologies, and righteous indignation lent an explosiveness to disagreements.

Parish priests generally did not attend the council. Yet, they, along with women and men religious, needed to indoctrinate congregations. For many older priests, self-reorientation was necessary. It was difficult to turn inside out early seminary training and subsequent lifelong experience and then to funnel theological changes to a congregation (Fichter 1968). Prompt liturgical alterations were called for; parish councils were established. Ecumenical overtures were expected. Many priests served on interracial commissions and exhibited pastoral concern toward parishioners with previously unresolvable religious problems, such as remarriage after divorce. For those who wanted slower change or none at all, the change-oriented priest became the target for dissatisfaction. For those who wanted rapid change, the slow or change-resistant priest was the foremost opponent.

Most issues evoking conflict during the mobilization-implementation stage were core to the movement. Discord centered on changes in authority structure, central symbolic acts, like the Mass, and symbolic roles, such as the duties and life-style of parish priests and other women and men religious. Bishops, parish priests, women and men religious were major protagonists (Seidler and Meyer 1989). Mobilization efforts were evident in the birth control controversy of 1968, attempts to organize priests' unions, and formation of interest groups such as black clergy (Kiely 1968; Stewart 1978). The traditionalist movement surged forward (Dinges 1983). From 1968 to 1971, there was an air of excitement stemming from attempts to win constituents or marshal strength for a particular orientation.

Priests rebelled. Ninety-three percent of American dioceses experienced some form of protest, albeit tame by secular standards (Seidler 1972). Authority relations were the issue. Rebellion flourished where bishops had nonconsultative leadership styles and where clergy felt a lack of autonomy in decision making. Dioceses that met rebellion with harsh disciplinary action got more of it (Seidler 1974a).

Priests resigned (Schoenherr and Greeley 1974; ; Seidler 1974b, 1979; Schallert and Kelley 1970). When high resignation rates were coupled with low replacement rates, net loss was about 14 or 15 percent when religious professionals including women religious are counted (Fichter 1974). Resignations were highest in large, urban dioceses which were regional centers and where there were many priests per parish, many categories of priests (religious clergy, teachers, nonparish workers), and long tenure at the assistant pastor level. These variables generally imply a cosmopolitan setting. High resignation rates were met with bureaucratic inertia in most dioceses; bishops maintained a no change policy (Seidler 1974b). In Rome, Pope Paul VI held to traditional ways in doctrine and discipline even while promoting the spirit of Vatican II in symbolic ways. Active and passive rebellion, discord surrounding key organizational members, and dispute over basic issues of structure, symbol and role gave evidence of continuing movement mobilization during implementation.

CHANGE DURING THE 1970S

Only in the 1970s did a less confounded implementation stage emerge. There were continuities, of course. Basic issues like authority, freedom, and liturgical change still dominated controversies. But they were extended and new issues emerged. Among them were marriage and family concerns, education policies, the charismatic movement, and women's issues (abortion, Equal Rights Amendment, ordination, role in the church). Issues of ecumenism and social justice also stirred some controversy. Key protagonists in the 1970s were lay Catholics, Catholic organizations, institutions, schools, parishes, newspapers, non-Catholic organizations, and hierarchy other than bishops and parish priests (e.g., pope, regional associations of bishops, National Conference of Catholic Bishops). Targets of conflict were external to the church more than they had been from 1965 to 1971 (Seidler and Meyer 1989).

As the implementation process proceeded during the 1970s, conflict centered on cultural, structural, and symbolic issues where disarticulations existed between the aggiornamento process and the currently operating church. Cultural norms clashed. For example, mentalities of top-down authority met norms of increased consultativeness. Priests complained that pastoral and priests' councils were asked to endorse bishops' plans rather than to deliberate over them. Norms of job placement according to preference, expertise, specialization, and competitive recruitment—endorsed particularly by younger priests—ran counter to norms routinely used to make clergy assignments, that is, seniority or simple appointment by the bishop. Expectations that priests work a nine to five day opposed the notion that the priesthood involved a 24-hour lifestyle and attentiveness. Differing viewpoints manifested themselves in different groups opposing each other in virtually every U.S. diocese. Sometimes the division was between philosophical liberals and traditionalists; sometimes the gap centered on differences in professional training; sometimes psychological tendencies to accept or resist change were germane; in one diocese, age divided the clergy. Occasionally, the gap was between bishop and priests.

Restructuring a hierarchical bureaucracy toward greater consultativeness was an enormous struggle. Clergy, bishops, and laity were not uniformly enthusiastic about it. Also, consultation is a time-consuming means of decision making. The process itself generated dysfunctions. Greater accountability often increased diocesan bureaucracy through the intermediate boards and consultative groups it generated. Duties and responsibilities among groups overlapped and were unclear. It took energy to attend to or consult these groups, once established. Coordinating them required information management systems.

In some dioceses, the role of the bishop was nebulous; team ministry was difficult; an ingroup of priests leading the change emerged, leaving others feeling disaffected from the process; and clergy became disillusioned with the slow pace of change. Priests searched to redefine their roles. Clergy shortages had become a structural fact in most dioceses. They increased clergy tension and stress and put limits on how many priests could be released for updating their educations. Foreign priests or priests from religious orders were recruited to fill vacancies which further lessened cohesion among diocesan priests. Shortages led to a maintenance mentality by diocesan administrators; further implementation of change seemed either undesirable, impossible, or both.

There was symbolic disarticulation. Symbols emphasizing community involvement were moved into liturgies, like the Mass, where symbols of personal piety had abounded. Theology emphasizing God's love and mercy, Jesus as brother and savior, and salvation overshadowed the earlier emphasis on Mary, Purgatory, sin, and a judgmental God. Devotions, such as novenas and Benediction, became uncommon events. Symbolic rewards were disrupted. Monsignorships were either phased out or rejected by potential recipients in the spirit of social leveling. Assignments to difficult or less desirable positions were not seen as stepping stones to future advancement as they had once been. Personnel boards had problems filling such positions or justifying such assignments.

The symbolic role of bishops, priests, women and men religious was contested. Some priests and laity wanted bishops to be strong leaders. That desire interfaced poorly with the role of a consulting, listening shepherd, articulated by Vatican II. Changes in clothing, life-style, and social involvement of priests and women and men religious symbolized changed roles for them. Some clergy and laity were dismayed. These disarticulations were more than psychological disorientations. They were disjunctures in symbols which serve to sustain religious involvement (Greeley 1981).

Normative, structural, and symbolic disarticulations implied continuing conflict over modernization during the implementation period of the 1970s. But the basis had shifted. The pre-Vatican II struggle about whether to modernize or not had basically been resolved in favor of aggiornamento. During implementation, proponents of radical change were pitted against those arguing for more moderate change.

By the end of the 1970s and into the 1980s, change was apparent. Dioceses had more specialized early and midcareer training for clergy. There were structures, such as personnel boards, priests's senates, grievance procedures, and continuing clergy education, which gave evidence of increased attention to clergy rights and of respect for them as professionals. Destratification was evident in various ways: team ministry, consultative structures like priests' senates and pastoral councils, and a decrease in honorific titles like monsignor. Consultative structures were in place, which attempted to implement collegiality, shared ministry, and the priesthood of the laity (Fichter 1977). Seminary education was more rigorous. In some chancery offices, there was a new administrative spirit where specialists interacted with bishops and administrators as equals. Many dioceses created a new status—pastoral planner, the person responsible for implementing Vatican II more fully. Some dioceses reflected a generally improved clerical climate (Seidler and Meyer 1989).

The implementation phase spilled over into the 1980s. It was characterized by a continued broadening of issues beyond authority, freedom, and liturgical change, and a continued inclusion of groups other than clergy and bishops in debates over updating. Some dioceses were attentive to continued aggiornamento; some were cajoled to modernize through a strong and progressive bishop; some pitted a relatively progressive and outspoken Catholic faction against a traditional bishop; and some demonstrated that all major diocesan factions resisted aggiornamento.

EVIDENCE OF COUNTERMOVEMENT

Evidence of traditionalist influences had been present throughout implementation. In the 1980s, when Pope John Paul II embraced aspects of Traditionalist Catholicism, it was clear that a countermovement was mobilized. John Paul II addressed issues that went to the heart of the movement for change: authority, freedom, liturgical change, theological doctrine, and the symbolic roles of priests, brothers, and women religious. Action was taken. Prominent theologians (Küng, Schillebeeckx, Curran, Boff) were questioned and/or banned from teaching. The Tridentine Mass was permitted under specified conditions; an African-American rite was disallowed. The Vatican intervened in the Jesuits' tradition of passing on the top leadership position and in the writing of a new constitution for the Discalced Carmelites. Priests were told to step out of politics (e.g., in the Sandinista government of Nicaragua and in the U.S. Congress). Women religious were disciplined for signing an announcement on pluralism and abortion in the *New York Times* and for serving in civil positions where birth control or abortion were options. Issues extending beyond those central to change also were treated. Traditional positions on birth control, in vitro fertilization, abortion, and homosexuality were reiterated. Women were banned as acolytes and lectors. Visible proponents of aggiornamento (e.g., Fox, Hunthausen, Callahan) were sanctioned. The Vatican Congregation for the Doctrine of the Faith warned against use of certain methods of meditation and prayer coming from Eastern religions. At least part of the traditionalist agenda was legitimated by John Paul II.

Movement organizations espousing different ideological reconstructions were obvious. Catholics United For the Faith (CUFF) and similar organizations were visible in many dioceses. Alongside these traditionalist groups, other types of groups grew. Charismatic Catholics were linked nationally and internationally and were close to a newly identified center of devotion, Medugorje. Call to Action, the Corps of Reserve Priests United for Service (CORPUS), and groups interested in furthering the image of a church consistent with the contemporary world developed and/or gained in strength.

In some ways, the struggle for ideological ascendancy mirrored that which occurred in the decades preceding Vatican II. Images of a traditionalist Catholicism vied with charismatic and contemporary visions. One notable difference was the obvious involvement of Catholic laity. Conflict extended beyond those central to church administration (bishops and clergy) not only to embrace others but also to feature them in leadership statuses. For example, former U.S. Treasury Secretary William Simon and theologian Michael Novak endorsed the free-market profit system as the most moral economic approach in 1984 after the American bishops developed their pastoral letter on Catholic Social Teaching and the U.S. Economy, which elaborated pitfalls of capitalist systems. Another notable difference was the use of secular media. For example, a full-page ad in the *New York Times* in November, 1989, by about 4,500 Catholics called for ordaining women, allowing married priests and optional celibacy, revising teachings on sexuality, providing a role for laity to select bishops, consulting parishioners about major decisions, opening financial records, and respecting controversy among theological teachings.

In the 25 years since Vatican II, the floor of controversy had shifted. Even a major legitimator of the traditionalist countermovement, Pope John Paul II, was not a complete traditionalist, especially about social issues and international conflict. He spoke out for human rights and liberation; opposed rigid capitalism; publicly supported Solidarity, the Polish workers' union; ordained married Anglican priests as Roman Catholic clergy; excommunicated Cardinal Lefebvre for elevating clergy to the rank of bishop; nearly reversed his earlier position on liberation theology; and moved to re-establish ties with the Soviet Union and Eastern European nations like Hungary. New structures were in place at both national and local levels (e.g., The National Federation of Priests' Councils, diocesan synods, Christian base communities). Shared ministry was evident in liturgies and in parish administration, where laity were visibly present. A norm of social responsibility ran through Bishops' statements on war and peace, nuclear buildup, and certain aspects of capitalism. The updating of the Catholic church from pre-Vatican II days to the present, through movements and conflict, spawned an organization startlingly different from the one that resisted modernity for basically five centuries.

REFERENCES

Aubert, R. 1978. *The Church in a Secularized Society,* vol. 5. *The Christian Centuries.* New York: Paulist Press.

Boyd, M. 1968. "Ecclesia Christi." Pp. 3-6 in *The Underground Church,* edited by M. Boyd. New York: Sheed and Ward.

Brown, R.McA. 1969. *The Ecumenical Revolution.* Garden City, NY: Anchor-Image.

Cullman, O. 1968. *Vatican Council II: The New Direction.* New York: Harper & Row.

Davis, C. 1967. *A Question of Conscience.* New York: Harper & Row.

Dinges, W.D. 1983 "Catholic Traditionalist Movement." Pp. 137-158 in *Alternatives to American Mainline Churches,* edited by J.H. Fichter. New York: Rose of Sharon Press.

Dulles, A. 1974. *Models of the Church.* Garden City, NY: Doubleday.

————. 1977. *The Resilient Church: The Necessity and Limits of Adaptation.* Garden City, NY: Doubleday.

Ellis, J.T. 1969. *American Catholicism.* Chicago: University of Chicago Press.

Etzioni, A. 1961. *A Comparative Analysis of Complex Organizations.* New York: The Free Press.

Fesquet, H. 1967. *The Drama of Vatican II: The Ecumenical Council, June 1962-December 1965.* New York: Random House.

Fichter, J.H. 1968. *America's Forgotten Priests: What They Are Saying.* New York: Harper and Row.

————. 1974. *Organization Man in the Church.* Cambridge, MA: Schenkman.

————. 1977. "Restructuring Catholicism." *Sociological Analysis* 38(Summer):154-166.

Freeman, J. 1983. "On the Origins of Social Movements." Pp. 8-33 in *Social Movements of the Sixties and Seventies*, edited by J. Freeman. New York: Longman.

Gamson, W. 1975. *The Strategy of Social Protest*. Homewood, IL: Dorsey.

Greeley, A. M. 1973. *The New Agenda*. Garden City, NY: Doubleday.

————. 1977. *The American Catholic: A Social Portrait*. New York: Basic Books.

————. 1981. "The Failures of Vatican II After Twenty Years." *America* 146 (February 6):86-89.

Hadden, J.K. 1969. *The Gathering Storm in the Churches*. New York: Doubleday.

Hall, D.T., and B. Schneider. 1973. *Organizational Climates and Careers: The Work Lives of Priests*. New York: Seminar Press.

Haughey, J.C. 1971. "Priest-Bishop Relations: American Perspective." *America* 124 (May 15):518-520.

Hennesey, J. 1981. *American Catholics: A History of the Roman Catholic Community in the United States*. New York: Oxford University Press.

Hoge, D.R., and J.W. Carroll. 1975. "Christian Beliefs, Nonreligious Factors, and Anti-Semitism." *Social Forces* 53(June):581-594.

Kaiser, R. B. 1963. *Pope, Council and World: The Story of Vatican II*. New York: Macmillan.

Kiely, P. 1968. "A Cry for Black Nun Power." *Commonweal* 88(September 27):650.

Killian, L. M. 1973. "Social Movements: A Review of the Field." Pp. 9-53 in *Social Movements: A Reader and Source Book*, edited by R.R. Evans. Chicago: Rand McNally.

Küng, H. 1968. *Truthfulness: The Future of the Church*. New York: Sheed and Ward.

————. 1976. *On Being a Christian*. Garden City, NY: Doubleday.

Lang, K., and G. E. Lang. 1978. "The Dynamics of Social Movements." Pp. 96-108 in *Collective Behavior and Social Movements*, edited by L.E. Geneviie. Itasca, IL: F. E. Peacock.

McBrien, R.P. 1973. *The Remaking of the Church*. New York: Harper & Row.

McCarthy, J.D., and M.N. Zald. 1977. "Resource Mobilization and Social Movements: A Partial Theory." *American Journal of Sociology* 82:1212-1241.

McKenzie, J.L. 1966. *Authority in the Catholic Church*. New York: Sheed and Ward.

McSweeney, W. 1980. *Roman Catholicism: The Search for Relevance*. New York: St. Martin's.

Meyer, K., and J. Seidler. 1978. "The Structure of Gatherings." *Sociology and Social Research* 63(October):131-153.

Mottl, T.L. 1980. "The Analysis of Countermovements." *Social Problems* 27(June): 620-635.

Murphy, F.X. 1981. *The Papacy Today*. New York: Macmillan.

Murray, J. C. 1960. *We Hold These Truths: Catholic Reflections on the American Proposition*. New York: Sheed and Ward.

National Opinion Research Center (NORC). 1972. *The Catholic Priest in the United States: Sociological Investigations*. (A.M. Greeley and R.A. Schoenherr, co-investigators.) Washington, DC: U.S. Catholic Conference.

Novak, M. 1964. *The Open Church*. New York: Macmillan.

Oberschall, A. 1973. *Social Conflict and Social Movements*. Englewood Cliffs, NJ: Prentice-Hall.

Pelikan, J. 1983. "The Enduring Relevance of Martin Luther 500 Years After His Birth." *The New York Times Magazine* (September 18), pp. 43-45, 99-104.

Perry, J.B., Jr., and M. D. Pugh. 1978. *Collective Behavior: Response to Social Stress*. West.

Poulat, E. 1969a. *Integrisme et Catholicisme Integral* [Integrism and Integral Catholicism]. Paris: Casterman.

————. 1969b. "'Modernisme' et 'Integrisme': Du concept polemique a l'irenisme critique" ['Modernism' and 'Integrism': From polemical concept to ironical criticism.]. *Archives de sociologie des religions* 27:3-28.

————. 1977. *Catholicisme, Democratie et Socialisme: Mgr. Benigni* [Catholicism, Democracy and Socialism: Mgr. Benigni]. Paris: Casterman.

Ruether, R.R. 1975. *New Woman, New Earth.* New York: Seabury.

————. 1977. *Mary, The Feminine Face of the Church.* Philadelphia: Westminster Press.

Rynne, X. 1968. *Vatican Council II.* New York: Farrar Strauss and Giroux.

Schallert, E. J., and J.M. Kelley. 1970. "Some Factors Associated with Voluntary Withdrawal from the Catholic Priesthood." *Lumen Vitae* 25:425-460.

Schoenherr, R. A., and A. M. Greeley. 1974. "Role Commitment Processes and the American Catholic Priesthood." *American Sociological Review* 39:407-426.

Schoenherr, R.A., and A. Sorensen. 1987. "Power and Authority in Organized Religion: Disaggregating the Phenomenological Core." *Sociological Analysis* 47:52-71.

Seidler, J. 1972. *Rebellion and Retreatism among the American Catholic Clergy.* Ph.D. dissertation, Department of Sociology, University of North Carolina, Chapel Hill.

————. 1974a. "Priest Protest in the Human Catholic Church." *National Catholic Reporter* 10(May 3):7, 14.

————. 1974b. "Priest Resignations, Relocations, and Passivity." *National Catholic Reporter* 10(May 10):7, 14.

————. 1979. "Priest Resignations in a Lazy Monopoly." *American Sociological Review* 44(October):763-783.

Seidler, J., K. Meyer, and L. MacGillivray. 1977. "Collecting Data on Crowds and Rallies: A New Method of Stationary Sampling." *Social Forces* 55(March):507-518.

Seidler, J., and K. Meyer. 1989. *Conflict and Change in the Catholic Church.* New Brunswick, NJ: Rutgers University Press.

Smelser, N.J. 1963. *Theory of Collective Behavior.* Glencoe, IL: The Free Press.

Spencer, A. E. C. W. 1966. "The Structure and Organization of the Catholic Church in England." Pp. 91-125 in *Uses of Sociology,* edited by J.D. Halloran and J. Brothers. London and Melbourne: Sheed and Ward.

Steeman, T. M. 1969. "The Underground Church." Pp. 713-722 in *The Religious Situation: 1969,* edited by D.R. Cutler. Boston: Beacon Press.

Stewart, J.H. 1978. *American Catholic Leadership: A Decade of Turmoil.* The Hague: Mouton.

Suenens, L.J. 1968. *Coresponsibility in the Church.* New York: Herder and Herder.

Tilly, C. 1978. *From Mobilization to Revolution.* Reading, MA: Addison-Wesley.

Tracy, D. 1981. *The Analogical Imagination.* New York: Crossroad.

Turner, R. H., and L. M. Killian. 1972. *Collective Behavior.* Englewood Cliffs, NJ: Prentice-Hall.

Vallier, I. 1969. "Comparative Studies of Roman Catholicism: Dioceses As Strategic Units." *Social Compass* 16:147-184.

Wilson, J. 1973. *Introduction to Social Movements.* New York: Basic Books.

Wood, J. R. 1981. *Leadership in Voluntary Organizations: The Controversy over Social Action in the Protestant Churches.* New Brunswick, NJ: Rutgers University Press.

PART IV

CATHOLICISM IN WORLD PERSPECTIVE

WESTERN EUROPEAN CATHOLICISM
SINCE VATICAN II

Karel Dobbelaere and Liliane Voyé

In his recent book *Ontwijding* [Profanation] (1989), the Belgian historian Van Isacker explains the "massive exodus" of the faithful and the "desertion of the priests" in the Western world as a result of the Second Vatican Council. He agrees with N. Trippen, head of the Seminary of Cologne, who stated that the crisis of the church is a consequence of the theological and reformatory impulses coming out of the Council; the pluralistic worldviews and the spiritual confusion of Western democracies are only secondary causes (Van Isacker 1989, pp. 25, 40). Typical consequences of the Council were the emphasis upon "humanism," "democracy," and "ecumenism," concepts which resulted from the infiltration into the church of masonic, relativistic ideas about God, truth, and religion and which created a climate of confusion (Van Isacker 1989, pp. 58-60). The profanation became eminently clear in the liturgical changes: the Tridentine Missal was banned, the sacred language and music replaced by the vernacular, jazz, folk, and electronic music; and the altar was turned to face the people. "Now, one sits comradely, 'democratically', and 'sans gêne' [unashamedly] before the unnameable God. And, immediately, the mystery that should surround the attitudes of humans toward their God is gone" (Van Isacker 1989, p. 67).

Religion and the Social Order, Volume 2, pages 205-231.
Copyright © 1991 by JAI Press Inc.
All rights of reproduction in any form reserved.
ISBN: 1-55938-388-7

Was the Council the cause of the changes or was the Council itself a consequence of the changing world? Without denying that the Council had a multiplying effect on some preexisting tendencies, we will argue that the second hypothesis is the more valid. Indeed, it was the explicit intension of Pope John XXIII to have an "aggiornamento" [updating] to open the church to the "signs of the times" (Latourelle 1988, p. 12). However, the question remains: To what extent is this purpose being actualized?

The hypothesis that the exodus of the faithful is explained by the Second Vatican Council has been rejected on empirical grounds by a study of Greeley and associates. Instead, they explained the exodus as a violent reaction of a large number of Catholics to the 1968 birth-control encyclical, *Humanae Vitae* [Concerning Human Life] (Greeley 1985, pp. 55-57; Greeley et al. 1976, pp. 116-152; Hout and Greeley 1987, pp. 332-335). However, a comparative analysis across countries demonstrates that the exodus from the church is explained neither by the Second Vatican Council nor by *Humanae Vitae*. In Belgium and the Netherlands, the sharp decline started before the publication of the encyclical (Dobbelaere 1988a, pp. 88-95) and in France the exodus began in the early 1960s, which was well before the impact of the Council was felt. Indeed, regular church attendance in France dropped from 38 to 20 percent between 1961 and 1966 (3.5 percentage points a year). It dropped even further to 10 percent by 1981 (Donegami 1984, p. 56; see also Hervieu-Léger 1986, pp. 19-65). In addition, the decline in church attendance was not limited to the Catholic church: it also occurred in the Protestant Churches (Van Hemert 1980, pp. 10-11). This fact can be easily documented with data from the German Federal Republic: from 1963 to 1967-69, regular church attendance for Catholics dropped seven percentage points from a high of 55 percent of Catholics 16 years and older to 48 percent. In the next five years, it dropped another 13 percentage points to reach 35 percent. Between 1973-1982, it leveled out at 32 percent. Church attendance figures for Protestants also declined: from 15 percent in 1963 to 10 percent in 1967-69 and further to 7 percent in 1973 and 6 percent in 1982 (Köcher 1987, p. 221). Furthermore, institutional factors do not explain why in Belgium, as in Canada, the attendance drop-off was far from uniform across these countries (Bibby 1987, 19-21; Dobbelaere 1988a, p. 96). An analysis of the available evidence points rather to the *contextual* factors of industrialization and modernization. The acceleration of these processes in Flanders and Quebec in the 1960s explains the belated and more dramatic declines that occurred there.

The purpose of this paper is threefold: (1) to present cross-national data on the extent of the exodus; (2) to explain the exodus on the basis of "modernity," "postmodernity," and the amplification given to it by a failing implementation of the "aggiornamento" by the church; and (3) to describe some hopes that were raised by the Council but that were not fulfilled.

AN EXODUS?

Research reports indicate that church attendance declined everywhere in Europe during the 1960s and early 1970s, most notably in the Catholic church (Dobbelaere in press). In 1981, according to the European Value Study, 37 percent of the Catholics and 9 percent of the Protestants still went to church weekly. However, this does not mean that people who do not attend weekly services have severed all ties with their church. Slighty more than a fifth of the self-declared Catholics and a third of the self-declared Protestants never go, while others go occasionally (Stoetzel 1983, p. 120).

Apart from going to church on weekends, many people go or are brought to church to sacralize important passages in their life: birth, adulthood, marriage, and death. The frequency of rites of passage is best recorded for Catholics in what Stoetzel (1983) called the European laicized region: France, the Netherlands, and Belgium. These data are often used by the Catholic church to point out that many people still behave religiously at important moments of their lives. Although a vast majority of children of Catholics are still baptized in this European region, a serious decline began in the 1960s. Since the 1970s, the number of religious marriages has also gone down (Maitre 1988, pp. 35-36, 38; Dobbelaere 1988a, pp. 88-89, 94-95). This indicates that now more and more young adults (i.e., those marrying and those having children) do not behave any more religiously on solemn occasions (see also Furlong 1988, pp. 121-122; Lambert 1988, pp. 50-53). Consequently, we may affirm that more and more young adults have become areligious. This is not the case for the older population: the number of Catholic burials was very stable in the Netherlands and Belgium over the last 20 years (Dobbelaere 1988a, pp. 88-89, 94-95). Other research confirms this trend. For example, in 1981, the European Value Study registered 12.7 percent of the Western European population as not affiliated with a church (Stoetzel 1983, p. 113). This number has been growing in the last decades and is more prevalent in the generation born after World War II than in the older generations (Dobbelaere 1988a, p. 87, 1986-87, p. 297; Harding et al. 1986, p. 42; Madelin 1988, pp. 60-63; Sasaki and Suzuki 1987, pp. 1065-1069; Wallis 1984, p. 61; Wadsworth and Freeman 1983, pp. 422-423). We may thus conclude that, in Western Europe, markedly fewer people born after World War II are affiliated with a church than in the older generations. Research reports also indicate that fewer persons of this generation who declare themselves to be Catholics or Protestants go to church on weekends than those of earlier generations (de Moor 1987, pp. 30-31; Dobbelaere 1984, pp. 103-104; Felling et al. 1986, p. 82; Harding et al. 1986, pp. 40-41; Köcher 1987, pp. 176-177; Stoetzel 1983, pp. 229-230).

Some might object that our analysis up to now has been based only on ritual behavior and self-declared church membership and that beliefs and ethical practices are more important to evaluate the religiosity of a person. However, the Belgian data of the European Value Study have shown that the way Catholics conceive of God has a strong relationship to their church involvement and to the other beliefs they hold. Indeed, the majority of Belgian Catholics believing in a "personal" God attend a church service weekly. Those conceiving of God as a "spirit" or "life force" and those who "do not really know how to 'conceive' Him" attend less frequently. Finally, people who doubt His existence or do not believe in Him overwhelmingly are not involved in the church. The predictability of a person's affiliation to and involvement in the church based on his conception of God was statistically higher than the reverse (Dobbelaere 1984, pp. 82-84). This relationship has been confirmed by research in other European countries for both Catholics and Protestants (de Moor 1987, pp. 38-39; Goddijn et al. 1979, p. 47; Harding et al. 1986, pp. 48-49; Köcher 1987, p. 229).

The belief in a "personal" God also correlates with the acceptance of traditional beliefs in life after death, the soul, hell, heaven, and sin. Again, the number of people accepting traditional Catholic beliefs has particularly declined among those born after World War II (Dobbelaere 1984, p. 73), a trend that has been confirmed by Lambert's (1988, pp. 36-58) analysis of French data. In fact, the situation is the same all over Western Europe for Catholics and Protestants (de Moor 1987, p. 39; Felling et al. 1986, p. 82; Goddijn et al. 1979, pp. 33, 66; Harding et al. 1986, p. 48; Köcher 1987, pp. 166-167, 202), although a higher number of Catholics than Protestants believe in a "personal" God (Harding et al. 1986, p. 48), a fact that correlates with their higher church attendance.

Similar results are found in Belgium between affiliation with a church and degree of ritual participation, on the one hand, and acceptance of moral guidelines for Catholics, on the other (Dobbelaere 1984, pp. 83-84). The same holds for Catholics and Protestants in Germany (Köcher 1987, pp. 185-194, 242-279). The closer Catholics and Protestants are to their church, the more conservative are their ethical standards. This relationship is also confirmed for Great Britain and the Netherlands (de Moor 1987, p. 31; Gerard 1985, pp. 77-79; Philips and Harding 1985, p. 108). Again, as for affiliation, involvement, and beliefs, moral attitudes vary with age in all the nations studied by the European Value Study: the younger the population, affiliated or not, the less orthodox they are in moral matters (de Moor 1987, pp. 30, 40; Dobbelaere 1984, pp. 87-89, 92-93; Harding et al. 1986, p. 66; Kerkhofs 1984, p. 53; Phillips and Harding 1985, p. 108 [who call the effect of age "pervasive"]; Stoetzel 1983, p. 253). The divergence of expressed beliefs concerning God also has implications for the ethical points of view people take: belief in a "personal" God tends to promote the acceptance of absolute moral guidelines as opposed to the notion that good and evil depend entirely upon the circumstances at the time. A "relativistic" perspective, in contrast, is more likely endorsed by those who believe in a "spirit" or "life force" and by those who either do not believe in God or are uncertain in their beliefs (Harding et al. 1986, p. 49).

We may conclude this descriptive section by stating that beliefs, church involvement, and ethical views for Protestants, as well as Catholics, are strongly correlated and that all these dimensions reveal a clear difference between the generation of those born after World War II and the older generations. While it is correct to state that the Catholic faith, in general, is still sustaining a greater commitment among young people than the Protestant faith (Harding et al. 1986, p. 70), changes are more pronounced within the Catholic population in the last three decades. Studies also make it clear that, if gender differences still exist, they are attributable to women not in paid employment. Women in full-time employment display an outlook on religious and moral matters close to those of men (de Moor 1987, p. 31; Dobbelaere 1966, pp. 190-192, 1984, p. 104; Harding et al. 1986, p. 63). All the other traditional social variables (such as level of education, income, social class, home ownership, and urbanization) have little or no impact (de Moor 1987, pp. 30-33; Dobbelaere 1984, pp. 102-105; Gerard 1985, p. 68; Harding et al. 1986, pp. 34-71; Stoetzel 1983, pp. 87-120), a finding that indicates a change since the 1950s and 1960s (e.g., Dobbelaere 1966; Voyé 1973).

Finally, was there really an exodus from the church? Most people do not leave the church suddenly. Rather than that, they first diminish their involvement. The number of Catholics with reduced involvement rapidly grew during the last several decades: an occasional mass, especially on the holidays, for some, but, most of all, a growing number who limited their relationship to the church to participating in a rite of passage, the so-called "festive Catholics." What will the future bring? Is this a new way of being Catholic or is it a hesitant "farewell" en route to disaffiliation? If we may generalize from Dutch data, the latter seems to be the most plausible hypothesis (Felling et al. 1986, p. 63). Consequently, we may predict that a growing exodus is most plausible.

EXPLAINING THE EXODUS

Our theory must explain the Catholic and Protestant decline, allowing for differences in rate. Indeed, the exodus affected both the Catholic and Protestant churches. Because the same social variables apply to the changes in both constituencies, several European researchers did not report on them separately. At first, the Catholic church withstood the societal pressures much better than did the Protestant churches. In France, due to a "clear split between militant faith and militant unbelief" (Martin 1978, p. 39), the latter being dominant, the great Catholic exodus of the faithful occurred in the early 1960s. Indeed, the culture of the center easily reached the periphery through mass media, especially television. In Belgium, West Germany, and the Netherlands, the Catholic exodus occurred much later: in the late 1960s and early 1970s. For example, in Belgium in 1967-73, the average decline of church attendance in the Catholic church was 2.3 percentage points a year. Before it was only .7, and, afterwards, nearly .9 percentage points a year into the 1980s. It seems, then, that in countries not split between laïcists and believers, a "collective religion" (Martin 1978), supported by an institutionalized pillar (cf. next section), could hold its constituency much longer than could "individualistic religions." However, once the "dikes" (Hoge 1986) gave in, the decline was much greater in a very short period of time. If the decline is now less dramatic, it is because the elderly remain faithful; the young, however, disaffiliate or are only marginally involved. Cohort replacement no longer occurs (Köcher 1987, pp. 174-177).

In recent publications (Dobbelaere 1988a, pp. 93-98; Dobbelaere and Voyé 1990), we have described our explanation of the decline, so we may be brief here. Our theory is based on the centrality of the belief in a "personal" God for the preservation of traditional beliefs, ethical viewpoints, and church behavior, and on the impact on that belief of functional or structural differentiation, rationalization, and societalization.

As a consequence of functional differentiation and rationalization, people, especially the young, conceive of the physical, psychic, and social world as more and more controllable and calculable. Consequently, many can no longer believe in God because "*they* have the world in *their* hands." And if, for some people, the notion of God still lingers on, He is more and more conceived of as a "higher power," "something vague and general," and not as a "personal" God. How could He be thought of as a "personal" God if people experience fewer and fewer "personal" relationships in public life? In a society where impersonal, segmented role relations prevail, belief in a "personal" God and, consequently, the celebration of a person's relationship with Him in religious services seem to be an anachronism for many modern women and men. As Durkheim suggested, the more general and vague God becomes, the more removed He is from the world and the more ineffective He is. At the same time, such a belief is very shaky. It is a belief in an abstract notion without any real impact on people's lives, and one that can easily be disposed of. Consequently, the functional differentiation of society and the related processes had an impact not only on the secularization of society but also on personal lifeworlds, which became compartmentalized. This is highly compatible with a functionally differentiated society. Of course, functional differentiation also produced the individuation of decisions (Luhmann 1977, pp. 232-248), an event that stimulated "religion à la carte" [a religious collage]. This had an exceptional appeal for the upper middle and upper classes and especially for intellectuals. They no longer accepted the "given" answers. Because the churches lost credibility as a consequence of scientific discoveries and because the process of secularization divested the churches of their capacity to legitimate the status of these upper classes, members of these classes dissociated from it. This explains why the well-established relationship between the upper classes and church involvement changed. Today all social classes practice very little.

Already in the early 1960s, the impact of modernity strongly undermined the belief in a "personal" God as well as belief in other articles of faith and the traditional ethical views of the faithful, but overt, traditional behavior simply continued under the impact of social control. A vast number of priests and religious persons together with the Catholic pillar regimented the faithful. However, Sunday Mass had become for many a "duty," a "tradition" not supported by strong beliefs.

In the second half of the 1960s, a discussion began about a number of issues raised in Robinson's *Honest to God* (1963), *Humanae Vitae* (1968), and the implementation of the conciliar resolutions. One could, for the first time, in public discourse and the mass media, acknowledge that the religious understanding of beliefs, church ethics, and church authority were very much undermined. Also in the secular world, institutions and authority came under heavy criticism. This discussion broke down the "dikes" the church had established to protect the faithful (e.g., the pillar, see next section). The clergy, in the same period, massively left the church, an event that had repercussions upon the beliefs, attitudes, and behavior of the lay people. The sharp decline in Sunday Mass attendance at the end of the 1960s and the early 1970s may, consequently, be seen as the collapse of traditional behavior that was no longer supported by the belief in a "personal" God and the traditional values that the church proclaims. What occurred was the convergence of *public* behavior and the *personal* general disbelief in the doctrines and values of the church. Since that time social control has increasingly had a completely different impact in that it started to keep people out of the church rather than induce them to attend.

Important historical changes, however, cannot be explained monocausally. Other factors, institutional as well as contextual, also had an impact. In the 1970s and the 1980s, the reactionary policy of the Holy See, blocking the "aggiornamento" [updating] discouraged a number of Catholics who wanted to adapt the church to the world in the light of the conciliar spirit (Schillebeeckx 1989, pp. 5-6; and pp. 215-224 in this volume). Moreover, structural changes were also important: in the 1960s and 1970s, an increasing number of people obtained more and more leisure time, not only more vacation time but also the so-called English week: Saturdays were freed from work and school, and a "leisure culture" developed. Consequently, in a period when, for a growing number of people Sunday Mass became a "traditional" behavior, a "sheer duty," an "obligation of little substance," it became more and more located in a period of extended leisure time. The feeling associated with leisure time, being primarily a time of "exemption from external pressures," heightened the awareness of "duty" associated with religious "obligations." Bit by bit, a culture emerged that conflicted directly with traditional religious values, which legitimated a "culture of duties and self-restraint" and was based on the notion of "community." In contrast, the leisure culture stressed freedom, individualism and "private niches," massification and emotionalism, pleasure and ecstasy. This culture is supported by consumerism and advertising, both of which stress novelty, new trends, new fashions, new products (Balandier 1985, pp. 184-195; Yonnet 1985). Religion, in contrast, is supported by collective rituals that "repeat" the same gestures and the same texts, stressing continuity and tradition.

Since the mid 1970s, not only "modernity" but also "postmodernity" had an impact on church behavior, the latter even underscoring more the individuation of the person than the former. Modernity still stressed collective identities (the proletariate, the bourgeois, the women, the consumers, the militants), which had a historic role to play in building a new society, a new world (Touraine 1984). However, the militant vanished and with it "les visions totalisantes" [meta-theories] (Balandier 1985, pp. 138-140) and "the grand narratives" (Lyotard 1984, p. 37). Now, more than ever, the person is thrown back on himself/herself in his/her confrontation with daily and existential problems and creates his/her own networks to handle them (Voyé 1985a, pp. 269-271, 1988a, pp. 129-130). Catholicism may offer him/her some help in coping with these problems: popular religion (pilgrimages, lighting candles, blessings, healing waters, charms, novenas), and the rites of passage allow people to ritualize problems and to petition God for help, especially through the Blessed Mother and particular saints (Voyé 1988b). Such forms of popular religion allow the individual not only to respond directly to his/her problems of everyday life but also to those of relatives and friends with whom he/she lives in close networks, the "private niches." According to a recent study on pilgrimages in Belgium (Robberecht 1986), it is especially those Catholics who practice irregularly who are motivated to go on pilgrimages to the Blessed Mother to alleviate their "actual needs." The subjective image of the Blessed Mother is very much related to "needs," most of all among the nonpracticing and irregularly practicing Catholics. For practicing Catholics, going on pilgrimage seems more a devotional exercise (Robberecht 1986, p. 64). Consequently, to come back to our first section, the functions of healing, of making sense of the contingent, and of uniting a compartimentalized life at certain moments of transitions (holidays and rites of passage) may well slow down the exodus from the church, because no well-integrated alternative meaning systems seem to be available at present (Felling et al. 1986, pp. 52-60).

PILLARIZATION

In the preceding section, reference was made to the protective function of the Catholic pillars in the Netherlands, West Germany, and Belgium. Traditionally, pillars have been defined as segmented and polarized organizational complexes that are religiously or ideologically legitimated and that strive toward autarky (self-sufficiency). In Europe, there are Catholic, Socialist, Liberal, and Communist pillars. Catholic pillars are usually the most autarkic, because they overarch so many sectors of life for which services are provided (Dobbelaere and Voyé 1990, pp. S6-S8). If we may suggest that the first building blocks of the Catholic pillars emerged in Europe at the end of the nineteenth century (Righart 1986), it took many decades before they were consolidated, in the Netherlands and Belgium not before the 1950s (Coleman 1978, pp. 67-77; Dobbelaere 1988a, pp. 82-83). By establishing these integrated organizations, Catholics built an organizational "dike" to protect the faithful from the secularized world, because the so-called profane functions (education, information, economy, health care, etc.) were progressively more and more differentiated from the church and organized by the state. By doing so, Catholics acknowledged, both internally and externally, the process of functional differentiation, but they reverted to an earlier process of differentiation, that is, segmented differentiation, to protect *and* to control the "sheep."

How, in the 1960s, did the Catholic pillars evolve under the pressures from, on the one hand, the *inside,* the crisis in the Catholic culture itself (cf. the preceeding sections), and, on the other hand, the *outside,* functional differentiation, the rationalization of the institutions, the Vergesellschaftung [societalization] of the organizational structures, professionalization, etcetera (Dobbelaere 1988a, pp. 83-87)? In the Netherlands, the Catholic pillar *disintegrated* to a large extent (Thurlings 1978). "From 161 national Catholic organizations which existed in 1960, about 35 had disappeared in 1970 and nearly 100 in 1980. . . . This process was typical of all societal sectors except education" (Duffhues et al. 1985, p. 270). Belgium represents an alternative pattern, the *universalization* of the ideological basis. In conferences and colloquia, a new "collective consciousness" developed in the late 1960s and early 1970s, which Billiet and Dobbelaere (1976) have called "socio-cultural Christianity," that is, the "civil religion" of the pillar (Dobbelaere 1986).

The core values of socio-cultural Christianity can be summed up by the concept of "social personalism." It refers to a humane approach to clients, the Gemeinschaftlichkeit [communal feeling] of Christian institutions, solidarity, social justice, etcetera (Billiet 1981; Billiet and Dobbelaere 1976, pp. 59-78; Dobbelaere 1986, pp. 658-660; Dobbelaere and Billiet 1983). This "sacred canopy" is symbolized by a "C," referring more and more to *Christian,* that is, evangelical, instead of Catholic, the latter being considered to be more confining and to have a restrictive, particularistic appeal. However, the proposed so-called Christian values are not typically Christian, either individually or in combination. Rather, they are European values with a universalistic appeal (Dobbelaere 1982, pp. 124-126). The only typical characteristic of socio-cultural Christianity is that it is anchored in the Gospel, a trait that gives it a sacred aura. This new collective consciousness is proclaimed *externally* and is used to attract clients and members who are, by and large, not regular churchgoers. It also functions *internally* to promote different programs, for example, a program for the humanization of Christian hospitals (Dobbelaere 1988a, pp. 84-86).

In Belgium, the Catholic, Socialist, and Liberal pillars make up the civil society. The state provides the legal framework and the financing; the pillars organize the services. This is especially the case of the Christian pillar with its broad range of services, attending people from cradle to grave. In a society where the public system has lost most of its credit by being impersonal, ineffective, and bureaucratic, Christian organizations, seen as "private" organizations, appeal more to people (Dobbelaere 1988a, pp. 84-85; Voyé 1979, p. 327; Voyé and Remy 1985a, pp. 237-238, 1985b). By changing the core values and losing its particular "Catholic" culture, the pillar survived. However, the "dikes" collapsed, and the pillar lost its protective function for "Catholic" identity and life.

At the start of the 1990s, a "secularized" consciousness has been able to maintain a flourishing corporate channel (Billiet 1981; Dobbelaere and Voyé 1990, pp. S7-S8). But, as Rokkan (1977, pp. 563-570) suggests, an institutionalized pillar has two channels: one corporate and the other electoral. Since the 1980s, the Christian electoral channel has been crumbling in Belgium (Billiet and Dobbelaere 1986, pp. 138-156; Dobbelaere 1988b, pp. 41-42; Van De Velde 1988, pp. 217-221). Is this the beginning of the desinstitutionalization of the Christian pillar or will the Christian corporate channel be able to adapt to the new political preferences and affiliations of its membership and members of the boards of its component organizations (Billiet and Dobbelaere 1986, pp. 156-158). The situation in Wallonia in Belgium seems to suggest that the latter could be the case.

Vatican II, as has been pointed out, cannot be held responsible for the past and present "exodus" from the church. At most, the Council amplified and accelerated preexisting trends. Indeed, Vatican II did allow the preexisting tensions to be openly expressed, and it did raise hopes in Europe that were rapidly abandoned, thereby contributing to the distancing of many Catholics from the church. Next, we want to stress some aspects of the hopes raised, sometimes unduly, by Vatican II and to show what happened to them.

A VAIN HOPE FOR DEMOCRACY

Without necessarily being founded on a close reading of the Conciliar texts, the success of the definition of the church as the "People of God" incontestably raised the hope of a democratic and decentralized church succeeding the hierarchical and centralized church. First, "Vatican II amply responded to the expectation of a promotion of the laity" (Magnani 1988, p. 586). Certainly, the theological debates on the significance of this promotion largely escaped the majority, but many Catholics, laity and clergy alike, saw in it a reduction, if not a disappearance, of the hierarchical difference between the clergy and the laity. Various concrete elements of daily life confirmed this interpretation, such as the disappearance of the cassock as a distinctive sign, the abandonment of the pulpit as the material and symbolic expression of domination, readings and preaching by lay people, and the reception of communion in the hands, the laity now being permitted to touch the host, a "privilege" previously reserved to priests. Thus, there rapidly developed the idea of an equality of importance that was accompanied by intense discussion on the diversity of ministries in the church. The laity saw themselves as being invested in certain ministries. Nevertheless, disappointment soon arose for those who wanted to become more involved. Certain functions, sacramental ones in particular, remained closed to them. The reaffirmation of the rule of priestly celibacy underlined the permanence of an indisputable difference, and women remained excluded from the sacerdotal ministry. These disappointments led to a progressive disengagement of many lay people. Their disenchantment was such that they hardly reacted when, during the Synod of the Laity of 1987, Rome reaffirmed the fundamental difference between priests and lay people and the supremacy of the former over the latter.

Moreover, some people had expected much from the participation structures recommended by the Council, in particular the Priests' Councils and the Pastoral Councils, even though they were defined at the outset as only consultative. In Belgium, the diocesan Priests' and Pastoral Councils were established very rapidly, in 1967 and 1969, respectively. The procedures of selection of their members were diverse, but, in some dioceses there was an election with universal suffrage and by secret ballot with publicity in the press, as is customary political practice in Belgium. The intention was to have councils that were as representative as possible not only of the various geographical zones but also of different sensibilities. Once installed, these councils debated many subjects such as the priest and his spiritual, intellectual, and emotional life; the new structures of pastoral care (pastoral teams composed of priests and lay people, parishes without priests, and pastoral workers, etc.); the youth and their estrangement from the church; economic problems (unemployment, strikes, etc.); and Christian identity. They also reflected on themselves, their role, and their powers. In the beginning, in fact, many members of these councils went beyond the given definition, envisaging their role not as consultative but as decision-making. They referred to the theme of co-responsibility, which was developed at that time by the church itself, and they were encouraged by the mood challenging all forms of authority that prevailed at the end of the 1960s and the beginning of the 1970s. At that time, the human sciences were often called upon, as, for example, in the long discussions held by the French-speaking Pastoral Council of Brussels on the distinction between "decision making" and "decision taking." And everywhere, the mode of functioning of the church was criticized by these councils with reference to the mode of political functioning of the democratic societies (Remy and Voyé 1973).

For several years, these councils worked eagerly and enthusiastically. However, disappointment increased as the non-decision-making character of the councils was confirmed, and the feeling grew that their advice would meet with little, if any, response. The result was often abandonment of these councils and a sharp reduction of their activity (Voyé 1985b).

A third aspect of the democratization expected from Vatican II was the power of the local church with respect to Rome. Apart from the debate on the question of whether the church is a strictly hierarchical pyramid or if it is to define itself as the "people of God" with the hierarchy viewed in function of service, the Council opened the door to the debate on the monarchical or collegial direction of the church, on the centralization or the decentralization of ecclesiastical power (Legrand et al. 1988).

At first, albeit to different degrees, the churches of Western Europe started to decentralize. It was the church of the Netherlands that would go the farthest in this direction, which led to serious conflicts with Rome and severe repression. In fact, as Laeyendecker (1987, p. 125) has shown, early on, the Dutch bishops were committed to decentralization in order to meet "the trends of renewal that were manifested before and during the Council." In passing, we note again here that the Council was not seen as the initiator of these trends but, in a way, as an instrument of their legitimation and thus as the signal for their actual recognition by the episcopacy. Thus, the Dutch bishops gave a mandate to write the "New Catechism for Adults," the publication of which in 1966 was the occasion of the first conflict with Rome.

However, it was the "Pastoral Council of the Ecclesiastical Province of the Netherlands" that provoked the most serious crisis. This council was held in order to obtain "opinions on the governing of the Church, in order to implement a necessary renewal by means of intense consultation on as large a scale as possible" (Laeyendecker 1987, p. 127). To do this, the bishops used several methods. Experts prepared reports on "questions affecting the whole of the ecclesiastical province" (p. 128): the conception and mode of exercising authority, ethical behavior, marriage and the family, ministry, peace, etcetera. More than 10,000 discussion groups were created and submitted their comments. A "letter box" was opened in which everybody could deposit opinions and questions. The media were largely kept informed. Thus, "the Council initiated an intense, mobilizing activity. . . . What was in progress, obviously, was the modern construction of a Church" (p. 130). At all levels and in every sector, bishops, priests, and lay people discussed together the route the church was to follow. A program to be implemented was drafted. Already disturbed by the democratic procedure, which, in the words of L. Laeyendecker (p. 127), "enlarged the collegial direction to the priests and the laity," Rome saw in this program and in the project of national consultation that accompanied it the danger of a seizure of local autonomy and a simultaneous attack on its centralized organization.

This fear was expressed in the conflict on the question of celibacy. Several polls had shown "that a strong majority did not oppose the suppression of the obligation of celibacy for priests, and a session of the Dutch Council affirmed in 1970 that celibacy should not be imposed as a condition for future priests" (Laeyendecker 1987, p. 136). A communiqué from the Secretariat of the Episcopal Conference stated that the bishops wanted to exercise their ministry in the line of the suggestions made by the Council. Rome could not fail to react: it first prohibited the continuation of the national consultation and drastically limited the role of the deliberating agencies by refusing that the members of these bodies be elected and by affirming their exclusively consultative role. But this was only the first step. Beginning in 1977, Rome stopped following the proposals of the Dutch Episcopal Conference in the appointment of new bishops. The Dutch Catholics were greatly demoralized, and these bishops, in whom the Dutch did not recognize themselves, met with growing skepticism if not outright opposition. This led to serious tensions with the remaining conciliar bishops in office, a growing indifference toward the church, and, among a minority, contramobilization, the vitality of which was manifested during the visit of the pope to the Netherlands in 1985.

The policy of episcopal appointments was directed everywhere in the same direction as that taken in the Netherlands. This is particularly the case in Germany, Austria, France, and Belgium. Even if, in Belgium, the influence of Cardinal Danneels has up to 1991 prevented a situation comparable to that of the Netherlands, it still required several years to designate a successor for the Bishop of Liège, the "local candidates" not having the approval of Rome and Rome's own candidate(s) being rejected locally. This appointment policy constituted for Goddijn (1987, p. 198, translation)

an important element of a new conception of authority. This new strategy is expressed, first of all, by a papalization of the church, a kind of presidential regime in which the Pope is the unique political subject in the church. The new type of bishop must . . . agree with the will of Rome to administer the church in a more centralized way by the mediation of the Pope and the Curia.

This desire for centralization is manifested equally in the debates concerning the status of the Episcopal Conferences. While Lumen Gentium [Light of Mankind] saw in them a modality of expression of collegiality (Thils 1986, p. 162), the Episcopal Conferences today engender the distrust of Rome and, in particular, of Cardinal Ratzinger, who, in his Entretien sur la foi [Discourses on faith], has more or less explicitly expressed his misgivings about them: the national level should not be an ecclesial dimension (should one see here the fear of a resurgence of Gallicanism?); they blur positions and give power to enterprising minorities; they undermine the personal responsibility of each bishop and the direct link of the bishop with the pope. This mistrust is also expressed just as clearly in the Code of Canon Law of 1983, which situates the attributions of the Episcopal Conferences short of that which the Council allowed one to expect.

These indicators tend to support the hypothesis of an attempt to reinforce the personal power of the pope, surrounded by his administration. What is happening is the recentralization of power in the church. In Europe, this is largely met with indifference.

This indifference seems, moreover, all the greater when the church, or rather, the Roman vision of the church, appears to cut itself off from the world, and more specifically from Western Europe, and the dominant traits of its culture.

KEEPING THE INTELLECTUALS AND SCIENCE AT A DISTANCE

For many European intellectuals, the Council had been in itself and in its effects an important turning point. A number of them had been called upon to participate in the elaboration of its content and its implementation. This was done with the openness required by scientific debate and in the perspective of an "ethic of the discussion," to use Habermas's expression. Thus, speaking of the Dutch Council, Laeyendecker (1987, p. 130, translation) stressed

> the mobilization included the intellectuals within the Dutch church. Probably never before had any other church succeeded in placing at the service of its authorities the most brilliant minds. Not only were theologians involved but also specialists in other disciplines, in particular the social sciences, became actively involved in the renewal of the church.

Progressively, however, these intellectuals were marginalized and even, in some cases, condemned. This was, first of all, the case of theologians whose debates with Rome were for a long time "à la une" [headline news] of the European media. The "affairs" [the cases] of Küng, Schillebeeckx, and others witnessed in public to the Roman refusal to debate and to accept theological divergence. But, more extensively and without bringing it into the foreground, there is the pushing aside of all those whom Jossua (1987, p. 237) calls "the theologians of renewal," who stimulated the Council "not so much by a modification of the systematic (theological) bloc as by the addition of associated disciplines." They insisted, for example, on the need to take into account "historical differences" in the interpretation of the basic texts and thus to pass from norm to reference. In a general way, a number of academic theologians were "disturbed" by the Roman reactions to them (Thils 1986, p. 21). Such disturbance was, for instance, shown by the "Cologne Declaration," whereby 163 German, Austrian, Swiss, and Dutch theologians (who were also joined later by Dutch-speaking Belgian theologians) argued for "an open Catholicism." Thus, they manifested their concern about Roman centralism, which was expressed not only in the appointment (or the dismissal) of bishops and professors of theology but also in the authoritarian imposition of responses on questions of faith and conscience (Brekelmans et al. 1989).

But it was not only theologians who were challenged when they dared to deviate from the Magisterium. The human sciences also became (and are becoming again) suspect. This concerned, in particular, sociology and sociologists whom Cardinal Ratzinger labeled as "computers, functionaries, planners applying their technical principles to an ecclesiastical reality which they wrongly consider to be their proper domain and about which they pretend to exert a real competence" (Thils 1986, p. 37).

In general, tensions increased with the scientific world, and the university as such saw itself directly challenged: "this glorious European institution that the church has engendered has shown itself incapable of developing an acceptable cultural project," said the Pope to the Bishops of Europe, assembled in Symposium in Rome in 1985.[1] This general declaration has been applied several times. Thus, the authorities of the Catholic Universities of Leuven and Louvain in Belgium, Lille in France, and Nijmegen in the Netherlands were called to defend themselves in Rome about the way they did or did not take into account the doctrine of the church in bioethical matters in the faculties of medicine and the hospitals associated with them. The Instruction of 1987 on "respect for human life and the dignity of procreation" went so far, according to Ladrière (1987c, pp. 276-277), as to "require politicians to be tutors of scientists" by requiring the state to intervene to prevent the dangers that "the new technological possibilities" could present to civil society from "researchers who pretend to govern humanity in the name of histological discoveries and of allegedly improved processes derived from them." Incontestably, science remains suspect and must be placed under surveillance. Is it not in this sense that the Catholic Universities are asked to recognize the new "profession of faith?" This profession concerns the duties inherent in the functions assumed in institutions linked to the church and thus, particularly, in the Catholic Universities. They are also to subscribe to the "loyalty oath required of each and every person called to exercise a responsibility in the name of the Church"

(Thils 1989, p. 7). Of course, several European Catholic Universities, including those just cited, distanced themselves from these documents, initiating discussions and developing counter proposals.

However, this distrust risks widening the gap between intellectuals and the church. This becomes all the more marked because a reversal has occurred since the Council. We have noted how the Council called upon intellectuals. Moreover, the period immediately following the Council was marked by a concern for intellectualization (and politization) of the religious. The "sociological Catholics" were reproached for practicing out of family custom, for being more sensitive to the festive and emotional dimensions of the religious acts than to a free and sincere adherence to the content of the faith. Thus, a new attitude led to the marginalization of all forms of popular religiosity and favored the austerity of the conviction personally acquired by a critical work of intelligence. This reconciliation with scientific reflection was brief, and today one can only be struck by the insistence placed upon "the superiority of the simple." During the recent canonization of a Belgian Brother of the Christian Schools, the emphasis was placed on the "simplicity, self-effacement, humility" of the new saint. His lack of professional success was explicitly noted, and the grandeur was stressed of his acceptance of this lack of success without anguish and without problems. There are a number of other examples showing the favor enjoyed by "devout ignorance," which is less suspect than critical study.

The figure of the pope himself goes in the same direction. His "charismatization," as Laeyendecker (1987, p. 132) noted, stresses the emotional dimension of religion and addresses directly the masses from which he solicits reactions, short-circuiting the local episcopacy (Grootaers 1981, p. 245). He claims that his successes with the crowds prove the error of those who are concerned with the exodus from the church referred to earlier and with Rome's apparent apathy with regard to the preoccupations of everyday culture. However, the legitimacy that is socially granted to him derives much more from the symbolic register, with its imaginary dimension, than from the register of daily life. His discourse escapes, consequently, the limits of time and space; it is intended to be universal and nontemporal because the Pope escapes the rational-functional order. His discourse is a ritual element of a feast, that is, of an event that breaks with the everyday routine and that, as such, can contradict it (Voyé 1988d, p. 14).

FROM THE "SIGNS OF THE TIMES" TO THE "COUNTERVALUES"

Vatican II affirmed unambiguously the need for the church to take into account the "signs of the times." Commenting on what Ladrière said in *La restauration catholique* [Catholic restoration] (1987b), Eslin (1989, p. 188) stresses that the 20th century has not ceased to question the compatibility between Catholicism and liberty (Tocqueville, Michelet, Quinet, Lamennais). It has not ceased to question the "form" of religion that would suit modern times and has imagined all the ways of reforming the Catholic church. However, this reform has never emerged, for none of these plans emanated from the sole authority that could authorize and conceive it. . . . With Vatican II, the reform emerged from the highest authority in the Catholic church. It seemed that the time, awaited for too long, had come.

However, after the enthusiasm of the first years after the Council, during which the Western world seemed to be regarded by the church with sympathy, there came a return to keeping it at arm's length, a return to condemnations of the Western World, what Schlegel (1989, p. 71) calls the "diabolicization of society" and a sectarian drift of Catholicism. The "signs of the times" to which the Council proposed to be attentive have become "countervalues" or "non-values." This negative evaluation of the contemporary world is addressed particularly to Western Europe. Thus, the 6th Symposium of the European Bishops' Conferences held in Rome in October 1985 had as the theme: "Evangelizing the Secularized Europe." Particular insistence was placed on the moral degradation of this Europe:

> The secularized European man . . . is a man so engaged in the task of building the earthly city that he has lost sight of, or even freely excludes, the city of God . . . . This man, who very much wants to be adult, mature, free, is also a man who flees from liberty to conform, a man who suffers from loneliness, who is threatened by diverse diseases in his soul, who tries to evacuate death and is marked by an appalling loss of hope.[1]

Such is the diagnosis proposed to the Bishops of Europe by the pope while he insists on the historical links of this Europe with the church. Historically the bearer of fundamental human values, Europe no longer has "the Absolute as point of reference." Cardinal Danneels of Belgium insisted during the course of the Symposium that this means that these values "secrete toxins, of which some may be mortal, that slowly poison the living tissue." Lay people, present as experts, reacted to this unilaterally negative vision of contemporary Europe. Without denying the existence of problems, they were particularly surprised at the more or less explicit opposition placed between a previous "Christian" Europe, based on an idealized vision of the past, and the present Europe, described as marked by "the practical atheism of the consumption society." Thus Professor de Moor of the University of Tilburg in the Netherlands asked the assembly: "The majority of Europeans consider that they live well and that these 'non-values' are, for them, values. Why this gap?" This reaction is an interesting indication of a feeling shared by a number of people, and particularly, by a number of Europeans who call themselves Catholics (or Christians) while maintaining a distance from the institution, which is seen as "a system of oppressive moral rules" (de Moor). While the church tends to accuse the world, this world organizes itself around new values and takes as its first reference: "the lived experience and no longer the rational and the 'comprehensible' of the positivist epoch" (Kerkhofs 1981, p. 19). Some others are surprised by the nostalgia, at least latent, generated by the disappearance of the previous docility—which was largely the result of social pressure— and the correlative growth of a "polemical relationship to the expressed truths" which is tied to "the banalization of knowledge and authority" (Defois 1981, p. 58). Still others questioned the effectivity of this previous docility and of the absolute subordination of civil society to the church. Indeed, they asked if the previous lack of opportunities for communication did not render this docility and subordination sometimes fictional. Lacking an effective ability to control, "the autonomy of the subject peoples was taken away in theory but not in practice" (Kaufmann 1988, p. 288). There is expressed in all these comments by committed Christian intellectuals a clear refusal of a unilaterally negative evaluation of Western Europe, this refusal being seen in terms of an increasing risk of marginalization of the church in this region of the world.

The occasions for the church to condemn Western Europe and its "countervalues" are of various types and clearly manifest a refusal to see in present Western European culture anything but the negative and an attempt to impose on everyone the viewpoints of the church. In this regard, Schlegel (1989) notes various recent events, which created considerable stir without, however, resulting in a change of behavior: the assembly of French bishops meeting in Lourdes gave a standing ovation to the decision of the laboratory that manufactured the abortion pill to withdraw it from the market; a "religious war" was conducted in France against the campaign by the government to encourage the use of condoms to prevent AIDS; the statements of the French bishops condemning Scorsese's film *The Last Temptation of Christ,* provoked, without intending it, acts of violence against the movie theatres. Each time, the positions taken by the church and published in the media were interpreted by many as "an attempt by the church to control morals" and to place the individual under a kind of tutelage.

The "denunciation of the illnesses of old Western Christianity" compared to the positive presentation of the "martyred churches" (Eastern Europe) and the "poor churches" (Third World) has not "sounded well in the ears of the ecclesiastical authorities of Western Europe" (Grootaers 1981, p. 41; Ladrière 1987a, p. 305). First, these comparisons confront Europeans with the loss of their cultural supremacy while they have hardly gotten used to the loss of their economic and political domination; moreover, the praise of poverty and martyrdom runs counter to their dominant cultural models. Certainly these Western European models are imperfect, but Vatican II proposed to take them into consideration and, by so doing, to "remove the church from its severe closure, from its mistrust of the modern world" (Martina 1988, p. 33). And today it is this same call that is repeated regularly in many local European churches by their authorities because they consider that the church cannot "fulfil its mission of hope" unless "it takes into account the human realities as they are today . . . in line with the pastoral perspectives outlined by Vatican II" (Message of the Bishop of Namur, Belgium, during the closing session of the Diocesan Assembly of 1985).

One aspect of these "human realities" is, without doubt, their internal diversity, which is linked to "the particularity and the diversity of historical and cultural conditions" (Menozzi 1987, p. 289). The importance of this diversity is felt all the more as exchanges intensify. Also this pluricultural society is being confronted with the proposal of a "universal catechism" and with the various facts that run counter to the ecumenical openings made by Vatican II.

A BLOCKED ECUMENISM

Even though the pope personally meets the leaders of the major religions, thus developing what Willaime (1989, p. 15) calls "a diplomatic ecumenism," a series of decisions have been made and concrete acts performed that hinder the ecumenical advances made by Vatican II. A number of particularly striking examples have marked Europe in recent years. First, there was the proclamation of a system of indulgences associated with the Holy Year of 1983. In view of the role they played in the Lutheran schism, one can understand the very negative reaction of Protestants and many Catholics, who were shocked not only by the fact itself but also by its symbolism—and this in the year of the 500th anniversary of the birth of Martin Luther! The president of the Federation of Evangelical Churches of Italy called this "coincidence" a dangerous "paradox." As for the French sociologist Mehl, he stressed in the journal *La Réforme* [The Reform] (April 9, 1983) how much that granting of indulgences was "a new manifestation of salvation by works" and also how much it reflected a view and an image of the pope that are radically rejected by Protestantism: "By granting indulgences to those who, for example, go to Rome, visit one of the great basilicas, . . . the Sovereign Pontiff clearly shows that he disposes of divine grace and that this is subordinated to the accomplishment of certain acts of piety." The sensitivity in this regard was probably greater in Europe than elsewhere, Europe being historically predominantly Catholic. The delicate rapprochements between Protestants and Catholics initiated since Vatican II suffered a very significant chill.

The European Protestant churches also reacted strongly to the Roman Instruction on Mixed Marriages, which only introduced adjustments in the usage of this legislation. The Synod of the Evangelical Church of Würtemberg, for example, opposed all participation of a pastor in a Catholic ceremony that did not guarantee true ecumenism, and the Evangelical Church of Austria was concerned about the maintenance of the obligation for mixed couples to commit themselves to give their children a Catholic education. As Bovay and Campiche stressed (1989, p. 183), mixed marriages (which actually are increasing) "have not given rise to progress in the dialogue between the religious institutions nor have they contributed to unity."

The rules concerning "eucharistic hospitality" have also profoundly irritated European Protestants. Thus, for example, a statement from the French Episcopal Commission for Unity was released while an ecumenical session was in progress in Chantilly (Paris 1983). Cardinal Etchegaray, who was present at the session, had much difficulty in tempering the criticisms and the disappointment of the participants. The radical maintenance of obligatory celibacy for priests has proved to be another obstacle, in particular with the Anglican church, with which reunification plans were well advanced. We add to these various points the question of the role of women in the church and that of canonizations, which, in many respects, regularly re-emerge in Europe as so many persistent hindrances to an advance of ecumenism, which the Council had seemed to have accelerated.

To the traditional points of friction between European Christian churches, Birmelé (1989, p. 240) sees another area of discord, that of ethical and sociopolitical problems. Cardinal Decourtray, Primat des Gaules [Primate of the Gaules], said that he "felt much closer to the world of Judaism than to the world of Protestantism in the debate on the new genetic possibilities" (Birmelé 1989, p. 241). Furthermore, Protestants are, in general, clearly more firm on questions such as apartheid in South Africa and disarmament, while the Catholic church has reduced these problems to classic doctrinal questions. The Reformed Church of the Netherlands, for example, has invited all of its parishes to give "an explicit no" to any use and retention of atomic weapons (Birmelé 1989, p. 236).

CONCLUSIONS

All the elements that were cited to try to depict the development of European Catholicism after Vatican II permit one to interpret "the actual Roman strategy" in the line of what Ebertz's (1980) analysis. He has shown that, in history, the Catholic church has always responded in the same way to that which it defines as a threat: reinforcement of centralization and of the hierarchical organization; a return to tradition, favoring devotional practices and mass manifestations; and charismatization of the figure of the pope.

This triple strategy is being applied today as in the nineteenth century. It remains to be seen if it will be successful. In our opinion, it will not succeed in reestablishing the church in its disciplinary role, influencing the daily lives of individuals, even if the church seems to extend its overarching ethical role on the public scene. Therefore, when in Europe one suggests a "return of the religious," we prefer to speak of a "return of the sacred." Indeed, this return refers rather to a certain redevelopment of practices of popular religion (pilgrimages, benediction, cults of particular saints, etc.) and, particularly, to the multiplication of groups and movements of all types, such as Communione e Liberazione [Community and Liberation] (Abbruzzese 1989), the Charismatic Movement (Cohen 1989, p. 142), and many small-scale movements with low visibility and generally wanting to remain so (Champion and Hervieu-Léger 1990; Hervieu-Léger 1989; Léger and Hervieu 1983; Voyé 1988c, forthcoming). Even when it is accompanied by an identification of oneself as Catholic, these practices and movements are situated at the margins of the institutional church. Indeed, it reflects a concern for independence with respect to the enclosure of the sacred in a definition imposed by the church (Zylberberg 1985); it expresses a quest for meaning that is emancipated from the universal and more or less mechanical institutional responses proposed by the church and whose results are not postponed to the beyond. Moreover, some offer the hypothesis, and we agree with them, that the rise of such groups and movements reflects the fulfilment of secularization (Hervieu-Léger 1989, p. 241; Schlegel 1989). Already eliminated economically, politically, and socially by the general process of secularization (Dobbelaere 1981, 1988b), the church is now also seeing its symbolic apparatus losing relevancy: collective significations, individual identification, and the quest for meaning no longer find a satisfactory expression in the church and in its language (Hervieu-Léger 1989, p. 243). Thus, people search outside the church for the foundations of plausibility suited to the modern world.

NOTE

1. This and the following citations refer to unpublished documents that were distributed at the 6th Symposium of the European Bishops' Conferences.

REFERENCES

Abbruzzese, S. 1989. *Comunione e Liberazione: Identité Catholique et disqualification du monde* [Community and Liberation: Catholic Identity and Disqualification of the World]. Paris: Cerf.
Balandier, G. 1985. *Le détour* [The Detour].Paris: Fayard.
Bibby, R.W. 1987. *Fragmented Gods: The Poverty and Potential of Religion in Canada.* Toronto: Irwin Publishing.
Billiet, J. 1981. "Kenmerken en grondslagen van het sociaal-kultureel katholicisme" [Characteristics and Foundations of Socio-cultural Catholicism]. Pp. 29-61 in *Van ideologie tot macht: Doorlichting van de bewustzijnsindustrie in Vlaanderen* [From Ideology to Power: Investigating the Consciousness Industry in Flanders], edited by J. Servaes. Leuven: Kritak.

Billiet, J., and K. Dobbelaere. 1976. *Godsdienst in Vlaanderen: Van Kerks Katholicisme naar Sociaal-kulturele Kristenheid?* [Religion in Flanders: From Ecclesiastical Catholicism to Socio-cultural Christianity]. Leuven: Davidsfonds.

——. 1986. "Naar een desinstitutionalisering van de christelijke zuil?" [Toward a Deinstitutionalization of the Christian Pillar]. Pp. 129-64 in *België en zijn Goden* [Belgium and its Gods], edited by K. Dobbelaere, L. Voyé et al. Leuven: Cabay.

Birmelé, A. 1989. "De l'hérésie doctrinale à l'hérésie éthique?" [From Doctrinal to Ethical Heresy]. Pp. 227-243 in *Vers de nouveaux oecuménismes* [Toward New Ecumenisms], edited by J-P. Willaime. Paris: Cerf.

Bovay, C., and R. Campiche. 1989. "Les mariages mixtes. Restructuration ou dilution des identifications confessionnelles" [Mixed Marriages: Restructuring or Dilution of Confessional Identifications]. Pp. 156-185 in *Vers de nouveaux oecuménismes* [Toward New Ecumenisms], edited by J-P. Willaime. Paris: Cerf.

Brekelmans, C., J. Bulckens, G. De Schrijver et al. 1989. "Probleemgebieden in de Kerk van Vandaag: Theologie en Kerk in nieuw perspectief" [Problem Areas in the Church of Today: Theology and Church in New Perspectives]. *Onze Alma Mater* 89:311-359.

Champion, F., and D. Hervieu-Léger, eds. 1990. *De l'émotion en religion* [On Emotion in Religion]. Paris: Le Centurion.

Cohen, M. 1989. "Les renouveaux catholique et juif en France" [The Catholic and Jewish Renewals in France]. Pp. 121-167 in *De l'émotion en religion* [On Emotion In Religion], edited by F. Champion and D. Hervieu-Léger. Paris: Centurion.

Coleman, J. A. 1978. *The Evolution of Dutch Catholicism, 1958-1974.* Berkeley: University of California Press.

Defois, G. 1981. "Critique des institutions et demande de participation" [Criticism of Institutions and Demand for Participation]. Pp. 57-64 in *Les églises après Vatican II. Dynamisme et prospective* [The Churches After Vatican II. Dynamism and Prospect], edited by G. Alberigo. Paris: Blanchesne.

de Moor, R. 1987. "Religieuze en Morele waarden" [Religious and Moral Values]. Pp. 15-49 in L. Halman, F. Heunks, R. de Moor, and H. Zanders, *Traditie, secularisatie en individualisering: Een studie naar de waarden van de Nederlanders in een Europese context* [Tradition, Secularization, and Individualization: A Study of the Values of the Dutch in a European Context]. Tilburg: Tilburg University Press.

Dobbelaere, K. 1966. *Sociologische analyse van de katholiciteit* [A Sociological Analysis of Catholicicity]. Antwerpen: S.W.U.

——. 1981. "Secularization: A Multi-Dimensional Concept." *Current Sociology* 29:1-213.

——. 1982. "Contradictions between Expressive and Strategic Language in Policy Documents of Catholic Hospitals and Welfare Organizations." *The Annual Review of the Social Sciences of Religion* 6:107-131.

——. 1984. "Godsdienst in België" [Religion in Belgium]. Pp. 67-111 in *De stille ommekeer, Oude en nieuwe waarden in het België van de jaren tachtig* [The Silent Revolution. Old and New Values in the Belgium of the 1980s], edited by J. Kerkhofs and R. Rezsohazy. Tielt: Lannoo.

——. 1986. "Sociaal-culturele christenheid en publieke religie: een vergelijking" [Socio-cultural Christianity and Public Religion: A Comparison]. *Tijdschrift voor Sociologie* 7:653-679.

——. 1986-7. "Vrijzinnigheid, kerkelijkheid en kerksheid in een geseculariseerde wereld: grensvervaging of nieuwe grenzen?" [Liberalism Church Membership, and Church Attendance in a Secularized World: A Blurring of the Borders or New Borders?]. *Tijdschrift voor de Studie van de Verlichting en het Vrije Denken* 14-15:283-311.

————. 1988a. "Secularization, Pillarization, Religious Involvement, and Religious Change in the Low Countries." Pp. 80-115 in *World Catholicism in Transition,* edited by T. M. Gannon. New York: Macmillan.

————. 1988b. *Het "Volk-Gods" de mist in? Over de Kerk in België* [Has the "People of God" Foundered? On the Church in Belgium]. Leuven: Acco.

————. In press. "Church Involvement and Secularization: Making Sense of the European Case." In *Secularization, Rationalism and Sectariarism,* edited by E. Barker et al. Oxford: Oxford University Press.

Dobbelaere, K., and J. Billiet. 1983. "Les changements internes au pilier catholique en Flandre: d'un catholicisme d'église à une chrétienté socio-culturelle" [The Internal Changes in the Catholic Pillar in Flanders: From an Ecclesiastical Catholicism to a Socio-cultural Christianity?]. *Recherches Sociologiques* 24: 141-184.

Dobbelaere, K., and L. Voyé. 1990. "From Pillar to Post-modernity: The Changing Situation of Religion in Belgium." *Sociological Analysis* 51:S1-S13.

Donegami, J-M. 1984. "L'appartenance au Catholicisme Français: Point de vue sociologique" [Belonging to French Catholicism: A Sociological Point of View]. Pp. 44-65 in *Regards sur le Catholicisme Français* [Views on French Catholicism], edited by J. Gellard, P. Valadier et al. Paris: Cahiers Recherches-Débat.

Duffhues, T., A. Felling, and J. Roes. 1985. *Bewegende patronen: Een analyse van het landelijk netwerk van katholieke organisaties en bestuurders 1945-1980* [Moving Patterns: An Analysis of the National Network of Catholic Organizations and Directors 1945-1980]. Baarn: Ambo.

Ebertz, M.N. 1980. "Herrschaft in der Kirche. Hierarchie, Tradition und Charisme im 19. Jahrhundert" [Power in the Church: Hierarchy, Tradition, and Charism in the 19th Century]. Pp. 89-111 in *Soziologie des Katholizismus* [Sociology of Catholicism], edited by K. Gabriels and F.X. Kaufmann. Mainz: Matthias-Grunewald Verlag.

Eslin, J-C. 1989. "Controverse: Vatican II n'a-t-il été qu'une illusion" [Controversy: Was Vatican II Only an Illusion?]. *Esprit* 148-149:188-190.

Felling, A., J. Peters, and O. Schreuder. 1986. *Geloven en Leven: Een nationaal onderzoek naar de invloed van religieuze overtuigingen* [Faith and Life: A National Study of the Influence of Religious Convictions]. Zeist: Kerckebosch BV.

Furlong, P. F. 1988. "Authority, Change, and Conflict in Italian Catholicism." Pp. 116-132 in *World Catholicism in Transition,* edited by T. M. Gannon. New York: Macmillan.

Gerard, D. 1985. "Religious Attitudes and Values." Pp. 50-92 in *Values and Social Change in Britain,* edited by M. Abrams, D. Gerard, and N. Timms. London: Macmillan.

Goddijn, W. 1987. "Qui est digne d'accéder à l'épiscopat?" [Who Is Worthy of Acceding to the Episcopacy?]. Pp. 194-217 in *Le retour des certitudes: Evènements et orthodoxie depuis Vatican II* [The Return of Certitudes: Events and Orthodoxy Since Vatican II], edited by P. Ladrière and R. Luneau. Paris: Le Centurion.

Goddijn, W., H. Smets, and G. van Tillo. 1979. *Opnieuw: God in Nederland* [Again: God in the Netherlands]. Amsterdam: De Tijd BV.

Greeley, A. M. 1985. *American Catholics Since the Council: An Unauthorized Report.* Chicago: The Thomas More Press.

Greeley, A. M., W. C. McCready, and K. McCourt. 1976. *Catholic Schools in a Declining Church.* Kansas City, MO: Sheed and Ward.

Grootaers, J. 1981. *De Vatican II à Jean-Paul II. Le grand tournant de l'Eglise catholique* [From Vatican II to John Paul II: The Great Turning Point of the Catholic Church]. Paris: Le Centurion.

Harding, S., D. Phillips, and M. Fogarty. 1986. *Contrasting Values in Western Europe: Unity, Diversity and Change.* London: Macmillan.

Hervieu-Léger, D. 1989. "Renouveaux émotionnels contemporains" [Contemporary Emotional Renewals]. Pp. 219-248 in *De l'émotion en religion* [On Emotion in Religion], edited by F. Champion and D. Hervieu-Léger. Paris: Le Centurion.

Hervieu-Léger D. with F. Champion. 1986. *Vers un nouveau christianisme? Introduction à la sociologie du christianisme* [Toward A New Christianity? Introduction to the Sociology of Christianity]. Paris: Editions du Cerf.

Hoge, D.R. 1986. "Interpreting Change in American Catholicism: The River and the Floodgate." *Review of Religious Research,* 27:289-299.

Hout, M., and A. M. Greeley. 1987. "The Center Doesn't Hold: Church Attendance in the United States, 1940-1984." *American Sociological Review* 52:325-345.

Jossua, J-P. 1987. "La condition des théologiens depuis Vatican II, vue par l'un d'entre eux" [The Condition of Theologians Since Vatican II As Seen by One of Them]. Pp. 235-257 in *Le retour des certitudes: Evènements et orthodoxie depuis Vatican II* [The Return of Certitudes: Events and Orthodoxy Since Vatican II], edited by P. Ladrière and R. Luneau. Paris: Le Centurion.

Kaufmann, F-X. 1988. "The Principle of Subsidiarity viewed by the Sociology of Organizations." *The Jurist* 48:275-291.

Kerkhofs, J. 1981. "Principaux changements dans les sociétés chrétiennes établies et dans les Eglises après Vatican II" [Principal Changes in Established Christian Societies and in the Churches After Vatican II]. Pp. 13-31 in *Les Eglises après Vatican II. Dynamisme et prospective* [The Churches After Vatican II: Dynamism and Prospect], edited by G. Alberigo. Paris: Beauchesne.

_____. 1984. "Ethische accenten" [Ethical Accents]. Pp. 39-65 in *De stille ommekeer: Oude en nieuwe waarden in het België van de jaren tachtig* [The Silent Revolution. Old and New Values in the Belgium of the 1980s], edited by J. Kerkhofs and R. Rezsohazy. Tielt: Lannoo.

Köcher, R. 1987. "Religiös in einer säkularisierten Welt" [Religious in a Secularized World]. Pp. 164-281 in E. Noelle-Neuman and R. Köcher, *Die verletzte Nation: Ueber den Versuch der Deutschen ihren Charakter zu ändern* [The Wounded Nation: On the Attempt of the Germans to Change Their Character]. Stuttgart: Deutsche Verlag Anstalt.

Ladrière, P. 1987a. "Note sur le Synode Extraordinaire" [Note on the Extraordinary Synod]. Pp. 300-308 in *Le retour des certitudes: Evènements et orthodoxie depuis Vatican II* [The Return of Certitudes: Events and Orthodoxy Since Vatican II], edited by P. Ladrière and R. Luneau. Paris: Le Centurion.

_____. 1987b. "La restauration catholique" [The Catholic Restoration]. Pp. 38-43 in *L'état des religions dans le monde* [The State of Religions in the World], edited by M. Clévenot. Paris: La Découverte/Cerf.

_____. 1987c. "L'appel à la loi naturelle" [The Appeal to the Natural Law]. Pp. 258-277 in *Le retour des certitudes: Evènements et orthodoxie depuis Vatican II* [The Return of Certitudes: Events and Orthodoxy Since Vatican II], edited by P. Ladrière and R. Luneau. Paris: Centurion.

Laeyendecker, L. 1987. "Du Cardinal Alfrink au Cardinal Simonis. Vingt ans de Catholicisme Hollandais" [From Cardinal Alfrink to Cardinal Simonis. Twenty Years of Dutch Catholicism]. Pp. 122-141 *Le retour des certitudes: Evènements et orthodoxie depuis Vatican II* [The Return of Certitudes: Events and Orthodoxy Since Vatican II], edited by P. Ladrière and R. Luneau. Paris: Le Centurion.

Lambert, Y. 1988. "Retour ou recul du religieux chez les jeunes?" [Return of or Retreat from the Religious by the Young] *L'année sociologique* 38:49-62.

Latourelle, R. 1988. "Introduction." Pp. 7-18 in *Vatican II Bilan et Perspectives: Vingt-cinq ans après (1962-1987)* [Vatican II. Balance and Perspectives. Twenty-five Years After (1962-1987)], edited by R. Latourelle. Montreal: Les éditions Bellarmin.

Léger, D., and B. Hervieu. 1983. *Des communautés pour les temps difficiles. Neo-ruraux ou nouveaux moines* [Communities for Difficult Times: Neo-rural or New Monks]. Paris: Le Centurion.

Legrand, H., J. Manzanares, and A. Garcia y Garcia, eds. 1988. "The Nature and Future of Episcopal Conferences." *The Jurist* 48.

Luhmann, N. 1977. *Funktion der Religion* [Function of Religion]. Frankfurt am Main: Suhrkamp Verlag.

Lyotard, J-F. 1984. *The Postmodern Condition.* Minneapolis: University of Minnesota Press.

Madelin, H. 1988. "The Paradoxical Evolution of the French Catholic Church." Pp. 57-79 in *World Catholicism in Transition,* edited by T. M. Gannon. New York: Macmillan.

Magnani, G. 1988. "La théologie du laïcat a-t'elle un statut théologique?" [The Theology of the Laity: Does it Have a Theological Status?]. Pp. 557-613 in *Vatican II. Bilan et Perspectives. Vingt cinq ans après (1962-1987)* [Vatican II. Balance and Perspectives. Twenty-five Years After (1962-1987)], edited by R. Latourelle. Paris: Cerf.

Maitre, J. 1988. "Les deux côtés du miroir: Note sur l'évolution religieuse actuelle de la population française par rapport au catholicisme" [The Two Sides of the Mirror: Note on the Current Religious Evolution of the French Population with Regard to Catholicism]. *L'année sociologique* 38:33-47.

Martin, D. 1978. *A General Theory of Secularization.* Oxford: Basil Blackwell.

Martina, G. 1988. "Le contexte historique dans lequel a surgi l'idée d'un nouveau Concile Oecuménique" [The Historical Context in which Emerged the Idea of a New Ecumenical Council]. Pp. 31-94 in *Vatican II. Bilan et Perspectives. Vingt cinq ans après (1962-1987)* [Vatican II. Balance and Perspectives: Twenty-five Years After (1962-1987)], edited by R. Latourelle. Paris: Cerf.

Menozzi, D. 1987. "Vers une nouvelle Contre-Réforme?" [Toward a New Counter Reformation]. Pp. 278-299 in *Le retour des certitudes: Evènements et orthodoxie depuis Vatican II,* [The Return of Certitudes: Events and Orthodoxy Since Vatican II], edited by P. Ladrière and R. Luneau. Paris: Le Centurion.

Phillips, D., and S. Harding. 1985. "The Structure of Moral Values." Pp. 93-108 in *Values and Social Change in Britain,* edited by M. Abrams, D. Gerard, and N. Timms. London: Macmillan.

Remy, J., and L. Voyé. 1973. "Eglise et partis. Le champs religieux peut-il s'organiser à la manière du champ politique?" [Church and Parties. Can the Religious Domain Be Organized Like the Political Domain?]. *Lumen Vitae* 28:609-616.

Righart, H. 1986. *De katholieke zuil in Europa: Een vergelijkend onderzoek naar het ontstaan van verzuiling in Oostenrijk, Zwitserland, België en Nederland* [The Catholic Pillar in Europe: A Comparative Study of the Development of Pillarization in Austria, Switzerland, Belgium, and the Netherlands]. Meppel: Boom.

Robberecht, P. 1986. *Mariaverering te Scherpenheuvel: Proeve van een hedendaagse pastoraal in een Mariaal bedevaartsoord* [The Veneration of Mary in Scherpenheuvel: An Example of a Contemporary Pastoral Activity in a Marian Pilgrimage Site]. Brussels: Lumen Vitae.

Robinson, J. A.T. 1963. *Honest to God.* London: SCM.

Rokkan, S. 1977. "Towards a Generalized Concept of 'Verzuiling': A Preliminary Note." *Political Studies* 25:563-570.

Sasaki, M., and T. Suzuki. 1987. "Changes in Religious Commitment in the U.S., Holland and Japan." *American Journal of Sociology* 92:1055-1076.

Schillebeeckx, E. 1989. *Mensen als verhaal van God* [People As a Story of God]. Baarn: H. Nelissen.

Schlegel, J-L. 1989. "L'Eglise catholique sur la mauvaise pente" [The Catholic Church on the Bad Slope]. *Esprit* 148-149:70-81.

Stoetzel, J. 1983. *Les valeurs du temps présent: Une enquête* [Contemporary Values: A Survey].
Paris: Presses Universitaires de France.

Thils, G. 1986. *En dialogue avec l"Entretien sur la Foi"* [In Dialogue With Discourses on Faith].
Louvain-la-Neuve: Peeters.

─────. 1989. "La profession de foi et le serment de fidélité" [The Profession of Faith and the
Loyalty Oath]. *Cahiers de la Revue Théologique de Louvain* 23:5-56.

Thurlings, J.M.G. 1978. *De wankele zuil: Nederlandse katholieken tussen assimilatie en pluralisme*
[The Tottering Pillar: Dutch Catholics Between Assimilation and Pluralism]. 2nd ed.
Deventer: Van Loghum Slaterus.

Touraine, A. 1984. *Le retour de l'acteur* [The Return of the Actor]. Paris: Fayard.

Van De Velde, V. 1988. "De netwerkanalytische benadering van lokale zuilstructuren: Een
toepassing" [The Network-Analytical Approach to Local Pillar Structures: An
Application]. Pp. 203-227 in *Tussen bescherming en verovering: sociologen en historici over
zuilvorming* [Between Protection and Conquest: Sociologists and Historians on Pillar
Formation], edited by J. Billiet. Leuven: Universitaire Pers.

Van Hemert, M.M.J. 1980. "*En zij verontschuldigen zich . . . ": De ontwikkeling van het
misbezoekcijfer 1966-79* ["And they accused themselves . . .". The Evolution of Mass
Attendance 1966-1979]. The Hague: KASKI.

Van Isacker, K. 1989. *Ontwijding* [Profanation]. Leuven: Davidsfonds.

Voyé, L. 1973. *Sociologie du geste religieux: De l'analyse de la pratique dominicale en Belgique
à une interpretation théorique* [The Sociology of the Religious Act: From the Analysis
of Sunday Practice in Belgium to a Theoretical Interpretation]. Brussels: Vie Ouvrière.

─────. 1979. "Situation religieuse des catholiques en Belgique. De l'adhésion écclésiale au
catholicisme socio-culturel en Wallonie" [The Religious Situation of Catholics in Belgium:
From Ecclesiastical Adhesion to Socio-cultural Catholicism in Wallonia]. Pp. 295-331 in
Actes de la 15éme Conférence Internationale de Sociologie des Religions: *Religion et
Politique* [Acts of the 15th International Conference on the Sociology of Religions: Religion
and Politics]. Lille: Conférence Internationale de Sociologie des Religions.

─────. 1985a. "Au-delà de la sécularisation" [Beyond Secularization]. *Lettres Pastorales:
Informations officielles du diocèse de Tournai* [Pastoral Letters: Official Information of
the Diocese of Tournai]. 1(21):253-274.

─────. 1985b. "Les Conseils Presbytériaux et Pastoraux diocésains" [Diocesan Priests' and
Pastoral Councils]. Pp. 233-254 in *La Belgique et ses dieux* [Belgium and Its Gods], edited
by L. Voyé, K. Dobbelaere et al. Louvain-la-Neuve: Cabay-Recherches Sociologiques.

─────. 1988a. "Prolongements et perspectives: le point de vue d'un sociologue" [Extensions
and Perspectives: The Point of View of a Sociologist]. Pp. 125-136 in *Le religieux en
Occident: Pensée des déplacements,* [The Religious in the West: Reflections of Shifts] edited
by J-L. Schlegel et al. Brussels: Facultés Universitaires Saint-Louis.

─────. 1988b. "Approche méthodologique du sacré" [Methodological Approach to the Sacred].
Pp. 255-277 in *Religion, Mentalité et Vie Quotidienne* [Religion, Mentality, and Daily Life],
edited by M. Cloet and F. Daelemans. Brussels: Archives et Bibliothéques de Belgique.

─────. 1988c. "Du monopole religieux à la connivence culturelle en Belgique. Un catholicisme
hors les murs" [From Religious Monopoly to Cultural Connivance in Belgium: An
Extramural Catholicism]. *L'Année sociologique* 38:135-167.

─────. "Vision of the Church, Vision of the World: The Bishop's Conferences and the Principle
of Subsidiarity." Paper presented at the Fiftieth Annual Meeting of the Association for
the Sociology of Religion, Atlanta, Georgia.

─────. Forthcoming. *From Institutional Catholicism to Christian Inspiration.*

Voyé, L., and J. Remy. 1985a. "Les évolutions divergentes du monde catholique Belge" [The
Divergent Evolutions of the Belgian Catholic World]. *La Revue Nouvelle* 81:227-241.

_____. 1985b. "Perdurance des clivages traditionnels et différences d'enjeux prioritaires" [The Continuation of Traditional Cleavages and Differences In Priorities]. Pp. 153-173 *La Belgique et ses Dieux*, edited by L. Voyé, K. Dobbelaere et al. Louvain-la-Neuve: Cabay.

Wadsworth, M.E.J., and S.R. Freeman. 1983. "Generation Differences in Beliefs: A Cohort Study of Stability and Change in Religious Beliefs." *The British Journal of Sociology* 34:416-437.

Wallis, R. 1984. *The Elementary Forms of New Religious Life*. London: Routledge and Kegan Paul.

Willaime, J-P., ed. 1989. *Vers de nouveaux oecuménismes* [Toward New Ecumenisms]. Paris: Cerf.

Yonnet, P. 1985. *Jeux, modes et masses: La société française et le moderne* [Games, Fashions and Masses: French Society and the Modern]. Paris: Gallimard.

Zylberberg, J. 1985. "Les transactions du sacré" [The Transactions of the Holy]. *Sociétés* 1:9-13.

THE POST-VATICAN II
CHURCH IN LATIN AMERICA

Madeleine Adriance

If there is a single phrase associated with the post-conciliar church in Latin America, it is the preferential option for the poor. This one term sums up the ideological and structural shift that the institutional church has made from its traditional alliances with the military and land-owning elites to an identification with the struggles of peasants and factory workers. It represents an official policy that has been expressed in the documents of national and continental conferences of bishops, and that has inspired both liberation theology[1] and the grassroots activism characteristic of base ecclesial communities (CEBs).[2]

These new developments in Latin America easily suggest contrasts with Catholicism in the United States. Three differences that are immediately evident relate to the social doctrine of Vatican II, the proportion of clergy in relation to the laity, and religious roles for the latter. Let us take a closer look at each of these three points of contrast.

In the United States, the issues that surfaced at the time of Vatican II mainly concerned individual freedom of conscience. This concern was less salient in

Religion and the Social Order, Volume 2, pages 233-245.
Copyright © 1991 by JAI Press Inc.
All rights of reproduction in any form reserved.
ISBN: 1-55938-388-7

Latin America for two reasons: (1) Socioeconomic problems were far more pressing there than in the United States, with as much as eighty percent of the population in some countries living in poverty; (2) for the majority of Catholic lay people in Latin America religion had been associated more with cultural identity and local customs than with the observance of specific behavioral norms. The absence of strong ecclesial control over people's behavior is related to the second important difference between the United States and the countries of Central and South America—that is, that the shortage of clergy that is now of concern to the North American church has always existed beyond our southern borders. In the absence of priests, frequent mass attendance, reception of the sacraments, and formal religious instruction were not possible, particularly in rural areas, where the majority of the population was located.

The third difference concerns the role of the laity. Throughout Latin American history, lay people have had institutionalized roles within the Catholic church, although those roles have taken different forms and have not been equally distributed among the various social classes. During the colonial period,[3] the rulers of Spain and Portugal had complete rights of patronage, including the power to recommend and approve appointments of bishops. After independence, the governments of several of the new countries managed to retain that prerogative.

On the local level, large landowners exercised control of the church through their influence over the parish priests, many of whom were virtually family chaplains for the wealthy. In addition, there were numerous official lay associations that developed at various times. These included, for example, the Congregation of Mary, the Apostleship of Prayer, Opus Dei and Catholic Action. Although officially under the control of the clergy, they would become important sources of lay leadership.[4] Because of the shortage of priests, these organizations would be entrusted with the task of extending the church's influence over people's lives. Although they developed mainly among the middle and upper classes, they were the forerunners of the Bible circles and rural chapels that emerged in the 1950s. These new groups, which drew their membership mainly from the peasant class, would provide a model for the base ecclesial communities, in which both rural and urban poor people would develop ministerial roles and input into decision making. This shift of emphasis to the poorer laity would become a conspicuous element of post-conciliar Latin American Catholicism.

The specific process by which change came to the Latin American church was facilitated by the spirit of renewal encouraged by Pope John XXIII before and during Vatican II.[5]

THE POPE, THE BISHOPS, AND VATICAN II

Pope John did not wait until the Second Vatican Council to attempt to bring religious renewal to Latin America. As early as 1958, he was urging the bishops of that region to take action to save their church. His message was pastorally weak, out of touch with the majority of the people, and threatened by the growing strength of both Evangelical Protestant churches and socialist movements. In a letter to the bishops written in 1961, the pope urged the setting up of national episcopal conferences, the writing of pastoral plans and the devoting of attention to social problems (Caramuru de Barros 1968, pp. 25-26). Some of these measures already existed in Chile and Brazil, where a few progressive members of the hierarchy had begun their own efforts for revitalizing the church. During the Second Vatican Council these bishops would have some influence in the writing of *Gaudium et Spes,* the Pastoral Constitution on the Church in the Modern World.

Nevertheless, in the mid 1960s, ecclesial renewal was not yet widespread. It was the Chilean bishop, Manuel Larraín, who, with the help of his Brazilian colleague, Dom Hélder Câmara, would bring together the bishops of the whole continent at Medellín, Colombia, in September, 1968 (Gómez de Souza 1982, p. 291). The purpose of this gathering was to apply the documents of Vatican II to the specific social context of Latin America.

MEDELLÍN

The Medellín Conference was the most important event of this century for the Latin American Catholic church. It has been a source of pastoral renewal and an inspiration of efforts toward social change, as well as a symbol of conflict and controversy. *Gaudium et Spes* was the conciliar document from which most of the inspiration for the conference was drawn. The specific elements of this document that would produce significant social and religious consequences were a concern about social problems, the encouragement of pastoral innovations, and new ecclesial roles for the laity.

A reform-oriented approach to social problems is evident from the following statement from the Medellín *Conclusions:*

> The Latin American Church encourages the formation of national communities that reflect a global organization, where all of the peoples but more especially the lower classes have, by means of territorial and functional structures, an active and receptive, creative and decisive participation in the construction of a new society (CELAM 1979, p. 35).

The Document on Justice goes on to encourage land reform, the development of unions for both urban and rural laborers, the reform of political structures, interfaith cooperation for working on justice issues and concientización (that is, facilitating the development of a critical consciousness and an orientation to social action among the poor).

In the specifically pastoral area, the Medellín Document on the Pastoral Care of the Masses encourage studying popular religion, purifying it of practices defined by the church as superstitious and then tying its practices more closely to Scripture:

> That all manifestations of popular devotion such as pilgrimages, processions and other devotions, be permeated by the Word of God . . . That devotions and sacramentals do not lead to semi-fatalistic acceptance, but that they educate man to become co-creator with God and master of his own destiny (CELAM 1979, pp. 94-95, 130).

In addition, there is the encouragement of the formation of base ecclesial communities, which would later come to be defined as "a new way of being church":

> That a greater number of ecclesial communities be formed in the parishes, particularly in rural and marginal urban communities. These must have as their foundation the Word of God and, insofar as possible, find their fulfillment in the Eucharistic celebration, always in communion and dependent upon the local bishop. The community will develop to the degree that its members have a sense of belonging that leads them to solidarity in a common mission, and accomplishment of common and active participation, conscientious and fruitful, in liturgical and community living (CELAM 1979, pp. 94-95).

It was in relation to the base communities that new roles for lay people, as well as for religious, were to be developed:

> For the formation required by the afore-mentioned communities, let the permanent diaconate be established, and let men and women religious, specially prepared catechists and lay apostles be called to a more active participation (CELAM 1979, p. 95).

There is also encouragement for lay movements within the church, with particular reference to their role in social reform:

> We recommend with special urgency the creation of apostolic teams or lay movements within functional structures in which the process of liberation and humanization of the society to which they belong is elaborated and decided. These groups must enjoy adequate coordination and a pedagogy based on the discernment of the current signs of the times manifested in the actual world (CELAM 1979, p. 130).

The Document on Lay Movements goes on to encourage the development of a lay spirituality.

Even before the Medellín conclusions were approved in Rome, they were being mimeographed and discussed by church people throughout Latin America (Berryman, 1984, p. 28). The resulting changes would be deep and extensive.

NEW STRUCTURES AND NEW
LIFE IN THE CHURCH

A consequence of Medellín which became evident within the next decade was the formation of new ecclesial structures. In some countries, the bishops set up organizations for dealing with social problems, such as the Pastoral Land Commission in Brazil and the Vicariate of Solidarity in Chile.[6]

In countries where the hierarchy was slower to move, lay people, women religious and priests who picked up the spirit of Medellín began to orient their ministry to the people of the poorer classes and to work for social and pastoral change at the grassroots level (Levine 1986, pp. 11-12). Networks of Christian activists began to emerge. These included the National Office of Information (ONIS) in Peru, Priests for the Third World in Argentina, the Golconda Movement in Colombia, ISAL in Bolivia, and the Justice and Peace Commission in Guatemala (Berryman 1986, p. 75; Cleary 1985, p. 45).

In several countries documentation centers were set up in order to maintain records of what was going on in the church. As repression by military—authoritarian governments began to affect church people, the documentation centers became important sources of information about human rights violations (Cleary 1985, p. 46).

Another significant change occurred in the relationship between priests and lay people. Traditionally, the function of the clergy in Latin America had been to dispense sacraments to essentially passive recipients. Following the spirit of Vatican II, Medellín encouraged a stronger institutional role for the laity, which included going beyond the old elitist lay organizations and recruiting religious leaders among the poorer classes. Programs began to be developed for training leaders, both in countries with progressive bishops, such as Brazil and Chile, and in some where the hierarchy was generally more conservative, such as Guatemala, El Salvador, and Nicaragua (Berryman 1986, p. 60). These leadership training programs would help to stimulate the growth of base communities. Although the original intent of the bishops at Medellín in encouraging the development of the communities may have been primarily pastoral (that is, finding a way to compensate for the shortage of priests in the face of Protestant evangelization), their political consequences have been wide-ranging. These have included labor union activity in Brazil, land struggles in Paraguay and Peru, and involvement in revolutionary movements in Nicaragua and El Salvador (Cleary 1985, pp. 116-120; Dodson 1986, p. 85).[7] It is also likely that CEB members were active in promoting progressive candidates in the recent presidential elections in Brazil and Chile.

DIFFERENCES WITHIN THE
LATIN AMERICAN CHURCH

The overall impact of Vatican II on institutional structures has not been consistent from one Latin American country to another and it has frequently been marked by conflict. The smoothness or difficulty in bringing about progressive policies has been at least partly affected by the sociopolitical contexts of the individual countries. When the Medellín conference took place in 1968, Brazil, for example, was entering a period of severe repression. Some church people, including bishops, were beginning to experience persecution because of their identification with the poor. Medellín encouraged that continuing identification, which led to the church's providing a space for dissent within Brazilian society (see Adriance 1986, pp. 129-152). When all other organizations that might challenge the military government had been suppressed, the bishops began to speak out on human rights. At this same time, however, bishops in Chile were more concerned about the consequences for the church of the growing strength of the Socialist Party. They had been lending indirect support in previous presidential elections to candidates who were running against Salvador Allende. Catholics moving in leftist directions were being censured by the hierarchy (Smith 1982, pp. 231-253). It was not until the coup of 1973 initiated a period of violent repression that the bishops and lay activists found themselves on the same side of a conflict. As in Brazil, the base communities in Chile provided a space for political dissent.

It seems ironic that the very country in which the Medellín Conference took place is also the one that appears to have been the least affected by it. Colombia's history of church-state relations has been characterized by stability and mutual support. Economic change has also come slowly to Colombia, which, unlike Brazil and Chile, has remained predominantly agricultural. Because Colombia has not experienced the type of social dislocation characteristic of those countries that underwent rapid industrialization, the church there has maintained its traditional power base and close ties with the elites. It is firmly entrenched in civil and political life, has not undergone major persecutions or threats to its authority and, consequently, has experienced little external stimulus toward change. In the aftermath of Medellín, the Colombian episcopate did write a document that suggested a rethinking of the church, its internal structure of authority, and its relationship to the larger world. However, there then appeared to be a pulling back from this progressive position. Documents written in the early 1970s reaffirmed the authority of the hierarchy (Levine 1986, pp. 193-194). At the present time sharp distinctions remain between lay and clerical roles. Although the bishops do support the formation of lay ministries, the promotion of base communities, and social action, these are tightly restricted. The hierarchy maintains central control and encourages the development of leaders who will be loyal to the institutional church (Levine 1986, pp. 193-199).[8]

Like Colombia, Argentina has had a history of close ties between church and state. However, in the aftermath of the Council, many bishops appeared to be open to change. They donated church land to the poor and supported those priests who were implementing pastoral innovations that would tie the church to the underclasses. At the same time, there was conflict between several members of the hierarchy and the Movement of the Priests for the Third World, whose members tended to use tactics of public confrontation in the struggle for social change. Furthermore, during the severe repression of the 1970s, the Argentine bishops took ambiguous positions regarding human rights violations, emphasizing forgiveness toward the perpetrators of the atrocities (Burdick 1989, p. 2). In general, they appeared to show tacit acceptance of violence on the part of authoritarian regimes that maintained institutional privileges for the church, but were critical of the subsequent democratically elected government of Raul Alfonsín, a human rights activist who did not seem inclined to support old systems of privilege. In addition to prosecuting members of the previous government, Alfonsín legalized divorce and also proposed a change in the church's constitutional status (Burdick 1989, pp. 8-9).

The conservatism of Venezuelan bishops has very different roots from the Colombian and Argentine cases. In Venezuela there was a long history of church-state conflict, with a period of 150 years in which the government exercised tight control over religion. The democratically elected government that came to power in 1960, however, freed the church of direct state control and provided some financing of religious activities. During the period immediately prior to Medellín, the institutional church flourished, with a rapid increase in the numbers of dioceses, parishes, and priests (Navarro 1988, pp. 302-305). As a result, the bishops have tended to be supportive of the government and have been reluctant to encourage any directions within the church that would lead to the questioning of political or religious authority. This position, however, has not been accepted by everyone within the Venezuelan church. During the 1960s some priests and lay people, inspired by Vatican II, were already taking initiatives in social action and church renewal. Seminary teachers began to introduce new directions in theology. Groups of young lay Catholics organized a national congress. There were open letters to the bishops demanding a commitment to the poor and questioning their support for the government. In response, the bishops shut down channels of communication, dismantled the clerical movement, purged the seminaries of reformist teachers, and postponed the implementation of a new pastoral plan. Most of the people in favor of change in the church have quietly held on to their beliefs, drawing support from networks that connect progressive Christians throughout Latin America and continuing to work with the poor (Navarro 1986, pp. 304-306).

The position of the Catholic church in Central America is difficult to define because of rapid changes in the political-economic context, shifts in the positions of members of the hierarchy, and deep divisions within the church itself that are further exacerbated by actions of the Vatican. One characteristic of the Nicaraguan church, in contrast to Brazil and Chile, is the split between the popular religion embodied in the base communities and the official Catholicism of the hierarchy. In Nicaragua, the base communities developed independently of the bishops' initiative, which may be one explanation for the latter's mistrust of them. In addition, these communities were developing their political analysis in the late 1970s, at the same time that the Sandinista opposition was gathering strength, which led to increasing identification, cooperation, and even some overlap between the religious and political movements (see Berryman 1986, pp. 67-74; Dodson 1986, pp. 84-91).

The split between the official and grassroots church may have been further widened by what appeared to many lay persons, women religious, and priests to be a shift in the position of the hierarchy. After Medellín, the Nicaraguan church acquired a progressive image because of its support of the preferential option for the poor, shown in the channeling of resources toward social welfare and grassroots evangelization (Crahan 1988, pp. 266, 269). At the same time, the abuses of the Somoza government led to an erosion of the church's support for it. In June, 1979, the Nicaraguan bishops stated in a pastoral letter that the insurrection of that time was moral and legitimate. After the victory of the Sandinistas, however, there was a shift. The bishops began to perceive the close identification of many base community members with the new political-economic order as evidence of independence from religious authority (Dodson 1986, pp. 87-91). They also accused the government of promoting materialist conceptions of the human being that alienate people from God. The position of the Vatican has deepened the split between the bishops and the popular church, with Pope John Paul II's support of opponents of the Sandinistas (particularly Cardinal Obando y Bravo, the Archbishop of Managua) and his public criticism of the popular church as too ideological and radical (Crahan 1988, pp. 173-276). At the time of this writing, it remains to be seen what arrangement of political and religious alliances and oppositions will occur under the Chamorro administration. It seems likely that the archbishop will now be more supportive of the government and that many progressive clergy and women religious will be in sympathy with the new opposition. In light of the results of the 1990 presidential election, one may wish to exercise caution in predicting the position of the majority of the Catholic laity.

In El Salvador, the much-publicized murders in the 1980s of an archbishop, four missionary women and a large number of priests, including six prominent Jesuits at the University of Central America, may create the impression that the official church tends to be progressive. However, the majority of the bishops are actually moderate-to-conservative, and such progressives as the late

Archbishop Romero and his successor, Archbishop Rivera y Damas, have tended to be isolated within the episcopate. As in Nicaragua, most of the post-Medellín initiatives have originated at the grass roots level, through the actions of priests and women religious who have organized leadership training programs and base communities. By the early 1970s, lay people began to become more active in the church, organizing meetings and courses and trying to solve community problems. As members of base communities became more activist, guerrilla groups began building alliances with them (Berryman 1984, pp. 101-105, pp. 223-225, 1986, pp. 60-65). Similar to the situation in Nicaragua in the 1970s, the revolutionary movement in El Salvador is supported by people in the grass roots church.

It should be evident that there is a wide range of experiences among the Latin American countries with regard to the implementation of the spirit of Vatican II. In those countries in which the preferential option for the poor has had its strongest impact (Brazil, Chile, Nicaragua, and El Salvador) there have been clear effects on the lives of church members. However, there have also been consequences in other places as well, because of communication channels that link individuals with similar commitments in different countries.

An important effect has been the encouragement given to women religious and priests who are inclined toward pastoral experimentation and the social-political empowerment of the poor. For many pastoral agents, the preferential option for the poor has become a taken-for-granted aspect of their religious commitment. This has naturally led to changes in the lives of poor people themselves, as they become accustomed to a more active role within the church and in efforts to transform their social environment. At the same time, there has been a disaffection by some of the wealthy, who believe that the church has abandoned them. However, there is nothing in the pastoral documents of any of the episcopal conferences that would seem to advocate attention to one class at the expense of another. In fact, Medellín devoted a whole document to pastoral concern for the elites (CELAM 1979, pp. 97-105). What may be disturbing to some people is that this document states that pastoral efforts should be directed to orienting elites toward a commitment to social change and that all classes of citizens should be encouraged to contribute to the common good (CELAM 1979, pp. 103-104). In other words, progressive elements in the church appear to be challenging privileged people to dedicate themselves to the creation of a just society. It is possible that this new message is perceived by some persons to be a threat to their economic interests.

The preferential option for the poor has certainly had an impact beyond the immediate experience of religious believers, since it has led the latter to question existing political-economic arrangements. This has resulted in efforts toward social and political reform, the weakening of ties between the church and oligarchies, repression of the church by right-wing governments, and revolutionary activity in those countries, especially in Central America, where the existing structures have been particularly resistant to change.

While these political consequences have been disturbing to a few bishops, the greater part of the resistance by some members of the hierarchy to new directions within the church has likely resulted from another factor—the inclination of many lay people, women religious, and priests to extend the desire for political democracy to greater participation in decision making within the church. Much of the reaction against the popular church has centered on the issue of ecclesial authority.

COUNTERFORCES

Puebla

In 1979, another general meeting of bishops was held, this time in Puebla, Mexico. During the eleven years since Medellín, there had been growing disagreement within the hierarchy over the question of whether the church should become involved in advocating social change, or whether it should limit itself to spiritual matters (Cleary 1985, p. 44). In 1972, the Latin American Bishops' Conference (CELAM) had undergone a conservative shift, when a Colombian archbishop, Alfonso Lopez Trujillo, became secretary general. He carefully selected the persons who would compose the preliminary documents for Puebla, excluding the progressive theologians who had been influential at Medellín (Cleary 1985, p. 47). The resulting documents emphasized a harmonious view of society and expressed criticism of base communities and of liberation theology (O'Shaughnessy 1986, p. 3).

This new direction was not accepted by all of the bishops and theologians. Episcopal conferences of individual countries criticized the preliminary documents as failing to address important societal issues. During the Puebla meeting itself, the excluded theologians organized themselves into a parallel conference. By serving as advisors to progressive bishops who were delegates to the official meeting, they were able to influence the direction of the final documents (O'Shaughnessy 1986, pp. 3-4). Consequently, those documents were even more radical than the conclusions from Medellín. Besides reaffirming base communities as the preferred pastoral strategy, they criticized unjust economic systems, the lack of land reform and the arms race (Cleary 1986, pp. 48, 110). They also presented a strong position on human rights.

Vatican Reactions

Since Puebla, there has been growing pressure from the Vatican to control grass roots groups, to define the limits of legitimate political action for church-linked organizations, and to reinforce ecclesial authority. Pope John Paul II has been urging the bishops to reaffirm institutional unity, to emphasize reconciliation over class struggle and to counter the "sociologization" of religious doctrine (Levine 1986, pp. 13, 248-249). Two of the most conspicuous ways in which this conservative direction has manifested itself are episcopal appointments and the censuring of theologians. The retirement of progressive bishops, such as Hélder Câmara of Recife, Brazil, and Raul Silva of Santiago, Chile, has resulted in their replacement by persons who are not supportive of the popular church or of strong positions on social issues. In appointing cardinals, Pope John Paul favored the conservative Archbishop Miguel Obando y Bravo of Managua over the more progressive Archbishop Arturo Rivera y Damas of San Salvador. The attack against liberation theology became official with the publication in 1984 of the "Instruction on Certain Aspects of the Theology of Liberation" by Cardinal Joseph Ratzinger, prefect of the Congregation for the Faith. Around this time, two Latin American theologians, Gustavo Gutierrez and Leonardo Boff, were summoned to Rome to account for their writings. Father Boff was later silenced for several months, during which he was required to abstain from his duties as editor of the *Revista Eclesiástica Brasileira* [Brazilian Ecclesiastical Review] and to refrain from all other activities as a writer and lecturer.[9]

While the present situation may appear to have some ingredients of a schism, this is not likely to occur. Most Latin American Catholics have a strong sense of loyalty to their church, a loyalty that goes beyond institutional structures, authority relations or dogma. It is deeply rooted in their sense of cultural identity. At the same time, it would be difficult for the hierarchy to suppress a grassroots Catholicism that has been integrated into such traditional forms as religious feasts, processions, stations of the cross and devotion to Mary, as well as the post-Vatican II practices of the study of Scripture, liturgical renewal and lay leadership. What is more likely to happen is that adherents to the liberationist interpretation of Catholicism will find ways to express their beliefs in forms that are acceptable to the official church.[10]

CONCLUSION

It should be clear that the consequences of Vatican II have been very different for Latin America, as compared with the United States. When Pope John XXIII opened the windows of *aggiornamento*, the winds of change in Latin America were blowing strong, not only for the Catholic church, but also for the societies in which it was embedded. In spite of counterforces that have attempted to slow down or stop that process of change, the church is now set on a course of action that is not entirely reversible. There is a lay dynamic that has been unleashed and that cannot be suppressed, although it may become more quiet. There is a whole generation of women religious and priests who have become accustomed to a new form of ministry—more participatory and more oriented to social problems—that they are not likely to unlearn. There are some progressive bishops who are still too young to be retired and replaced by conservatives. Finally, there is the church's own established social gospel that cannot be denied. The option for the poor has been institutionalized as an integral part of Catholic belief and practice, making it ecclesial as well as Biblical. Whatever may happen to or within the church in Latin America, it cannot return to the past.

ACKNOWLEDGMENT

I am grateful to Michael Burdick for his helpful comments on an earlier draft of this chapter.

NOTES

1.   Liberation theology may be defined as the intellectual articulation of the belief that people's eternal salvation is inseparable from their participation in the struggle for social and economic justice.

2.   CEBs (*comunidades eclesiales de base*) are groups of ten to thirty people who gather for Scripture study and community activism, based on the method of action and reflection articulated by Paulo Freire (1970). Estimates for the number of CEBs in Latin America run in the vicinity of a hundred thousand, with the largest proportion of them in Brazil (see Lernoux 1980, p. 41).

3.   For a historical perspective on church-state relations, see Meacham (1966). For accounts of religious-political developments in specific countries in the twentieth century, see Bruneau (1974), Levine (1981), Smith (1982), Berryman (1984).

4.   In Brazil, certain elements of the Catholic Action movement developed such a strong independent lay initiative by the 1960's that they were suppressed by the bishops. See Bruneau (1974, pp. 125-126).

5.   This is not meant to imply that change came to the Latin American Catholic church from exclusively religious sources. For analyses that integrate political-economic with religious-institutional factors, see Adriance (1986) and Mainwaring (1986).

6.   For a description of the development and the activities of the Vicariate of Solidarity, see Smith (1982, pp. 318-319).

7.   The exact nature of the consequences of CEBs in a particular country is largely determined by its political-economic context. For example, in Brazil at the present time, where some measure of democratic change may be achieved in a non-violent manner, members of CEBS are likely to be involved in community mobilization, legal tactics and electoral politics to achieve social goals. In other contexts where attempts at change have been met by violent repression, such as in Central America, members of CEBs may become involved in an armed uprising.

8.   Levine (1986, pp. 209-210) does mention one possible exception—some CEBs on the periphery of the city of Cali that have been organized by a group of women religious and have benefitted from the laissez-faire attitude of the local bishop.

9.   For more details about the situations of Gustavo Gutierrez and Leonardo Boff, see Brown (1990) and Cox (1988).

10. This possibility does not seem unlikely on a continent where African and indigenous religions have long been disguised by the symbols of Christianity.

REFERENCES

Adriance, M. 1986. *Opting for the Poor: Brazilian Catholicism in Transition.* Kansas City, MO: Sheed and Ward.

Berryman, P. 1984. *The Religious Roots of Rebellion: Christians in Central American Revolutions.* Maryknoll, NY: Orbis Books.

————. 1986. "El Salvador: From Evangelization to Insurrection." Pp. 58-78 in *Religion and Political Conflict in Latin America,* edited by D.H. Levine. Chapel Hill, NC: The University of North Carolina Press.

Brown, R. McA. 1990. *Gustavo Gutierrez: An Introduction.* Maryknoll, NY: Orbis Books.

Bruneau, T. C. 1974. *The Political Transformation of the Brazilian Catholic Church.* New York: Cambridge University Press.

Burdick, M. A. 1989. "The Greater Value of Mercy: Religion and Human Rights in Argentina." Paper presented at the annual meeting of the Association for the Sociology of Religion, San Francisco, August 6-9.

Caramuru de Barros, R. 1968. *Brasil: Uma Igreja em Renovação.* Petrópolis, Brazil: Vozes.

CELAM (Latin American Bishops Conference). 1979. *The Church in the Present-Day Transformation of Latin America in the Light of the Council,* vol. 2. *Conclusions.* Washington, DC: United States Catholic Conference, Secretariat for Latin America.

Cleary, E. L. 1985. *Crisis and Change: The Church in Latin America Today.* Maryknoll, NY: Orbis Books.

Cox, H. 1988. *The Silencing of Leonardo Boff: The Vatican and the Future of World Christianity.* Oak Park, IL: Meyer-Stone.

Crahan, M. E. 1988. "Cuba and Nicaragua: Religion and Revolution." Pp. 265-282 in *World Catholicism in Transition,* edited by T.M. Gannon. New York: Macmillan.

Gómez de Souza, L. A. 1982. *Classes Populares e Igreja nos Caminhos da História.* Petrópolis, Brazil: Vozes.

Lernoux, P. 1980. *Cry of the People.* Garden City, NY: Doubleday.

Levine, D. H. 1981. *Religion and Politics in Latin America: The Catholic Church in Venezuela and Colombia.* Princeton, NJ: Princeton University Press.

————. 1986. "Religion, the Poor and Politics in Latin America Today." Pp. 3-23 in *Religion and Political Conflict in Latin America* edited by D.H. Levine. Chapel Hill, NC: The University of North Carolina Press.

Mainwaring, S. 1986. *The Catholic Church and Politics in Brazil, 1916-1985.* Stanford, CA: Stanford University Press.

Meacham, J. L. 1966. *Church and State in Latin America.* Chapel Hill, NC: University of North Carolina Press.

Mignone, E. 1988. *Witness to the Truth: The Complicity of Church and Dictatorship in Argentina.* Maryknoll, NY: Orbis Books.

Navarro, J. C. 1988. "Too Weak for Change: Past and Present in the Venezuelan Church." Pp. 297-307 in *World Catholicism in Transition,* edited by T.M. Gannon. New York: Macmillan.

O'Shaughnessy, L. N. 1986. *The Church and Revolution in Nicaragua.* Athens, OH: Ohio University, Center for International Studies.

Smith, B. 1982. *The Church and Politics in Chile.* Princeton, NJ: Princeton University Press.

PART V

LOOKING TO THE FUTURE OF THE CHURCH IN THE UNITED STATES

U.S. CATHOLICISM:

THE NOW AND FUTURE CHURCH

Joseph H. Fichter, S. J.

Two Christian voices that sounded the alarm about the deterioration of American culture spoke with a Russian accent and delivered their dire predictions at Harvard University. The "crisis of our age" was a central theme of Pitirim Sorokin's sociology lectures for almost four decades. He saw us moving into the sensate stage of Western civilization, materialistic and irreligious. Our atomized selfish values were progressively destructive, "representing a museum of sociocultural pathology rather than the imperishable values of the Kingdom of God" (Sorokin 1957, p. 699).

Aleksandr Solzhenitsyn was also an emigre from the Soviet Union and an acclaimed hero in America, until his 1978 Harvard commencement address scolded Americans for their selfish individualism. He described the calamity of our "autonomous irreligious humanistic consciousness." He declared that "all the celebrated technological achievements of progress, including the conquest of outer space, do not redeem the twentieth century's moral poverty." We have neglected religion. "We have placed too much hope in politics and social reform, only to find that we were being deprived of our most precious possession: our spiritual life" (Solzhenitsyn 1978, p. 57).

Religion and the Social Order, Volume 2, pages 249-265.
Copyright © 1991 by JAI Press Inc.
All rights of reproduction in any form reserved.
ISBN: 1-55938-388-7

In the twenty years since Sorokin's death, and in the decade since Solzhenitsyn's Harvard exhortation, American society has witnessed moral delinquency at the highest levels of our citizenry. We had long known "crime on the streets," which has hardly abated; but we were not ready for the sinful extravagances of the Pentagon, the peddling of influence among government officials, the naked greed of money changers in banking and finance, the venality of the munitions industry, the chicanery and duplicity in the exercise of foreign affairs. Perhaps most embarrassing of public moral failures is that of notorious television preachers. We are witnessing an unexpected display of decadence among the very people, the educated and well-placed, the "social authorities," who are normally expected to represent the solid ethical values of the American society.

Whatever the failings of selfish individualism in public life, there seems also to be a relaxation of the nation's social conscience. We can recite the litany of social problems: an unrealistic low norm of minimum wages, the expanding numbers of homeless people, the decline of labor unions, the neglect of affirmative action programs, the flare-up of racial conflict. Public commitment to the commonweal is promised in every political campaign but is seldom seriously implemented after the election.

Catholic moralists and church leaders have made their share of complaints about America's social morality. Pastoral letters on the concerns of women, on the economic system, and on the nuclear weapons controversy have clarified important areas of public morality. Cardinal Joseph Bernardin's lectures on the "Seamless Garment" emphasize the sacredness of life in the face of secular movements about euthanasia, abortion, warfare, and the death penalty. The pastoral on the U.S. economic system struck directly at the areas of greed and graft that reflect public social inequity. The impact of the Bishops' moral teaching may be measured in the degree of criticism by conservatives and in the degree of praise by progressives.

The moral crises of contemporary society have long been the concern of the Holy See and have been given even greater prominence during and since the Second Vatican Council. The greatest religious leader of the century, Pope John XXIII, expressed foreboding when he convoked the Council in 1961. "Today the Church is witnessing a crisis underway within society." The world exalts its tremendous progress in the technical and scientific fields, in a temporal order that excludes God. "Modern society is earmarked by a great material progress to which there is not a corresponding advance in the moral field" (Abbott 1966, p. 703). These are "painful considerations," said the Pope, but we must not be pessimistic and distrustful; we must "reaffirm all our confidence in our Savior, who has not left the world which He redeemed."

THE MILLENIALISTS

The words of the Pontiff were upbeat and were heeded by the Fathers of the Council who ushered in what has come to be known as *aggiornamento*, a movement of progressive change. Almost immediately, dissent was expressed by traditionalists whose voices have gradually become stronger. Their protests seem to have grown within the church under the provocation of Cardinal Ratzinger, and outside the church by the followers of the excommunicated Archbishop Lefebvre. American Catholic traditionalists have their own leaders, clerical and lay, and their own propaganda vehicle through the public media. The increasing numbers of quasi-fundamentalists among American Christians now include many members of the Catholic church.

The politically influential "moral majority," founded by the Reverend Jerry Falwell in 1980, and disbanded by him in July, 1989, attracted large numbers of Catholics. Whether they knew it or not, their ideology reflected the "premillenial" theology of the fundamentalists. All Christians anticipate, at least vaguely, the millenium in the words of the Lord's Prayer, "Thy Kingdom Come," but many traditionalists warn that the end is imminent because of our sinfulness. The premillenialists expect the Second Coming of Christ "only when the degenerating effects of man's sinful rebellion againt God reached the depths" (Marsden 1987, p. 150ff).

The burgeoning popularity of the Medjugorje pilgrimage is seen by some as a kind of premillenial fundamentalism, sparked by the alleged messages emerging from the apparitions. American Catholic visitors returning from the parish of St. James are impressed with the significance of penance, prayer, fasting, and mortification. Many are ready to say that they have had a conversion experience, a new awareness of the conditions of salvation, and an urgency for repentance and spiritual renewal. Informal groups of returned pilgrims hold regular prayer meetings and Bible sessions centering around the prophecies of the Blessed Mother. Their devotions are kept alive by attendance at so-called Medjugorje Masses.

Another expression of this premillenial enthusiasm was identified with the Catholic Charismatic Renewal, instituted among midwestern college students in the late 1960s. The Charismatics were among the first, in 1981, to recognize the religious importance of Medjugorje. An interesting split has occurred in the movement. One large and active branch, identified mainly as the "Sword of the Spirit," subscribes to an ideology of "gloom and doom," of dire predictions of proximity of the final judgment. The contrasting Charismatics, aligned with the "People of Praise," generally stay aloof from Medjugorje, and intend to do so until the Vatican has given approval to the apparitions.

Catholic traditionalists, who admit to the fundamentalist ideology, are among the pessimists who believe that our moral decadence is hastening the day of judgment. On the other hand, Catholics who have faith in the positive affirmations of Vatican II may be called "postmillenialists." They are optimistic Christians in the wake of Pierre Teilhard de Chardin, with this firm belief that we are making spiritual progress toward the Parousia and the thousand-year Kingdom of Christ. "We do not know the time for the consummation of the earth and of humanity. Nor do we know how all things will be transformed" (Abbott 1966, p. 237). Yet, the Council Fathers assured us of the Coming of the Kingdom, which will be a Kingdom of "truth and light, of holiness and grace, of justice, love and peace" (p. 237).

The hectic complaints of the traditional premillenialists are in sharp contrast to the quiet confidence of postmillenial Catholics. Christian hope prevails even in the avalanche of public immorality, which cannot drown out the *aggiornamento*. Vatican II warns us that "earthly progress must be carefully distinguished from the growth of God's Kingdom" (Abbott 1966, p. 237). Nevertheless, "on this earth that Kingdom is already present in mystery. When the Lord returns it will be brought into full flower" (p. 238). The gradual moral progress of human society is setting the stage for the thousand-year reign of peace and justice, *after* which Christ will return.

The scriptural language of the millenial prophecy is readily converted to the secular language of the sociologist. The literature on social problems distinguishes clearly between the "conflict" theorists who focus on "what is wrong" and the "order" theorists who want to know "what works." The ongoing social order is measured from the perspective of group consensus which reflects the general stance of the religious postmillenialist. Society is constantly undergoing change, and the premillenialist Catholic preserves tradition while he senses disaster in *aggiornamento*.

Much of what is happening in United States Catholicism can be interpreted as a consequence of, and a reaction to, the imapct of Vatican II. The laity have become more active in the affairs of the church, while the church professionals have diminished in numbers. It was no accident that the traditional diaconate was reconstituted and that at least a narrow concession was made for the ordination of married convert priests. Ecumenical outreach has made some cautious progress even as the "Americanized" church continues to deal with its minority members, its poor people, and immigrants.

PARTICIPATORY RELIGION

American Catholics who forgot their history give the impression that the enormous measurable success of the Catholic church in this country was the exclusive achievement of bishops, monsignors, and pastors. Popular commentators on the contemporary church seem to have "discovered" that lay people began to participate in church activities only as a consequence of the Second Vatican Council. Up to that point everybody knows that "Roman

Catholics were part of an autocratic, hierachically structured religious organization which expected unquestioning obedience from its adherents" (D'Antonio et al. 1989, p. 5). This caricature is belied by social historians, pointing to the energetic Catholic laity who built an enormous network of parishes, schools, hospitals, colleges, welfare agencies, and spiritual associations, unparalleled in the so-called Catholic countries elsewhere (Dolan 1985).

This stereotype was belied also in the first sociological parochial studies we made just after World War II. We reported at that time that "every parish developed a number of 'societies,' or formal sub-groupings, through which the more zealous and interested parishioners may carry on the general and specific functions of the parish" (Fichter 1954, p. 154). The successful parish had priests willing and competent to cooperate with the energetic Motherss Club, the bustling CYO, the zealous Vincent de Paul Society. It was the people who made the parish and who did the work. They exemplified the best traditions in both personal morality and social awareness.

There were some sad exceptions, where the priests operated "more on the patterns of the secular community than on the social teaching of the Church." One Southern urban parish we studied exhibited well-defined negative social attitudes concerning low-cost housing, organized labor, free school lunches, and race relations. The pastor reflected and supported these bourgeois attitudes because they were the convictions of his closest advisers: socially prominent businessmen (Fichter 1950, pp. 495-500). In this instance, the best and most Christian efforts of the parishioners were frustrated by the clergy.

Where the parish clergy are competent and cooperative, lay participation seems most notable at the heart of the parish: celebrtion of the Eucharist. Obviously, the liturgy in the English language opens up a wide understanding of collective prayer. The central complaint of traditionalists is that the priest has been replaced by the congregation as the celebrant of the Holy Sacrifice. The priest is the "presider" who now faces the people, often shares the ceremonies with a permanent deacon, a religious sister or other unordained person. Eucharistic lay ministers help in the distribution of the sacrament at Mass and bring Communion to the sick of the parish. The "kiss of peace," which is usually a handshake with the next person in the pew, is especially objectionable to traditional Catholics.

The trend toward greater lay participation is more than a shift to the English language or the introduction of guitar Masses. Catholicism is now manifested in a more confident and joyous spirit. Gone is the Salve Regina, which depicted Catholics as "poor banished children of Eve, mourning and weeping in this vale of tears." The sorrowful prayers of the Way of the Cross have gone out of style; the sacrament of penance has become the act of reconciliation; even the funeral Mass has dispensed with black vestments, and turned the requiem into a joyful paean to the Resurrection. These changes were opposed by men like Gommar De Pauw and Francis Fenton, who launched Catholic traditionlist movements in the United States.

Aside from religious and spiritual activities, the laity now also takes part in organizational and administrative tasks previously reserved for the parish clergy. The parish council elects parishioners, both men and women, who are "working in close union with their priests" (Abbott 1966, p. 501). Finance committees share the decisions that maintain the physical plant. Critics are out of date who continue to say that lay people are excluded from all parochial tasks except to "pay and pray." They have failed to observe the modern operation of the typical American parish.

VANISHING CHURCH PROFESSIONALS

The increasing number of lay Catholics who are actively engaged in church work constitutes a response to diminishing number of priests, sisters, and brothers in the church. The empty seminaries and convents have been sold in many instances to evangelical and other Protestant churches that have growing numbers of candidates. It is a strange coincidence that the divinity schools of certain conservative churches are overcrowded with ministerial candidates of both sexes. The obvious answer to the problem is to imitate the Protestants, as suggested by sociologist Dean Hoge. The least radical solution, he thinks, is that "Bishops ordain people to the priesthood who are not celibate or not male" (Hoge 1987, p. 212).

The "shortage" of priests seems to have attracted the most attention of both prelates and people because attendance at Mass is still the main way of counting Catholics. Remove the priests and you remove the Eucharist. The increasing number of priestless parishes not only breaks the pattern of church attendance; it also decreases the availability of other sacerdotal services. Pastoral ministry is being provided more and more by ordained deacons and religious sisters, who must refrain, however, from the priestly functions of Mass, reconciliation, and anointing.

The decline in the number of nuns has been statistically more dramatic. There are about eighty thousand fewer religious sisters than there were at the time of Vatican II. Even so, Catholic sisters are a phenomenon unequaled in any other American religious community, and the decline marks the practical "disappearance" of the sisters in their religious garb. It probably goes unnoted by youthful Catholics who have never seen a dozen sisters in full religious habit ushering school children to morning Mass. One has to watch television now for the sighting of a nun like Mother Angelica, and for news stories about Mother Teresa of Calcutta and her followers, who wear distinctive religious garb.

In the days before the Second Vatican Council the person who left the religious life, and especially the priesthood, was considered a "failure." There were proportionately fewer departures from the total religious commitment in those days, and they often suffered the pejorative term, "defections," upon "Giving Up the Vocation" (Fichter 1961). The formal procedure for leaving is still termed a "dismissal," suggesting that it cannot be an honorable and voluntary resignation. Rather than "blame" the resigning religious, Sister Marie Augusta Neal (1984, p. 23) suggests that "the overall trends in numbers leaving are more social than psychic, caused by concomitant trends in the conditions of society, and the Church's response to them, the changing apostolic needs in relation to population shifts and new calls for prophetic and institutional service."

Most Catholics no longer consider it a "disgrace," or an act of immorality, to leave the convent or the priesthood. The church vocation has not been completely secularized, but the flood of resignations has made the experience almost commonplace. The choice of an alternative vocation and life-style is not now "unthinkable." The general attitude of American Catholics does not condemn the resignee as a derelict, a deserter, a deviant. In a research project about ex-priests, Hernan Vera (1982) found that practicing priests tend to give a positive rating to resigned priests. "The surprisingly positive rating of the deserter" is a recognition of the dramatic changes that have occurred in the Church and in the priesthood.

For the most part, the stigma of defection has been removed from the ex-nuns and former priests who now mingle almost unnoticed among the Catholic population. They are often employed in dioceses and parishes, in schools and hospitals, under the auspices of the church, a type of employment that would have been unthinkable a generation ago.

The decline in numbers of church professionals suggests that the laity must take over the necessary functions of the church and thus decrease the significance of the clergy. This is probably a negative way of saying "democratization" of the church, but it looks at a de-emphasis of the clerical culture rather than an emphasis of lay activities in the church. Unfortunately, the terms, "church" and "clergy," have been so intimately linked for so long that when some people say "church" they tend to mean "clergy." People who disagree with the clergy sometimes show their anger by leaving the church.

The post-conciliar crisis of the clergy revolves around two distinct, if not contradictory, conceptions of the priesthood. One idea is the widespread notion that the clergyman should narrow his functions to the strictly cultic and sacramental activities that keep him close to the altar and the pulpit. This is his specialty, the reason why he was ordained. The other defintion "de-clericalizes" the clergyman by placing him at the service of the people wherever their needs are greatest and most apparent. He has a concern for the larger community, for the people in the secular city. He is still the man of God, but he has become also a man of the people of God in a much broader sense than ever before.

What is confusing about this de-clericalization process is the different kind of relationship that is developing between the clergy and the people. There has never been a genuine anti-clericalism in the American church, mainly because there has never been a genuine clericalism. The status differential between ordained and laity was quite clear, but the personal relationship has been close. Now the level of familiarity is changing; "the priest wants to be called by his first name, do away with the clerical collar, involve himself in the secularity of things" (Fichter 1974, p. 83).

DIACONATUS REDIVIVUS

The counterpart of this change in clerical functions has been the extent to which the laity have taken over clerical tasks. The active role of lector at church services was once reserved to men in holy orders. Now the pulpit is occupied by both women and men, as is the service of minister of the Eucharist. Permanent deacons are ordained clergymen, performing all former priestly duties except the sacraments of reconciliation, Eucharist and sacrament of the sick. There are no "lay" deacons in the Catholic church. The extent to which lay people are allowed to become "clericalized" depends on the will of the local pastors, who are in some places fighting off this invasion. Traditionalists are sure that this is a way of "Protestantizing" the Catholic church in America.

Hardly anyone paid attention over the years to the fact that at a solemn High Mass the second and third celebrants at the altar, subdeacon and deacon, were actually identified as fully ordained priests. Seminarians preparing for priestly ordination became clerics by tonsure and received the minor orders of porter, acolyte, and lector, before taking the temporary passage through the steps of subdiaconate and diaconate. These stages were always known as transitional. Nobody remained in the status of deacon until the 1967 Apostolic Letter of Pope Paul VI, *Sacrum Diaconatus Ordinem*, decreed that permanent deacons could be ordained, but with no expectation of becoming priests.

This papal *motu proprio* fulfilled the promise of the conciliar document, *Lumen Gentium*, issued November, 1964, which said that "the diaconate can in the future be restored as a proper and permanent rank of the hierarchy." The authorized duties of the deacon are specified: "to administer baptism solemly, to be custodian and dispenser of the Eucharist, to assist at and bless marriages in the name of the church, to bring Viaticum to the dying, to read the sacred scripture to the faithful, to instruct and exhort the people, to preside at the worship and prayer of the faithful, to administer sacramentals, and to officiate at funeral and burial services" (Abbott 1966, p. 55).

In his apostolic letter, *Ministeria Quaedam*, of 1972, Pope Paul VI abolished minor orders and the subdiaconate. "First tonsure is no longer conferred. Orders, which up to now have been called 'minor,' will henceforth be known as 'ministries.'" While the ministries of lector and of acolyte are conferred on diaconal candidates during their formation program, they may be conferred also on lay men who will not advance to the diaconate. On the same date, 15 August, 1972, the Pope issued *Ad Pascendum*, containing the norms for the order of diaconate, both transitional and permanent. The rite of installation to the two "new ministries" of lector and acolyte is not ordination, but institution. Father Komonchak (1985, p. 20) suggests that in many parishes "all of the functions of the instituted ministries" are carried out by both laymen and laywomen.

Even before these papal norms were published, the Bishops of the United States, through the National Conference of Catholic Bishops (NCCB), in the Spring of 1968, petitioned the Holy See for approval to start the diaconal program. They received almost immediate consent from the Apostolic Delegate that they could proceed. The Bishops saw the need of a training program that was relatively uniform for all dioceses in the country, and, in 1971, published a book of *Guidelines* for formation and ministry, which was revised in 1984 (*Permanent Deacons* [1971]1985). Church statistics in 1989 count over nine thousand U.S. deacons, who are sometimes mistakenly identified as "lay" deacons, even though they are authentic clergymen and they belong, as Vatican II said, "to a proper and permanent rank of the hierarchy." Their status as clergymen seems to be "played down" by both laity and priests. One Bishop, who decreed in 1986 that "clerical attire (Roman collar, vest, or clerical shirt) are not to be worn under any circumstances," said that the Diaconate must be identified "with the ordinarty lifestyle of the faith community from which the deacon comes and continues to live." This leads to the conclusion that "for pastoral reasons it is essential that he continue to identify closely with the faithful, even in his public attire" (Hannon 1986).

The ministry of permanent deacons in any diocese requires the approval of the Ordinary, which is not universally granted. In about a dozen smaller dioceses, like Salina, Steubenville, and Winona, the Bishop has not yet ordained permanent deacons. The official *Catholic Directory* lists their names in each diocese and in many instances the parish to which they are assigned by the Bishop. The deacon signs a written agreement with his pastor, specifying his functional obligations, which usually include the tasks that pastors do not care to do, like attending wakes, visiting the sick, giving convert instructions, performing baptisms. If he continues in full-time gainful employment his diaconal ministry is usually limited to ten hours a week. This limitation is understandable because "commitment to wife and family has clear priority over ministry" (*Permanent Deacons* 1971, n. 127). Because he works for the church without pay he must also give priority to his occupational commitments, his means of "making a living."

Permanent deacons are unpaid volunteers who receive no stipend from the diocese during the several years of preparatory study and training. In most instances they have to pay for their textbooks, for the retreats and workshops they make with their wives, and for whatever vestments they will need. The educational requirements for candidates are tightening up, but about one out of four (23%) has not attended college. The faculty for preaching is granted by the bishop, or withheld, on the basis of background education.

What seems of some sociological significance is the fact that the permanent diaconate has introduced for the first time in modern America a married Catholic clergy. Only one out of ten is unmarried and vowed to celibacy; all the others are married men who must become celibate in the event of the wife's death. The ordination cannot take place without the wife's consent. In most cases she participates in the lectures and classes of the diaconal formation program. In what manner and to what extent the wife gets involved with her husband's ministry are still questions open to experimentation. Many priests and bishops seem to find the wife's presence awkward, with the result that a significant minority (37%) of the wives say that they do not participate in their husband's ministry.

Nevertheless, Leonard Doohan (1986) writes that "the ministry of most deacons is already a team ministry with their wives. In fact, we must honestly acknowledge that in some cases the ordination of a deacon is beneficial to the Church precisely because it brings to the Church the ministry of his wife. The wives of many deacons are unquestionably the insightful and dedicated ministers the Church needs." This wondrous description is probably the exception rather than the rule among diaconal couples. It is still a novelty to deal with the ministry of a married clegyman; it is even more novel to cope with the ministry of the deacon's wife.

MARRIED PRIESTS

The married diaconate had existed for about a decade before the first married man was ordained to the priesthood, in 1982, in this country. The official document, under the title, "Pastoral Provisions," was issued by the Vatican in June, 1980, at the request of Episcopal priests and parishioners who applied for admission to the Roman Catholic Church in the late 1970s. Some appealed to Archbishop Jean Jadot, then Apostolic Delegate at Washington; others went directly to Cardinal Franjo Seper, Prefect of the Congregation for the Doctrine of the Faith at the Vatican. Archbishop John Quinn, President of the NCCB, received the Vatican document and promulgated it (Fichter 1988a, pp. 177-180).

This ecclesiastical experiment, which introduced two exceptional innovations, has been handled with a degree of caution that almost amounts to secrecy. it was played down, and the participants were asked to "keep it quiet." It was, after all, a most adventuresome idea that American Catholic priests should be allowed to have wives. It was also an unexpected notion that an Anglican parish could transform itself almost intact into a Catholic congregation under the jurisdiction of the local Bishop. For these very reasons the pastoral provisions were expected to attract some sensational attention and were best introduced without fanfare.

One of the ways to keep this innovation quiet was the stipulation that the married priests were not to be given a direct pastoral assignment that would bring them into close contact with parishioners. Catholic lay people would thus be protected from the "scandal" of a married priest celebrating Mass. Our research has unearthed two interesting facts: first, very few Catholics even know of the existence of these married priests; and second, the majority of lay adult Catholics are in favor of married clergy.

Although Archbishop Quinn insisted that the provisions must in no way interfere with the ongoing process of ecumenical relations between the Roman and the Anglican church, some Episcopal Bishops immediately saw the acceptance of married Episcopal priests as a direct insulting response to their ordination of women. They were disturbed also by the refusal of the Roman authorities to recognize the validity of Anglican Holy Orders. Each converting priest had to submit to Catholic ordination. This complaint had been made as early as 1837 by John Henry Newman, still an Anglican and writing about Rome: "We admit her Baptism and her Orders; her custom is to re-baptize and re-ordain our members who chance to join her" (Newman 1901, pp. 212-213). Catholic authories insisted that the "provisions" were not ecumenical; each person was an individual convert. The Episcopal Bishops complained also that the establishment of so-called Anglican-use communities was a threat to ecumenical relations.

Another sociological problem threatened internal relations in the Catholic church. This is the so-called double standard in the contrast between married Catholic men who were called upon to resign the priesthood, and married Episcopal priests whose wives could stay with them. This contrast is kept alive by the energetic leaders of CORPUS (Corps of Reserve Priests United for Service) who are organized to represent thousands of American resigned priests. They welcome the married priests converted from the Episcopal church but declare that they themselves are willing to return to the ministry under some similar "provisional" program.

One must assume that the limited response to the pastoral invitation is a disappointment to its enthusiastic proponents. Only six small congregations for Anglican-use have been established, with an estimated total of less than two thousand parishioners. The program is young and the number of convert priests is few. In the short period of seven years, from June, 1982, when the first was ordained, to May, 1989, the most recent ordination, only forty-two married clergymen transferred from the Episcopal Church and were ordained to the Roman Catholic priesthood.

The reason these married clergymen gave for switching to the Catholic church is their conviction that the fullness of Christian faith is to be found in the Roman tradition. They had lived in hopes of ultimate corporate unity, but the 1976 decision of the General Convention to ordain women priests seems to have destroyed their dream of ecumenical unity. The small number of converts may also be explained by the stringent requirements placed on their acceptance (Fichter 1989, p. 68). As one priest remarked, "they sure don't make it easy to become a Catholic married priest."

ECUMENISM

The transfer of Episcopalians, whether clergy or laity, is carefully described by Roman authorities as a personal and individual profession of faith in the truths of the Catholic faith. This is not "ecumenism" if the term implies a recognition of "parity," or equal status between the churches in dialogue. In the conventional language of ecumenical dialogue there is no question that in the United States ecumenical relations have achieved a high degree of mutual respect and appreciation among the Christian churches. Nevertheless, from an ecumenical perspective, it is still the fact of membership in the Roman church that marks the distinction from the "separated" Christian believers. The church officially still keeps its distance from Protestant churches. There appears to be less likelihood than ever that the Roman church will accept an invitation to join the National Council of Churches in Christ.

The ecumenical movement is pointed at the "restoration of unity among all Christians" because, as the Second Vatican Council tells us, "Christ the Lord founded one Church and one Church only" (Flannery 1984, p. 452). From the traditional Catholic perspective, this *Unitatis Redintegratio* means a corporate, or organic, unity envisioned by the 1928 Encyclical of Pope Pius XI, *Mortalium Animos*, according to which the unity of Christians could be achieved only by the submission of non-Catholics to the one true Church of Rome. Ecumenical dialogue does not lead to integration, or assimilation, of Protestant Churches into Catholicism. It means, at best, a kind of separate-but-equal relationship.

Lest there by any doubt about what is meant by "union" with Rome, the doubt has been removed by the fathers of the Second Vatican Council. The dogmatic constitution on the Church, *Lumen Gentium*, issued in November, 1964, states clearly that the Catholic church is "necessary for salvation." How extensive then is the membership in this necesary church? Does it really include Protestants? "They are fully incorporated into the society of the Church who, possessing the Spirit of Christ, accept her entire system and all the means of salvation given to her, and through union with her visible structure are joined to Christ, who rules her through the Supreme Pontiff and the Bishops. This joining is effected by the bonds of professed faith, of the sacraments of ecclesiastical government, and of communion" (Abbott 1966, p. 33).

Nevertheless, the Fathers of the Council pointed out that "many elements of sanctification and of truth" can be found in other religions, and Catholics must have love and respect for all other believers. Subsequently, interested Catholic theologians have scheduled discussions with various church groups: Lutherans, Presbyterians, and Baptists. Much progress in understanding has been claimed in the mutual agreements on Baptism, Eucharist, and Ministry, but the optimistic consultations with the Anglicans (Anglican-Roman Catholic International Commission [ARCIC]) came to a halt after the Episcopalian General Convention of 1976 allowed the priestly ordination of women. This raised strenuous objections on the part of Episcopalian clergymen who had long anticipated corporate unity with the Roman church.

When the Vatican agreed to accept married priests under certain "pastoral provisions," Anglican objections were voiced by some bishops and theologians. A certain ambiguity arises, as the representatives of both churches seem to be talking at cross-purposes. From the beginning of the pastoral provisions in 1980, the Catholic authorities were saying: "This is not an ecumenical action, and we don't want it to interfere with our ecumenical relations" (Fichter 1988b, p. 18). The Anglican representatives were saying: "Your pastoral provisions are anything but ecumenical, and they are really destructive of ecumenical relations." Catholic authorities clearly anticipated a negative reaction from Episcopal churchmen, and they made an effort to "play down" such ecumenical interpretations.

The Pope of Rome and the Archbishop of Canterbury had corresponded in an ecumenically friendly way over the past decade, but the ordination of women had raised an unnecessary barrier between the churches. This barrier became even more troublesome when a woman, Barbara Harris, was consecrated Bishop suffragan of the Massachusetts diocese. If there ever was hope for the ultimate union of the Anglican and Roman churches, this hope now appears completely forlorn.

These decisions and discussions at the upper level of the church hierarchy appear to have relatively little influence among the ordinary lay people. For the most part, questions about religion are not asked and theological disputations do not occur in everyday life. People live in the same neighborhood, work in the same office or factory, shop at the same stores, and do not know or care about anyone's church or denomination. Pastors sometimes exchange pulpits; their parishioners attend services at other churches. For some churchgoers, the distinctions are breaking down. The tendency to invite Protestant Christians to intercommunion was recognized by the Catholic bishops who issued an official prohibition against this practice. "As a consequence of the sad divisions in Christianity we cannot extend to them a general invitation to receive Communion."

AMERICANIZED CATHOLICS

Certain social commentators have spread the word that we Catholics have now "arrived" in the American society. By occupation, education, income, and place of residence, we have matched all the criteria of the upwardly mobile. After all, a Catholic was elected President, and no other church has as many members of the Congress. Our families have moved into the suburbs, sharing the affluence of the middle class, and joining the country club. We are college graduates, working on Wall Street and in corporative executive offices. We are no longer identified with the organized labor movement, so naturally we have changed our national party affiliation.

These statistics on upwardly mobile Catholics may beguile us as long as we ignore the facts of racial, ethnic, and social-class differences in the Catholic population. The perennial existence of racial discrimination was again publicized by Father George A. Stallings, when he gave reasons for establishing the Imani Temple African-American Catholic Congregation. What is at issue, says this African-American priest, "is the failure of a Euro-American White male hierarchy to be culturally sensitive to the needs of minorities." Another long-standing ethnic problem for the Catholic church is the continuing exodus of Latin (Hispanic) Catholics from the church, attracted in large numbers to evangelical Protestant churches.

Racial and ethnic minorities have been within the Catholic church in America for a long time, and they have not vanished with the gradual "Americanization" of the old-line Irish, Germans, Italians, and Poles. The demographic facts suggest strongly that we are still—or we are again—the immigrant church. More than a fifth of our people belong to minority groups— sixteen percent Hispanics, three percent Blacks and three percent Asian. Nonterritorial language parishes still exist in the large cities, and are increasing on the West Coast.

The common element among these newest minorities is not only their Catholicism, but their proverty. They may or may not, want to retain their ethnic identity and traditional culture, but they do not want to be kept among the underprivileged and oppressed minorities of the American Catholic church. Most descendants of nineteenth-century immigrants no longer take seriously their traditional mores and folkways. Even the more recent immigrants, like Vietnamese and Haitians, and the continuing stream of Mexicans and Central Americans, have less interest in preserving their culture than they have in escaping poverty. They want jobs and income, a decent place to live, schooling for their children, and a parish that welcomes them.

The simple demographic fact is that large numbers of Catholics have not "made it" into the comfortable upper-middle class of individualism and acquisitiveness. We learn from the U.S. Census Bureau that "the gap between rich and poor families is now at its widest level in forty years." This widening chasm between the poor and the well-to-do is not an exclusively Protestant or Anglo-Saxon phenomenon. It is an American phenomenon that reflects also the persistent social-class difference in the American Catholic population. The proportion of poor and needy Catholics is growing steadily. In other words, the Catholic population in this country now contains more poor people and more immigrants than at any time in our history.

SECULARISM

When Sorokin and Solzhenitsyn deplored the materialism, individualism, and irreligion of Western culture, they were describing the process of secularization. When the dispensational fundamentalists predict that total depravity and degeneracy precede the end of time and the Second Coming of Christ, they envision the nadir of secularism. There is a sense in which the Second Vatican Council launched the church itself into the secular culture. Immense changes have "modernized" the church in America, which has become "worldly" without becoming irreligious.

Worldliness is a fact of modern life in the secular city, and the polar religious responses tend to be either defense or accommodation. Both of these are occurring in the U.S. Catholic Church. Defense against encroaching secularism can be an "escape" into the Charismatic covenant community, into the more "observant" religious congregations, or even into one of the numerous so-called "cults." Pastors complain that evangelical and fundamentalist preachers are winning over their parishioners, many of whom are dissatisfied with the liberal modern trends in the church.

This dissatisfaction with the "secularized" church is fed by organized and archaic "defenders of the Faith," like the members of *Opus Dei*, the Wanderer Forum, Catholics United for the Faith (CUF), and similar groups who are constantly railing against the secular humanism that has invaded the church since, and through, the Second Vatican Council. Defense of the faith can also mean "holding the line" against further change and modernization. This is what John Paul seems to be doing through the voice of Josef Ratzinger. The condemnation of progressive scholars and theologians, the demand for the academic Oath of Fidelity, the oversight of American universities, the attempt to weaken the collegial magisterium of regional Bishops' conferences—are all attempts to "stem" the secularist tide (Fichter 1988, p. 152).

The religious response of accommodation to modern secular developments has earned the charge of "secular humanism." It was the solemn intention of the Second Vatican Council to update the Roman Catholic Church, and the American church authorities have tried to implement this intention. Secularization has generally meant that religion adapts to the culture, but this adaptation has been selective. National programs of social justice have been reflected in Catholic opposition to militarism, racism, sexism, and capital punishment. The American Bishops have been in the forefront in the pastoral letter on nuclear deterrence and on the economy.

There is an affirmative way of defining the church's secularist attitude as one of concern for the needs of society. Historically, the Church was the first to establish hospitals, orphanages, homes for the aged, soup kitchens for the hungry and homeless, half-way houses, and rehabilitation centers. American Catholics continue to involve themselves in movements for a better world. The civil rights movement, peace marches, Bread for the World, demonstrations for amnesty, boycotts, and picket lines are expressions of social awareness promoted by Church people, laity, clergy, and religious sisters.

A more deep-seated concern, however, goes beyond accommodation to worldly concerns and actually represents a counterculture movement. This is a growing recognition by church people-theologians, administrators, clergy, and laity—that the very structures of society and the institutions of culture are in need of reform. This has been a hard lesson to learn, but it emerges logically from the experiences of protest movements. Reform has been urged in and through these movements, but the protests have not gone far enough. They raised the moral consciousness of the American people and moved in the external procedures of social justice, but the radical changes have yet to be made. The fact is that the causes of these social problems lie not only in the immoral attitudes and actions of the people, but also in the institutional system that perpetuates social inequities.

In conclusion, what I see as the absorbing future task of American Catholicism is the attempt to transform the concupiscent institutions of the larger society. Relations and confrontations will continue between clergy and laity, conservatives and progressives, Catholics and Protestants, Christians and non-Christians, the Spirit-filled and the conventional Christians. In a sense, all of these antiphons are internal to organized American religion. Historically, we have moved from a Christendom that attempted a universal embrace of society, to a situation where organized religion became a recognized institution alongside other major institutions of the cultural system. We are already in the next phase, and increasingly so, where religion must stand in judgment of the whole complex social structure of the modern world. I see no other force outside of religion that will intelligently challenge the institutionalized inequities, inequalities, and discriminations of Western society.

REFERENCES

Abbott, W. M., S. J., ed. 1966. *The Documents of Vatican II*. New York: America Press.
D'Antonio, W., et al. 1989. *American Catholic Laity*. Kansas City, MO: Sheed and Ward.
Dolan, J. 1985. *The American Catholic Experience*. Garden City, NY: Doubleday.

Doohan, L. 1986. "Ministry and Spirituality for Deacons and Their Wives." *Deaconate Magazine* (January/February), pp. 15-19.

Fichter, J.H. 1950. "Social Role of the Parish Priest." *The Catholic Mind* (August), pp. 495-500.

_____. 1954. *Social Relations in the Urban Parish.* Chicago: University of Chicago Press.

_____. 1961. *Religion as an Occupation.* South Bend, IN: Notre Dame University Press.

_____. 1974. *Organization Man in the Church.* Cambridge: Schenkman.

_____. 1988a. "Rome Welcomes Married Priests." *Commonweal* (March 25), pp. 177-180.

_____. 1988b. "The Ordination of Episcopal Priests." *America* (September), pp. 17-24.

_____. 1988c. *A Sociologist Looks at Religion.* Wilmington: Glazier.

_____. 1989. *The Pastoral Provisions-Married Catholic Priests.* Kansas City, MO: Sheed and Ward.

Flannery, A., ed. 1984. *The Conciliar and Post-Conciliar Documents.* Northport, NY: Costello.

Hannon, P. 1986. Letter to the Permanent Deacons of the Archdiocese, June 4. New Orleans, LA.

Hoge, D. 1987. *Future of Catholic Leadership.* Kansas City, MO: Sheed and Ward.

Komonchak, J.A. 1985. "The Permanent Dioconate and the Variety of Ministries in the Church." Pp. 12-38 in *Diaconal Reader.* Washington, DC: U.S. Catholic Conference.

Marsden, G. 1987. "The Confines of Premillenialism." Pp. 150ff in *Reforming Fundamentalism.* Grand Rapids, MI: Erdmans.

Neal, M.A. 1984. *Catholic Sisters in Transition.* Wilmington, DE: Glazier.

Permanent Deacons in the United States: Guidelines on Their Formation and Ministry. (1971)1985. Washington, DC: National Conference of Catholic Bishops (NCCB).

Solzhenitsyn, A.I. 1978. *A World Split Apart.* New York: Harper and Row.

Sorokin, P.A. 1957. *Social and Cultural Dynamics.* Boston: Porter Sargent.

Vera, H. 1982. *The Professionalization and Professionalism of Catholic Priests.* Gainsville: University Press of Florida.

VATICAN II AND THE RECONCEPTUALIZATION OF THE CHURCH

Helen Rose Ebaugh

While 1990, the twenty-fifth anniversary of the close of the Second Vatican Council, provided the impetus for various evaluations of the effects of the Council on the Catholic world, there has been continuous debate in the intervening years of whether the changes initiated by the Council have, in fact, revitalized and strengthened the church or, rather, weakened the solidarity and control the church traditionally exercised over its members. Liberal critics bemoan the compromises that the progressive bishops had to make in the Council debates and the slow implementation of changes that were made while more conservative critics are quick to point out the anomie and unrest that many Catholics have experienced since their taken-for-granted Catholic culture was disrupted by changes created by the Council. Despite these varied and sometimes hostile reactions to the Council, as the papers in this volume make clear, the Catholic world was disrupted and changed as a result of the Council. The Council represented an event that challenged centuries old thinking in the church and replaced it with new ideas of the church and its role in society.

Religion and the Social Order, Volume 2, pages 267-284.
Copyright © 1991 by JAI Press Inc.
All rights of reproduction in any form reserved.
ISBN: 1-55938-388-7

In this concluding paper, I argue that what happened at the Second Vatican Council was the development and legitimation of a new conceptualization of the church. Using Wallace's (1956, 1957) analysis of revitalization movements in which he sees shifts in mazeways as central to such movements, I will discuss two major mazeway shifts that were legitimated at the Council and institutionalized in its decrees. The fact that these reformulations involved central notions of the church and the relationship of individual members to the church meant that the ramifications of these shifts would affect every aspect of Catholic living. It is these shifts in the basic theology of the church and their ramifications in terms of structural changes that lead to the Council's becoming a landmark event in church history.

The Council itself was not an isolated event that erupted as a total surprise upon a nonsuspecting world. As I argue in the first chapter, the Council was rather one event in the entire revitalization movement that began as the First Vatican Council ended in 1870. The Second Vatican Council mobilized various national reform movements in the church into a more highly organized international movement and legitimated some of the ideologies and goals that had sustained these national movements for decades. In addition to serving as a legitimating agency, the Council also established structures by which the institutionalization and implementation of new ideas would be translated into the everyday life of the church.

In a very real sense, the Council is a prime example of the type of movement that Wallace (1956, p. 256) described when he defined a revitalization movement as a "deliberate, organized, conscious effort by members of a society to construct a more satisfying culture." In fact, he argued that revitalization is a special kind of culture change phenomenon characterized by three elements: (1) persons involved in the process of revitalization must perceive their culture as a system; (2) they must feel that this cultural system is unsatisfactory; and (3) they must innovate not merely discrete items, but a new cultural system, specifying new relationships as well as, in some cases, new traits.

The key to revitalization, in Wallace's analysis, is the shift that takes place in the "mazeways" or mental images that people have of the society and its culture. When old mazeways are no longer consistent with lived experience, stress sets in. As large numbers of people become discontent with the "fit" between cultural mazeways and daily experience, the potential exists for effecting change in the mazeway. Changing the mazeway involves changing the total gestalt or nature of images of self, society, culture, and ways of action. The collaboration of a number of persons in the effort toward changing mazeways is what Wallace calls a revitalization movement.

The two major mazeway shifts that were legitimated by Vatican II and that resulted in a new conceptualization of the church and constituted the rationale for many of the structural changes effected by the Council were: (1) aggiornamento or adaptation of the church to changing social conditions; and

(2) the church as the People of God. I will discuss how each of these mazeway shifts came about, their formulation at the council, the structural changes that followed from them, and, finally, how successful their implementation has been in the twenty-five years since the council. The basis for evaluation of the success of the implementation of these mazeway shifts is primarily the data presented in the chapters in this book.

AGGIORNAMENTO

When Pope John XXIII, on Janurary 25, 1959, announced his intention to call an ecumenical council, he made it clear that the purpose of the council was to update and renew the church in the light of contemporary social conditions. He outlined the goal of the council as one of aggiornamento, an Italian word which indicates updating, modernization and adaptation to modern conditions. His program for the upcoming council was in stark contrast to the stance against modernization that was evident on the part of the Vatican in the one hundred years since the First Vatican Council in 1870.

Pre-Vatican II Conception of the Church

As the nineteenth century came to a close, the church seemed to be at war with the modern world (Kurtz 1986). Beginning with the French Revolution, the church's status in European society had eroded (Burns 1990). A number of crises had challenged the church throughout the century. Darwin's theories of evolution and the rise of historical critical methods challenged the validity of Catholic teachings. The authority of the church as well as the orthodox interpretation of Scripture were called into question in the light of new archeological discoveries and the literary Biblical movement that was popular in Europe in the latter half of the nineteeth century (McSweeney 1980).

The church was bombarded by a host of new ideas that challenged her authority to speak definitively on issues. Notions of cultural relatively and scientific truth often clashed with traditional Catholic teachings. In an attempt to define the enemy, church authorities rallied against what they called "modernism." Pope Pius X, in 1907, condemned modernism as the "synthesis of all heresies" and required all clergy to take an anti-modernist oath (Lyng and Kurtz 1985). Books were placed on the *Index of Prohibited Books* and a secret organization, the *Sapiniere,* was created to coordinate efforts to stamp out modernism by reporting suspicious activities and persons to Rome so that appropriate action could be taken against offenders (Hebblethwaite 1968; Kurtz 1986).

For the Vatican, modernism summed up a series of attacks aimed at church doctrine from various sources: questions regarding the authorship of the scriptures, the authority of the church, the virgin birth, and the very notion of dogma itself (Lyng and Kurtz 1985; McSweeney 1980). In response to these threats, the church became more authoritarian and entrenched in its orthodox positions, and persecuted offenders with censure and excommunication.

The two most dramatic and consequential responses of Rome to the perceived attacks of the modernists was the proclamation of papal infallibility at the First Vatican Council and the official approbation of Thomism as the accepted theology of the church by Pope Leo XIII at the end of the nineteenth century. By defining papal infallibility as a central dogma of the church, the bishops at Vatican I laid to rest the disputes within the church on the question of authority. Papal authority was reaffirmed and, with it, the reestablishment of centralization in the church.

While Pope Leo XIII (1878-1903) is best remembered as the pope of social reform, one of his major agendas as pontiff was to reestablish and further the control and centralization of the church both in the Catholic and secular worlds. His major strategy was the restoration of the philosophy and the theology of Thomas Acquinas as the basis of Catholic teaching (McSweeney 1980). The rediscovery and official promulgation of Thomism as the acceptable Catholic theology had a two-fold purpose: (1) to provide an intellectually valid basis for the beliefs of Catholics in the face of widespread scepticism about the church and religion in the nineteenth century, and (2) as a political strategy intended to bring about the restoration of a Christian social order, a hierarchic society united by common values and common faith under the temporal kingship of secular rulers and under the ultimate authority of the Pope (Burns 1990; McSweeney 1980). According to Pope Leo XIII, it was the genius of Thomas Acquinas to show that no contradiction existed between the teaching of the church and the findings of modern science and to reestablish the church as the final arbiter in the interpretation of scientific findings. As McSweeney (1980) argues, Thomism provided the church with the most refined instrument of intellectual discipline and papal imperialism.

Throughout his pontificate, Leo XIII was deeply concerned with what he saw as the evils of modern society, especially the threat of socialism. He was certain that the church alone was capable of restoring the ruins of society by reestablishing its primacy. It was only in Catholic doctrine that he saw a viable alternative to the growing threat of socialism.

Anti-modernism and rivalry with secular society dominated the teaching of the church from the time of Leo XIII to the death of Pope Pius XII in 1958. The term "seige mentality" is used by a number of scholars (Fesquet 1967; Kaiser 1963; Rynne 1968) to characterize the church's stance during this period, a term that implies a church that saw itself as beseiged by the threats of modern society. By periodically reaffirming its authoritarian position and condemning the attacks of the modernists, the church presented itself as safe from the challenges of modern science and secular humanism that were rampant in the first half of the twentieth century.

Despite its image of organizational stability and confidence of doctrine, by the time Angelo Roncalli (Pope John XXIII) was elected to the papacy in 1958 a number of reform movements were quite well organized in various countries and challenging the outdated teachings and structures of the church. The worker-priest movement in France had called attention to the plight of workers in industrialized countries. While Catholic Action was under the strict control of the church, it did raise the consciousness of lay people of their potential contributions to the work of the church and caused some among the laity to challenge the clericalism that existed in the formal church structures (Abell 1960; Hennesey 1981; Vaillancourt 1980). Along with Catholic Action, the Social Gospel movement, both in Europe and the United States, challenged Catholics to be more aware of the needs of poor and dispossessed peoples (Ellis 1969).

The Catholic Scriptural renaissance (Ahlstrom 1975) opened a whole range of questions relating to the origins and interpretation of Scripture as well as the integration of Scripture with the recent archeological discoveries relating to the origins of man and the universe. Contemporary theologians such as Chenu, Congar, de Lubac, Rahner, Schillebeecx, Teilhard de Chardin and John Courtney Murray were struggling to interpret Catholic doctrine in the light of new scientific discoveries and humanistic philosophies (McSweeney 1980). The rapid evolution of mass communication made it possible for their ideas to be disseminated to clergy, nuns, and lay people around the world.

This was the situation that John XXIII inherited as he ascended the papacy in 1958. Rather than ignoring the contemporary issues or reverting to authoritarian, dogmatic, and traditional means of responding to the crisis that had arisen in the church, he boldly called for the reevaluation of the church's stance in the modern world. From his opening speech at the first session of the council, it was evident that he wanted a distinction made between the content of church doctrine and its form of expression in the modern world, in other words, the aggiornamento of the church.

Adaptation to the Modern World

In his opening remarks to the Council, it was clear that Pope John XXIII was calling for a total reevaluation of the church in the light of modern conditions. He condemned the "prophets of doom" within the church, and especially among his advisors, who maintained that "our era, in comparison with past eras, is getting worse, and they behave as though they had learned nothing from history, which is nevertheless the great teacher of life" (Abbott 1966, p. 712). He then proceeded with ideas that either alarmed or gratified his listeners, depending upon their theological outlook. He said he had not called the Council to discuss particular articles of church doctrine but rather to study and expound doctrine "according to the methods of research and literary forms of modern thought" (Abbott 1966, p. 715). In other words, doctrine was to be interpreted to contemporaries in the light of advances in biblical, theological, philosophical, archeological, and historical findings of modern science.

In his bold way, the Pope then went on to distinquish the substance of doctrine and its expression, a distinction that was unacceptable in traditional Catholic theology. He maintained that "The substance of the ancient doctrine of the *depositum fidei* [deposit of faith] is one thing; the way in which it is expressed is another" (Abbott 1966, p. 715). The task of the Council, he told the assembled delegates, was to find the best expressions for our times.

The Pope's opening address to the Council, in which he established renewal and reform as the agenda, marked an end to the closed mentality and traditionalism that characterized the church since the sixteenth century. He put an end to the condemnations of modernism that plagued the church during the previous fifty or more years and established updating, adaptation to the modern world, and aggiornamento as the primary stance of the renewed church. In these opening remarks, he created a new conceptualization of the relationship of the church to the modern world and set an agenda that was reflected in every document that resulted from the next four sessions of the Council.

The Pastoral Constitution on the church in the Modern World (Abbott 1966) laid out the new conceptualization of the church most clearly and dramatically. In the decree, the Council delegates declared their respect for the truth and benefits that modernization brought into the world. The decree stated that we are witnesses to the birth of a new humanism in which people are conscious of their responsibility to one another for the future of the world. The faithful must "live in close union with their contemporaries" and must "blend modern science and its theories and the understanding of the most recent discoveries with Christian morality and doctrine" so that the church may keep pace with the times and enter fully into the twentieth century (Abbott 1966, p. 262).

The traditional conceptualization of the church as an unchanging, set apart and superior monolithic institution that must fight the dangers of modernization gave way to the new idea of the church as part of the modern world. This new conceptualization of the church not only permeated the theological debates at the Council, but became the rationale for a host of structural changes that were made in the course of the council sessions.

Structural Implementation of the Mazeway Shift

The new conceptualization of the church as part of the modern world was most evident in three major structural changes that resulted from the Council: (1) liturgical changes, (2)Biblical scholarship, and (3)moral issues.

Liturgical Changes

The first completed work of the Council was the Constitution on the Sacred Liturgy. For decades, a vigorous liturgical movement had been going on, especially in Europe and the United States(Ellis 1969; McNaspy 1966). Serious scholarly work was part of the movement so that the Council delegates had before them a well-prepared proposal for liturgical reform. At the heart of the movement was the call for more active participation on the part of the laity in the rituals of the church which had as its offshoot adaptation of the liturgy to the language and customs of the people so that participation would be meaningful. The acceptance of the vernacular in the Mass as well as musical expressions meaningful to the local people were among the first structural changes brought about by the Council that affected the religious lives of ordinary Catholics.

While the Council held in Rome was far removed and often esoteric for the layman in the pews of their local parish churches, the liturgical changes that occurred soon after the Council were felt by every Catholic. While some local parishes welcomed the changes and others resisted them vehemently, over a very short time span, Catholics around the world were aware that the Council had radically altered the ways in which Catholics joined together to worship. Hardest to accept for some Catholics, especially older ones, was the very notion that the Mass and sacraments could change. Since Pope Pius V, in 1570, laid down the liturgical norms for the Latin church and added severe warnings against any deviations from them, Catholics have enjoyed the security of a ritual unchanging through time and place. Suddenly, after 400 years, what Catholics were taught was sacred and unchanging was changed for the sake of relevancy and adaptation to modern conditions. The changes in the liturgy, as well as the change in the norm of not eating meat on Friday as a sacrificial commemoration of Christ's death, caused many Catholics to question what teachings of the church were divine and unchanging truths and which ones were adaptable to modern circumstances. The idea that church doctrine and teaching could be adapted to changing times and circumstances constituted the mazeway shift that caused a whole new way of thinking for many Catholics after the Council.

Biblical Scholarship

The Biblical renaissance (Ahlstrom 1975; Kurtz 1986) that was endorsed by the Council also had far reaching and profound effects on the post Vatican II Catholic world, although the Biblical movement was felt more by the intelligentsia in the church than by the ordinary layman. The Catholic Biblical movement paralleled a similar movement that was prominent in Protestant scholarship for several decades prior to the Council. The movement raised a range of questions that challenged traditional Catholic teaching such as the story of creation, dates and authencity of old Testament events, the traditional story of the events surrounding Christ's birth, and the origins of the New Testament accounts. Archeological finds, such as ancient Troy, Peking Man, and the Dead Sea scrolls threw new light on earlier civilizations and the development of man. Carbon dating allowed more precise calculation of ancient events. Scientific advances in astronomy and geology also raised naturalistic explanations of such Biblical events as the parting of the Red Sea, the crumbling walls of Jericho, and the Star of Bethlehem (Seidler and Meyer 1989).

Biblical scholars were also aware of the new discoveries of ancient tongues and literary forms that were common in Old Testament times and paralleled literary forms in the Bible. Bible stories came to be seen as part of ancient mythology rather than Divine revelation. The realization that religious truths were cloaked in historical forms common at a particular period of history challenged scholars to sort out the essential message and adapt it to expressions that were more understandable and meaningful to contemporary people. Again, the realization that what was taken for granted as unchangeable could now be changed jolted the old mazeways of post-Vatican II Catholics and established relevancy rather than certainty and stability as a new conceptualization of the church.

Vatican II strongly endorsed the Biblical perspective, both in terms of the importance of Scripture in liturgy and daily prayer and also the new interpretations of Scripture. Almost every document that came out of the Council reflected the new approach to Scripture (Rynne 1968). The notions of aggiornamento and relevancy were operationalized in the very interpretation of the source of Catholic teaching, the Bible itself.

Moral Issues

The third area that reflected the impact of aggiornamento or adaptation of the church to modern times was in issues of morality. While the initial intention of the Council planners was to include a document on the church and morality, the debate among the Council delegates on this issue was so intense that all efforts to reach a compromise were abandoned (McSweeney 1980). However, embedded in several other Council documents, particularly in the Dogmatic Constitution on the Church and the Declaration on Religious Freedom, is found the church's new teaching on morality. The striking feature of the church's position was a shift from the objective to the subjective in defining morality and from the level of the individual to that of the community in establishing conditions for moral behavior (McSweeney 1980). The Declaration on Religious Freedom stated clearly that morality, like faith, is a free response of the individual acting according to his conscience and that "every man has the duty, and therefore the right, to seek the truth in matters religious, in order that he may with prudence form for himself right and true judgments of conscience, with the use of all suitable means" (Abbott 1966, p. 680).

Social circumstances were acknowledged as an important factor in determining the moral response of the individual. The Council fathers emphasized the relation of social structure to moral commitment and recognized social factors as variables in determining moral decisions. Overall, there was a strong resistance among the Council delegates to the notion of individualistic piety which encouraged the traditional focus on objective conditions of sin and sinfulness and an emphasis on social conditions that might facilitate or inhibit conditions of individual responsibility (McSweeney 1980). The implementation of the mazeway shift from conceptualizing the church as an unchanging, monolithic, authoritarian institution to a church that adapted its doctrine and forms of expression to conditions of the modern world was most evident in the changes that were brought about in the three areas discussed earlier: liturgical changes, the Scriptural movement, and issues of morality. How effective and successful was the church in its implementation strategies? That is the subject of the next section.

Indications of the Success of the Mazeway Shift

As Wallace (1956) points out, a successful revitalization movement will inevitably encounter some resistance and, in the process of responding to the resistance, will further develop and refine the nature of the mazeway shifts that are occurring. Resistance may in some cases be slight and fleeting but more commonly, is determined and resourceful. The revitalization movement uses various strategies of dealing with the resistance: doctrinal modification, political and diplomatic maneuvers, and force. In the course of dealing with resistance, the new mazeways are usually better defined and even reworked to make them more acceptable to special interest groups. One function of resistance movements is to highlight and accentuate the fact that a mazeway shift has occurred in the cultural system.

Catholic Traditionalism, a resistance movement that arose shortly after the Council closed, is the most vociferous expression of opposition to the Council (Dinges 1983, 1989). It is a social reaction to the humanistic, horizontally oriented, world view construction that had been legitimated during the Council. The movement is a collective protest against the modernist transformation of Catholicism and the abandonment of many religious patterns, values, symbols and norms that characterized pre-Vatican II Catholicism.

The Catholic Traditionalist Movement focused its efforts most dramatically in terms of protest of the liturgical changes effected by the Council, most notably the substitution of the vernacular for the centuries old Latin Tridentine Mass. Traditionalist Catholics gathered privately in homes, hotel rooms, meeting halls, and chapels to celebrate Mass in Latin, at an altar where traditionalist priests continued to wear traditional garb and perform the rite with their backs to the people. They performed this rite without the official sanction of Rome and in defiance of the Vatican II Constitution on the Sacred Liturgy.

While there are several Traditionalist organizations, by far the largest and best known is the Society of St. Pius X, a religious order founded in 1970 by French Archbishop Marcel Lefebvre. A major reason that Lefebvre's organization posed a serious resistance threat to the church is the fact that, as an Archbishop, he maintained the authority to ordain priests, thereby maintaining a means of producing a resource critical to the survival of the Traditionalist Movement (Dinges 1983).

A major ideological theme of the Traditionalist Movement was the accusation that the Council, in its program of aggiornamento, had condoned Modernism after condemning it as a heresy for more than a century and a half. In particular, they argue, the adaptation of the liturgy to contemporary conditions has seriously weakened the Catholic faith, as is evident in the decline in Mass attendance and the use of devotional practices on the part of Catholics since the council. The Traditionalists go so far as to argue that the Mass, in the vernacular, is an invalid rite (Dinges 1983).

After twenty years of responding to Lefebvre in various ways, including accommodation, reprimands, removal of canonical status of his Society, and the suspension of ordaining privileges, he was formally excommunicated from the Catholic church in June, 1988. The actions against Lefebvre and his Traditionalist Movement was clear indication that Rome was serious in its efforts toward aggiornamento, especially as it relates to the adaptation of the liturgy to contemporary times. Even though Pope John Paul II made efforts for rapprochement with Lefebvre and even went so far, in 1983, as to allow the Tridentine liturgy under "strictly controlled conditions," the resistance movement was not only unsuccessful in challenging the legitimacy of the "new Mass," but was the occasion for Rome to reaffirm the fact that the renewed liturgy was the official rite of the church. Aggiornamento, in so far as it was implemented in liturgical reform, was successful and had become the firm policy of the church.

As Meyer descibes in her chapter in this volume, there were other conservative reactions to the changes initiated by the Council. Pope John Paul II embraced aspects of traditional Catholicism as seen in his censoring prominent liberal theologians, allowing the Tridentine Mass under specified conditions, intervening in the Jesuit's tradition of passing on the top leadership position, telling priests to step out of politics and disciplining women religious women for signing an announcement on abortion.

McSweeney (1980) argues that the major effect of Vatican II was the "authority to dissent." By introducing the principle of relativity in terms of doctrinal expression, forms of worship, and matters of moral conscience, the

Council legitimated dissent based on social circumstances and personal conscience. The dissent among the bishops at the Council that Pope John allowed to be displayed to the world via mass communication set an example for Catholics that soon replaced the outdated catechism that Catholics had memorized and lived by for centuries. It was in the area of morality, more than any other, that Catholics experimented with their right to dissent.

The fact that a shift in the church's approach to morality had filtered to the laity by the time Pope Paul VI issued his birth control encyclical, *Humanae Vitae* (1968), was one factor that caused both confusion and hostility toward the encyclical both on the part of clergy and laity (Greeley 1977). The encyclical seemed to contradict the stance of aggiornamento and relevancy created by the Council. For many Catholics, the encyclical was a return to the objective conditions of morality that had been rejected in many Council documents and contradicted the use of modern science and social circumstances in arriving at moral decisions. The fact that the Pope disregarded the advise of the experts whom he had commissioned to study the issue also lead many Catholics to disregard the church's teaching as out of line with the spirit of aggiornamento that motivated and permeated the recent Council. The spirit of the Council had created a mazeway shift that was incompatible with the authoritarianism of the new encyclical. Greeley's (1977) data demonstrates that most Catholics (78%) felt that the church had no right to teach them what they should think about birth control and simply ignored the Pope's encyclical on the basis of its irrelevancy in the modern world. The widespread rejection of the encylical, especially on the part of American Catholics, is evidence that a shift in mazeway had occurred and Catholics no longer viewed their church as a monolithic institution with absolute truth and authority.

The fact that many Catholics were noncompliant with the moral demands of the encyclical and yet considered themselves "good Catholics" shows a kind of "selective Catholicism" (D'Antonio et al. 1989; Greeley 1990; Gremillion and Castelli 1987) in which people pick and choose what they want to believe. As Kelly's chapter in this volume shows, American Catholicism is characterized by a seeming paradox: strong dissent and stable loyalty. Because many of the traditional moral teachings of the church are difficult to adapt to contemporary conditions, they have required organizational innovations that engaged many Catholic laity, both as paid staff and volunteers. Programs in family planning, pre-Cana and Cana marriage conferences, marriage encounter, dignity groups for Catholic homosexuals and church organizations for AIDS patients have enlisted the participation of thousands of Catholics. Kelly concludes that moral dissent prodded organizational innovation which increased participation and stimulated vitality on the part of lay Catholics.

In summary, the sixteen Council decrees and the structural changes they effected in the church are evidence of the fact that the aggiornamento or adaptation of the church to the modern world that Pope John XXIII envisioned has been felt throughout the Catholic world. Regardless of one's evaluation of whether these changes add to the vitality of the church or weaken its structures of commitment, there is little disagreement that the church has changed and is more in tune with the modern world.

Church As People of God

There is widespread agreement among those who have analyzed the Council documents that the image of the church as the "People of God" is the dominant ecclesial image throughout the Council documents (Dulles 1988). The Council delegates arrived at this new image of the church after prolonged and heated discussions that carried over into all four sessions of the Council, a fact that testifies to the importance and consequential nature of the shift in image of the church (Rynne 1968).

Pre-Vatican II Conceptualization of the Church

It is almost a platitude to assert that the Catholic church from the Middle Ages until Vatican II was pyramidal in structure. A military analogy best describes the social organization of the church as it existed in the five or six centuries preceding the Second Vatican Council with the pope as commander-in-chief, the primary arbiter of truth and holiness. The cardinals and bishops served as subordinate officers carrying out the orders of the Pope with parish priests implementing decisions made above them. In this system, ordinary laity had no power and very little involvement in any decision-making functions. They were visualized as recipients of the truth and goodness provided them by Holy Mother church.

Buttressing this military image of the church was an ecclesiastical juridical system that administered the laws and norms of the church. Canon law was a rigid system of rules that embodied the requirements of being a Catholic in "good standing" with the church. The elaborate system of authority relationships and legal specifications created an image of a church that was highly bureaucratic and complex as well as transcendant and removed from the daily lives of ordinary Catholic people.

A sense of "institutional awe" functioned as one of many control mechanisms that the church used to assure that members remained obedient and subservient to the hierarchy of the church. The notion of papal infallibility, which theologically applies only to doctrinal pronouncements of the Pope, carried for the laity the generalized notion that the Pope had the God-given authority to speak the truth in all matters, spriritual and temporal. The aura of authority filtered down through the hierarchical ranks such that bishops and local priests were also considered dispensers of truth even in the minutest matters of faith and morals.

In the several decades prior to the Council, pressure mounted in various countries to redefine the traditional image of the church to allow greater collegiality and power both on the part of clergy and laity in the church. The experience of democracy in the Western countries and the rumblings toward greater democracy in the Third World countries caused many people to begin to question the rigid and authoritarian structures that still prevailed in the church. In addition, movements like the worker-priest movement in Europe and the growing Catholic Action movement around the world gave priests and laity a sense of greater participation in church affairs. There were pressures from German, Dutch, French, Eastern and other Catholics for a modernization of the way the church was structured and was handling its internal problems. Some groups were agitating for a reorganization of the Roman Curia, an inner circle of clerics that were running the affairs of the church in Rome. Other Catholics wanted changes in the laws and regulations affecting marriage and education, the Mass, the sacraments, the inquisitorial and condemnatory procedures of the Holy Office, and a redefinition of the rights and duties of bishops, priests, and laymen in the church's structure (Rynne 1968). Many of these concerns and pressures came to a head during the first session of the Council as the delegates began to debate the schema on the church. The fact that the debate lasted a week and was one of the most heated of the debates and resulted in sending the document back to the committee for significant revisions before the second session indicated the seriousness of the issue. What was at stake was a total reconceptualization of the nature and structure of the church.

Vatican II Reformulation of the Image of the Church

Cardinal Suenens of Brussels is credited with challenging the conservatives at the Council who favored retaining the traditional hierarchical image of the church and suggesting that a totally new image be substituted, one that visualized the church as the People of God, working together to accomplish God's kingdom on earth (Rynne 1968). His proposal was met with loud applause in the meeting hall, indicating widespread agreement with his proposal.

The progressives at the Council won a major victory in their insistence that the hierarchical image of the church be replaced by one that visualized the church as a chosen people, clerics and laity alike, called by means of their Baptism and Confirmation to work together to spread God's kingdom on earth. The final document on the church devotes an entire chapter to the description of the church as the "new people of God" and emphasizes the human and communal side of the church rather than the institutional and hierarchical aspects that characterized previous conceptualizations.

Structural Implementation

A major reason that the new conceptualization of the church caused such debate was the fact that the council delegates anticipated and openly discussed some of the major structural consequences that logically followed from redefining the church. Among the most important of the structural changes were: (1) the principle of collegiality, (2) focus upon the poor and disadvantaged of the world, and (3)the role of women in the church.

Collegiality

While Vatican II did not deny the primacy of the pope in the authority structure of the church, it did put the papacy into a significantly new context. The college of bishops, together with the pope as its head, was seen as having ultimate authority and power. Just as the pope exercises authority in consultation with bishops, each bishop governs his diocese in consultation with his priests, religious, and laity. So, too, each pastor was mandated to establish parish councils and consultative bodies of lay parishioners. Thus, the principle of collegiality was mandated for all levels of the church.

Within a short time after the close of the Council and the promulgation of the document on the church, the principle of collegiality was implemented on practically every level: the establishment of a worldwide synod of bishops to consider on a continuous basis issues and problems in the church; national and regional episcopal conferences; national and diocesan pastoral councils; priests senates and parish councils. Along with liturgical changes, one of the most dramatic structural changes following the Council was the implementation of the notion of collegiality by means of these various consultative and, in some instances, policy making bodies. As Dobbelaere and Voye demonstrate in their chapter in this volume, there has been much criticism of the effectiveness of many of these groups. However, the fact remains that the church had established mechanisms for participation and involvement that were unheard of in the pre-Vatican II church. As Fichter's article in this volume points out, the laity now take part in organizational and administrative tasks previously reserved only for the parish clergy, even participation in the sacred rite of the Eucharist. As more and more priests and nuns abandoned their religious roles, the laity filled the void by taking over many of the necessary functions of the church. Hoge, in his chapter, suggests that one option for filling the void left by the decline in priestly vocations is to expand lay ministries in the church.

Interestingly enough, the demise of the clerical culture and the humanizing of convent life simultaneously brought about both greater collegiality and the era of "vanishing professionals," to use Fichter's term. Paradoxically, as collegiality was introduced as the new mazeway of the church, a kind of relative deprivation set in. As the data in Schoenherr and Young's chapter shows, some priests left the priesthood and others became unhappy with the lack of collegial structures in the contemporary church, even though, compared with pre-Vatican days, priests and nuns exercised significantly greater voice. The high defection rates among nuns that Marie Augusta Neal describes in her chapter are due, in part, to nuns' dissatisfaction with the lack of democratic structures in the church.

While Vatican II , in the spirit of aggiornamento, responded to many of the challenges of modern society, Baum and Vaillancourt, in their chapter, argue that the church failed to insert modern values into its own self organization. This contradiction between social teachings and self structure caused confusion and frustration for many in the church, particularly for many clergy and nuns.

Focus on the Disadvantaged

In addition to collegiality, a second area in which the shift in image of the church was felt was renewed attention to the poor of the world, especially in Third World countries. The bishops at the Council made explicit the fact that the People of God included not only the materially fortunate in the church, but also those who are materially disadvantaged. The apostolate of peace and social justice was defined as a requirement of the church's mission to carry on the work of Christ, who had compassion for the poor and the oppressed. The struggle for justice and the transformation of society were seen as constitutive dimensions of evangelization (Dulles 1988). Fitzpatrick's chapter shows that attention to the Social Gospel has historically been a part of the church's doctrine. At Vatican II the Council delegates reaffirmed this focus in principle. However, the impact of the church's Social Gospel was felt in the decade after the Council, especially in Latin America as a result of the Medallín Conference of Bishops, where the church's solidarity with the poor was translated into the policy of a "preferential option for the poor." As Adriance describes in her chapter, the affiliation of the church with the materially poor in countries like Brazil, Mexico, and Argentina reversed centuries-old patterns of the identification of the church with the ruling elites in these countries and has had tremendous social and political consequences.

The concern and positive response of the Catholic church in the United States to the growing numbers of new immigrants, especially Catholics from Mexico and Central America, has lead to various types of church-sponsored organizations, established to help immigrants accommodate to their new surroundings. As Christiano's chapter shows, the Catholic church in America is one of the largest providers of services to immigrants. However, simultaneously, as Greeley points out in his chapter, the Catholic church in the United States is losing large numbers (approximately 60,000 people a year) of Spanish origin Catholics to Protestant denominations each year. He sees the defection of these immigrant Catholics as a major problem which the American church must address in the decade of the 1990s.

Role of Women in the Church

In regard to the third structural change that resulted from the redefinition of the church as People of God, namely, women, the council itself had almost nothing to say directly to the topic. The minor changes that occurred in relation to the place of women in the church came primarily on the diocesan and local levels as notions of collegiality and participation were implemented. As Wallace's chapter indicates, among the 2,540 voting members of the Council, there was not a single woman! It was only toward the end of the Council that 22 women were finally included among the observers who had no vote and could not speak.

Interestingly, during the second session of the Council, Cardinal Suenens urged that the number of lay auditors should be increased and women should be invited to join their ranks, for, he argued, "women make up one half of the world's population" (Rynne 1968). At his urging, women were finally admitted as observers at the fourth and last session of the council.

Despite the lack of attention to women by the Council itself, as the council documents began to be implemented, especially in the United States, women began to work their way into the newly created collegial structures (see Wallace's chapter in this volume). In many parishes, they began to serve as alcolytes, readers in liturgical services, Eucharistic ministers, on parish councils, and, most recently, as associate pastors. As Wallace shows, however, their mobility and power is structurally blocked by the fact that they are prohibited from the rite of ordination. As long as this is the case, women will remain second-class citizens among the People of God.

Success of the New Conceptualization of Church As People of God

One of the most powerful indicators that the new concept of church took hold and was implemented in numerous structural changes that took place after the Council is the intense evaluation of the change that occurred at the Extraordinary Synod of Bishops held in Rome in 1985. Pope John Paul II called this unusual synod to measure how the council had been interpreted and implemented in different countries. While the synod titled its first report, "The Message to the People of God," nearly all commentators have remarked on the almost total absence of the new conceptualization in its documents. Some reporters have suggested that the virtual omission of this theme was due to some outside agents who put pressure on the synod to rework the council in this crucially important point (Hebblethwaite 1968). However, Dulles (1988) maintains that the omission of the concept was due to the lack of consensus among the bishops regarding the positive effects of the concept for the church. The Dutch and Belgium bishops complained that the idea of People of God was encouraging civil democratic thinking among Catholics in their countries. Cardinal Daneels, in his report, noted the tendency to make false oppositions between the hierarchical church and a "people's church," a fact that he bemoaned (Dulles 1988). The fact that the synod bishops expressed such concern over the ways the new church image was being implemented in their countries is indication that a new mazeway had caught hold among church members and was producing far reaching effects in terms of structural implementation.

The fact that Pope John Paul II used a synod of bishops as a means of evaluating the effects of the Council twenty years after its completion was, in itself, indication that the notion of collegiality had become standard procedure. In fact, in preparation for the synod he asked each episcopal conference to submit a report dealing with specific questions, a procedure that differed significantly from the commission structure that prepared for the Council itself, commissions that were dominated by Roman curia members (Rynne 1968). Interestingly, most of the 95 reports that were submitted by episcopal conferences reflected deep gratitude and positivism for the work of the council, thus demonstrating that most bishops were happy with the changes effected by the Council (Dulles 1988). Only reports from continental Europe represented a more pessimistic view that the church has been declining since the council. This was an accurate representation of the situation of the church in certain European countries. As Dobbelaere and Voyé show in their chapter, various empirical indicators such as Mass attendance, religious marriages, involvement in church activities, and orthodoxy of moral beliefs show a decline in religious behavior in Western European countries.

By the time the Synod convened in 1985 it was obvious that the concept of church as People of God had caught hold as the predominant image of the church. The increase in lay participation in all aspects of the church is indication that structural changes had accompanied the conceptual shift.

The revitalization movement that preceded and eventuated in the Second Vatican Council in Roman Catholicism had as its goal a shift in basic mazeways that constituted the church's self image and role in the modern world. The Council delegates legitimated the movement goals in two ways: (1) by accepting the notion of aggiornamento or the need for adaptation of the church to changing social conditions, and (2) by redefining the church as the People of God. These two mazeway shifts lead to far reaching structural changes in all aspects of church life.

Despite the changes that have occurred, the chapters in this volume make clear that the process of implementation is far from complete. Most evident is the need for self reorganization in order to more closely align the church with the principles of collegiality and participatory power.

REFERENCES

Abbott, W. M., S. J., ed. 1966. *The Documents of Vatican II.* New York: Guild Press.

Abell, A. 1960. *American Catholicism and Social Action.* Garden City, NY: Doubleday.

Ahlstrom, S. E. 1975. *A Religious History of the American People.* Vol. 2. Garden City, NY:Doubleday (Image Books).

Burns, T. 1990. "The Politics of Ideology: The Papal Struggle With Liberalism." *American Journal of Sociology* 95:1123-1152.

D'Antonio, W. V., J.D. Davidson, D.R. Hoge, and R.A. Wallace. 1989. *American Catholic Laity in a Changing Church.* Kansas City, MO:Sheed and Ward.

Dinges, W. 1983. "Catholic Traditionist Movement." Pp. 137-158 in *Alternatives to American Mainline Churches,* edited by J.H. Fichter. New York: Rose of Sharon Press.

————. 1989. "The Quandry of Dissent on the Catholic Right." Pp. 107-125 in *Sociological Studies in Roman Catholicism: Historical and Contemporary Perspectives,* edited by R. O'Toole. Lewiston, NY: The Edwin Mellen Press.

Dulles, A. 1988. *The Reshaping of Catholicism.* New York: Harper and Row.

Ellis, J. T. 1969. *American Catholicism.* Chicago: The University of Chicago Press.

Fesquet, H. 1967. *The Drama of Vatican II: The Ecumenical Council, June 1962-December 1965.* New York: Random House.

Greeley, A. M. 1977. *The American Catholic: A Social Portrait.* New York: Basic Books.

————. 1990. *The Catholic Myth.* New York: Scribner's.

Gremillion, J., and J. Castelli. 1987. *The Emerging Parish: The Notre Dame Study of Catholic Life Since Vatican II.* New York: Harper and Row.

Hebblethwaite, P. 1968. *'Inside' the Synod: Rome, 1967.* New York: Paulist Press.

Hennesey, J. 1981. *A History of the Roman Catholic Community in the U.S.* New York: Oxford University Press.

Kaiser, R. B. 1963. *Pope, Council and World.* New York: Macmillan.

Kurtz, L. 1986. *The Politics of Heresy: The Modernist Crisis in Roman Catholicism.* Los Angeles, CA: University of California Press.

Lyng, S., and L. R. Kurtz. 1985. "Bureaucratic Insurgency: The Vatican and the Crisis of Modernism." *Social Forces* 63:901-921.

McNaspy, C.J. 1966. "Liturgy." Pp. 133-136 in *The Documents of Vatican II,* edited by W. M. Abbott, S.J. New York: Guild Press.

McSweeney, W. 1980. *Roman Catholicism: The Search for Relevance.* New York: St. Martin's Press.

Rynne, X. 1968. *Vatican Council II.* New York: Farrar, Straus and Giroux.

Seidler, J., and K. Meyer. 1989. *Conflict and Change in the Catholic Church.* New Brunswick, NJ:Rutgers University Press.

Vaillancourt, J-G. *Papal Power: A Study of Vatican Control Over Lay Catholic Elites.* Berkeley, CA: University of California Press.

Wallace, A. F.C. 1956. "Revitalization Movements." *American Anthropologist* 58:264-281.

————. 1957. "Mazeway Disintegration: The Individual's Perception of Sociocultural Disorganization." *Human Organization* 16:23-27.

DATE DUE